THE ULTIMATE

BOOK ON

STOCK MARKET TIMING

VOLUME 2

GEOCOSMIC CORRELATIONS TO INVESTMENT CYCLES

THE ULTIMATE

BOOK ON

STOCK MARKET TIMING

VOLUME 2

GEOCOSMIC CORRELATIONS TO INVESTMENT CYCLES (LONG-TERM STOCK MARKET CYCLES)

BY
RAYMOND A. MERRIMAN

MMA PUBLICATIONS, P.O. BOX 250012 WEST BLOOMFIELD, MI 48325

DISCLAIMER

All information provided herein is based upon original research and observations of Raymond A. Merriman. It is written with sincere and reliable intent.

Although these methods and techniques have proved reliable over the years, there cannot be and therefore is no guarantee that these same methods will continue to work in the future. Therefore, neither the publisher nor the author assume any responsibility whatsoever for any reader's activities or decisions regarding trading or investing in any stocks or financial vehicles.

1st printing: January, 1999

ISBN: 0-930706-27-7

THE ULTIMATE BOOK ON STOCK MARKET TIMING, VOLUME 2: GEOCOSMIC CORRELATIONS TO INVESTMENT CYCLES

Published in the United States by:

MMA/Seek-It Publications
P.O. Box 250012
West Bloomfield, MI 48325
1-248-626-3034
Fax 1-248-626-5674
E-Mail: mmacycles@email.msn.com
Internet: http://www.mmacycles.com

TABLE OF CONTENTS

FIGURES AND DIAGRAMS

TABLES

APPENDICES

ACKNOWLEDGMENTS

It is — as always — impossible to write a book of this scope without the assistance and support of several very special people.

First of all, a technical book of this nature requires a large amount of accurate historical data. Procuring price data for the stock indices of the United States is no simple matter, particularly prior to 1880. The Foundation for the Study of Cycles has made yearly data (yearly high, low, and close) available for the period prior to 1880. However, since this book attempts to correlate cycle crests and troughs with astronomic movement, and since planets are always moving in their orbits around the Sun, the lack of anything shorter than yearly data would subject this study to considerable error.

However, the author is very fortunate to have a friend and colleague who has gathered monthly data on the U.S. stock market from its inception in 1789 through the period in question — through 1880. The author is deeply indebted to the generosity of well-known cycles analyst James Jones of Dallas, Texas, for providing this information. Without Jones' contribution to this effort, the level of accuracy in the studies involving geocosmic correlations to long-term stock market cycles would not have been possible.

Secondly, every writer knows the value of being able to work in a distraction-free environment. Concentration and focus are the hallmarks of every successful endeavor, and perhaps more so when the endeavor requires a creative expression, such as writing. Unless one has actually pursued this type of effort to any meaningful degree (i.e. written a book), it is perhaps difficult to understand just how important the setting is. To accomplish the proper state of mind — to achieve a conducive atmosphere for the task of intense research and writing — this author finds it necessary to work in secluded locations surrounded by natural beauty, absent of other human beings.

Such a location was made available to the author by his own family. The author wishes to thank his sister and her husband — Joan and Bob Tewes — for allowing him the use of their northern Michigan retreat. Located deep in the woods, on a high plateau overlooking the nearby mountains covered in evergreen and pine trees, oftentimes high above clouds providing a rather surreal appearance, the author was able to complete the greatest and most significant body of this work. It helped immensely that there was no telephone in this beautiful lodge.

The author is also grateful to his brother and sister-in-law — Dane and Julie Christy — who every summer abandon their beautiful home in Bloomfield Hills, Michigan in order to live mostly on their boat on the Great Lakes. When summer comes, they leave and kindly allow the author to take over their large home, where he becomes inspired as he works diligently in the Florida room overlooking the woods and quiet pond in the back of their estate. And for this, all they require is that the garden be properly watered!

Finally, every author knows that the writing of a book is not truly completed until it is edited properly. In the past, I have been more concerned with getting the material out before it was obsolete, and in the process, failed to catch several grammatical and numerical slights. Furthermore, the formatting of chapter titles, sub-chapter titles, tables, and figures could have been improved upon. Although this did not in any way detract from the principles being presented, it was of concern that the final product was not 100% perfect. In this Volume, I have taken the time to find an extremely competent and trustworthy editor in Geraldine Hatch Hannon of Venice, California. Ms. Hannon has a solid grounding in both astrological and financial languages, and astrological readers may be familiar with her role as editor of *The Mountain Astrologer* magazine, America's top astrological magazine for professional astrologers. She is also a financial planner and very knowledgeable in the specialty of financial astrology. The author is indeed grateful for her willingness to take on the editing of the first two drafts of this work. The reader should also understand, therefore, that any errors in editing rests solely on the author, who for reasons of wishing to get this book published more quickly, edited the last draft himself.

FORWARD: "WHAT IF?"
THE TRUTH IS OUT THERE

"What if there was a correlation between cycles in nature and cycles in the U.S. stock market? What if some of the biggest turns in the history of the U.S. stock market happened close in time to some of the longest-term planetary pair cycles known to humankind? What if there were one or two — or more — long-term planetary pair cycles that coincided every time to the beginning (and end) of a major bull or bear market in U.S. stocks?" These are questions I asked myself when I began the research required in writing this book.

Now follow along with this simple exercise. First of all, open to the three-page fold out in Appendix 5 at the back of this book. Turn to Exhibits 1 and 2, titled: **Foundation U.S. Stock Index: Yearly High-Low-Last 1789–1995,** and **Foundation Long-Term Stock Index: Yearly Averages 1695-1995.** If you have a copy of Volume 1 of this work, you may also wish to turn to pages 37–39, which consist of a table, and filtered wave charts, of the eleven 18-year cycles in the history of the U.S. stock market.

Now look at the list of dates below. These are the 11 cases of Saturn in conjunction and opposition to Uranus since 1761 to the time of the writing of this book (1998).

1. **May 14, 1761 – January 3, 1762**
2. **February 15, 1782 – December 2, 1783**
3. **November 17, 1805.**
4. **August 26, 1828 – July 9, 1829**
5. **March 15, 1852**
6. **April 7, 1873 – November 18, 1875.**
7. **January 6, 1897 – September 9, 1897**
8. **October 1, 1918 – June 7, 1920.**
9. **May 3, 1942**
10. **April 1, 1965 – January 6, 1967**
11. **February 12, 1988 – October 18, 1988**

Compare these dates to the charts before you. What do you notice?

Pretty amazing, isn't it?

Now that I have your attention, let's proceed with the work at hand. And that is quite simply no longer a question of "What If?" We can leave that question to those skeptics who are at least open-minded enough about the possibility to consider the question. As for the majority of others who won't consider the possibility on the simple assertion that *It doesn't work because it shouldn't work,* this is truly a case where ignorance is not bliss, but rather "missed opportunity."

So instead of wondering whether or not there *is* a correlation between the two studies (geocosmics and stock market cycles), this book will focus upon *what* those correlations are. Sit back, turn off the phone, get out your yellow highlighter pens, and prepare for a truly exciting journey.

The Truth is out there.

INTRODUCTION

How many times have you said: "If I knew then what I know now, I'd be wealthy"? Well, with the information to be imparted in this book, that may indeed be possible. That is, of course, assuming that certain astronomical cycles continue to coincide with long-term cycles in U.S. stock prices as they have in the past. As you will soon discover through reading this book, there are indeed some remarkable "coincidences" to the end and beginning of some very long-term cycles in the U.S. stock market — coincidences which if repeated, have every possibility of allowing one to attain enormous profits. This is not just some slick marketing verbiage. Through reading and understanding the material presented in this book (and the previous first volume of this book), you will feel as if you do know what you need to know about timing the stock market. You will feel as if you have just entered a time capsule, and fortunately this time capsule is one towards the future that involves many, many geocosmic signatures that have a remarkable correlation to the end and beginning of very prominent long-term stock market cycles.

Welcome to Volume 2 of this five-part series on *The Ultimate Book on Stock Market Timing.* In Volume 1, the concept of cycles in the U.S. and Japanese stock markets was introduced. In that work, the presence of several consistent long-term and short-term cycles pertaining to the history of these stock markets was shown. In addition, it was demonstrated how each of these cycles consisted of sub-cycles, known as "phases" of the greater cycle, and that these phases made up three basic patterns within the greater cycle. Each phase of a cycle had distinctive characteristics which could be very useful to an investor or trader, depending upon whether the cycle was a long-term or short-term type. Each pattern also exhibited distinctive characteristics, which could furthermore enhance one's profitability, regardless of whether it was a long-term or short-term cycle.

However, another one of a cycle's characteristics is that it has an orb of time in which it can occur. Cycles do not unfold precisely to the day, or even week, of their length. In fact, their length is simply a "median" time period. The actual cycle usually unfolds within an orb of about one-sixth of this median periodicity. Hence an 18-week cycle would actually have a time band of 15-21 weeks. In actuality, though, the extent of this orb differs with each cycle, as disclosed in Volume 1.

The criteria used for determining a cycle's median length and its orb consisted of identifying all the historical instances of each cycle — based upon a combination of patterns that unfolded within approximate intervals of a similar time band — and finding the average length of all these instances. Then the number of instances was reduced by eliminating approximately 15-30% of those that unfolded at the extreme short or long end of the entire time band. Once it was determined where 70-85% of the instances unfolded, the midpoint of that range was labeled as the correct cycle length. The distance between the beginning (or end) of that time band which contained the majority of instances, and the actual "median" length of that majority time band, was deemed to be the "orb" of that cycle.

To illustrate this point, please refer back to Chapter 14 in Volume 1, titled "The 50-Week Cycle In U.S. Stocks." Tables were presented that identified 71 instances of this cycle, with a range of 29-78 weeks. Using the entire field, one could say there is a 53.5-week cycle in U.S. stocks, with an orb of 24.5 weeks. The problem with using the entire field is that it produces a very wide time band in forecasting when future instances of this same cycle might unfold. This wide of an orb reduces its usefulness as an investing or trading tool. To overcome this problem, it is necessary to shorten this field to include only those cases in which 70% or more instances unfolded. Thus those instances that were extremely short or extremely long in their interval were eliminated. After this process of elimination was completed, it was observed that 64 instances — or slightly over 90% of the entire field — unfolded between weeks #34-67. This then created a median cycle interval of 50.5 weeks, with an orb of 16.5 weeks. Further refinement showed that 52 instances (73.24%) unfolded between 38-62 weeks. Once again the median is narrowed down to a 50-week cycle with an orb of 12 weeks. This then became the "high probability" time band for the 50-week cycle. In other words, 73.24% of 50-week cycles have historically unfolded between weeks #38-62, so we use this cycle length for forecasting the "most probable time band" in future projections. But it would also be technically correct to state that 90.14% of 50.5-week cycles have historically unfolded between weeks #34-67. One could then use that longer time band to project future "high probability" zones for this cycle. However, as one can see, this higher probability zone also contains a considerably wider time band, and the wider the time band, the less useful it becomes as an actual investing or trading tool.

This then brings to light the need — and value — for tools that will further reduce the time band in which a cycle is due. To some extent, this concern was addressed in Volume 1. The study of "patterns" within cycles pointed out the presence of sub-cycles, or "phases" that made up those greater cycles. By overlapping the time bands of several sub-cycles over the time band of the greater cycle, one can narrow the expected time frame in which greater cycles are due. Furthermore, by utilizing certain technical indicators within these time bands of expected cycle occurrences, one can usually see the cycle bottoming or topping just as — or shortly after — it forms (see Chapter 12 of Volume 1).

The market timing tools presented in Volume 1 provided the reader with a firm foundation in market timing. It provided the tools to effectively outline high probability time bands in which future market highs and lows would likely form. Yet there are other market timing tools that can narrow the time band for a cycle even further. Fibonacci time ratios and W.D. Gann techniques are two such methodologies. Numerous books on each method (which are carried by the publisher of this book) have been written by such modern-day authors as Robert Miner, Jeanne Long, and Robert Krausz, to name just a few.

But perhaps the most effective, precise, and consistently reliable tool for timing reversals in financial markets is in a field that is less used and less accepted than any of the so-called arcane areas introduced so far. It is the area of geocosmic studies, or astrology. This is not the astrology of sun-signs and horoscopes as read in the daily newspapers and popular magazines, but the part of astrology that studies the mathematical relationships between *planets*, and the correlation of certain of those mathematical relationships to *cycles* in human activity (like financial markets).

The purpose of this book (Volume 2 in Stock Market Timing) is to examine the relationship of geocosmic signatures to long-term cycles in the U.S. stock market. In this process, specific signatures will be identified that have the highest correlations to timing the most important types of cycles. One thing the reader will instantly discover is that not all geocosmic signatures have the same degree of "influence," or same degree of consistency, to long-term cycle crests or troughs in the stock market. Some are historically more consistent, and more powerful, than others. Those that qualify as consistent and powerful, though, will be found to be extremely valuable to investors and analysts alike. They will help narrow the time band for an expected cycle crest or trough considerably, in some cases from several years to just a couple of weeks. In Volume 3, we will examine the correlation of geocosmic signatures to trading cycles. Here we will find it is possible to narrow the time band of a short-term cycle trough or crest from several weeks to just a couple of trading days.

DESIGN OF STUDIES

This book is divided into two parts: Trends, and Long-Term Market Reversals. The correlation of geocosmic signatures to stock market trends is very difficult. One reason for this is because the time parameters for a "trend" are so elusive. A bull or bear market just doesn't last 9-18 months in every instance. Another is due to the fact that in the entire history of the U.S. stock market, there has never been an *extreme* bear market lasting more than 3-7 years. Yet bull markets have lasted 30-72 years, based upon the same long-term parameters. Therefore, geocosmic trend correlations to a financial market that has historically been one big long-term bull market is thwarted by this inherent obstacle: there are not enough long-term bearish trends to compare against long-term bullish trends.

Even if one examines the more intermediate or shorter-term trends (i.e. less than 2 years), there are difficulties to overcome. These may be related to the underlying assumption as to why geocosmic studies have any correlation to financial markets whatsoever. Briefly, the marketplace is comprised of individuals who bid and offer prices to buy and sell a particular good (stocks, financial instruments, or commodities). Geocosmic studies, on the other hand, deal with the movement of planets and their correlation to human activity. The supposition is that when certain geocosmic signatures are in force, they will coincide with an effect upon the psychology of the collective and possibly correlate to a "change" in trend, or an event of collective significance. When the price of a stock or commodity is rising, it will supposedly peak when one of these geocosmic signatures comes into force, and then prices will begin to decline. That decline will continue until the next important geocosmic signature comes into effect, at which time the decline will end and a rally will commence. In actual practice, this theory works quite well. Put quite simply, geocosmic signatures provide an excellent tool for identifying times of a *market reversal* — those times when the collective psychology makes a general "shift" in focus. However, it does not seem to do a very adequate job of measuring the *direction — trend* — of the market in between those times of reversals. For this reason, it has been the author's position that astrology (geocosmic studies) is not a strong tool for identifying the underlying trend of a market — which is why *trend analysis* via geocosmic studies is such a difficult subject matter to master. Astrology is an exceptional tool for timing cyclic troughs and crests in any market. Its greatest value is thus as a market timing tool, not as a trend indicator tool. Nevertheless, this book will delegate its first section to those possible geocosmic correlations to trends in the stock market.

The major portion of this book — and Volume 3 — will be dedicated to "Market Timing." It will be designed along the lines of *The Gold Book: Geocosmic Correlations to Gold Price Cycles,* written by the author. That is, instances of every geocosmic signature — which includes aspects and retrograde/direct motions — will be correlated to all cycle types to determine *strength.* A value will be given to each cycle where the longer the cycle, the greater the strength value. The number of times each signature coincides with a certain type of cycle will be observed to determine *consistency.* The strength and consistency figures will then be combined to generate a C/S (consistency/strength) value. Those that have the highest strength and consistency values will be categorized as Level One signatures. In other words, it will be found that in a high percentage of occurrences, these Level One signatures have the strongest correlation to the longer-term cycles in the U.S. stock market. Those that have consistent correlations to intermediate and shorter-term cycles in the U.S. stock market will be categorized Level Two or Three signatures. The criteria for each will vary between Volume 2 and 3, because of the difference between long-term, intermediate-term, and short-term planetary cycles.

References

It is assumed that the reader of this book is already familiar with the language of cycles and astrology, as they pertain to financial markets. If not, the following books by the author are highly recommended before reading this study

1. ***Basic Principles of Geocosmic Studies For Financial Market Timing***. This book is a beginning introduction to astrology and market timing. It includes basic astrological terminology, how to read an ephemeris, how to calculate aspects, and how to determine a "cluster" as a potential market-timing reversal date.

2. ***Merriman on Market Cycles: The Basics***. This is a beginning book on the study of cycles for market timing as used by the author. It includes basic cycles terminology, basic technical analysis, cycle characteristics, cycle periodicities in a variety of markets, and explanation of how to integrate cycle time bands with technical analysis studies.

3. ***The Ultimate Book On Stock Market Timing, Volume 1: Cycles and Patterns in the Indexes.*** A "must" prior to reading this book. All the charts and cycles to which these studies pertain are presented in this book.

Each of these books are available through MMA/Seek-It Publications, and several of the publisher's distributors. For a list of these distributors, please contact the publisher at address shown on the copyright page of this book.

In addition, the reader may also find the following books and tools useful in understanding the material presented in this book

1. Neil F. Michelsen, *The American Ephemeris for the Twentieth Century,* San Diego, CA: ACS Publications, 1980.

2. Neil F. Michelsen, *Tables of Planetary Phenomena,* San Diego, CA: ACS Publications, 1990.

3. Raymond A. Merriman, *The Gold Book: Geocosmic Correlations to Gold Price Cycles*, W. Bloomfield, MI: MMA/Seek-It Publications, 1982.

4. Raymond A. Merriman, and Jeanne Long, *FAR for the Galactic Trader* market-timing software program, Ft. Lauderdale, FL: PAS and MMA, 1996-97.

5. Raymond A. Merriman, John Woodsmall, *The S.O.S. (Stock Optimizing Selector)* software program, W. Bloomfield, MI: MMA/Seek-It Publications, 1996.

Each of these books and software programs are also available through MMA/Seek-It Publications.

CHAPTER ONE

TRENDS

Trends are one of those market concepts that mean different things to different people. Nearly every market participant agrees that one should trade primarily "in the direction of the trend." Traders are also fond of the maxim: "The trend is your friend." Everyone knows that when prices are rising over a prolonged period of time, the trend is up. And when prices are falling over an extended period, the trend is down. If a market rises for a longer time than it falls, it is considered an uptrend, or bull market. Conversely, if a market declines for a longer period of time than it rallies, it is considered a downtrend, or bear market. Yet nowhere in the literature of market studies can one find a consensus as to what defines the *time* parameters of a bull and bear market trend.

This issue was addressed at length from a cycles' perspective in Chapter Two of Volume 1. Cycles are measured from trough (low) to trough. Each cycle has an uptrend phase and a downtrend phase. The time between the start of the cycle (low) and the crest of the cycle (its highest price) is its uptrend, or bullish, phase. The time between that crest and the end of the cycle (the following trough) is its downtrend, or bearish, phase.

Generally speaking, though, each cycle itself is either bullish, bearish, or mixed in trend, depending upon 1) where its crest falls in relation to the length of the entire cycle, and 2) whether the ending price is lower or higher than the beginning price. If the crest falls before the midpoint of the entire cycle, it is said to be a "left translation" pattern, or a bearish cycle. If the crest falls in the second half of the cycle (past its midway point), it is said to be a "right translation" pattern, or bullish cycle (see Volume 1, page 12, Figure 4). Also, if the trough that ends the cycle is *lower* in price than the trough that began the cycle, it is said to be a bearish cycle, whereas if the ending trough is *higher* in price than the start, it is said to be a bullish cycle. In those cases where one signature contradicts the other, the market is said to be "mixed." For instance, if the cycle forms a crest before the midway point (which is left translation and a bearish signature), but the ending trough is higher in price than the beginning (bullish signature), then the cycle exhibited mixed trend signals.

However, every cycle is also part of a greater cycle, and one of the most important keys to understanding markets from either a cyclical or technical viewpoint is *tying in multiple time frames*. Said another way, the sum of the parts make up the whole. By understanding the parts — or "phases" — of a cycle, one can more easily grasp the whole of the cycle. Furthermore, knowledge of the greater cycle will always give an advantage in understanding the likely trend of the smaller cycles, or phases, which make up the larger cycle. This is because, in most cases, the first phase (or smaller cycle) of the greater cycle will exhibit a bullish trend. The last phase of a cycle, however, will usually exhibit bearish signatures. This principle was clearly demonstrated in Volume I, and in fact was one of its basic premises.

If the first task of this book (Volume 2) is to identify geocosmic correlations to stock market trends, then the first question to ask is: the trend of which cycle? If it is the 17-week primary cycle (with a 13-21 week probability orb), then one will want to study those geocosmic cycles that are relatively shorter-term in their periodicities, such as the lunar cycle, or maybe even certain sectors of the orbital cycles of the Sun, Mercury, Venus, or Mars as seen from the Earth — or Earth, Mercury, Venus, or Mars as seen from the Sun. The relationship of these planets to each other may also be significant, for they too are cyclical. But if it is longer-term trends that the reader wishes to explore, then the research must involve the further-out planets of the solar system.

In attempting to design geocosmic studies to analyze stock market trends, the author considered two types of analysis. The first was to study the relationship of planets in signs, or sectors of the zodiac. Do certain planets in certain signs correlate with bullish or bearish trends in the U.S. stock market? Do certain planets in specific sectors of the zodiac correlate with uptrends or downtrends? The second type of analysis examined the cycles of *planetary pairs*. As planets orbit the Sun, they form cycles with another. There are times when two planets, as seen from Earth, come into an alignment together known as a *conjunction.* The interval of time between a conjunction of any two planets is said to be the cycle period of that planetary pair. And, just as market cycles are comprised of phases, so too are planetary cycles comprised of phases. For instance, when the two planets separate 90° (of a 360° cycle) from one another, it is called a "first quarter cycle," or *waxing square aspect.* When two planets are 180° apart, it is the halfway point of the cycle, or *opposition aspect.* The last quarter cycle (270° into the cycle) is called a *waning square aspect.* Note that in the waxing square, the two planets are 90° apart *following* the conjunction. In the waning square, they are also 90° apart, but *prior to* the next conjunction. The goal here is to determine whether there might be a preponderance of one trend or another depending upon the phase — or a sector — of any particular planetary pair cycle.

These of course do not make up the whole of all possibilities for geocosmic correlations to stock market trends. There might, for instance, be a relationship of trends to planetary declinations or latitudes, aphelion and perihelion, the Saros cycles of eclipses, retrogrades and directs, sunspots, and many other geocosmic phenomena. However, every study must have limitations on what it can practically research, and this book (as well as the next) has chosen the two methods just mentioned, because they are 1) the most obvious areas to examine and 2) the most familiar areas for those who study astrology.

Please refer to Figure 1 on the next page for a list of geocosmic symbols that will be used throughout this book.

Figure 1

SIGNS BY QUALITIES

CARDINAL	*FIXED*	*MUTABLE*
♈ Aries	♉ Taurus	♊ Gemini
♋ Cancer	♌ Leo	♍ Virgo
♎ Libra	♏ Scorpio	♐ Sagittarius
♑ Capricorn	♒ Aquarius	♓ Pisces

Planets in "hard aspect" to one another are usually in the same quality by sign. When they are in cardinal signs, the potential for a significant trend reversal is greatest.

ASPECTS

MAJOR ASPECTS	*MINOR ASPECTS*
☌ - **Conjunction (0°)***	∠ - **Semi-square (45°)**
□ - **Square (90°)***	⚹ - **Sextile (60°)**
△ - **Trine (120°)**	⚼ - **Sesquiquadrate (135°)**
☍ - **Opposition (180°)***	

***The fourth harmonic types are known as "hard aspects", and are probably the most critical. They are the conjunction, square, and opposition. The eighth harmonic aspects are also known as "hard aspects," but not as critical. They are the semi-square and sesquiquadrate. The third and sixth harmonics are known as "soft aspects," and include the trine and sextile. The trine is the stronger of the two.**

CHAPTER TWO

THE VERY LONG-TERM TRENDS IN THE U.S. STOCK MARKET

It is possible to look at the history of the U.S. stock market and proclaim that it has been in a singular long-term bull market since its inception in the later part of the 18th century. As shown in Exhibit 1 of Appendix 5 of the fold out charts in the back of this book (same as Figure 1 in Volume 1), the U.S. stock market has generally moved higher and higher over every 20-year period. All the long uptrends shown on the yearly charts are greater than the downtrends.

Upon closer examination, though, one can clearly see two periods of multi-year down markets. By inserting these down markets, it doesn't take much stretch of the imagination to see three basic periods of long, strong upward trending markets. These are as follows:

1. 1797 – 1835 (38 years)
2. 1842 or 1857 – 1929 (72 or 87 years)
3. 1932 or 1942 – present

The years between these uptrends consist of a severe decline that lasted 3-7 years, followed by congestion in which neither the previous high nor the low were taken out for many years. In fact, these lows were never taken out, so it would be more accurate to say that once the 3-7 year decline was completed, it would still be several years before new all-time highs would be achieved.

After the high of 1835, prices declined 7 years, losing 80% of the market's value before completing its low in 1842. Yet it would not be until 1863 before prices would make a new all-time high. After the high of 1929, it took 25 years before the Dow Jones Industrial Averages recovered the 90% decline it had suffered during the Great Depression.

The crests of 1835 and 1929 — and the following declines — were without a doubt the most spectacular in the entire history of the U.S. stock market, as of this writing (1998). Each of those crests were the culmination of the greatest bull market runs in history. And the third one of these mighty bull market runs — comparable to those of 1797-1835 and 1857-1929 — is arguably in effect now, and has been since 1932 or 1942. Yet there appears to be no regularity, or "consistent interval of time," in these three runs. The first is at least 38 years. The second is a whopping 72 or 87 years (1857-1929, or

1842-1929). If we measure the third as having started in 1932, it is already 66 years long as of this writing (1998). If the measurement of the third bull market begins from the secondary low in 1942, we still have a minimum 56-year bull run in force, which is about the average of the previous two instances (38 and 72 years).

The problem with identifying a "pattern" here in the history of the U.S. stock market might be created by the fact that the history itself is limited. What if 1797 was not the correct starting place for the beginning of a great bull market in U.S. stocks? In all likelihood, it was not. If instead of just the U.S. stock market history, we appended the British stock prices that were in effect prior to 1797, we would discover a different picture that supports a clearer pattern. Exhibit 2 of Appendix 5 of the fold-out charts in the back of the book (same as Figure 2 in Volume 1) shows the yearly averages of the Foundation for the Study of Cycles Long-Term Stock Index, which includes the British stock prices from the Course of the Exchange prior to 1789. Here we can see a more clearly identifiable long-term bear market trough in 1784, or even 1762. It would appear, then, that one of these two dates would represent a better starting point for the first bull market run in the U.S. stock market than that of 1797, even though the U.S. stock market was not in existence in 1762 or 1784.

If 1762 is used as the starting point for the first great bull market, which ended in 1835, it can be seen that this bull market lasted 73 years. This is nearly as long as the second great bull market as measured from 1857, which lasted 72 years. However, just as the period between 1842-1857 was considered "congestion" and not really part of the greater long-term trend, so too might the period between 1762-1784 be considered a congestion zone and not part of the greater long-term trend. It is interesting to note that this first period of congestion lasted 22 years, and in the second case, the congestion period lasted 15 years, and in the third (current case), it could be argued that there was a 10-year congestion period (1932-1942) before the new bull market run commenced. This itself suggests a pattern that begins the extremely long bull market runs in U.S. (and perhaps world) stock indices. That is, after several decades of rising prices, stocks will decline for multiple years (3-7 years at the end of Cycles 1 and 2 so far in U.S. stocks only). They will then enter a period of congestion in which previous all-time highs are not exceeded for several years (25-28 years so far). During the congestion period, there will be a secondary bottom, usually 10-22 years later. From this secondary low, the next great bull market run commences.

Therefore, we could have two ways of determining the length — and character — of the great bull market runs in the U. S. stock market. The first could start with the absolute low in price (or first low). The second could start with the secondary low that ended the congestion zone and truly began the bull market run. Here is how each would look.

Bull Market Runs in the U.S. Stock Market Starting from First Trough (Absolute Low)

1762–1835 (73 years)
1842–1929 (87 years)
1932–present (66 years as of 1998)

Bull Market Runs in the U.S. Stock Market Starting from Secondary Trough (End of Congestion)

1784–1835 (51 years)
1857–1929 (72 years)
1942–present (56 years so far)

In the first case, we have two completed instances of bull markets which lasted 73-87 years, or 80 years with an orb of 7 years on either side. If this is a valid bull market cycle (and two cases does not make it a high probability by any means), then we could outline a time band in which the next (current) bull market would be due to culminate: 2005-2019. After that, if the pattern of the first instances were to repeat, the U.S. stock market would lose 80-90% of its value over the next 3-7 years. The fourth great bull market would then get underway and could be expected to last 73-87 years.

Readers should keep in mind that because there are only two completed cases to study in the history of U.S. stocks, that these projected time bands could change. For instance, an 80-year cycle does not necessarily have an orb of only 7 years. In studies of many cycles throughout the history of financial markets, it seems the average orb is about 1/6 of the cycle's median length. Thus, per the first study, it would not be surprising to see future instances of bull market runs to last anywhere from 66-94 years (80 years +/- 14 years). Furthermore, the two instances of bear markets lasting 7 and 3 years, respectively, may not hold up in future cases. Perhaps an orb of 1-9 years may become the norm after several centuries of data have unfolded.

The second study yields slightly different projections, but not so different that it cannot be used in combination with the first. If 1784 is used as the correct starting point for the first great bull market, then we can see it lasted 51 years. If 1857 is used as the staring point of the second great bull market run, then it lasted 72 years. Thus if we take the shortest of these cycles (51 years) and the longest (72 years), we can calculate the midpoint (61.5 years) and have the beginnings of a potential very long-term cycle in terms of bull market runs. It would be a 61.5-year cycle with an orb of 10.5 years. This isn't bad, because most valid cycles will have an orb of up to 1/6 their median cycle length. In this case, a 61.5-year cycle would be expected to have an orb of slightly over 10 years. Now if time proves this to be a valid historical cycle, then we can project a time band in the future of 51-72 years to determine the likely period for the end of future bull market runs. Thus if the third such great bull cycle in U.S. stocks began with the secondary low of April 1942, then the current 61.5-year bull market run cycle is already near the midpoint of its due period: mid-2003, +/- 10 years. This gives us a probability time band of 1993-2011 for a crest, to be followed by a steep decline. The duration of this decline will likely be 3-7 years (but those are the only two cases in the past, and perhaps it could be 2 years in either direction, i.e. 1-9 years).

As the reader will soon see, these time bands suggesting a crest prior to the end of 2011 and a 1-9 year severe decline to a trough have some very remarkable geocosmic parallels to the prior historical instances of these same cycles. For instance, between 2008-2013 (and mostly 2008-2010), Saturn, Uranus, and Pluto will form a T-square in first mutable, then cardinal, signs. Pluto will be the midpoint planet. These same three planets last formed this same astrological pattern in cardinal signs between 1930-1932, which just so happened to follow the end (crest) of the last completed cycle of this potential series. But just as amazing is the fact that these same three planets were involved in hard aspects* to one another back in the 1835-1842 "crash."

Let us now look at some of the geocosmic signatures that occurred at these historical turning points and see if we can't begin to appreciate the interplay between investor psychology (measured by extreme highs and lows in market prices) and re-occurring celestial patterns.

** See Figure 1 on page 10 for an explanation of "hard aspects."*

CHAPTER THREE

CORRELATION OF PLANETARY CYCLES TO LONG-TERM TRENDS

Tables 1 and 2 on the following pages provide a list of the geocentric positions of Saturn, Uranus, Neptune, Pluto, and the Moon's North Node at the times of the beginning (low) and end (crest) of each great bull market cycle in the U.S. stock market. The first table uses the absolute, or first low, as discussed in the previous chapter. The second table uses the secondary low from which the bull market started in earnest. When dates prior to 1789 are used, they pertain to British stock indices. In these cases, the middle of the year (July 1) was chosen. Thus these planetary positions may be off by a few degrees, depending upon when that actual low or high formed during the year. For example, in the case of Uranus, it may be off by as much as 8°, which is the extent of Uranus' range in one year. It will be less in the case of Neptune and Pluto (perhaps 4-5° maximum), and more in the case of Saturn and the Moon's Node. In the case of the Moon's Node, it moves with regularity about 18° per year. So it is not likely to be off by more than 9°.

In cases prior to 1928, the exact week or month was known, but not the exact date. In cases in which only the month as known, the planetary positions for the middle (15th) of that month were used. In cases where only the nearest week was known, the planetary positions of the middle of that week were chosen

Even before examining the planets, the first step is to determine the most probable time band for the top of this current bull market. This is done by overlapping the two time bands for the projected tops (Table 1 and Table 2). The projected time band for the end of the current bull market, based on the starting dates used in Table 1, is 1998-2026. The projected time band for the crest based on the starting dates used in Table 2 is 1992- 2014. Both projections overlap between 1998-2014. This, then, is the optimal time band for the crest of this third great bull market in U.S. stocks, based upon two different starting points of the two prior instances of great bull market runs.

Now let's see if there are any geocosmic correlations between the previous two great bull market trends, the down trends which followed, and even the congestion periods that followed those absolute lows. For this, we will study both tables, examining the distances traveled by the major planets, the degree sectors from which the reversals began, and the relationship of the planets in their planetary pair cycles with one another.

Table 1

ABSOLUTE FIRST LOWS

	Start (Low)			End (Crest)		
1.	*July 1, 1762*			*May 15, 1835 (73 years)*		
	Saturn	23°	Aries	Saturn	17°	Libra
	Uranus	13°	Aries	Uranus	0°	Pisces
	Neptune	22°	Leo	Neptune	3°	Aquarius
	Pluto	0°	Capricorn	Pluto	14°	Aries
	North Node	10°	Taurus	North Node	8°	Gemini
2.	*February 15, 1842*			*September 3, 1929 (87 years)*		
	Saturn	11°	Capricorn	Saturn	23°	Sagittarius
	Uranus	22°	Pisces	Uranus	10°	Aries
	Neptune	17°	Aquarius	Neptune	1°	Virgo
	Pluto	19°	Aries	Pluto	19°	Cancer
	North Node	29°	Capricorn	North Node	14°	Taurus
3.	*July 8, 1932*			*Crest due 2012 +/- 14 years*		
	Saturn	2°	Aquarius	Saturn	??	
	Uranus	23°	Aries	Uranus	Aquarius-Taurus	
	Neptune	5°	Virgo	Neptune	Aquarius-Pisces	
	Pluto	21°	Cancer	Pluto	Sag.-Cap.	
	North Node	18°	Pisces	North Node	??	

Table 1: Planetary positions on or near day of absolute beginning and end of the three great bull markets in history of U.S. stocks.

THE PLUTO EFFECT

The problem with studying the furthest-out planet in the solar system is that it moves so slowly. In fact, it takes Pluto about 248 years to make one complete orbit around the Sun. It has yet to complete an entire cycle since the U.S. stock market started trading. Nevertheless, there are some remarkable astrological correlations that have appeared.

Looking at Table 1 above, one can see that the first bull market began with Pluto near the Capricorn ingress (0° Capricorn in 1762). That bull run continued until 1835, when Pluto was near the middle of the next cardinal sign of Aries. When the market dropped in 1842 and the next major bull market commenced, Pluto was still in Aries (about 21°).

Table 2

SECONDARY LOWS

	Start (Low)			End (Crest)		
1.	*July 1, 1784*			*May 15, 1835 (51 Years)*		
	Saturn	21°	Capricorn	Saturn	16°	Libra
	Uranus	12°	Cancer	Uranus	0°	Pisces
	Neptune	9°	Libra	Neptune	3°	Aquarius
	Pluto	11°	Aquarius	Pluto	14°	Aries
	North Node	1°	Pisces	North Node	8°	Gemini
2.	*October 15, 1857*			*September 3, 1929 (72 years)*		
	Saturn	16°	Cancer	Saturn	23°	Sagittarius
	Uranus	27°	Taurus	Uranus	10°	Aries
	Neptune	22°	Pisces	Neptune	1°	Virgo
	Pluto	6°	Taurus	Pluto	19°	Cancer
	North Node	1°	Aries	North Node	14°	Taurus
3.	*April 29, 1942*			*Crest due 1992-2014*		
	Saturn	29°	Taurus	Saturn	??	
	Uranus	29°	Taurus	Uranus	Aquarius-Aries	
	Neptune	27°	Virgo	Neptune	Aquar.-early Pisces	
	Pluto	3°	Leo	Pluto	Sag.-early Cap.	
	North Node	18°	Virgo	North Node	??	

Table 2: Planetary positions on or near date of secondary low which began the three great bull markets in U.S. stocks, and positions on date of crests which ended those bull market runs.

The second great bull market did not end until Pluto had entered the middle section of Cancer, the next cardinal sign, in 1929. Three years later the collapse was over, and the current third great bull market began. Pluto was still in Cancer at the time. *In all cases of the absolute trough and crest (beginning and end) of each bull market, Pluto was in a cardinal sign. In fact, the beginning trough of each bull market found Pluto in the next successive cardinal sign.*

The secondary lows from which the bull markets really lifted off, as depicted in Table 2, are also quite interesting. The first secondary low unfolded in 1784 as Pluto was in early Aquarius, the fixed sign following the Capricorn low of 1762. The second bull market witnessed the secondary low taking place in 1857, when Pluto was in early Taurus, the fixed sign following Aries, which is where the absolute low took place 15 years earlier (1842). Likewise in 1942, 10 years after the absolute low that began the third great bull market, Pluto was in the next fixed sign, early Leo.

So far, these cases have formed an astrological correlation. That is, the absolute bottom from which great bull markets commence occur when Pluto moves through a cardinal sign of the tropical zodiac. A few years later, as Pluto enters the early degrees of the next fixed sign, the market makes a secondary low, after which the bull market begins in earnest. It lasts until Pluto enters the next cardinal sign.

However, according to this pattern, a crest and a severe decline were due to unfold when Pluto entered Libra. Such a crest and ensuing decline did in fact happen. On January 11, 1973, the stock market made a new intraday all-time high at 1067, via the Dow Jones Industrial Averages. Pluto was at 4° Libra. The market then lost nearly 50% of its value (46.6%) in the following 23 months, as it bottomed on December 9, 1974. At the time of the bottom, Pluto was indeed still in the successive cardinal sign of Libra (see Table 3). The market did not recover its 1973 all-time high levels again until late 1982, some 9 years later. A secondary low was registered in August 1982, as Pluto hovered around 24° Libra. Following that secondary low, the great bull market of 1982 through the present commenced.

These time lengths do not fit our linear conception of a cycle time band as described in the previous chapter. That is, they do not coincide with an 80 or 61.5-year bull market trend cycle. However, due to Pluto's elliptical orbit around the Sun, these dates do fit nicely into an astrological time sequence. Unlike the other planets, which orbit in a more circular and thus rhythmic pattern, Pluto does not spend the same amount of time in each zodiac sign. For instance, it only spends 12-13 years each in the signs Libra, Scorpio, and Sagittarius; 15 years in the signs Capricorn and Virgo; 19-20 years in Leo and Aquarius; and 25-31 years in Pisces, Aries, Taurus, Gemini, and Cancer. Since the first two of the three great bull markets took place between 1762-1929, when Pluto transited between Capricorn and Cancer (the slowest part of its orbit), the cycles would appear longer. But between 1956-2008, Pluto transits through the signs where it spends only half as much time, and thus cycles related to Pluto seem much more contracted. As a digression, this might astrologically explain why everything in life seems so speeded up in recent years, for Pluto is now in that sector of the zodiac where it moves so quickly in comparison. Between 1971-2008, a period of only 37 years, it will complete its passage through three zodiac signs (Libra, Scorpio, and Sagittarius). In comparison, it took 90 years, from 1822-1912, to pass through three signs (Aries, Taurus, and Gemini).

This later period (1822-1912), when Pluto sojourned through the most elongated part of its elliptical orbit, corresponded fairly well to the longest of the three great historical bull markets in U.S. stocks (1842-1929). But at the same time, it is possible to interpret 1932-1973 as a complete bull market against the time frame of Pluto's orbit. If so, this bull market lasted only 41 years, or the shortest of what would then be three completed bull markets on record. *Taking this one step further, it is possible that a fourth bull market*

Table 3

ABSOLUTE FIRST LOWS
PLUTO EFFECT

Start (Low)			End (Crest)		
1. *July 1, 1762*			*May 15, 1835 (73 years)*		
Saturn	23°	Aries	Saturn	17°	Libra
Uranus	13°	Aries	Uranus	0°	Pisces
Neptune	22°	Leo	Neptune	3°	Aquarius
Pluto	0°	Capricorn	Pluto	14°	Aries
North Node	10°	Taurus	North Node	8°	Gemini
2. *February 15, 1842*			*September 3, 1929 (87 years)*		
Saturn	11°	Capricorn	Saturn	23°	Sagittarius
Uranus	23°	Pisces	Uranus	10°	Aries
Neptune	17°	Aquarius	Neptune	1°	Virgo
Pluto	19°	Aries	Pluto	19°	Cancer
North Node	29°	Capricorn	North Node	14°	Taurus
3. *July 8, 1932*			*January 11, 1973 (41 years)*		
Saturn	2°	Aquarius	Saturn	14°	Gemini
Uranus	23°	Aries	Uranus	23°	Libra
Neptune	5°	Virgo	Neptune	6°	Sagittarius
Pluto	21°	Cancer	Pluto	4°	Libra
North Node	18°	Pisces	North Node	16°	Capricorn
4. *December 9, 1974*			*Crest due 2008-2023*		
Saturn	17°	Cancer	(Pluto in Capricorn)		
Uranus	0°	Scorpio			
Neptune	9°	Sagittarius			
Pluto	8°	Libra			
North Node	10°	Sagittarius			

Table 3: Planetary positions on or near day of absolute beginning and end of the four great bull markets in history of U.S. stocks, per Pluto studies.

Table 4

SECONDARY LOWS
PLUTO EFFECT

	Start (Low)			End (Crest)		
1.	*July 1, 1784*			*May 15, 1835 (51 Years)*		
	Saturn	21°	Capricorn	Saturn	17°	Libra
	Uranus	12°	Cancer	Uranus	0°	Pisces
	Neptune	9°	Libra	Neptune	3°	Aquarius
	Pluto	11°	Aquarius	Pluto	14°	Aries
	North Node	1°	Pisces	North Node	8°	Gemini
2.	*October 15, 1857*			*September 3, 1929 (72 years)*		
	Saturn	17°	Cancer	Saturn	23°	Sagittarius
	Uranus	28°	Taurus	Uranus	10°	Aries
	Neptune	20°	Pisces	Neptune	1°	Virgo
	Pluto	6°	Taurus	Pluto	19°	Cancer
	North Node	27°	Pisces	North Node	14°	Taurus
3.	*April 29, 1942*			*January 11, 1973 (41 years)*		
	Saturn	29°	Taurus	Saturn	14°	Gemini
	Uranus	29°	Taurus	Uranus	23°	Libra
	Neptune	27°	Virgo	Neptune	6°	Sagittarius
	Pluto	3°	Leo	Pluto	4°	Libra
	North Node	12°	Virgo	North Node	16°	Capricorn
4.	*August 9, 1982*			*Crest due 2006-2012*		
	Saturn	17°	Libra	(Pluto late Sagittarius-early Capricorn)		
	Uranus	0°	Sagittarius			
	Neptune	24°	Sagittarius			
	Pluto	24°	Libra			
	North Node	13°	Cancer			

Table 4: Planetary positions on or near day of secondary trough beginning the four great bull markets in history of U.S. stocks, per Pluto studies.

began with the absolute low of late 1974, and would be due to top out — and form its next absolute low as well — while Pluto transits through Capricorn. This will take place from 2008-2023. That is, if indeed there is a Pluto correlation to these long-term cycles in U.S. stocks, then this current bull market would end between 2008-2014, after which a severe decline would commence and end before 2023. The market would then likely enter into a congestion period for a number of years, forming a secondary low as Pluto entered the sector of the zodiac between very late Capricorn and early Aquarius (probably between 2020-2030). Afterwards, the next major bull market would be due to commence. According to Pluto's orbit, it would last approximately 50 years, or until Pluto entered Aries (2066-2095).

Using Pluto's history as a guide, it may be possible to obtain yet a more narrow time band for a potential crest. Looking at Table 4, one can note that the duration of time it took for the bull market to unfold (based upon the secondary low as a starting point) was 61°-73° of Pluto's movement. That is, in the first bull market (1784-1835, or 51 years), Pluto moved from 11° Aquarius to 14° Aries (63°). In the second bull market (1857-1929), Pluto transited from 6° Taurus to 19° Cancer (73°). And if we use the third bull market from 1942–1973, Pluto transited from 3° Leo to 4° Libra, or 61°. Thus in every case, the duration of a powerful bull market lasted 61°-73° degrees of Pluto's orbit through the zodiac.

If we add this same spatial relationship to the position of Pluto at the start of the last secondary low (August 1982, or 24° Libra), we get a zodiac sector of 25° Sagittarius to 7° Capricorn. Pluto will be in this sector from 2006-2012. If Pluto unfolds in the cardinal sign of Capricorn at the time of this next bull market's climax, it will maintain the consistency of past instances. **Therefore, the highest probability zone for a peak in U.S. stock prices based upon the historical correlation of Pluto's transit would be 2008-2012.** Of course readers must keep in mind that these calculations involving Pluto pertain to only two to three completed historical cycles. But in the case of long-term bull markets in U.S. stocks, that is all that history has allowed us as of this writing.

THE NEPTUNE EFFECT

Neptune's orbital cycle around the Sun lasts 164 years. Unlike Pluto (which is unlike all other planets), Neptune's orbit through the zodiac is fairly constant. It spends 13-14 years in each sign of the zodiac.

There is not much evidence of a Neptune correlation to the beginning and end of the greatest bull markets in the history of U.S. stocks. One possible relationship may be Neptune approaching one of the equinox signs (Aries and Libra). In the three cases of secondary lows, Neptune was within 10° of its ingress into Libra (twice) or Aries (see Table 2). Neptune next ingresses into Aries in 2025. The 10° orb segment would be in effect from 2020-2030, which represents a potential time band for the next secondary trough from which a great bull market might commence. This is exactly the same time band in which a secondary trough was due to form according to the studies just discussed under the Pluto effect!

Another interesting observation is that each of the bull market's tops and bottoms (both absolute and secondary bottoms) since 1857 have unfolded when Neptune transited a mutable sign (Gemini, Virgo, Sagittarius, and Pisces). The 1857 secondary low was with Neptune in 20° Pisces; the 1929 crest found Neptune at 1° Virgo; the 1932 absolute low had Neptune at 5° Virgo, while the 1942 secondary trough found Neptune at 27° Virgo. Even if we use the 1973 crest as valid, Neptune was at 6° Sagittarius, the absolute low which followed saw Neptune at 9° Sagittarius, and the secondary trough of 1982 occurred when Neptune was at 24° Sagittarius — all mutable signs. **The next mutable occurrence of Neptune will be through Pisces, between 2011-2025.** If this signature unfolds again as it has since 1857, the stock market would end its bull run, form an absolute trough, and a secondary trough, all during this time band. This, too, fits well with the projections based on the Pluto effect. **In fact, both studies show an overlap of 2011-2012 as a potential end to this current long-term bull market, which also fits into the cyclic time band for a long-term crest.**

THE URANUS EFFECT

What can one observe about the relationship of Uranus to these significant market events? *For one thing, all three absolute lows have unfolded while Uranus transited in — or just before — the sign of Aries* (see Table 1). **The next transit of Uranus through Aries (or just before) will take place between 2008-2018, and if this phenomenon happens again as it has in the past, an absolute long-term cycle trough could form during that period.**

All secondary lows (three cases) formed in a rather narrow time band extending from 28° Taurus through approximately 12° Cancer. Perhaps most interesting about this are cases two and three, in which the secondary low formed at 28° Taurus (1857) and 29° Taurus (1942), respectively. Since the absolute lows formed in, or just before, Aries, this suggests that the financial community — as represented by the value of the U.S. stock index — was in a state of "flux" during the 7 years in which Uranus transited through Taurus. In astrology, Taurus rules money and values, while Uranus is the principle of sudden changes and unpredictability. When a market is in congestion, it is in a sense without a trend. Once Uranus left the money sign of Taurus, the "great bull markets" in U.S. stocks got underway in earnest. The stock market developed a clear, long-term uptrend that lasted until Uranus reached the Pisces/Aries sector. In a very real sense, then, Uranus has so far coincided with strong upward trends in U.S. stocks when it transits through the Gemini-Aquarius sector of the zodiac. That upward trend peaks as Uranus transits somewhere between Pisces and Aries. Once the top is in, it declines sharply to form an absolute low while Uranus is still in Aries. Throughout Taurus the stock market tends to trade up and down in a wide congestion zone. After leaving Taurus, the market returns to its strong upward trend for several years.

Uranus will enter these various signs of importance, as follows, in the next few decades. The overlap of years at the end and beginning of successive signs is due to the apparent retrograde motion of the planet as it moves through the signs. Uranus moves into a new sign, then retrogrades back out for a few months, and then re-enters the new sign for about 7 years before moving back and forth into the next sign.

Aquarius	1995–2003
Pisces	2003–2011
Aries	2010–2019
Taurus	2018–2026

The fact that the prior two secondary lows which preceded great bull markets happened when Uranus was about to ingress a new sign brings up an interesting possibility. Perhaps the ingress of Uranus might be a critical market-timing indicator by itself. Theoretically, this would make sense, for the astrological principle of Uranus correlates with the concept of reversals and sudden changes. The principle of any planet ingressing into a new sign correlates with the concept of a shift in collective psychology — a change in collective values, goals, and even beliefs. Thus Uranus ingressing into a new sign has the astrological qualities of what might coincide with changes of trends in financial markets — like stocks.

To test this theory, one need only to observe the relationship of Uranus ingress periods to long-term cycles in the U.S. stock market since 1872 (see Table 5). In all, this table shows 19 completed periods of Uranus ingress (1872-1996). These are evenly divided into long-term crests (11) and troughs (11) that unfolded nearby. The reason there are more than 19 troughs and crests is because in three instances, both types occurred nearby. In all cases, the minimum cycle period used was the 4-year cycle. Thus the cycles chosen are indeed meaningful, for they represent a major change in the underlying bear or bull market trend, as measured by the 4-year cycle. Readers of Volume 1 may remember that the 4-year cycle was described as perhaps the ideal cycle to use for an investment strategy (as opposed to the "buy and hold" strategy of the long-term investor, or the short-term "trader's" strategy).

Perhaps the most outstanding characteristic is the fact that each of these 4-year cycles (tops or bottoms) unfolded when Uranus was in the last 10° or first 10° of a sign (each sign has 30°). *There were no instances of major reversals shown here that unfolded when Uranus was posited in the middle third of any sign.* In fact, 17 of these 22 cases (77.27%) unfolded when Uranus was between 23° of one sign and 5° of the next sign. If we look just at the 19 dates themselves, 15 occurred in this same sector of each sign (77.95%).

More to the point, when an orb of only 3° on either side of the ingress is used, eight of these Uranus ingresses (42%) coincided with major trend reversals (minimum 4-year cycle), which is quite remarkable. Perhaps even more remarkable is that 16 of these cases had an "ingress zone," occur during a *central time band*, where Uranus spent 9-10 months retrograding back and forth over an ingress point. In eight of these cases (50%), a long-term cycle reversed in this zone (asterisks in Table 5).

Table 5

URANUS INGRESSES AND LONG-TERM CYCLES

Uranus Ingress Dates	Actual Cycle Culmination	Uranus Position At Cycle Turn
1. June 29, 1872	Feb. 1874, 18-year Crest	7° Leo
2. Aug. 1878	June 1877, 18-year Trough	21° Leo
3. Oct. 1884-July 1885	June 1884, 9-year Trough	24° Virgo
4. Dec. 1890-Sep. 1891	May 1890, 18-year Crest	23° Libra
5. Dec. 1897-Sep. 1898	Aug. 1896, 18-year Trough	20° Scorpio
6. Dec. 1904	Nov. 1903, 9-year Trough	23° Sagittarius
	Jan. 1906, 18-year Crest	5° Capricorn
7. Jan. 1912-Nov. 1912	Oct. 1912, 4-year Crest	29° Capricorn*
8. Apr. 1919-Jan. 1920	Oct. 1919, 9-year Crest	28° Aquarius*
9. Mar. 1927-Jan. 1928	Sep. 1929, 18-year Crest	10° Aries
	Nov. 1929, 4-year Trough	7° Aries
10. June 1934-Mar. 1935	July 1932, 18-year Trough	23° Aries
11. Aug. 1941-May 42	Apr. 1942, 9-year Trough	29° Taurus*
12. Aug. 1948-June 1949	June 1948, 4-year Crest	26° Gemini
13. Aug. 1955-June 1956	Apr. 1956, 4-year Crest	28° Cancer*
14. Nov. 1961-Aug. 1962	Nov. 1961, 9-year Crest	0° Virgo*
15. Sep. 1968-June 1969	Dec. 1968, 4-year Crest	3° Libra*
16. Nov. 1974-Sep. 1975	Dec. 1974, 18-year Trough	0° Scorpio*
17. Feb. 1981-Nov. 1981	Apr. 1981, 9-year Crest	29° Scorpio*
	Aug. 1982, 9-year Trough	0° Sagittarius
18. Feb. 1988-Dec. 1988	Oct. 1987, 18-year Trough	23° Sagittarius
19. Apr. 1995-Jan. 1996	Nov. 1994, 4-year Trough	23° Capricorn
20. Mar. 2003-Dec. 2003	??????	Aquarius-Pisces
21. May 2010-Mar. 2011	??????	Pisces-Aries

Table 5: List of all Uranus ingress periods since 1872, the long-term cycle(s) that unfolded closest to the ingress, and the actual position of Uranus on the date of that long-term cycle. The asterisk (*) represents cycles which unfolded during the ingress zone, in cases where the retrograde period caused this zone to last 9-10 months.

In terms of months away from the ingress, Table 5 shows that there were nine cases in which the reversal unfolded during the central time band of a Uranus ingress zone, and four instances when it unfolded within 5 months prior to the first ingress. That means that a 4-year cycle either bottomed or topped out within 5 months prior — or during — a Uranus ingress zone in 13 of 16 historical instances (81.25%). More recently, since 1912 we see this correlation present in 11 of the past 13 instances (84.62%). The conclusion is that there is a much higher than usual probability that a 4-year cycle or greater will either top out or bottom between a period that starts 5 months prior to the first pass, through the month of the final pass of a Uranus ingress into a new sign. If the next Uranus ingress zone is March-December, 2003, then this study suggests a four-year cycle will either bottom or top out as Uranus transits between 20° Aquarius and 10° Pisces (April 2000-December 2006), with the greatest probability being between October 2002-December 2003 (5 months before the first ingress commences, until the very last instance of that same ingress — the end of the ingress zone).

THE SATURN EFFECT

Saturn's cyclic orbit around the Sun lasts approximately 29 years. It takes approximately 2-1/2 years for Saturn to transit each sign individually. Its quarter cycles last about 7-1/4 years each.

The preponderance of long-term cycle troughs which commenced the greatest bull markets in the history of U.S. stocks happened when Saturn was in a cardinal sign. It did not matter whether it was the absolute or secondary low from which these great bull runs began. The results were the same. It did not matter whether one used the three great bull markets as identified by Tables 1 and 2, or the four great bull markets based upon the Pluto Effect as shown in Tables 3 and 4. The results were the same. Saturn was predominantly in a cardinal sign when these great bull runs began. However, what is most remarkable is that Pluto was also in a cardinal sign when these absolute bottoms formed. This strongly suggests a Saturn-Pluto relationship as a planetary pair correlation to long-term trends.

Let's review Tables 1, 2, 3, and 4 with the positions of Saturn and Pluto in mind. In the first great bull market in U.S. stocks, the absolute bottom in 1762 (starting point) witnessed Pluto ingressing into Capricorn. At that same time, Saturn was in Aries, another cardinal sign which by sign relationship, is square to Capricorn. Another interesting celestial signature in effect was Uranus in Aries as well. The secondary low of that sequence unfolded in 1784. By that time, Saturn's 29-year cycle had transited three-fourths of the way through the zodiac and was posited in the cardinal sign of Capricorn — the same cardinal sign where Pluto was positioned at the time of the absolute low. Pluto by this time had moved forward into Aquarius. But by interesting synchronicity, Uranus was in Cancer, yet another cardinal sign, and in opposition to Saturn. Neptune was in Libra, squaring both. This then launched a 50-year great bull run that did not end until Saturn had traversed one and three-fourths times around the zodiac to Libra in 1835. Coincidentally, by then Pluto had entered its next cardinal sign of Aries and was opposing Saturn (in cardinal signs, of course).

The market then declined sharply, losing 80% of its value over the next 7 years. The decline finally ended with the absolute bottom of 1842, which began the second great bull market in U.S. stocks. Once again, both Saturn and Pluto were in cardinal signs, this time in Capricorn and Aries respectively — another square-by-sign relationship. One other interesting observation is that Uranus was also in a cardinal sign then (Aries). The market stayed in a wide congestion zone for several years before finally completing its secondary trough in 1857. By that time, Saturn had advanced halfway through the zodiac to yet another cardinal sign, Cancer.

From this point the market launched its longest bull market ever, lasting until the great climax in September 1929, 72 years later. Both Pluto and Uranus were in cardinal signs, Cancer and Aries respectively at the time, but Saturn was 7° away from ingressing into Capricorn. However, by the time the Crash had ended and the market put in its long-term absolute low in July 1932, Saturn had indeed transited through the cardinal sign of Capricorn, and in fact, was just barely 2° into the next sign, Aquarius. Uranus and Pluto were in very close square to one another from Cancer and Aries respectively. In fact, just a couple of months before this, both were in T-square formation with Saturn in Capricorn.

The market then entered a 10-year congestion period. The secondary bottomed ended on April 29, 1942. At this time, Saturn, Pluto, and Uranus were not in cardinal signs. They were in fixed signs, and Saturn and Uranus were conjunct in the last degree of Taurus (right before the Gemini ingress). The third great bull market was launched then.

This study could stop here and be impressive enough. However, if we now consider a fourth great bull market, per the Pluto Effect supported by Tables 3 and 4, we see the that relationship continues. The crest of the next great bull market culminated on January 11, 1973. The market then declined sharply for the next 23 months, ending in the absolute low, which began the fourth great bull market on December 9, 1974. Once again, both Saturn and Pluto were in cardinal signs, Cancer and Libra respectively. Once again, these two signs were square-by-sign to one another. An 8-year congestion period began. It ended with the secondary bottom on August 9, 1982, from which the current bull market began. At the secondary low, Saturn had transited around to yet another cardinal sign, Libra, as it approached a conjunction to Pluto.

Using the four cases of absolute lows and four cases of secondary lows (Tables 3 and 4), six of the eight lows found Saturn in a cardinal sign. One other (1932) found Saturn just barely past Capricorn, which would have made it seven out of eight possibilities. What is also quite remarkable is the fact that in each of the four secondary lows, Saturn had transited to a sign that was square or opposite to the sign it was in at the absolute low. *In fact, in the cases of cardinal signs, the secondary low was in almost the exact degrees of its absolute lows (square or opposition by degrees).* In the absolute low of 1762, Saturn was approximately 23° Aries at mid-year. In its secondary trough of 1784, it was in approximately 21° Capricorn. At the absolute low beginning the second great bull market (1842), Saturn was around 11° Capricorn. By the time of the secondary low in 1857, it was opposite, around 16° Cancer. In the 1932-42 sequence, Saturn moved from 2° Aquarius to 29° Taurus, which is square by sign. However, more significant was the fact that it was exactly conjunct Uranus at 29° Taurus at that secondary trough. In the fourth case, Saturn was at 17° Cancer during the absolute low. At the secondary low, it was exactly 90° further — at 17° Libra.

Yet the most remarkable of all is Saturn's correlation with Pluto — and to some extent Uranus — at these absolute (and even secondary) lows. All four troughs shown in Tables 1 and 3 (representing the absolute lows from which each great bull market began) found Saturn and Pluto in cardinal signs (except 1932, in which case Saturn was just past cardinal Capricorn at 2° Aquarius). The study on the Pluto Effect showed that the great bull runs began from absolute bottoms which coincided to the time Pluto was in each successive cardinal sign. However, during those 12-29 year periods in which Pluto transited each cardinal sign, it took the transit of Saturn through a different cardinal sign (never the same as Pluto's, so far) to launch the long-term trend reversal, to end the trough, and to start the rebuilding process of the stock market. It was during this time that the carnage was in process and then completed, and that the base-building of prices began in which the 8-22 year consolidation stage, or congestion zone, began.

Glancing ahead into the future, this signature unfolds again at the end of the first decade of the next millennium.

Pluto enters Capricorn (cardinal sign)	2008–2023
Uranus enters Aries (cardinal sign)	2010–2018
Saturn enters Libra (cardinal sign)	October 2009–October 2012
Saturn enters Capricorn (cardinal sign)	December 2017–July 2020

Somewhere, in the overlap of these periods (October 2009-October 2012, or December 2017-March 2019), there is a higher than average probability of an absolute low forming, based upon past correlations of geocosmic signatures to only four such lows in the past. When these three planets are in cardinal signs together, history has shown that stock prices have collapsed, formed a bottom, started an 8-22 year congestion period, after which a long-term super bull market commenced.

There is one more oddity about Saturn's correlation to long-term cycles in U.S. stocks. Starting with the first 18-year cycle trough in U.S. stocks, which unfolded in 1797, every <u>other</u> (every second) occurrence of Saturn in Cancer has correlated with an 18-year or longer cycle trough. These instances include the long-term cycle troughs of 1797, 1857, 1914, and 1974. The 1914 trough actually occurred in 28° Gemini, during the period when Saturn retrograded out of Cancer for a short period after having ingressed into Cancer just 4 months earlier. The next occurrence of this planetary signature will take place July 2032-May 2035.

The in-between instances of Saturn in Cancer also produced long-term troughs nearby, as often in late Gemini or early Leo as in the sign of Cancer itself. Furthermore, very long-term cycle troughs were noted frequently with Saturn in either Capricorn or early Aquarius, such as in the cases of 1784 (21° Capricorn), 1813 (16° Capricorn), 1842 (11° Capricorn), 1903 (3° Aquarius), and 1932 (2° Aquarius). In the most recent two instances of Saturn in Capricorn or early Aquarius, 4-year cycle troughs unfolded. These occurred in June 1962 (10° Aquarius) and October 1990 (19° Capricorn). The only instance of Saturn in either Capricorn or early Aquarius that failed to produce an impressive cycle trough was the one of December 1870–December 1873, although in November 1873, with Saturn at 27° Capricorn, it did coincide with a 4-year trough. However, it was a modest trough, for just 3 months later the market was back up to the level of the 4-year cycle crest of January-May 1873. In fact, it was a little higher and formed the crest of the next 4-year cycle then, as Saturn was in 7° Aquarius. Nevertheless, all eight of these cases produced at least a 4-year cycle trough while Saturn was in Capricorn or early Aquarius. In fact, it seems that the zodiac sector between 11° Capricorn and 3° Aquarius is the most likely area for Saturn to be positioned during such a trough (six of eight instances). In addition, five of these eight instances coincided with cycle troughs that were of the 18-year type or greater. **The next instance of Saturn in Capricorn will unfold December 2017-December 2020. It will be in early Aquarius in 2021. It would appear that 2018-2021, then, is a high probability zone for another significant long-term cycle trough in U.S. equities.**

THE MOON'S NORTH NODE EFFECT

The Lunar Nodal cycle through the zodiac lasts 18.73 years. It's quarter cycle phase is about a 4-1/2-year interval. It spends about 18-19 months transiting through each sign of the zodiac, and in one year its average rate of motion is about 18°-19°. A numerologist might find some significance in the frequency of the numbers 18-19 pertaining to various lengths of time regarding the Moon's North Node. A student of geocosmic studies, though, will find more interesting the fact that three Lunar Nodal cycles take about the same amount of time as two Saturn cycles (56-58 years). As a slight digression, three Saturn cycles take approximately the same amount of time as one Uranus cycle (84 years); two Uranus cycles last about as long as one Neptune cycle; and three Uranus cycles last about as long as one Pluto cycle. That is why this chapter is focused upon these five signatures: The Moon's Nodes, Saturn, Uranus, Neptune, and Pluto all have cyclic orbits that are mathematically (symmetrically) related to one another. More importantly (and related, of course), these five geocosmic cycles also have significant correlations to long-term cycles — and trends — in the U.S. stock market.

It would seem natural that the 18-year long-term cycle in U.S. stocks would correlate to the 18.73-year lunar nodal cycle. However, the "fit" is not as tight as one would hope. First of all, the 18-year cycle in stocks is not a consistent 18-year interval of time. It has a range of 15-21 years. Furthermore, when it is part of the greater 54- or 72-year cycles, it tends to distort (contract or expand beyond the normal 15-21 year range). Consequently there is no consistency between 18-year cycle troughs in U.S. stocks and the sign position of the Moon's North Node.

Looking only at the U.S. stock market since 1789, let's create a table of the approximate (before 1870) and actual positions of the Moon's North Node at the time of the 18-year cycle troughs and crests.

Table 6

MOON'S NODAL CORRELATION TO STOCK MARKET CYCLES

18-Year Trough	North Node	Crest	North Node
1. 1797	13° Gemini	1806	25° Sagittarius
2. 1813	19° Leo	1824	6° Capricorn
3. 1829	11° Libra	1835	8° Gemini
4. 1842	29° Capricorn	1853	28° Gemini
5. 1857	27° Pisces	1874	8° Taurus
6. 1877	4° Pisces	1890	9° Cancer
7. 1896	24° Aquarius	1906	21° Leo
8. 1914	28° Aquarius	1929	14° Taurus
9. 1932	18° Pisces	1953	12° Aquarius
10. 1953	1° Aquarius	1973	16° Capricorn
11. 1974	10° Sagittarius	1987	2° Aries
12. 1987	2° Aries		

Table 6: List of positions for Moon's North Node at troughs and crests of 18-year cycles.

At first glance, nothing may stand out in Table 6. On second glance, one may notice that of these 23 instances, 12 unfolded rather close (within 22°) to the Aries (spring), Cancer (summer), and Capricorn (winter) ingress points. Only one happened close to the Libra (autumnal) ingress. There were also three instances of troughs occurring while the Moon's North Node transited through Aquarius, and two instances of long-term cycle crests unfolding while the Node was in Taurus (the money sign). In fact, the last nine (of the total of 12) troughs unfolded while the Moon's North Node transited (retrograde) between 2° Aries through 10° Sagittarius (or roughly, between the fire signs Aries-Sagittarius third of the cycle, or 0° Aries to 0° Capricorn quarter of the cycle). Conversely, seven of the 11 long-term crests unfolded between the 21° Leo and 2° Aries sector of the zodiac. This, too, covers yet another third of the zodiac measured by the fire sign segment of Aries-Leo. The other four crests unfolded within one sign of the Capricorn ingress (one in Sagittarius, two in Capricorn, and one in Aquarius).

This table, thus, suggests several things. Let's divide the Nodal cycle into three astrological sectors, starting with 10° Aries, with each sector lasting about 6 years. The first sector covers 10° Aries through 10° Sagittarius. The second covers 10° Sagittarius through 20° Leo. And the final sector would cover 20° Leo through 10° Aries. The first contains a high number of long-term cycle troughs (nine of the 12 cases possible in Table 6). However, the area surrounding the 0° Capricorn ingress part of this sector also contains a number of crests (three), suggesting an extremely sensitive point in the zodiac sector for the Moon's North Node regarding major long-term reversals in stock prices. The second sector contained only one very long-term cycle reversal — the 18-year cycle trough

Table 7

MOON'S NORTH NODE BETWEEN 20° LEO AND 0° ARIES

Dates	18-Year Cycle Crest
1. 1831–1838 (approx)	1835: 8° Gemini
2. Mar. 1850–July 1857	1853: 28° Gemini
3. Nov. 1868–Mar. 1876	1873: 28° Taurus
4. June 1887–Oct. 1894	1890: 24° Gemini
5. Jan. 1906–June 1913	1906: 20° Leo
6. Sep. 1924–Dec. 1931	1929: 14° Taurus
7. Apr. 1943–June 1950	1946: 20° Gemini*
8. Nov. 1961–Mar. 1969	1966: 1° Gemini*
9. May 1980–Dec. 1987	1987: 2° Aries
10. Mar. 1999–June 2006	??????

Table 7: Time bands when the Moon's North Node transited 20° Leo - 0° Aries sector, and the long-term crests that unfolded therein. The asterisks* pertains to the 1946 crest, which may or may not be an 18-year crest, depending upon which count one uses, and the 1966 crest, which may or not be an 18-year crest, depending upon which index one uses.

of January 1829. This might make sense based upon astrological principles, for this sector surrounds the Libra cardinal ingress point — the halfway point of the zodiac's range. Libra represents the principle of "balance," according to astrological studies, and thus the idea of a major reversal or sudden change in trend may be less expected in this sector. The third sector, though, (Leo-Aries) has extremely promising correlations. The table suggests that there may be a greater likelihood of very long-term cycle crests forming when the North Node transits between approximately the 20° Leo through 0° Aries — and especially between the 21° Leo through 8° Taurus sector (suggesting the significance of the area surrounding the 0° Cancer ingress point).

Let's explore these indications a little more closely. Let's create a table of those periods when the Moon's North Node transited the 20° Leo to 0° Aries sector of the zodiac, starting in 1831 (see Table 7). We will also identify the crest of the 18-year or longer cycle that formed during this period — which in fact happened in all nine instances. We will then list the dates in which the North Node crossed the 0° Cancer and 0° Capricorn ingress points since 1890, the 4-year or greater cycles that topped out or bottomed close by, and the degree of the Moon's North Node at those times (Table 8).

As one can observe, these time bands corresponding to long-term cycle crests occur every 18.73 years and last about 7 years. During that 7-year period, the sector that covers 14° Taurus - 28° Gemini contained seven of the nine instances of these crests. The Moon's North Node passage through this sector of the zodiac usually lasts less than 3 years. **The**

Table 8

MOON'S NORTH NODE INGRESS INTO 0° CANCER-CAPRICORN

Node Ingress Dates	Actual Cycle Culmination	Node Position At Cycle Turn	
1. Feb. 1890	May 1890, 18-year Crest	24°	Gemini
2. June 1899	Apr. 1899, 4-year Crest	2°	Capricorn
3. Sept. 1908	Nov. 1907, 4-year Trough	24°	Gemini
4. Feb. 1918	Dec. 1917, 4-year Trough	1°	Capricorn
5. Apr. 1927	Apr. 1926, 4-year Trough	20°	Cancer
6. Sept. 1936	Mar. 1937, 4-year Crest	20°	Sagittarius
7. Dec. 1945	May 1946, 4-year Crest	20°	Gemini
8. Apr. 1955	Apr. 1956, 4-year Crest	9°	Sagittarius
9. Aug. 1964	Feb. 1966, 4-year Crest	0°	Gemini
10. Oct. 1973	Jan. 1973, 18-year Crest	16°	Capricorn
11. Mar., 1983	Aug. 1982, 4-year Trough	12°	Cancer
12. Aug. 1992	Jan. 1994 4-year Crest	0°	Sagittarius

Table 8: Listing of Moon's North Node ingressing the 0° Cancer-Capricorn axis since 1890, and their proximity to a nearest 4-year cycle crest or trough.

next instance of the transit through this more narrowly defined sector will be April 2001-March 2004. Thus even though the next Nodal long-term crest is due March 1999-June 2006, the most likely time in that period is April 2001-March 2004, according to this study.

Table 8 displays how close the Moon's North Node ingressing over the Cancer-Capricorn ingress points corresponds closely to a 4-year cycle trough or crest. The idea here is to see whether or not this single signature really is so significant in timing long-term trend reversals. The results show that in all cases, a 4-year or greater cycle trough or crest unfolded when the Moon's Nodes was within 30° of an ingress into Cancer or Capricorn. Ten of the 12 instances observed since 1890 found the 4-year cycle had either topped out or bottomed when the Moon's North Node was within 21° of these two critical ingress points. And 8 of these 12 instances coincided with a 4-year cycle (top or bottom) when the Moon's Nodes was within only 12° or less of this ingress. In four of the six instances of the Node ingressing the 0° Cancer point, the actual reversal happened in the sector of 12° Cancer through 20° Gemini. In the six Capricorn ingress instances, the actual reversal unfolded four times in the sector of 16° Capricorn through 20° Sagittarius. Thus the Moon's North Node ingressing within 16° of the Cancer-Capricorn axis has about a 67% correlation to the culmination of a 4-year or greater cycle trough or crest. It thus has some promise as a trend analysis tool, but not so much as other indicators shown previously in this chapter. What may be more significant is the observation that every third Lunar North

Node cycle over the Cancer ingress has coincided nearby with a multi-year crest: 1835 (8° Gemini), 1890 (24° Gemini), and 1946 (20° Gemini). If this continues, the next multi-year crest indicated by this signature would unfold within a few months of October 2001.

SUMMARY

This chapter analyzed the astrological correspondences to the three — and possibly four — major bull markets in U.S. stock market history. When a possible geocosmic signature was found in all cases, other instances of the signature were examined to see if similar correspondences existed. The following relationships were found to be present.

Pluto

1. Each successive transit of Pluto in a cardinal sign corresponded with an absolute long-term cycle low from which the greatest bull markets commenced.

2. Each bull market lasted for an interval of 60°-73° of Pluto's transit (from secondary low to the end of the long-term bull market run).

Neptune

3. Secondary lows from which the bull market runs began found Neptune posited within 9° of the Aries-Libra equinox points.

4. Since 1857, Neptune in mutable signs has been in evidence at every absolute or secondary low, and crest, defining each long-term bull market.

Uranus

5. Each absolute long-term low preceding each bull market found Uranus posited in the sign of Aries.

6. Each secondary low found Uranus posited between 28° Taurus and 12° Cancer.

7. In every instance of Uranus within 10° of an ingress, a 4-year or greater cycle type has topped or bottomed. There were no such instances of long-term cycle culminations when Uranus was in the middle third of a sign.

8. When Uranus retrogrades back and forth over an ingress point (known as the "ingress zone"), there is a 56.25% probability that a 4-year or greater cycle type will reverse during that 9-10 month time band.

9. There is a 77% probability that a 4-year or greater cycle will reverse when Uranus is between 23° of one sign and 5° of the next.

Saturn

10. Absolute or secondary lows preceding great bull markets tend to unfold when Saturn is in a cardinal sign (75% probability).

11. Saturn between 11° Capricorn and 3° Aquarius tends to coincide with a long-term cycle trough (eight of eight cases, or 100%).

12. Every other instance of Saturn in Cancer tends to correspond with very long-term cycle troughs.

Saturn-Pluto

13. The most powerful geocosmic signatures corresponding with an absolute low in U.S. stocks preceding a major bull run is when Saturn and Pluto are both in cardinal signs. The most extreme combination tends to happen when Uranus is also in Aries at the same time (or possibly in late Pisces, or another cardinal sign).

Moon's North Node

14. Long-term cycle crests tend to culminate when the Moon's North Node transits from 20° Leo through 0° Aries, and in particular, 28° Gemini through 14° Taurus.

15. There is a 67% probability that a 4-year or greater cycle will reverse when the Moon's North Node is within 16 degrees of an ingress over the Cancer-Capricorn ingress point.

CHAPTER FOUR

THE WEIGHTING AND VALUES OF GEOCOSMIC SIGNATURES

How does one measure the strength and consistency of a geocosmic signature in regards to financial market prices?

Perhaps the most difficult task in trying to determine possible correlations between geocosmic signatures and market prices is that of establishing some sort of accurate measuring method. One's first impression might be to simply measure percentage changes in values that either start or end at the time of (or nearby to) a geocosmic signature. But this presents several problems. First of all, what percentage change would be acceptable? 3%? 5%? 10%? 20%? Secondly, would one choose that percentage of change from the move that begins at the time of the signature, or from the move that ends at the time of the signature? For instance, the market might end a 20% decline at the time of the signature, but the following rally only finds prices increasing 5% before another decline starts. Third, does one only accept the exact day of an aspect (or signature) as important? Or does one allow an *orb of time*, say 3 or 8 days? Or does one allow an *orb of spatial movement* between planets (or ingresses), like say 3° or 8° applying or separating? Last — and perhaps most importantly — what happens in those instances where the market is in a long-term congestion pattern? Are highs and lows within congestion ignored simply because they failed to produce the correct or minimum amplitude in price change? What if a signature did correlate with a crest that was not seen again for one year, but during that long interval of time, prices never dropped more than, say, 4%, and our criteria was 10%? Would it be any less important than another time when that same signature produced a crest from which prices fell 10%, but the interval of time from the crest to trough was only 3 weeks (instead of, say, 4% and one year later)?

In an effort to create a type of measurement that would most closely depict a possible correlation between market prices and geocosmic signatures, a method of weighing both time and strength values was adopted. The method is similar to that used in *The Gold Book: Geocosmic Correlations to Gold Price Cycles*[1]. In *The Gold Book*, market cycles were given various values from 1-5 based upon their median time length. This was known as the *relative strength*, or RS, value. The greater the cycle (i.e. the longer its median periodicity), the greater the RS value. All RS values were then added and divided by the number of instances of the geocosmic signature to produce a single RS value for that signature. Thus if there were 10 instances of a particular geocosmic signature, and five correlated with an RS value of 5, three correlated with an RS value of 4, and two correlated with an RS value of 3, the sum total of the RS values would be 43. Divided by 10 instances, this would produce an RS value for this geocosmic signature of 4.30.

Next, signatures were measured according to their frequency of occurrence nearby to a defined market cycle. The percentage of times in which a particular geocosmic signature unfolded nearby to a cycle in the gold market was multiplied by 5. The number 5 was chosen to compliment the values used in the *relative strength* calculations (1-5). This, then, produced the value known as *consistency*. As an example, if the 10 cases used in the above example produced prominent cycles within the allowable time orb in all 10 cases, then its *Consistency* value would be 5.00 (5 x 10 = 50, divided by 10 instances). But if only six cases produced a prominent cycle within the allowable time band of the signature, then its *Consistency* value would be 6 x 5, divided by 10, or 3.00.

Finally the two values were added together to produce a combined total of *Relative Strength* and *Consistency*, known as the *C/S Index (Consistency + Strength Index)*. This index could have a potential value anywhere from 0.00 to10.00, with 10.00 being the most valid correlation. A 10.00 C/S Index would mean that the strongest cycles were present in the allowable time band of every instance that the geocosmic signature unfolded.

In this study on geocosmic correlations to stock market cycles, it is necessary to distinguish between three groups of cycles. The studies presented in this book relate to those cycles known as *long-term and intermediate-term, or investment cycles*. As defined in Volume 1, a long-term cycle in U.S. stocks will refer to all those of the 4-year types or greater. Intermediate-term cycles will pertain to all those with a periodicity greater than a primary cycle, but less than a 4-year cycle (i.e. 50-week or 22.5-month cycles). The third group will be known as the *short-term, or trading cycles*, and will refer to all those cycles that comprise the primary cycle (primary, half-primary, major, and trading cycles), as defined also in Volume 1. The studies on these cycles will be presented in Volume 3 of this series, subtitled *Geocosmic Correlations to Trading Cycles (Short-term Cycles in Stock Indexes)*.

CONSIDERATIONS IN DEVELOPING THE MODEL

This book will focus upon correlations between geocosmic signatures and both the long-term and intermediate-term cycles in the U.S. stock market. Specifically this volume will examine the correlation of various aspects of long-term planetary pair cycles to long and intermediate-term stock market cycles (crests and troughs). Even within the context of long-term stock market cycles, though, a distinction has to made between those that are the longest of the intermediate-term, and those that are the shortest of the long-term types. In other words, there is a considerable difference in time between an 18-year cycle and a 4-year cycle. Likewise, there is a considerable difference between the longest of the long-term planetary pair cycles (like Neptune and Pluto, which takes 492 years to make a complete cycle), and the shortest of the intermediate-term planetary pair cycles (like Jupiter and Pluto, which take 13 years to complete a cycle). Obviously when using

Neptune and Pluto cycles, a longer time band must be allowed in determining their potential correlation to a long-term stock market cycle than if one were to use something like a Jupiter-Pluto cycle. Therefore, a different set of criteria will have to be used for time bands when determining Relative Strength and Consistency values which involve the longer of the planetary pair cycles from the shorter ones. In this book, one set of criteria will be used for correlating long-term stock market cycles involving Saturn, Uranus, Neptune, and Pluto in aspect to one another. A different set of criteria will then be used for determining Strength and Consistency values involving Jupiter in aspect to one of the aforementioned planets (beyond Jupiter's orbit). And in Volume 3, another criteria yet will have to be used for all shorter-term planetary pair cycles. Each of the criteria used in determining C/S values for the various planetary pair cycles will be clearly defined in its appropriate section. This first section will now define the criteria used for determining C/S values for the longest of the planetary pair cycles — those involving Saturn and beyond in aspect to one another.

CENTRAL AND EXTENDED TIME BANDS

Many of the long-term geocosmic cycles (like planetary aspects involving Jupiter and beyond to one another) will extend over a several month period due the retrograde motion of the faster-moving planet. As two planets enter an aspect to one another, the faster moving planet begins to separate from this relationship. However as the faster moving planet reverses its motion (i.e. turns retrograde), it will oftentimes return to the same aspect as before with the slower moving planet. When it returns to direct motion again, it may enter into this same aspect yet a third time. These will be referred to as "hits," or "contacts," or "passes," or even "passages." In some cases involving Saturn to planets beyond its orbit, the same type of aspect might even form a fourth and fifth contact due to the retrograde motion, and it may take as much as 2 years or more to complete the aspect in some cases. In fact, in the case of Neptune and Pluto, a sextile aspect in effect at the time of this writing will actually remain in force approximately one century. But in most cases, the duration of an aspect due to retrograde motion between Saturn and planets beyond will usually last about 9 months to one year. There are some occasions when Saturn and planets beyond in aspect to one another may last up to 2 years.

When an aspect between two planets involves a series of contacts (or passes) due to retrograde motion, then that entire period from the first to the final pass will be referred to as the *central time band* of the signature. In fact, an orb of one month before the first contact through one month after the last contact will be considered within the influence of the central time band. However, an *extended time band* of up to one year outside of this central time band may be allowed if the study involves aspects between Uranus, Neptune, and Pluto. An orb of 9 months either side of the first or last passage of an aspect will be allowed for the extended time band in cases involving Saturn to Uranus, Neptune, or Pluto in most cases. In some cases, this has been expanded to as much as 11 months.

There will also be instances in which an aspect between two of the furthest out planets only happen once. There are no retrograde contacts in these cases, and thus there is no central time band as defined above. There is only the single date — also known as a contact, or pass, or passage — in which the aspect unfolds. In these cases, the central time band will be considered in effect up to 4 months either side of a single passage instance involving Uranus, Neptune, or Pluto to one another, and 3 months if Saturn is involved. The extended time band, however, will have an allowable orb of one year from the exact date of the single passage of the aspect in cases involving Uranus, Neptune and Pluto to one another, and only nine months in cases involving Saturn to those same three planets, unless otherwise indicated.

The results of the values pertaining to *Central Time Band* will be shown in the first of three columns in the tables that follow each aspect. The results of these values pertaining to *Extended Time Band* will be shown in the center column in the tables that follow each aspect. This column will actually be denoted in terms of months away from the actual aspect(s) actually used for the extended orb in the study. The third column in the tables under each aspect will be titled *Totals.* The totals section will take only the greatest of the values that existed between the central or extended time band for each case.

Since the purpose of this chapter is to determine correlations of planetary cycle to long-term stock market cycles, and since instances of 22.5-month cycles were sometimes difficult to locate prior to 1885 (see the section on *Inherent Difficulties with this Model),* it was decided *not* to use instances of intermediate-term cycles (i.e. 22.5-month and 50-week cycles) in the calculations involving the extended time band, unless there were no other longer-term cycles nearby. If a 22.5-month cycle unfolded within the central time band, however, it was used in these longer-term studies of Saturn to planets beyond. It is the author's opinion that this will yield more reliable and useful results.

LONG-TERM CYCLES AND RELATIVE STRENGTH

Volume 1 of *The Ultimate Book on Stock Market Timing: Cycles and Patterns in the Indexes* identified several long-term cycles in the U.S. stock market. The longest of these cycles were the potential 72, 54, and 36-year cycles. However, there were not enough instances in the history of the U.S. stock market to confirm the validity of any of these long-term cycles, and therefore they remain only as potential cycles. Nevertheless, each of these cycles had in common the factor of 18 years. Upon further analysis, it was determined that there was indeed a valid 18-year cycle in U.S. stocks. Therefore, all 18-year (and greater potential) cycles must be considered as the strongest, or most important, of all long-term cycles in the U.S. stock market. Each of these cycle types (troughs or crests) will thus be given an RS value of 5, the highest weighting possible in this part of the study involving the longest planetary pair cycles. Almost as important as these long-term cycle tops and bottoms would be either double bottoms to them, or the secondary troughs (or crests) that began (or ended) the long-term bull markets discussed earlier in this book. These were given a value of 4.50.

Next in strength were the phases of the 18-year cycle (i.e. its half-cycle, or third of a cycle). In the case of half cycles to the 18-year cycle, an RS value of 4.00 would be assigned. In the case of a three-phase pattern to the 18-year cycle, each phase top or bottom would be assigned a value of 3.00.

The 4-year cycle itself would be as important as a third phase to the 18-year cycle. Oftentimes it was in fact one of the three phases to the 18-year cycle, and hence an RS value of 3.00 would be given here as well.

Following that in importance (and hence strength) would be the phases of the 4-year cycle, which would usually be a 22.5-month cycle. Their weighted values would be slightly less than the 4 or 18-year cycles, and hence they were assigned values of 2.00.

Below is a list of long-term cycles and the weighted values — *Relative Strength (RS)* — assigned for the long-term cycles part of this study.

18-year or longer cycles	**5.00**
Secondary trough or crest to long-term bull market	**4.50**
Double top or bottom to 18-year or longer cycle	**4.50**
Half-cycle to the 18-year cycle	**4.00**
Double top or bottom to half-cycle of 18-year cycle	**3.50**
"Phase" (third) to an 18-year cycle	**3.00**
4-year cycles	**3.00**
Double top or bottom to 4-year cycle	**2.50**
22.5-month cycle	**2.00**

As in *The Gold Book*, a plus (+) value will be assigned to crests, and a minus (-) value to troughs.

LONG-TERM CYCLES AND CONSISTENCY VALUES

The Consistency value will be determined in exactly the same manner as reported in *The Gold Book*. That is, the percentage of instances in which an acceptable cycle unfolds within the allowable time bands, will be multiplied by 5. Thus, if a cycle unfolds 12 of 15 times, then the Consistency value will be 4.00 (12/15, or 80%, x 5).

INHERENT PROBLEMS WITH WEIGHTING MODEL

There will be some inherent difficulties in applying this model of determining strength and consistency in U.S. stock market cycles to long-term geocosmic cycles. This is due to the manner in which data on U.S. stock market indices is available. Prior to 1885, dates and prices used were obtained through the data collected by James Jones of HALCO Commodities in Dallas, Texas. This was a compilation of various stock indices done through a study known as the Cowles Commission. Only the highs and lows of each year was available. However the data did indicate the month in which the high and the low of the year occurred. For instance, Jones data might indicate that the high for the year 1859 was 9.88 and it occurred in January, while the low was 8.33 and it occurred in June.

From 1885 through 1928, a combination of data provided by Securities Research Company (101 Prescott Street, Wellesley Hills, MA 02181) was used. According to their references, this data was itself procured from various sources, including the Foundation for the Study of Cycles, U.S. Department of Commerce, the Federal Reserve Board, Alfred Cowles III & Associates, and the National Bureau of Economic Research. Both monthly and weekly data format was available for this period. However, in all cases, the index was the same: the Dow Jones Industrial Averages. Following 1928, daily, weekly, and monthly data on the Dow Jones Industrial Averages was available through the generosity of Ray Reed, formerly of Commodity Services Incorporated (CSI), Boca Raton, Florida.

The problem, then, becomes one of identifying cycles of a correct 4-year or lesser periodicity prior to 1885. Different indexes may yield different times for these cycle troughs and crests. It wasn't until after 1885 that the data involved a singular index - the Dow Jones Industrial Averages. Prior to that, there are a mixture of indices that were used according to the various sources quoted here. Furthermore, with the data made available to this author, it was not possible to "see" if significant lows or highs fell during the year in which the record stated either January or December as the high or low of that year. In other words, if the record said the low of the year was in January, and the high was in June, this could very well imply there was another low between June and the end of the year. Although that low may not have been as low in price as the first of the year, it could very well have qualified for, say, a 22.5-month cycle trough. The author simply couldn't ascertain exactly where these lows (or highs) might have fell during years in such cases as these, prior to 1885. In these cases, the author implemented his "best effort" to either choose approximate months that would come closest to the most valid results for the objective of this study, or simply not include those cases where it seemed the results were too uncertain and could therefore "taint" this study. This was mostly in the case of using 50-week cycles prior to 1885, and in a just a few cases, even 22.5-month cycles. The author believes the choices of 4-year and greater cycles, even with the aforesaid limitations, are valid. The choices of 22.5-month cycles used prior to 1885 are mostly valid, in the author's opinion, but possibly incomplete.

Even after 1885, a case could be made that the DJIA (Dow Jones Industrial Averages) may not be the most appropriate index for measuring U.S. stock market cycles. Even if it is acceptable, it is certainly not the only acceptable index — and other indices will frequently result in different exact dates for the same cycle type being examined. In other words, not all stock indices bottom at the same time. In fact, very frequently there can be a considerable interval of time between the long-term cycle low on one index and that of another. As pointed out in Volume 1, this is known as "intermarket divergence," and is a valuable technical indicator in forecasting a change in trend.

It would, of course, be better to report only those instances that were analyzed from the same type of data. Or better yet, if *all* indices could be examined and measured for cycles, instead of choosing just one index. However, that would produce other problems.

Most notably it would be cumbersome and extremely time-consuming to perform such studies. In addition, it turns out that the very long-term cycles are usually relatively close in time from one index to another. In other words, they seldom occurred more than one year apart from one index to another. This would not produce a great difference in the results of the long-term market cycles and long-term planetary studies of this book, although it could make a difference in the results produced with the intermediate-term market and planetary cycles.

It would also, perhaps, be more reliable to give a report based upon only those cycles which unfolded after 1885, when monthly data was available, and the same index was used in all studies. But the problem then becomes one of not enough data to yield anything at all potentially significant, since some long-term planetary pair cycles only occur every 35 years or more. Since the purpose of this part of the book is to determine which geocosmic signatures (if any) have a strong correlation to long-term cycles, it is necessary to include those years prior to 1885, even if it means approximating (or even not using) some potential cases of the 22.5-month cycle.

Hence the decision was made to use the available data with these limitations in mind, but with the belief that even the data prior to 1885 would be reasonably sufficient to identify long-term cycles. Where it might be somewhat lacking is in its ability to accurately identify the intermediate-term cycles, since cycles this small might not show up as clearly on monthly charts as they would on weekly or daily charts.

THE STRUCTURE OF VALUES AS IT APPEARS IN THE LONG-TERM CYCLES SECTION OF THIS BOOK

Once again, the purpose for implementing this weighted values method is to enable the reader to see exactly what — if any — correlation each geocosmic signature has to stock market cycles. Simply identifying the dates and describing the nearby cycles may be enough for some students. However, this work would be far easier to use as a reference tool if one is able to see the figures actually calculated — figures for strength of cycle, consistency of occurrence of a cycle, and the combined "score" of these values. Thus — at a glance — one can quickly see what type of correspondence has existed in the past between each geocosmic signature and the U.S. stock market.

In the next section of this book, each chapter will focus on each long-term planetary pair cycle (a type of geocosmic signature known as an aspect). The date in which each planetary pair aspect unfolded will be listed in chronological order, along with the zodiacal (geocentric) position of the faster moving planet (that closest to the Sun) when involved in either a "hard aspect" (conjunction, square, or opposition, which have in common the same *quality* of sign), or a trine (which has in common the same *element* of sign). A brief description will follow, describing which long-term cycles unfolded nearby to this aspect date, or series of dates in the case of retrogradation. Other interesting information, including mundane events around that time (i.e. depressions, wars, etc.), and/or amplitude of price movements that preceded or followed this cycle, may also be displayed here. When amplitude of price changes are indicated in this description, *they are based on the measurement from the actual intraday highs and/or lows, and not based upon the closing prices.*

The structure of this part of the analysis will be as follows:

Dates & Position	**Long-term Cycles**

Following this, the calculations of the weighted values will appear. This breaks down the market cycles, according to their strength and consistency, as described previously in this chapter. The actual structure of this method of measuring values for long-term cycles will be as follows:

Relative Strength	**Central**	**+/- 9 Months**	**Total**
All			
Crest			
Trough			
Consistency			
All			
Crest			
Trough			
C/S Index			
All			
Crest			
Trough			

In each category, three sections appear. The first is called **Central** and pertains to the time band in which all passages of the aspect occurred, including the retrograde time band. Or it pertains to a defined period of time close to the date in which the aspect unfolded only once (i.e. single passage instances). In cases of multiple passages due to retrograde motion, a one-month orb prior to the first passage and following the last aspect was allowed. A 3-4 month orb of time either side of the aspect was allowed in those instances of single passages.

The next column pertains to long-term cycles that occurred outside of the central time band of the geocosmic signature, but which probably relate to the long-term market cycle. This is known as the extended time band, and its orb prior to the first (or only) passage or following the last (or only) passage is indicated by the title of this column. If it says **+/- 9 months**, this means an orb of time covering 9 months prior to, through 9 months following, the occurrence of any instance of this aspect.

The final column, **Total,** assumes the average value of the strongest (longest) cycles which unfolded in either the Central or Extended Time Bands. Each of these columns are further broken down according to crests or troughs, or both (All) combined.

In the **Relative Strength** category, the value of each cycle type is added, and then divided by the number of instances in which it occurred. In the **Total** columns, only the strongest (longest-term) cycles present in either the Central or Extended Time Bands were used (in cases where more than one cycle type unfolded). Thus if a 4-year cycle unfolded in the Central Time Band, but an 18-year cycle unfolded in the Extended Time Band, then only the 18-year cycle's value (5) was used in the **Total** calculations.

In the **Consistency** category, the percentage of long-term cycles that actually unfolded in each time band, multiplied by 5.00, was used. In other words, this category measures the total number of long-term cycles that are probably related to this geocosmic signature, as a percentage of the number 5.

The **C/S** category simply adds the values of the prior two categories together, and thus achieves the value of 0.00 to10.00.

References:

1. Raymond A. Merriman, *The Gold Book: Geocosmic Correlations to Gold Price Cycles*, W. Bloomfield, MI: MMA/Seek-It Publications, 1982.

CHAPTER FIVE

THE "CENTURIANS": CORRELATION OF TRANS-URANIAN PLANETARY PAIR CYCLES TO LONG-TERM CYCLES

Chapter 3 analyzed the relationship of slow-moving planets (and Moon's North Node) through the *signs* of the zodiac to long-term trends in the U.S. stock market. This chapter will analyze the relationship of the slowest-moving planets to one another at the time of major long-term cycle crests or troughs. These relationships are known as phases, or *aspects*, of the planetary pair cycles.

As stated earlier, the planets in our solar system orbit the Sun at different rates of motion, depending upon their distance away from the Sun. The further away from the Sun, the longer it takes that planet to make its orbit. Or said another way, the further a planet is removed from the Sun, the longer its cycle. Yet in their orbit around the Sun, planets will "align" with one another as seen from either the Earth (geocentric) or Sun (heliocentric). These periods of alignment are known as a *conjunction aspect*, and represent the *beginning* point of each planetary pair cycle. As the faster moving planet separates from the slower one, it forms various phases — or aspects — to the slower moving planet. The assumption in astrology is that the psychological dynamic pertaining to the two planets reaches a climax when those planets enter these various aspects with one another. An event, or collective psychological mood, tends to unfold nearby to these times, depending upon the principles of the two planets involved in the aspect and the nature of that aspect.

Although aspects are exact spatial relationships, their potential "influence" is in effect slightly before and after that precise moment. In other words, there is an "orb of influence" to each aspect. That orb can be defined by spatial distance. Some astrologers may use a 3° orb, while others may use a much greater orb — perhaps 8-12° or more, depending upon the planets involved, and the type of astrology being used. Those interpreting a natal chart might use a wider orb for aspects than those analyzing transiting aspects for forecasting purposes. Additionally, the terms "applying" and "separating" are used to refer to aspects that are either moving towards or away from exactness, respectively.

This leads to a very important consideration. Since planets have different cycle lengths in their orbit around the Sun, so too will they have different lengths of time during which their orbs of aspect are in effect. Two fast-moving planets like Mercury and Venus, for instance, will spend much less time in aspect to other planets than say Saturn, Uranus, Neptune, and Pluto to one another. In the first case, Mercury and Venus might stay within 3° of an aspect to any planet for perhaps 2-3 days. Any of the further-out planets (Saturn and beyond) might stay within a 3° aspect to one another for several months. In the case of Uranus, Neptune, and Pluto, the aspect may remain in effect for a year or more. Therefore, aspects between further-out planets to one another will happen much less frequently and remain in force for longer intervals of time, than those involving closer-to-Sun planets. It is thus reasonable to think that geocosmic correlations to long-term cycles and trends in U.S. (and even world) stock indices would involve these planetary cycles of the further-out planets in our solar system.

Additionally, in their orbits around the Sun, these planets will make numerous aspects to one another. In traditional astrology, the same name is assigned to certain aspects, regardless of whether they are moving towards or away from conjunction. For instance, a 120° distance between two planets is referred to as trine, regardless of whether they are 120° *past* the conjunction or 120° *prior* to a conjunction (which means 240° after the prior conjunction). For purposes of convenience, these studies will use the same distinctions found in *The Gold Book: Geocosmic Correlations to Gold Price Cycles.*[1] That is, planetary distances will be measured according to how far away the two planets are from their *last conjunction*, and be differentiated by the terms *waxing* and *waning*. Thus the first trine between two planets following their conjunction will be referred to as a *waxing trine*, and represented as a 120° aspect, because it has moved 120° from its last conjunction. The last trine before the next conjunction, however, will be referred to as a *waning trine* and a 240° aspect. This problem of assigning two different degrees of the 360° zodiac affects all aspects *except* the conjunction and the opposition, the only two aspect types which occur just once.

With that in mind, this chapter will explore possible relationships between long-term stock market cycles and the planetary pair cycles of Uranus, Neptune, and Pluto. For this, the *yearly* charts of the U.S. stock market (and in some cases, even the British stock market going back to the late 1600's) will be studied. Each of these complete planetary pair cycles have lengths of 100 years or greater. We will work inwards from the longest to the shorter cycles and we will examine all the conventional aspects — all the major and some of the more frequently used minor ones, using a geocentric approach. The dates used for these aspects are to be found in *Tables of Planetary Phenomena*[2] by Neil F. Michelsen, and/or via the *Pathfinder Astrology System* by AstroCybernetics[3], a software program created by John Woodsmall of Los Angeles, California. The "Hit List" feature of this program will indicate the date and transiting position for the planets involved in each aspect, based upon the time zone of one's choice. The *Tables of Planetary Phenomena* book provides a chronological order of all major aspects other than the sextile, basis Greenwich Mean Time (GMT).

NEPTUNE-PLUTO CYCLE

Dates	Aspect	Long-Term Cycles
1. 1776-1786	240° Waning Trine	72-year cycle trough (1784)
2. 1817-1820	270° Waning Square	18-year cycle trough (1813—7° applying) 18-year cycle crest (1824—5° separating) Half-cycle crest to 18-year cycle in 1819. Half-cycle trough to 18-year cycle in 1820.
3. 1844-45	300° Waning Sextile	4-year cycle crest in May 1844, and 4-year cycle trough in June-August 1845. The 72-year cycle trough was in February 1842, with double bottom January-March 1843.
3. 1856-1857	315° Waning Semi-square	72-year cycle trough (October 1857).
4. 1891-92	Conjunction	Double top to 18-year cycle crest, March 1892.
5. 1930-1932	45° Waxing Semi-square	72-year cycle trough in July 1932.
6. 1949-2032	60° Waxing Sextile	Too long an orb to identify just one or two long-term cycles.

	Central	+/- 1 Year	Total
Relative Strength			
All	4.42	4.50	4.67
Crest	+3.83	+0.00	+3.83
Trough	- 4.40	- 4.50	- 4.70
Consistency			
All	5.00	0.83	5.00
Crest	+ 2.50	0.00	+2.50
Trough	- 4.17	- 0.83	- 4.17
C/S Index			
All	9.42*	5.33	9.67*
Crest	+ 6.33	0.00	+6.33
Trough	- 8.57	- 5.33	- 8.87

* *Indicates a C/S value of 9.00 or greater, which means it has a consistent correlation to powerful, long-term cycles. These, then, would be the strongest signatures discovered in the studies of this book. More discussion of this in a later chapter.*

The Neptune-Pluto planetary pair cycle lasts 492 years. However, due to the elliptical and erratic orbit of Pluto, the interval of time between its various phases — or aspects —

is not regular. In fact, as a result of its irregular orbit, the amount of time it spends in orb of aspect also varies greatly with each aspect. For instance it moves back and forth in almost exact sextile over an 83-year period (1949-2032). However, the duration of its exact conjunction (6-8° Gemini) lasted all of 8 months!

Obviously there is not much history to observe with this planetary pair cycle. In the available history of the stock market, these two planets were in *waning trine* to one other between **1776-1786**. During that time band, there was the long-term cycle low in stocks (1784) that preceded the first great bull market in the United States.

The second aspect of these two planets was their 270° *waning square* (last quarter cycle) which unfolded between **1817-1820**. At the 18-year cycle trough in 1813, they were 7° away from the exact square (applying). At the 18-year crest in 1824, they were only 5° apart (separation). In 1820, there was a half-cycle trough to the 18-year cycle that unfolded, but the amplitude of the decline from the crest of the prior year (1819) was not very great. In all, it may be that this aspect was not a very strong correlation in this instance. Of all the Neptune-Pluto signatures, other than the waning sextile, it was certainly one of the weakest — in terms of cycle types occurring within the central time band.

The *waning sextile* occurred next in sequence, in **1844-1845**. During this time band, there was a 4-year cycle crest (1844) followed by a 4-year cycle trough (1845). However, the more dominant stock market cycle nearby was the absolute long-term low in 1842, followed by its double bottom in January-March 1843.

Yet another phase of this cycle — the last one-eighth phase — unfolded with the *waning semi-square* (315° between **March 1856-December 1857**). 1857, of course, was the year of the secondary low to the 1842 bottom, which began the second great bull market run in U.S. stocks.

The planetary cycle itself started anew with the **1891-92** *conjunction.* In March 1892, the stock market formed a double top to the 18-year cycle crest of 1889-90. Following that, prices collapsed the next 4 years, forming the 18-year cycle trough in 1896. Thus the conjunction kept prices up, but once completed, a decline of 45% ensued.

The first one-eighth phase of the new cycle (the 45° *waxing semi-square* aspect) unfolded between **November 1930 and September 1932**. Interestingly, the third great bull run began with the absolute low that formed in July 1932. That bull run continues as this is being written in 1998.

The sixth and final aspect of this cycle is the 60° *waxing sextile*. Again, due to Pluto's bizarre orbital pattern, this aspect remains in effect for over 80 years. It started in 1949 and continues into 2032. Thus, with such a long time band in force, it is impossible to isolate one long-term cycle with this signature.

Thus, even though there are very few instances of Neptune-Pluto cycles or phases in the U.S. stock market history, they do seem significant. All three of the great bull runs began when one of the phases of this planetary pair cycle was in effect — either the absolute or secondary low. In fact, if one broke up the second great bull run from 1857-1929, a half-cycle could be observed right in the middle, with the low of 1896. In other words, one could make a case that there was a great bull run between 1857-1892, and then another between 1896-1929. The Neptune-Pluto conjunction and 45° aspects occurred very close to the major reversal in each. It corresponded to the low of 1857, the high of 1892, and the low of 1932. In terms of our lifetime (those living at the end of the 20th century), the next phase of this cycle will not happen again. The square will unfold in the last half of the next century. The only instance that did not produce a long-term reversal during the period of exactness was the square of 1817-1820. All of the other four instances coincided with at least an 18-year or longer cycle in U.S. stocks.

URANUS-NEPTUNE CYCLE

Dates	Aspect	Long-Term Cycles
1. 1783-1785	270° Waning Square	72-year cycle trough (1784)
2. 1795-1797	300° Waning Sextile	18-year cycle crest (1795) 18-year cycle trough (1797)
3. 1801-1802	315° Waning Semi-square	1st phase trough of 18-year cycle (1802)
4. 1821	Conjunction	18-year crest (1824— 6° separating) Half-cycle trough of 18-year cycle in 1820. 4-year cycle crest Nov. 1821.
5. 1845-1847	45° Waxing Semi-square	1st phase crest of an 18-year cycle (1847). 4-year cycle trough in 1845.
6. 1853-1856	60° Waxing Sextile	18-year cycle crest (1852-53); 72-year cycle trough (1857). 4-year cycle trough (1854) and crest (1856).
7. 1868-1870	90° Waxing Square	2nd phase trough, 18-year cycle in December 1869, following 4-year crest in July-August 1869.
8. 1880-1883	120° Waxing Trine	Half-cycle crest of 18-year cycle (1881).
9. 1886-1889	135° Waxing Sesquiquadrate	36-year cycle crest (early 1890).
10. 1906-1910	Opposition	18-year cycle crest (1906). Double top in November 1909.

11. 1931-1936	225° Waning Sesquiquadrate	72-year cycle trough (1932)
12. 1939-1943	240° Waning Trine	Secondary trough to great bull market run. Also half cycle trough to 18-year cycle (1942).
13. 1954-1956	270° Waning Square	18-year cycle trough (September 1953). 4-year cycle crest April 1956.
14. 1966-1968	300° Waning Sextile	Double top to 18-year crest (1966).
15. 1972-1973	315° Waning Semi-square	18-year cycle crest (1973).
16. 1993	Conjunction	2nd phase crest of 18-year cycle (Jan. 1994)
17. 2017-2019	45° Waxing Semi-square	

	Central	**+/- 1 year**	**Total**
Relative Strength			
All	4.06	4.67	4.375
Crest	+3.96	+5.00	+4.125
Trough	- 3.94	- 4.67	- 4.25
Consistency			
All	5.00	0.94	5.00
Crest	+ 3.75	+0.31	+3.75
Trough	- 2.50	- 0.94	- 3.125
C/S Index			
All	9.06*	5.61	9.375*
Crest	+ 7.71	+5.31	+7.875
Trough	- 6.44	- 5.61	- 7.375

This planetary pair cycle has a periodicity of 171 years. Its quarter cycle (squares and oppositions) unfolds at 40-48 year intervals. As one can see, though, many important longer-term cycles coincide with other phases of its interval. In all, a 4-year or greater cycle unfolded in every case within the year(s) that Uranus aspected Neptune.

In the history of the U.S. stock market, there has only been two instances of a conjunction: 1821 and 1993. In neither case did a very long-term cycle trough or crest unfold. In the first case, a half cycle trough to the 18-year cycle occurred in 1820, followed by a 4-year cycle crest in 1821. There was also an 18-year cycle crest which unfolded 3 years later, but the BIG crest (from which the market subsequently lost 80% of its value) was not to be seen until 14 years later in 1835. In the second instance, once again there was no long-term cycle that unfolded. A 4-year crest was completed in January 1994, a good 3 months after the final conjunction. But even then the decline was not severe — only a 12% drop in value to the 4-year cycle low in April 1994.

In nine of the other 14 instances, an 18-year or greater cycle crest or trough — or a double bottom or top to one — occurred during the period of the Uranus-Neptune aspects. Of these, the sextile, sesquiquadrate, and opposition appear to be most consistently significant in their correlation to long-term (18-year or greater) cycle troughs or crests. The semi-square, square, and trine (and conjunction) did not seem to be consistent.

In all, there were slightly more crests than troughs under these aspects (the opposite was true with the Neptune-Pluto signatures). They seemed to run in groups: if a trough occurred at one aspect, then the next two or three aspects in succession would also be troughs. Then they would switch to crests for the next two-four aspects in succession. The total C/S value of 9.375 means that this signature has a fairly strong correlation to cycles somewhere between 4-year and 18-year types within 1 year of occurrence (and 75% of the time, within the central time band), which is very powerful and very consistent. This signature was also very consistent with its correlation to a long-term cycle within the year in which it unfolded.

URANUS-PLUTO CYCLE

Dates	Aspect	Long-Term Cycles
1. 1792-1794	Opposition	18-year cycle crest (1795), with a double top in 1794. 4-year cycle trough in September 1792.
2. 1805-1807	225° Waning Sesquiquadrate	18-year cycle crest (1806); half cycle trough to 18-year cycle in 1807.
3. 1810-1811	240° Waning Trine	3rd phase crest of 18-year cycle (1809). Double top to it in 1810.
4. 1820-1821	270° Waning Square	Half-cycle trough to 18-year cycle (1820). Also 4-year cycle crest in 1821.
5. 1830	300° Waning Sextile	18-year cycle trough (1829).
6. 1835	315° Waning Semi-square	72-year cycle crest (1835).
7. 1850-1851	Conjunction	18-year cycle crest (1852-53). 4-year cycle trough in 1851.
8. 1864-1865	45° Waxing Semi-square	Half-cycle crest of 18-year cycle (1864). Half-cycle trough of 18-year cycle (1865).
9. 1868-1869	60° Waxing Sextile	2nd phase crest of 18-year cycle (1869). 4-year cycle trough in December 1869.

10. 1876-1877	90° Waxing Square	36-year cycle trough (1877).
11. 1884-1885	120° Waxing Trine	Half-cycle trough to 18-year cycle (1884).
12. 1888-1889	135° Waxing Sesquiquadrate	36-year cycle crest (1889 & 1890). 4-year cycle trough in 1888.
13. 1901-1902	Opposition	4-year cycle crest (1901); it was a double top to crest of 18-year cycle .
14. 1916-1917	225° Waning Sesquiquadrate	4-year cycle crest (1916), and 4-year cycle trough (1917).
15. 1921-1922	240° Waning Trine	Half-cycle trough to 18-year cycle (1921).
16. 1932-1933	270° Waning Square	72-year cycle trough (1932).
17. 1943-1944	300° Waning Sextile	Secondary 72-year cycle trough (1942).
18. 1949-1950	315° Waning Semi-square	3rd phase trough, 18-year cycle (1949).
19. 1965-1966	Conjunction	Double top, 18-year cycle crest (1966). 4-year cycle trough in October 1966.
20. 1986-1987	45° Waxing Semi-square	54-year cycle crest and trough (1987).
21. 1995-1997	60° Waxing Sextile	22.5-month cycle and trough in August, then October, 1997.
22. 2012-2014	90° Waxing Square	

	Central	+/- 1 year	Total
Relative Strength			
All	3.97	4.58	4.12
Crest	+3.88	+ 4.50	+4.07
Trough	- 3.625	- 4.75	- 3.75
Consistency			
All	4.52	1.42	5.00
Crest	+3.09	+ 0.95	+3.33
Trough	- 3.81	- 0.48	- 4.29
C/S Index			
All	8.49	6.00	9.12*
Crest	+6.97	+5.45	+7.40
Trough	-7.44	- 5.23	- 8.03

In the 21 cases to date of aspects between Uranus and Pluto, a 4-year cycle or greater (or double top/bottom to it) occurred in the central time band in every case but three. Nine of these instances correlated with 18-year or greater cycle crests or troughs, or double bottom/tops to them. If the time band was extended by 1 year, then 12 cases involved 18-year or greater cycle crests or troughs (or double top/bottoms), which is roughly about half the time. On the surface, this may not appear to be very significant. However, let's look at the individual aspects separately and see if there might not be something relevant.

In the history of this 126-year planetary pair cycle, there have been two instances of conjunctions: 1850-51 and 1965-66. Both coincided with long-term crests. In the first instance, the crest unfolded 1 year after the aspect, in 1852 (and again in early 1853). In the second case, the Dow Jones Industrial Averages surpassed the 1000 mark for the first time as it touched 1001.10 in February 1966. From there the market declined to 627.50 over the next 4 years. It then soared back above 1000 to the ultimate 18-year cycle crest in January 1973. Thus the crest of 1966 was a double top to the 18-year cycle crest of 1973. It thus appears that the conjunction between Uranus and Pluto coincides — so far — with long-term cycle crests from which the market reverses sharply.

The waxing semi-square has also unfolded twice: 1864-1865 and 1986-87. In both instances major crests were followed by major troughs within this aspect period. In the first case, the first phase crest of an 18-year cycle unfolded in 1864. By the next year, while the aspect was still in force, stock prices lost 20% in value to complete the trough of the first half-cycle of the 18-year cycle. Similarly in August 1987, the stock market completed its then all-time high — the 18-year cycle crest. Within 2 months the market lost over 40% of its value as it dropped to an 18-year cycle trough (October 1987). So in both of these cases, the U.S. stock market unfolded in a similar fashion: first a significant crest, and immediately after, a significant and long-term cycle trough.

The waxing sextile may also have features in common with each other. Once again this signature has unfolded twice in the history of U.S. stocks: 1868-69, and then again 1995-1997. In the first case, stocks completed a significant crest — the second-phase crest to an 18-year cycle (1869). By the end of that year, the trough of that same cycle unfolded as prices declined about 19%. In August and October 1997, the U.S. stock market may have completed a similar crest and trough respectively of the 22.5-month cycle type. Nevertheless, the stock market did make a significant crest, followed by a 16% decline to a significant trough, shortly thereafter. In both cases, important crests did unfold — but in both cases, they were not the 18-year cycle themselves, but possibly "phases" of it.

The waxing square has only unfolded once (1876-1877), but it was an extremely significant cycle. It happened to coincide with one of the worse financial panics in the history of the United States. It also coincided with a 36- or 54-year cycle trough (1877). The next waxing square will unfold in 2012-2014.

The waxing trine also occurred only once, in 1884-1885. This instance coincided with the first phase trough of 1884, which was part of the 18-year cycle that began with the powerful trough of 1877 (under the square).

The only instance of the waxing sesquiquadrate occurred in 1888-1889. Like the semi-squares that preceded it, this signature too coincided with a long-term crest. In this case, it was the crest of a 36-year cycle in 1889-90. However, a 4-year cycle trough preceded this crest in 1888.

The first of two oppositions between Uranus and Pluto unfolded right near the opening of the New York Stock Exchange, in 1792-1794. Using the backdrop of British stock prices, it appears that this period coincided with an 18-year cycle crest in 1795, and the double top to it in 1794. There was also a 4-year cycle trough in 1792. However, due to lack of sufficient data, this interpretation may not be reliable. It may have just been a phase of the 18-year cycle. The second instance of an opposition unfolded in 1901-1902. A 4-year cycle crest occurred in 1901, arguably the crest of the first phase of the new 18-year cycle, but also a double crest to the half-cycle crest of the 18-year cycle which occurred in 1899. So once again there may be a similarity of cycle types with this aspect, for in both instances crests of some degree of magnitude occurred.

The waning sesquiquadrates followed the oppositions, and once again there appear to be similar cycle types that unfolded. In the first case (1805-1807) an 18-year cycle crest occurred (1806), followed by a half-cycle trough in 1807. In the second case (1916- 1917), a 4-year cycle crest unfolded (it may have been the crest of the first phase of a new 18-year cycle), followed by a 4-year cycle trough in 1917. Thus in both cases — as with all the previous sesquiquadrates and semi-squares (divisions of the zodiac by the number 8, or 8th harmonic signatures) — the U.S. stock market put in a long-term cycle crest.

The first difference in cycle types corresponding with the same type of Uranus-Pluto signature shows up with the waning trine. In the 1810-11 instance, there is a noticeable crest — the third phase crest of an 18-year cycle — in 1809. In the second case, 1921-1922, there is a well-defined half-cycle trough to the 18-year cycle, the first phase trough of a new 18-year cycle. Thus the trines were important — probably 4-year cycle types — but not distinguishable between crests or troughs.

The waning square once again shows similarity of a cycle type — both instances were significant troughs — but a vast difference in cycle length. The first case occurred in 1820-21. This coincided with the first half-cycle trough of an 18-year cycle, in 1820, followed by a 4-year cycle crest in 1821. However, the second instance was far more serious. The square of 1932-1933 coincided with the very long-term 72-year cycle trough, and the end (or bottom) of the Great Depression (1932).

The waning sextile also appears to correlate with significant troughs in U.S. stocks, although once again the degree of the cycle type differed in both cases. In the first instance (1830), there was an 18-year cycle trough that unfolded 1 year earlier (1829). In the second case (1943-44), another important trough unfolded 1 year earlier (1942). That was the time of the secondary trough to the 72-year cycle. Thus it seems that this sextile is actually bullish — prices are already rising from a trough that occurred just before this aspect.

The final aspect is the waning semi-square. The first instance of this signature occurred in 1835 and was a very dominant cycle crest — the crest of the 72-year cycle. Following this crest that the stock market began a 7-year decline in which it lost over 80% of its value. The second instance occurred in 1949-1950. This too was significant. It was the third phase trough of an 18-year cycle, but more importantly, it represented the last low before the U.S. stock market began its very powerful bull market to new all-time highs in the 1950's — the first time that prices finally recovered to levels seen in 1929.

In summary, then, the Uranus-Pluto aspects are indeed significant. They haven't always coincided with 18-year or greater cycles, but in an uncanny number of cases, aspects of the same type have correlated with similar lows or highs from which powerful reversals have unfolded. The conjunctions, waxing semi-squares, and sextiles have all coincided with powerful crests. The waxing squares, trines, and sesquiquadrates have only unfolded once, but in the case of the square and sesquiquadrate, 36-year cycle troughs and crests, respectively, have unfolded. The oppositions and waning sesquiquadrates correlated with important crests in all cases (18-year or greater, or secondary tests), whereas the waning trine appeared the least potent of all aspects. The waning square and sextile were again correlates to significant cycle troughs, while the waning semi-square correlated with long-term cycles, but a 72-year cycle crest in the first instance, and 4-year cycle trough in the second.

Putting it together, it seems that powerful crests unfold when Uranus and Pluto are in a conjunction, semi-square, and sextile in the waxing phase. Powerful troughs then unfold at the waxing square. The waxing trine seems weak (as does the waning trine), and therefore can probably be ignored in terms of long-term cycle formations. But the aspects between the 135° to 225° sector of the Uranus-Pluto cycle all appear to coincide with long-term cycle crests! These would include both sesquiquadrates and opposition. The waning square and sextile again correlate with troughs, while the waning semi-square could be either a powerful trough or crest. All that remains now is to analyze the long-term cycles outlined in the beginning part of the book, and see how often Uranus-Neptune-Pluto signatures were present at these most important reversals.

CORRELATIONS OF URANUS-NEPTUNE-PLUTO SIGNATURES TO LONG-TERM CYCLES IN U.S. STOCKS

So far this chapter has only analyzed the occurrence of aspects between Uranus, Neptune, and Pluto, and the stock market cycles that unfolded during those times. In some cases these correlated with very long-term cycles, like the 18-year cycle or greater crests and troughs. In other cases they correlated with lesser cycles, like phases of the 18-year cycle (for instance, 4-year cycles). It is the very important long-term cycles — and trends — that are of most interest to the investor. However, the very long-term cycles do not unfold often — certainly not as often as aspects between Uranus, Neptune and Pluto, which are the slowest moving planets in the solar system. Thus it should not be too surprising that there was not a higher correlation of very long-term cycles to these aspects. And yet if we study the most important feature of the weighting of values - the "Total of All" cycles in the C/S index - we will notice something quite significant: all had values of 9.00 or greater. This means that either 18-year cycles, or their phases, unfolded very consistently when these signatures were present, +/- 1 year. It is also very interesting to note that the longer the planetary pair signature cycle, the more powerful its correlation was to the longest of the longer-term cycles. For instance, the C/S value of Neptune-Pluto (the longest planetary pair cycle) was 9.67. Next strongest was Uranus-Neptune, the second longest planetary pair cycle whose C/S value was 9.375. And third strongest was Uranus-Pluto at 9.12, and Uranus-Pluto is the third longest cycle.

But what happens if the aspects were analyzed from the point of view of the cycles? That is, what would happen if the long-term cycles were identified, and then instances were observed (and counted) in which one of these Uranus, Neptune, or Pluto aspects occurred? Would a high proportion of these major trend changes in the history of the U.S. stock market be found to have unfolded when one of these signatures was present?

To find out, let's examine those dates of long-term cycle troughs (and secondary troughs) and crests, as shown in Table 9. These will include the troughs and crests of the major long-term bull market runs in the U.S. stock market, as identified in "The Pluto Effect" of Chapter 3, as well as those including the "Panic cycle" lows of 1877 and 1896, which were referred to in parts of this chapter. Those that correlated with the three greatest bull market runs — as identified in Chapter 2 — will be signified with an asterisk after the date. Additionally, major aspects involving Saturn and beyond will also be included in a separate line.

These results are rather remarkable. Perhaps the most remarkable of all implications is this: of the 19 cases in which very long-term trends ended and started, 17 (nearly 90%) occurred with a "hard aspect" in effect between either Saturn, Uranus, Neptune, or Pluto to one another. A hard aspect is a conjunction, square, or opposition. The only instances in which one of these long-term planetary signatures was not present were the secondary low of 1857 and the second crest (and absolute crest) of January 1973. In other words, there was another low and high respectively nearby in which one of these signatures was indeed present.

The Uranus-Neptune-Pluto signatures were not always present at the end or beginning of the longest trends in the history of the U.S. stock market as originally suspected. In fact, of the eight most important dates of long-term trends indicated in Chapter 2 (with asterisks here), only five of them (slightly more than half) unfolded with one of these three planets in one of the aspects studied in this chapter. Of the 19 total trend endings and beginnings listed here, only 12 (63%) found Uranus, Neptune, and Pluto in any of the aspects used in this chapter. This supports the earlier results shown in the astrologically-based study. That is, a long-term trend doesn't necessarily require aspects of Uranus, Neptune and/or Pluto — the longest planetary pairs in our solar system — to one another to begin or end.

Table 9

LONG-TERM CYCLES - AND THE GREAT "BULL MARKETS" - IN U.S. STOCKS

Dates	Aspects	Long-term Cycles
1. July 1762*	♄☌♅, ♄□♇ (90°)	Absolute low preceding bull market
2. July 1784*	♆△♇ (240°), **♅□♆ (270°)**	Secondary low preceding bull market.
3. May 1835*	♅∠♇ (315°),	Crest of bull market
	♄☍♇, ♄△♅ (240°), ♄□♆ (270°)	
4. February 1842*	♄∠♆ (315°), ♄□♇ (270°)	Absolute low preceding bull market
5. October 1857 *	♆∠♇ (315°), ♅⚹♆ (60°)	Secondary low preceding bull market
6. January-May 1873	**♄□♆ (270°), ♄☍♅**	Crest of bull market
7. June 1877	♅□♇ (90°)	Absolute low preceding bull market
8. June 1884	♅△♇ (120°)	Secondary low preceding bull market
	♄□♅ (270°)	
9. May 1890	♅⚼♆ (135°), ♅⚼♇ (135°)	Absolute crest of bull market
	♄□♆ (90°)	
10. March 1892	♆☌♇	Double top to the bull market
	♄△♇ (120°), ♄△♆ (120°)	
11. August 1896	♄☌♅	Absolute low preceding bull market
12. November 1903	♅☍♇	Secondary low preceding bull market
	♄∠♅ (45°), ♄⚼♇ (225°)	
13. Sept. 3, 1929*	♄△♆ (120°), **♄□♅ (270°)**	Absolute crest of bull market
14. July 8, 1932*	♆∠♇ (45°), ♅⚼♆ (225°)	Absolute low preceding bull market
	♅□♇ (270°), ♄☍♇	
15. April 29, 1942*	♅△♆ (240°), ♅⚹♇ (300°)	Secondary low preceding bull market
	♄☌♅, ♄△♆ (240°)	
16. February 9, 1966	♅⚹♆ (300°), ♅☌♇	Double top to the bull market
	♄☍♅, ♄☍♇, ♄△♆ (120°)	
17. January 11, 1973	♅∠♆ (315°)	Absolute crest of bull market
	♄△♅ (240°)	
18. December 9, 1974	**♄□♇ (270°)**	Absolute low preceding bull market
19. August 9, 1982	♄∠♅ (315°), **♄☌♇**	Secondary low preceding bull market

Table 9: List of the 19 instances of long-term trend changes, with their troughs and crests, and any secondary lows or highs made to these. Hard aspects that occurred in cardinal signs are highlighted in bold type. Asterisks (*) follow the dates of the three greatest bull market runs (absolute, or secondary, lows).

However, when you add aspects involving Saturn to these same planets, the probabilities of a long-term trend culmination increase remarkably. In fact, using all the aspects (not just hard aspects) between Saturn, Uranus, Neptune, and/or Pluto resulted in a 100% correlation of their presence at the time of long-term trend culminations.

The next question is obvious. Does the presence of Saturn in all aspects to Uranus, Neptune, or Pluto correlate with a long-term trend change in the U.S. stock market? It has now been demonstrated that it works from a market point of view. That is, when a long-term trend changes, one or more of these signatures are present. But does the aspect itself *cause* the change? If so, then every time (or at least most of the time) the signature arises, there should be some dramatic reversal in stock prices. That will be the subject of the next chapter.

But before progressing to that subject, let's note how many instances of these long-term trend culminations occurred with more than one of the trans-Saturnian aspects present. Once again note that in 17 of these 19 cases, there were more than one of these signatures present. Again the correlation is nearly 90%. The two instances in which multiple aspects were not present occurred in 1877 and 1896. In each of those two cases, there was only one trans-Saturnian aspect evident. But in each instance, it was a powerful hard aspect. In 1877, Uranus formed a waxing square to Pluto. This is a signature which by itself frequently coincides with financial panics — and 1877 was indeed the bottom of a very significant financial panic in the United States. In 1896, Saturn was in conjunction to Uranus. As will be shown shortly, this too corresponds to a period of political and, hence, economic difficulties in the world. It is a time of international tensions, and even wars, or threats of wars. Such threats oftentimes have a depressing effect upon stock prices around the world.

SUMMARY

Uranus, Neptune, and Pluto — three big planets far out in our solar system. Each has a long orbit around the Sun. The orbit of Uranus is 84 years, Neptune 164 years, and Pluto 248 years. Their cycles to one another are also very long. The Uranus-Pluto cycle lasts 126 years; Uranus-Neptune lasts 171 years; and the Neptune-Pluto cycle lasts 492 years. Whether we divided these cycles into sub-cycles by the 4th, 6th, or 8th harmonic, there was not an extremely high correlation between their presence and the beginning or end of long-term trends in U.S. stock prices (about 63%). Sometimes these signatures were enough to "break the trend," and sometimes they were not.

The philosophical question that arises from this is the following: Why do these long-term planetary pair cycles correlate with long-term trend changes some times and not others? The answer might lie in two considerations. First, these three planets are not enough for such a study. When you add Saturn to the study, the frequency of such correlations jumps incredibly — to nearly 90%. Second, the answer may lie in the study of cycles as presented in Volume 1. That is, rhythmic cycles (linear cycles) like stock prices, are not necessarily "due" to bottom or top out when these geocosmic signatures occur. All financial market cycles have a time band when their crest or trough is due. If these geocosmic signatures unfold outside of that rhythmic time band, they will not correlate with that cycle's top or bottom. They may coincide with a "phase" of that cycle, but not the entire cycle itself.

Thus it is important to understand how cycles themselves work, outside of astrology. It is important to know where the market is, in terms of its long-term cycle. And then knowing when the cycle is due to top or bottom, the presence of a trans-Saturnian signature can help narrow that time band down.

In this manner, one learns to understand the nature of reality, and then to use the study of the cosmos to apply to the nature of that reality. The other way doesn't seem to work. You can't apply knowledge of astrology onto reality, and expect astrology to alter reality from its natural evolution. To be useful in market analysis and forecasting, astrology must relate to the market's already existing structure and evolution. In that regard, astrology becomes an excellent market-timing tool. Without that structure, astrology by itself is more of a hit-and-miss proposition, for the dynamics of planetary signatures do not always translate only onto the world of finances. Planetary mechanics work — they have a correlation to changes in human activity. But human activity is more inclusive of other fields in life than just finances. There are other cycles of human activity than the world of economics. When a long-term planetary signature unfolds, it affects many areas of human activity — and especially those whose natural cycle time band is in effect. If it happens to be the "time band" for a cycle top or bottom in the stock market, then the presence of certain geocosmic signatures will do as fine a job of pinpointing that time as any study know to humankind.

References

1. Raymond A. Merriman, *The Gold Book: Geocosmic Correlations to Gold Price Cycles,* W. Bloomfield, MI: MMA/Seek-It Publications, 1982.

2. Neil F. Michelsen, *Tables of Planetary Phenomena*, San Diego, CA: ACS Publications, 1990.

3. John Woodsmall, *Pathfinder Astrology System for Windows,* Los Angeles, CA: AstroCybernetics, 1995.

CHAPTER SIX

THE "30-SOMETHING" GROUP: CORRELATION OF TRANS-SATURNIAN PLANETARY PAIR CYCLES TO LONG-TERM TRENDS

The interaction of Saturn to the planets beyond its own orbit is a vital key to understanding long-term cycles in the U.S. stock market. This may not be a novel discovery to students of astrology, for the principle of Saturn is known to be synonymous with "contraction." When a market is making a long-term cycle low, the economy of a nation is oftentimes at the depth of a "contraction" phase. Even when a market is making a top and about to reverse downwards, it is oftentimes coincident with the collective perception that the best of the "good times" is coming to an end, and an era of concern and apprehension about the future is commencing. In both cases, a Saturn signature is probably at hand.

Saturn's orbit around the Sun lasts 29 years. Thus, it too is a long-term cycle. Even the quarter phase of its cycle (sometimes referred to as the "4th harmonic") lasts a relatively long 7-1/4 years. During this orbit — in fact, beyond its 29-year orbit — Saturn will align with those planets further out in the solar system: Uranus, Neptune, and Pluto. Its planetary pair cycle with Uranus lasts approximately 45 years (43-47), and thus their quarter cycle is approximately 11 years. Its cycle with Neptune lasts about 36 years (35-37), and their quarter cycle lasts approximately 9 years. Its cycle with Pluto is more erratic due to Pluto's elliptical orbit. That cycle can vary from 31-37 years, and their quarter cycle is from 7-10 years, depending upon where Pluto is in its orbit. Thus each of these three cycles are referred to in this chapter as the "30-something group," meaning that their planetary pair cycles last 31-47 years. They are not as long as the planetary pair cycles of Uranus, Neptune, and Pluto to one another (the "Centurions," because their cycles to each other last over 100 years), but they are just as important to the study of long-term stock market trends. Additionally, this chapter will examine the Jupiter-Saturn planetary pair cycle, which has a 20-year periodicity.

The minor cycles (8th harmonic, or division of the cycle by the number 8, and of course, the soft aspects of the 3rd and 6th harmonics) can also be used to produce other contacts between Saturn and these further-out planets. Their occurrence in aspect formations is not very frequent, but they occur often enough to provide an excellent area of study for possible correlations between astrology and long-term cycles in the U.S. stock market. In the case of Jupiter and Saturn, however, these minor aspects occur more frequently. Therefore, only the conjunction, square, trine, and opposition aspects will be analyzed for correlations to long-term cycles.

In this chapter, some of these longer-term Saturnian aspects will be examined from the study of yearly charts prior to 1789, and monthly charts afterwards, to ascertain whether or not there was any correlation to 4-year or greater stock market cycles. In this effort, the focus will be upon whether a Saturnian aspect unfolded nearby to the time of a long-term cycle trough or crest. The term "nearby" has to be used, because there will be instances where an aspect may unfold on three or more occasions over a relatively long period of time (i.e. 9-10 months, and in some cases, more) due to a retrograde factor, while in other instances there will be only one contact, because the planets involved do not retrograde back into the same aspect again.

SATURN-URANUS: LONG-TERM CYCLES

This may be one of the most powerful of all cycles in mundane astrology. The dynamic of Saturn pertains to the foundation, tradition, or that which is known and expected. Uranus, on the other hand, refers to that which is new and different. When they come together, it is a clash of the old and the new, and typically the foundation (i.e. trend) is changed. The "old way" gives to the "new way." As mentioned earlier, the Saturn-Uranus cycle lasts 43-47 years with the quarter phases (conjunction, square, and opposition) occurring approximately 11 years apart. In this part of the chapter, the historical correlation between each Saturn-Uranus aspect will be studied from the perspective of whether or not such an aspect unfolded nearby in time to a major long-term cycle in U.S. stocks as outlined in *Volume 1* of this series.

Conjunctions (0°)

	Dates & Position of Saturn		**Long-Term Cycles**
1.	May 14, 1761 Oct. 28, 1761 Jan. 3, 1762	07°♈42' 06°♈03' 05°♈23'	Absolute low (72-year cycle) preceding great bull market run began in 1762.
2.	Nov. 1, 1805	21°♎32'	18-year cycle crest unfolded August 1806. This crest was over a 100% gain from low in 1802. Decline which followed lasted about one year, and loss was about 60%. 22.5-month cycle trough in September 1805.
3.	Mar. 15, 1852	02°♉10'	18-year cycle crest unfolded in January 1853, with double top in October-November 1852. Prices gained 80+% from low 4 years earlier (1848). Prices then declined over 40% to low 2 years later (1854). There was a 4-year cycle trough in October 1851.

4.	Jan. 6, 1897 June 1, 1897 Sep. 9, 1897	27°♏40' 26°♏26' 25°♏35'	36-year cycle trough unfolded in August 1896, preceding great bull market run that lasted into . 1929. 22.5-month cycle crest in September 1897.
5.	May 3, 1942	29°♉20'	Secondary low (and 4-year cycle trough) in April 1942, that preceded the great bull market run. World War II underway. This was end of 18-month decline (34%), and beginning of 4-year rally in which prices gained 130%.
6.	Feb. 13, 1988 June 26, 1988 Oct. 18, 1988	29°♐55' 28°♐47' 27°♐49'	18 and possibly 54-year cycle trough unfolded with the stock market crash of October 20, 1987. The global economy was extremely "worried" and vulnerable during this period. From this low, prices rallied over 80% to crest in 1990, 3 years later.
7.	June 28, 2032	28°♊01'	

Relative Strength	**Central**	**+/- 10 months**	**Total**
All	2.83	5.00	4.92
Crest	+2.00	+5.00	+4.00
Trough	- 3.25	- 4.50	- 4.08
Consistency			
All	2.50	4.17	5.00
Crest	+0.83	+1.67	+2.50
Trough	- 1.67	- 3.33	- 5.00
C/S Index			
All	5.33	9.17	9.92*
Crest	+2.83	+6.67	+6.50
Trough	- 4.92	- 7.83	- 9.08*

This is obviously one of the most powerful signatures correlating to long-term cycles in the U.S. stock market, as illustrated in the forward of this book. In every case, an 18-year or greater cycle, or a secondary low preceding a great bull market run, unfolded within 10 months of the aspect. However, only once did it unfold within the central time band as defined in this study (twice it unfolded 4-5 months *prior to* the first of three instances of the aspect, and twice it unfolded 7-10 months *after* the last passage). The one time it wasn't an 18-year or greater cycle occurred in 1942, which was the year of the secondary low from which one of the three great bull market runs began. That was also the one time in which it occurred in the central time band (1 month following the cycle trough). The instances of long-term troughs occurred twice as frequently as crests. There did not seem to be a difference as to what sign the conjunction occurred. It was strong regardless of sign type. In every case, there was a cycle trough recorded, although in two of the cases, it was not the strongest of the cycles present.

<u>Conclusions</u>: In all cases, very long-term trends in the U.S. stock market either started or ended nearby the Saturn-Uranus conjunctions. This is truly one of the most reliable and remarkable geocosmic indicators of long-term cycles in U.S. stocks, given an orb of 10 months preceding or following the first and/or last instance of this aspect. Investors may use this signature to time the culmination of very long-term cycles in U.S. stocks, like the 18-year or greater cycle. It is especially relevant if an 18-year or greater cycle trough is forming, in which case investors may use this aspect as a market-timing indicator to purchase stocks for the very long-term.

Waxing Semi-Square (45°)

	Dates & Position of Saturn		Long-Term Cycles
1.	Apr. 3, 1812 June 24, 1812 Jan. 14, 1813	07°♑52' 04°♑49' 11°♑58'	18-year cycle trough in March 1813; War of 1812 is underway. Stock market begins an 11-year bull market. Prices triple in 6 years.
2.	Aug. 15, 1856	09°♋55'	4-year cycle crest in December 1856. Market then declined sharply to 18-year cycle trough, and secondary low preceding great bull market run, in October 1857.
3.	June 2, 1903 June 29, 1903 Feb. 23, 1904	09°♒11' 08°♒05' 14°♒14'	Half-cycle trough to 18-year cycle in November 1903. This preceded the great bull market run that lasted through September 1929. Prices gained nearly 100% in next 18-months.
4.	Oct. 2, 1946 Mar. 4, 1947 June 30, 1947	06°♌47' 02°♌46' 07°♌54'	4-year cycle trough in October 1946; this followed 4-year crest of May 1946. Decline from crest to trough was about 25%. Market then advanced about 17% over next 9 months.
5.	May 16, 1994 Sep. 23, 1994 Feb. 20, 1995	11°♓15 07°♓25 13°♓22	4-year cycle troughs, double bottoms, in April & November 1994. Stock market soared over 100% the following 4 years.

Relative Strength	**Central**	**+/- 4 months**	**Total**
All	3.33	5.00	3.60
Crest	+0.00	3.00	+3.00
Trough	- 3.33	- 5.00	- 3.75
Consistency			
All	3.00	2.00	5.00
Crest	+0.00	+1.00	+1.00
Trough	- 3.00	- 1.00	- 4.00

C/S Index			
All	6.33	7.00	8.60
Crest	+0.00	+4.00	+4.00
Trough	- 6.33	- 6.00	- 7.75

In all five cases of this signature, 4-year or greater cycles have unfolded within four months of the central time band (100%). In the two cases in which it did not unfold in the central time band, a four year cycle crest unfolded just 4 months before a single passage instance, and an 18-year cycle trough unfolded just 2 months after the last passage of a three-series pass. In four of these five cases (80%), the dominant long-term cycle was a trough. In two cases, Saturn was in cardinal signs and both correlated nearby to 18-year cycle troughs (given an orb of 16 months). In the other instances, this signature correlated with smaller cycles (4-year cycle troughs). Thus the correlation was strongest to the longer-term cycles when Saturn was in a cardinal sign. These cycles were not as powerful as under the conjunction aspect, but important due to their correlation to important troughs nonetheless, especially if given a 16-month orb, in which case powerful troughs were present every time.

Conclusions: In all cases, 4-year or greater cycles bottomed nearby to the waxing semi-square between Saturn and Uranus. It has a remarkable correlation to the end of bear trends, and the beginning of substantial bull moves. Investors may therefore use this signature to identify a long-term cycle trough, and thus an opportunity to make long-term purchases of stocks.

Waxing Sextile (60°)

	Dates & Position of Saturn		Long-Term Cycles
1.	May 14, 1814 June 28, 1814 Feb. 24, 1815	00°♒45' 29°♑02' 06°♒48'	4-year cycle crest in September 1815. This followed 18-year cycle trough in March 1813, which began 6-year rally in which market tripled in price.
2.	Oct. 26, 1857 Jan. 7, 1858 July 31, 1858	28°♋10' 25°♋29' 02°♌50'	18-year cycle trough and secondary low preceding great bull market run in October 1857. End of 5-year decline in which market lost over 60% in value. Beginning of rally in which prices more than tripled in next 7 years. 22.5-month cycle crest in February 1858.
3.	June 8, 1905 Aug. 7, 1905 Mar. 20, 1906	02°♓52' 00°♓40' 08°♓14'	18-year cycle crest in January 1906. End of 3-year rally in which prices appreciated over 140%. Start of 1-year decline of almost 50%.
4.	Sep. 23, 1948	00°♍30'	4-year cycle crest, June 1948. Prices dropped 17.4% in 1 year.

5.	May 19, 1996	04°♈32'	22-month cycle crest, May 1996. End of 18-month rally in which prices rose 47%. Prices then dropped to 22-month cycle trough in July 1996 — loss of 11.3% in 2 months.
	Nov. 10, 1996	01°♈03'	
	Mar. 1, 1997	06°♈38'	

	Central	+/- 7 months	Total
Relative Strength			
All	3.75	3.00	3.60
Crest	+3.00	+3.00	+3.00
Trough	- 3.50	- 0.00	- 3.50
Consistency			
All	4.00	1.00	5.00
Crest	+4.00	+1.00	+5.00
Trough	- 2.00	- 0.00	- 2.00
C/S Index			
All	7.75	4.00	8.60
Crest	+7.00	+4.00	+8.00
Trough	- 5.50	- 0.00	- 5.50

80% of the long-term cycles associated with this Saturn-Uranus signature unfolded during the central time band. The one that fell outside was a 4-year cycle crest, which unfolded 7 months after the last passage of a three-pass series. However, there was also an 18-year cycle trough of 1813, which was just 14 months prior to the aspect. Two of other instances correlated with 18-year cycles (one trough, one crest). Another coincided with a 4-year cycle, and the other with a 22.5-month cycle (crest and trough). In every case a cycle crest unfolded, but in one case (1857-1858) it was not the dominant long-term cycle.

Conclusions: Long-term cycles reversed nearby to the time of the waxing sextile between Saturn and Uranus. However, in some of the earlier cases, it is difficult to tell whether or not these cycles correlated with the semi-square or sextile, since both unfolded nearby to one another. In the last three cases, this signature has coincided with a long-term cycle crest, whereas in all cases of the semi-square, the correlation was to a long-term cycle trough. In fact, in every case there was a cycle crest of importance, though in one case it was not the strongest cycle. The strength of the cycles correlating to this sextile was not as powerful as those corresponding to the conjunction. Nevertheless, investors may use this time band for identifying a possible end and beginning of 22.5-month or greater cycles, especially crests.

Waxing Square (90°)

	Dates & Position of Saturn		Long-Term Cycles
1.	Oct. 15, 1770	14°♌30'	18-year (or greater) cycle crest in 1770-71.
	Feb. 11, 1771	11°♌53'	
	Aug. 13, 1771	19°♌43'	

2.	June 13, 1818	18°♓01'	Half-cycle crest of 18-year cycle in May 1819. End of 6-year rally. Half-cycle trough of 18-year cycle in January 1820. Prices lost 25% from crest one year earlier.
	Aug. 21, 1818	16°♓10'	
	Apr. 10, 1819	24°♓28'	
	Dec. 6, 1819	24°♓02'	
	Jan. 27, 1820	27°♓03'	
3.	Dec. 13, 1860	09°♍30'	U.S. Civil War. 4-year cycle trough in May 1861. This was the end of the decline that began from 4-year cycle crest 8 months earlier (and outside of central time band) in September 1860.
	Jan. 29, 1861	08°♍06'	
	Oct. 3, 1861	16°♍18'	
	May 30, 1862	15°♍59'	
	July 16, 1862	18°♍40'	
4.	June 7, 1909	20°♈23'	4-year cycle crest in November 1909 (double top to the 18-year cycle crest of 1906). Prices declined 37% over the next 8 months to double bottom of 4-year trough, July 1910.
	Nov. 8, 1909	17°♈51'	
	Apr. 7, 1910	25°♈00'	
5.	Dec. 8, 1951	13°♎02'	22.5-month cycle trough in May 1952. Prices rose 15.86% in next 8 months to 18-year cycle crest in January 1953. Korean War was underway during this transit.
	Apr. 18, 1952	10°♎20'	
	Oct. 15, 1952	18°♎30'	
6.	July 18, 1999	15°♉37'	
	Nov. 14, 1999	13°♉04'	
	May 13, 2000	20°♉46'	

	Central	+/- 3 months	Total
Relative Strength			
All	3.70	3.67	4.30
Crest	+4.50	+4.00	+4.30
Trough	- 3.00	- 3.00	- 3.00
Consistency			
All	5.00	3.00	5.00
Crest	+3.00	+2.00	+5.00
Trough	- 3.00	- 1.00	- 4.00
C/S Index			
All	8.70	6.67	9.30*
Crest	+7.50	+6.00	+9.30*
Trough	- 6.00	- 4.00	- 7.00

This is a signature which has correlated with very powerful mundane events, such as wars, and always to at least a 4-year or greater cycle in U.S. stock prices within 3 months of one of its passes. In only two instances was there an 18-year or greater cycle present, but in a third (1909) there was a double top to an 18-year cycle crest. In fact, in only one instance was a 4-year cycle the strongest cycle present (1860-1862). All other instances corresponded with greater cycles (80%). In all five cases in which long-term cycles unfolded, there was a significant crest within 3 months (100%), either during the central time band, or within three months of the last pass of a three-series passage. In each case, it was a four-year or greater cycle crest. However, there were also significant troughs in 80% of these cases as well, which points out the volatile nature of the market around the time of this waxing square. In other words, within a three-month extended period from the central time band, both crests and troughs of significance unfolded in all cases (in the U.S. stock market, for in the first case during 1770-1771, this cannot be confirmed).

Conclusions: *This is a very powerful cycle, usually correlating with cycles greater than 4-year types (80%). It seems to correlate with more than stock market reversals — in two cases, times of great military tensions and wars (U.S. Civil War and the Korean War) occurred. In fact, international tensions were high during each of these periods. There was no preponderance of crests over troughs, as both types occurred in every instance in the U.S. stock market history, given an extended time band of only three months from the central time band. But the crest cycles were usually longer-term in nature than the troughs. In fact in four of the five cases, a half-cycle crest to the 18-year cycle, or greater, unfolded. The troughs on the other hand consisted of a 22.5-month, 4-year, and a half-cycle to the 18-year cycle, which is considerably weaker in nature than the crest cycles. When crests did coincide with this signature, the decline which followed was usually very severe, lasting about 8 months, and falling outside the central time band. Investors, therefore, need to be alert as to whether or not a long-term cycle is topping out, or forming a double top within 3 months, or during the central time band, of this signature. If so, it may be prudent to sell stocks. If instead it looks like a 4-year cycle trough is forming, then investors can look to purchase stocks for the move up to the next large cycle crest. However, cycles of both types are possible in a short span of time.*

Waxing Trine (120°)

	Dates & Position of Saturn		**Long-Term Cycles**
1.	June 11, 1822 Nov. 18, 1822 Apr. 20, 1823	06°♉02' 05°♉12' 11°♉36'	4-year cycle trough in September 1822. Prices then rallied to 18-year cycle crest in September 1824, 17 months afterward.
2.	Dec. 13, 1864 Apr. 23, 1865 Oct. 31, 1865 July 26, 1866 Aug. 23, 1866	27°♎41' 26°♎31' 03°♏43' 05°♏52' 07°♏16'	Half-cycle trough of 18-year cycle in March 1865, following half-cycle crest of 18-year cycle in March 1864. Prices more than tripled from the low in 1857 to the crest in 1864. Then prices declined about 20% to the trough in 1865, before resuming their uptrend that lasted the next 8 years.
3.	July 23, 1912 Nov. 25, 1912 May 28, 1913	01°♊33' 00°♊26' 07°♊27'	4-year cycle crest in September-October 1912. Prices then declined 44% to the 36-year cycle trough of December 1914. 22.5-month cycle trough in June 1913.

4.	Jan. 17, 1956	00°♐26'	4-year cycle crest in April 1956. Note that this was also the time in which Saturn ingressed into a new sign, back and forth from Scorpio and Sagittarius. 4-year cycle trough in October 1957. Market went straight down to end of aspect.
	May 24, 1956	29°♏15'	
	Dec. 8, 1956	06°♐41'	
	Aug. 6, 1957	07°♐42'	
	Oct. 20, 1957	11°♐19'	
5.	Aug. 21, 2002	26°♊48'	
	Dec. 16, 2002	25°♊40'	
	June 24, 2003	02°♋42'	

Relative Strength	**Central**	**+/- 9 months**	**Total**
All	3.25	4.00	3.25
Crest	+3.00	+4.00	+3.33
Trough	- 3.00	- 0.00	- 3.00
Consistency			
All	5.00	1.25	5.00
Crest	+2.50	+1.25	+3.75
Trough	- 5.00	- 0.00	- 5.00
C/S Index			
All	8.25	5.25	8.25
Crest	+5.50	+5.25	+7.08
Trough	- 8.00	- 0.00	- 8.00

In every case, a 4-year or greater cycle unfolded within the central time band. However in only one case was it stronger than a 4-year cycle type. In every case, a trough formed within the central time band, but it was not always the strongest cycle present. What is interesting is that in the last three cases, a 4-year or greater cycle crest occurred either just before the central time band, or in the early part of it, and was followed by a significant decline before the aspect ended. Thus the market seemed to rally very smartly if there was a trough near the time of the square, into a crest in the early part of the trine's time band. From the low at the square 2-3 years earlier, prices appreciated 67%- 200% in three of the cases. In the fourth (1909-1912), the stock market made a 25% gain in the last year.

Conclusions: *Although we only have four instances to draw from at the time this book is being written, there seems to be a fairly wide correlation to long-term cycle troughs within the central time band of Saturn in waxing trine to Uranus. Furthermore, this trough oftentimes follows a crest that occurred early in the extended or central time band. This is interesting, because this trine follows the square by about 3-4 years. Under the square, economic and/or political matters tend to be strained. However, those problems appear to be resolved shortly thereafter, and by the time Saturn forms the trine to Uranus, both economic and the political arenas tend to be running more smoothly, as reflected in rising stock prices from the square to the trine. Thus if the market is forming a 4-year or greater cycle trough at the time of the waxing square, investors may look to make purchases in anticipation of a healthy rally into a time band of 9 months prior to or in the early stages of the central time band of the trine aspect 3-4 years later. Investors may then wish to sell holdings if indeed a 4-year or greater cycle crest appears to be forming. However, keep in mind that these crests are then followed by significant troughs before the signature's influence ends, so investors may wish to hold onto stocks and just add to these positions on the trough.*

Waxing Sesquiquadrate (135°)

	Dates & Position of Saturn		Long-Term Cycles
1.	Aug. 9, 1823	23°♉13'	18-year cycle crest, September 1824. Prices rose over 60% from half-cycle trough of 18-year cycle in 1820 (4 years prior), and then declined 30% into low in 1829 — 5 years later.
	Oct. 10, 1823	22°♉52'	
	June 7, 1824	29°♉53'	
	an. 12, 1825	01°♊15'	
	Apr. 10, 1825	04°♊53'	
2.	Jan. 2, 1867	21°♏08'	22.5-month cycle trough in April 1867. Prices rose almost 50% from low 4 years earlier in 1865 to 4-year cycle crest in July 1869.
	May 12, 1867	20°♏48'	
	Nov. 24, 1867	27°♏19'	
	July 22, 1868	29°♏09'	
	Oct. 7, 1868	02°♐19'	
3.	July 13, 1914	25°♊27'	36-year cycle trough in December 1914. End of 5-year decline in which prices lost nearly 50% of value. Prices then rallied 120% to high 2 years later.
	Jan. 25, 1915	26°♊15'	
	May 17, 1915	00°♋40'	
4.	Feb. 16, 1958	23°♐53'	22.5-month cycle crest and 1st phase crest of 18-year cycle in August 1959. Prices rose 64% from low just 2 years earlier (1957), then dropped 17% into low 1 year later. 4-year cycle trough unfolded in October 1957, and a 22.5-month cycle trough occurred in September 1959.
	May 30, 1958	23°♐26'	
	Jan. 8, 1959	00°♑24'	
	Aug. 3, 1959	01°♑17'	
	Dec. 2, 1959	06°♑04'	
5.	Aug. 7, 2004	20°♋36'	
	Feb. 17, 2005	21°♋20'	
	June 12, 2005	25°♋46'	

Relative Strength	**Central**	**+/- 9 months**	**Total**
All	3.50	+3.00	4.00
Crest	+3.50	+3.00	+3.33
Trough	- 3.00	- 3.00	- 3.33
Consistency			
All	5.00	2.50	5.00
Crest	+2.50	+ 1.25	+3.75
Trough	- 3.75	- 1.25	-3.75

C/S Index

All	8.50	5.50	9.00*
Crest	+6.00	+4.25	+7.08
Trough	- 6.75	- 4.25	- 7.08

Two of these four instances have coincided with 18-year or greater cycles within the central time band. The other two instances correlated with 22.5-month cycles within the same central time band. This cycle was evenly split between crests and troughs, and all (100%) occurred within the central time band. There was also two 4-year cycle that unfolded 9 months after and 4 months before central time bands that contained 22.5-month cycle troughs.

<u>Conclusions</u>: *The waxing sesquiquadrate between Saturn and Uranus tends to be a significant correlation to long-term cycles in U.S. stock prices. In all cases to date a cycle of significance unfolded during the central time band. However, there is no consistency as to whether or not it will coincide with a longer-term cycle or an intermediate-term one, nor whether it will coincide with a crest or trough. Thus investors may use this time band to enter new stock positions if a long-term trough appears to be forming.*

Opposition (180°)

	Dates & Position of Saturn		**Long-Term Cycles**
1.	Feb. 15, 1782	29°♐00'	72-year cycle trough in 1784.
	May 9, 1782	00°♑31'	
	Jan. 5, 1783	04°♑56'	
	July 13, 1783	08°♑24'	
	Dec. 2, 1783	11°♑01'	
2.	Aug. 27, 1828	29°♋04'	18-year cycle trough (maybe 54-year) in January 1829. End of 5-year decline in which prices lost 30% value. Starts 6-year bull market in which prices gained over 130%.
	Jan. 10, 1829	01°♌41'	
	July 9, 1829	05°♌08'	
3.	Apr. 7, 1873	01°♒45'	36-year cycle crest in February 1874. End of 16-year bull market as prices rose 350%. Start of 4-year financial "panic" in which prices declined over 35% to low in 1877. 4-year cycle trough in November 1873.
	May 23, 1873	02°♒37'	
	Feb. 16, 1874	07°♒43'	
	Aug. 3, 1874	10°♒56'	
	Jan. 13, 1875	14°♒03'	
	Oct. 21, 1875	19°♒25'	
	Nov. 18, 1875	19°♒58'	
4.	Oct. 1, 1918	24°♌14'	Half-cycle crest of 18-year cycle in October 1919. Prices rose almost 90% from low 2 years earlier in December 1917. Prices then declined over 45% into
	Jan. 25, 1919	26°♌24'	
	Aug. 13, 1919	00°♍08'	

	Apr. 26, 1920	04°♍54'	low 1 year later, in December 1920. 22.5-month cycle trough in February 1919.
	June 7, 1920	05°♍40'	
5.	Apr. 1, 1965	11°♓37'	Double top to 18-year cycle crest in February 1966. First time DJIA crossed 1000 mark. This ended a 4-year rally in which prices nearly doubled. It began 8-month decline to 4-year cycle low in October 1966 in which prices fell over 25%.
	Aug. 27, 1965	14°♓33'	
	Feb. 24, 1966	18°♓07'	
	Nov. 8, 1966	23°♓12'	
	Jan. 6, 1967	24°♓24'	
6.	Nov. 4, 2008	18°♍58'	
	Feb. 5, 2009	20°♍39'	
	Sep. 15, 2009	24°♍43'	
	Apr. 26, 2010	28°♍46'	
	July 26, 2010	00°♎25'	

Relative Strength	**Central**	**+/- 9 months**	**Total**
All	4.625	5.00	4.70
Crest	+4.50	0.00	+4.50
Trough	- 3.25	- 5.00	- 3.60
Consistency			
All	4.00	1.00	5.00
Crest	+3.00	0.00	+3.00
Trough	- 4.00	- 1.00	- 5.00
C/S Index			
All	8.625	6.00	9.70*
Crest	+7.50	0.00	+7.50
Trough	- 7.25	- 6.00	- 8.60

This is one of the most powerful signatures of all. The only one stronger has been the Saturn-Uranus conjunction. Most of these oppositions coincided with powerful periods in world history, such as the American Revolution (1781), a major financial "Panic" (1873-77), World War I (1918-19), and the Vietnam War (1965-67 and beyond). Each of these periods also correlated to very long-term cycle changes right within their central time band, with the exception of possibly the first instance (1782-1783), which took place before the United States stock market began (figures based upon British stock prices). This of course may be due to the fact that these signatures oftentimes unfolded five times. Once they unfolded only three times, and once they unfolded a whopping seven times (1873-75). Thus these signatures last an unusually long 2-3 years. This signature coincided with troughs in every case, but they have not always been the strongest cycle present. In fact, very long-term crests have been the rule in the last three instances. It will be most interesting to see what happens in the next occurrence in 2008-2010, as that is the same period outlined in the earlier part of this book as being a likely time band for a long-term cycle crest or trough (of the 36-year or greater variety).

<u>Conclusions</u>: *The opposition of Saturn to Uranus is an extremely powerful signature correlating with the culmination of long-term cycles in U.S. stocks. In every case it*

coincided with at least the half-cycle of the 18-year cycle. In two of the five cases, it coincided with an even longer-term 36- and 72-year cycle. In another case it coincided with an 18-year cycle, and in another yet, with a double top to the 18-year cycle (and the first time the DJIA crossed the 1000 mark). It is thus one of the most powerful geocosmic correlations to long-term cycles in U.S. stock prices. Investors may use this time band to either 1) purchase stocks for the long-term if it appears that prices are declining into a long-term cycle trough, or 2) sell stocks if the market is rising into what looks like a long-term cycle crest.

Waning Sesquiquadrate (225°)

	Dates & Position of Saturn		Long-Term Cycles
1.	Oct. 14, 1833 Mar. 8, 1834 Aug. 29, 1834	03°♎43' 08°♎56' 09°♎38'	Half-cycle trough to 18-year cycle, February 1834. 72-year cycle crest in May 1835. Prices soared 85% in that year between 1834 low and 1835 crest. Then they began a 7-year collapse where prices dropped 80%. There was a half-cycle crest to 18-year cycle that unfolded in June 1833, as well.
2.	Apr. 19, 1880 Oct. 6, 1880 Mar. 7, 1881	20°♈05' 26°♈28' 26°♈31'	4-year cycle trough in June 1880, followed by half-cycle crest to 18-year cycle in June 1881. End of 4-year rise in which prices gained over 60%. Prices then declined about 25% over next 3 years.
3.	Dec. 5, 1923 Feb. 29, 1924 Oct. 13, 1924 May 19, 1925 Aug. 27, 1925	28°♎42' 02°♏03' 03°♏22' 09°♏45' 09°♏18'	4-year cycle crest in February 1926. This followed 22.5-month cycle trough in October 1923, with a double bottom in May 1924. Most important factor was that prices "broke out" to upside and doubled in value as new all-time highs were made (1924-26).
4.	July 10, 1970 Sep. 7, 1970 May 10, 1971 Dec. 5, 1971 Mar. 22, 1972	20°♉00' 22°♉37' 25°♉02' 02°♊15' 01°♊54'	4-year cycle trough in May 1970. Prices rose over 80% to 22.5-month cycle crest in April 1971, then declined over 17% to 22.5-month cycle trough in November 1971.
5.	Dec. 3, 2014 May 4, 2015 Oct. 22, 2015	27°♏43' 03°♐00' 03°♐05'	

Relative Strength	Central	+/- 6 months	Total
All	3.00	3.75	3.75
Crest	+2.00	+4.00	+3.50
Trough	- 3.00	- 2.50	- 3.00

Consistency	**Central**	**+/-6 months**	**Total**
All	3.75	5.00	5.00
Crest	+1.25	+3.75	+5.00
Trough	- 3.75	- 2.50	- 5.00
C/S Index			
All	6.75	8.75	8.75
Crest	+3.25	+7.75	+8.5o
Trough	- 6.75	- 5.00	- 8.00

The main feature of this signature appears to be volatility. In all four cases, long-term cycle crests *and* troughs occurred in a rather short amount of time. During the central time band there were no instances of 18-year or greater signatures, so it is not nearly so strong as the opposition. In every case (100%), a significant trough occurred within the central time band (or within just two months), although in two cases, they were intermediate-term troughs (22.5-month cycles), and not the long-term types. However, in three cases, long-term cycle crests unfolded 3-9 months *after* the last passage of the aspect.

Conclusions: The waxing sesquiquadrate between Saturn and Uranus is volatile, and tends to coincide with both crests and troughs nearby. However, these cycles are usually not as powerful as those coinciding to the conjunction or opposition. In all cases 4-year or greater cycles unfolded within an extended 9-month time band. But in three cases, the stronger cycle was slightly after the last passage, and it was a crest. Within the central time band, there was a greater likelihood of at least an intermediate-term market cycle trough unfolding. Therefore, investors may use this time band to identify these possible troughs and then purchase stocks for the rally of the next phase of the long-term cycle.

Waning Trine (240°)

	Dates & Position of Saturn		**Long-Term Cycles**
1.	Oct. 25, 1835	26°♎41'	72-year cycle crest in May-August 1835. Prices then declined 80% to bottom 7 years later. Double top in August 1835.
	Apr. 7, 1836	03°♏03'	
	Sep. 7, 1836	02°♏02'	
2.	July 18, 1881	11°♉16'	Half-cycle crest to 18-year cycle in June 1881. End of 4-year rally in which prices gained over 60%. Beginning of 3-year decline in which prices lost close to 25%. 22.5-month cycle trough in June 1882.
	July 31, 1881	11°♉55'	
	Apr. 28, 1882	14°♉40'	
	Nov. 16, 1882	22°♉33'	
	Mar. 10, 1883	21°♉24'	
3.	Dec. 20, 1925	21°♏43'	4-year cycle crest in February 1926, and 4-year cycle trough in March 1926. The crest was the end of 2-year rally in which prices nearly doubled in price. The one month decline to 4-year trough represented loss of 17%.
	Mar. 23, 1926	25°♏49'	
	Oct. 30, 1926	26°♏03'	
	June 12, 1927	03°♐08'	
	Sep. 10, 1927	02°♐02'	

4.	July 4, 1972 Oct. 30, 1972 May 12, 1973	14°♊16' 19°♊53' 19°♊47'	36-year cycle crest, January 1973. End of 14-month rally in which prices gained 70%. Beginning of very sharp 23-month decline in which prices dropped 46%.
5.	Dec. 25, 2016 May 19, 2017 Nov. 11, 2017	20°♐34' 26°♐23' 25°♐38'	

Relative Strength	**Central**	**+/- 5 months**	**Total**
All	4.00	5.00	4.25
Crest	+4.00	+5.00	+4.25
Trough	- 2.50	0.00	- 2.50
Consistency			
All	3.75	1.25	5.00
Crest	+3.75	+1.25	+5.00
Trough	- 2.50	0.00	- 2.50
C/S Index			
All	7.75	6.25	9.25*
Crest	+7.75	+6.25	+9.25*
Trough	- 5.00	0.00	- 5.00

This is a powerful and consistent signature to long-term cycle crests. In each instance a four-year or greater cycle crest unfolded in — or within 2 months of — the central time band (100%). One was the 72-year cycle crest and the end to the first great bull market in U.S. stocks (1835). The last instance was the crest of yet another long-term cycle and the end of the fourth bull market run if we use the Pluto effect described in an earlier chapter (1973). In each case, prices rallied for at least 14 months, and the gain was over 60%. In each case prices declined sharply afterwards. In three cases, the decline lasted 2-7 years and fell 25-80%.

Conclusions: Long-term cycle crests tend to end during the central time band of the waning trine between Saturn and Uranus. In each case, this crest is the result of a one-year or greater rally in stocks, in which prices tend to gain at least 60%. It is also the beginning of a substantial decline. Investors may look to sell holdings if the market is indeed rising into a long-term cycle crest into this time band, then wait for a substantial decline into a long-term cycle trough several months later as an opportunity to re-purchase stocks at potentially much lower prices.

Waning Square (270°)

	Dates & Position of Saturn		**Long-Term Cycles**
1.	July 9, 1794 Sep. 3, 1794	26°♉16' 29°♉36'	18-year cycle crest in April 1795, followed by 18-year cycle trough 2-1/2 years later in 1797.

Apr. 23, 1795 29°♉10'
Jan. 4, 1796 07°♊47'
Feb. 5, 1796 06°♊46'

2. Dec. 3, 1839 12°♐33'
May 20, 1840 19°♐52'
Oct. 10, 1840 17°♐16'

This was in the middle of the 7-year collapse of stock prices from 1835-1842. There was a 22.5-mo. cycle crest in October 1840, which followed the 22.5-mo. cycle trough in November 1839.

3. June 28, 1885 29°♊01'
Nov. 30, 1885 06°♋54'
Apr. 29, 1886 04°♋19'

22.5-mo. cycle crest in February 1886 followed half-cycle trough in year earlier in June 1884. Market then dropped to 22.5-mo. cycle trough in May, 1886, followed by 4-year cycle crest in December 1886.

4. Feb 22, 1930 09°♑15'
Apr. 9, 1930 11°♑45'
Dec. 12, 1930 11°♑28'
July 21, 1931 19°♑22'
Oct. 16, 1931 17°♑10'

72-year cycle crest in Sept. 1929 ended the second great bull market run, and began decline into 72-year cycle trough in 1932. There was a 4-year cycle trough in November 1929, followed by 4-year crest in April 1930. But this period was mostly known for its great "breakout" downwards - the breakout of the "Great Depression" 1929-1932.

5. Oct. 4, 1975 01°♌27'
Oct. 17, 1975 02°♌14'
July 1, 1976 03°♌04'
Feb 23, 1977 11°♌45'
Apr. 22, 1977 10°♌05'

4-year cycle crest in September 1976. End of 2-year rise in which prices gained 80%. Start of 18-month decline in which prices fell nearly 30%. There was a 22.5-month cycle trough in November 1976.

6. Feb 17, 2021 07°♒14'
June 14, 2021 13°♒07'
Dec. 24, 2021 11°♒06'

Relative Strength	**Central**	**+/- 8 months**	**Total**
All	3.00	4.00	3.60
Crest	+3.00	+4.00	+3.60
Trough	- 2.00	- 5.00	- 2.75

Consistency	**Central**	**+/- 8 months**	**Total**
All	5.00	2.00	5.00
Crest	+5.00	+2.00	+5.00
Trough	- 3.00	- 1.00	- 4.00

C/S Index			
All	8.00	6.00	8.60
Crest	+8.00	+6.00	+8.60
Trough	- 5.00	- 6.00	- 6.75

The waning square seems to have an important correlation to crests signatures, like the waning trine. However these are not always long-term cycles. Only 3 long-term cycles unfolded in the central time band (60%). Only two of the cycles associated with this signature were 18-year or greater types, and one of those happened five months prior to the central time band. However that one was the crest which defined the beginning of the Great Depression (1929-1932). So given an orb of 8 months either side of the beginning or end (and usually before), this is a powerful signature. It is frequently present when a "crash" is starting. Sometimes this "crash" starts just before the aspect begins, and at other times, it starts shortly after the aspect has occurred. This is consistent with the principles of the planets and the aspect. The planets represent a break of the foundation, and the last square is the "pain of death", or of an ending to something. That certainly seemed to be the case in two or three of these instances, where the economy was just in a free-fall (1839-1840 and 1930-1931). There was only one instance (1885-86) where prices rose from a trough that happened just before the aspect. The strongest cycle coincident with this signature occurred when both planets were in cardinal signs (1930-31)

<u>Conclusions</u>: *The waning square of Saturn to Uranus appears to be very powerful, and oftentimes is in effect during the "crash" period of U.S. stocks. It may correlate with a reversal of a long-term cycle, but it may just as often correlate with a breakdown — or breakout — in prices, as in a "crash." This is historically most true when both planets are in cardinal signs. In every case studied so far there has been an intermediate or long-term cycle crest which unfolded in the central time band, but it has not always coincided with the end of long-term trends. Investors may prepare to take profits, therefore, on long positions if indeed an intermediate or longer-term cycle crest appears to be unfolding within the central time band.*

Waning Sextile (300°)

	Dates & Position of Saturn		**Long-Term Cycles**
1.	June 23, 1798	13°♋54'	18-year cycle trough in November 1797, seven months before aspect.
	Jan. 21, 1799	22°♋02'	
	Mar 31, 1799	19°♋24'	
2.	Jan. 30 1844	29°♑30'	4-year cycle crest in May 1844.
	June 24, 1844	06°♒08'	
	Nov. 21, 1844	02°♒29'	
3.	Sep. 27, 1888	16°♌48'	Double top to 36-year cycle crest in September 1889. Prices fell 28% in next year. A 4-year cycle trough unfolded in April 1888, 5 months before aspect series began.
	Nov. 25, 1888	20°♌19'	
	June 27, 1889	17°♌52'	
4.	Jan 25, 1935	27°♒39'	No long-term cycles culminated here. This was in the middle of rather large rise from 1932 low to
	Oct. 7, 1935	04°♓17'	

	Oct. 21, 1935	03°♓45'	1937 crest, following "Great Depression." February 1935 was 50-week cycle crest and March 1935 was 50-week cycle trough.
5.	Sep 17, 1979 Feb 17, 1980 July 4, 1980	18°♍05' 25°♍30' 21°♍45'	Double bottom to 4-year cycle low in March 1980. 22.5-month cycle crest in February. This was the "Granville Decline", brought on by analyst Joseph Granville's sell signal. Market fell 20% in one month.
6.	Apr. 4, 2025 Aug. 11, 2025 Jan 20, 2026	24°♓55' 01°♈11' 27°♓33'	

Relative Strength	**Central**	**+/- 7 months**	**Total**
All	2.75	4.75	3.75
Crest	+2.50	+4.50	+3.17
Trough	- 2.50	- 4.00	- 3.50
Consistency			
All	2.00	2.00	4.00
Crest	+2.00	+1.00	+3.00
Trough	- 1.00	- 2.00	- 3.00
C/S Index			
All	4.75	6.75	7.75
Crest	+4.50	+5.50	+6.17
Trough	- 3.50	- 6.00	- 6.50

Only one long-term cycle unfolded in the central time band (20%), and only two others within a seven-month extended time band. There were two instances where no long-term cycle could be discerned, even using the extended time band of 7 months. Thus this is not a very reliable correlation to long-term stock market cycles.

Conclusions: The waning sextile between Saturn and Uranus is not a strong nor consistent signature correlating to long-term cycles in U.S. stocks. This signature may not be very useful to investors, based on lack of firm historical correlations to long-term cycles, except to correlate with rising prices during the aspect's reign.

Waning Semi-Square (315°)

	Dates & Position of Saturn		**Long-Term Cycles**
1.	June 21, 1800	08°♌11'	4-year cycle crest in October, 1800.
2.	Feb. 27, 1846 July 27, 1846	23°♒26' 29°♒13'	First phase crest of 18-year cycle in August 1847. End of 5-year rally in which prices gained about

	Dec. 6, 1846	25°♒43'	250%. Start of 1-year decline in which prices lost about 30%. 4-year cycle low occurred in August 1845.
3.	Sep. 25, 1890 Jan. 26, 1891 June 30, 1891	10°♍34' 16°♍22' 12°♍18'	36-year cycle crest in May 1890. 4-year cycle low in December, 1890. Prices rose 30% from that bottom, then fell nearly 45% 5 years after double top in 1892.
4.	Feb. 7, 1937	20°♓54'	Half-cycle crest to 18-year cycle one month later in March 1937. Market then dropped nearly 50% to low one year after in March 1938.
5.	Oct. 3, 1981 Apr. 3, 1982 July 10, 1982	12°♎33' 19°♎22' 15°♎56'	Secondary low to start of big bull market that began in August 1982, less than 1 month after last aspect.
6.	Apr. 12, 2027 Oct. 15, 2027 Jan. 12, 2028	18°♈20' 24°♈34' 21°♈22'	

Relative Strength	**Central**	**+/- 8 months**	**Total**
All	3.625	4.00	3.90
Crest	+3.50	+4.00	+3.75
Trough	- 3.75	- 3.00	- 3.50

Consistency	**Central**	**+/- 8 months**	**Total**
All	4.00	2.00	5.00
Crest	+2.00	+2.00	+4.00
Trough	- 2.00	- 1.00	- 3.00

C/S Index			
All	7.625	6.00	8.90
Crest	+5.50	+6.00	+7.75
Trough	- 5.75	- 4.00	- 6.50

This is a fairly strong and consistent aspect. In 80% of cases, a 4-year or greater cycle unfolded within the central time band. In the other case, a four-year cycle trough and crest unfolded 6-8 months outside the central time band of a three-passage series (1845-47). In fact, in most cases this signature coincided with either a 4-year cycle and/or one of the phases to the 18-year cycle (like the double top to the 18-year cycle in 1891) It is a volatile signature, suggesting a fairly strong reversal from a top (or bottom) that forms in this period.

Conclusions: *The waning semi-square between Saturn and Uranus is a fairly reliable signature, usually correlating to 4-year cycles, and sometimes longer. Most of the time the cycle unfolds within the central time band, and in fact, in the last three instances within 1 month of one of the aspects. Thus investors may look to take appropriate action if a 4-year cycle crest (sell) or trough (buy) is forming within the central time band.*

Summary of Saturn-Uranus Signatures

The following represents the ranking order of Saturn-Uranus aspects in correlation to long-term stock market cycles. This first ranking order is based upon Total C/S values, which includes a time band of up to 11 months (but usually no more than nine) outside of the aspect. In parentheses are those instances in which that particular signature correlated more times with a crest (+) or trough (-), and the respective values of each. Also included is a column indicating how many instances of cycles greater than four-year types which were associated with each aspect (again, within an eleven-month orb of time either side of the aspect), and the percentage of times this represents. In the last column, titled **Orb,** are the number of months used outside of the central time band for the extended time band upon which the Total C/S values were based

Aspect	Total	Cycles > 4-Years		Orb
1. Conjunction	9.92* (- 9.08*)	6/6 =	100%	10 mo
2. Opposition	9.70* (- 8.60)	5/5 =	100%	9
3. Waxing Square	9.30* (+9.30*)	4/5 =	80%	3
4. Waning Trine	9.25* (+9.25*)	3/4 =	75%	5
5. Waxing Sesquiquadrate	9.00*	2/4 =	50%	9
6. Waning Semi-Square	8.90 (+7.75)	3/5 =	60%	8
7. Waning Sesquiquadrate	8.75	2/4 =	50%	6
8A. Waning Square	8.60 (+8.60)	2/5 =	40%	8
8B. Waxing Sextile	8.60 (+8.00)	2/5 =	40%	7
8C. Waxing Semi-Square	8.60 (- 7.75)	2/5 =	40%	4
11. Waxing Trine	8.25 (- 8.00)	1/4 =	25%	9
12. Waning Sextile	7.75	2/5 =	40%	7

In a class all by themselves are the conjunction and opposition. In all but one instance, each of these aspects between Saturn and Uranus correlated to an 18-year or greater cycle, double top to it, or one of the secondary troughs preceding one of the major bull runs in U.S. stocks. In the other instance, it was a half-cycle to the primary cycle (a 7-11 year cycle crest).

At least three of the other aspects were also powerful and consistent, as signified by a C/S value of 9.00 or greater. These involved the waxing square, waning trine, and waxing sesquiquadrate. That means nearly half of the signatures are very powerful and consistent correlates to long-term cycles in U.S. stocks, given an orb of about 9 months (in most cases, the cycle unfolded within 5 months of one of these aspects).

Very close to approaching this study's level of significance (9.00 or greater) was the waning semi-square, which had a C/S value of 8.90. Four other signatures had values between 8.60-8.75. In fact, only two of these were not really consistent or strong — the waxing trine and the waning sextile.

In the history of the U.S. stock market, there have been 11 completed instances of 18-year cycles. If we use the British stock price charts and go back to 1760, we can spot 13 instances of these cycles — 13 troughs and 13 crests. The 14th one began in 1987, so actually there are 14 troughs and 13 crests. A Saturn-Uranus signature was present in 10 of these troughs (71.4%) and 11 of the crests (84.6%). Although 12 aspects were studied, only four are considered "hard aspects" (conjunction, square, and opposition). Six of the 10 long-term cycle troughs unfolded under a "hard aspect" between Saturn and Uranus, and five of those were the conjunction or opposition (50%). One of the secondary lows preceding a great bull market also happened under a conjunction (1942). There were also six of the hard aspects present when the crests formed, and four of these were the conjunction and opposition. Once again, this study, too, illustrates the importance of Saturn and Uranus in either a conjunction or opposition as a reliable correlation to long-term (18-year or greater) cycles in U.S. stocks.

There were also strong correspondences to crests or troughs in several of these aspects. For instance, the waxing square and waning trine had a surprisingly high correlation to crests, with C/S values of +9.30 and +9.25 respectively. Furthermore, these crests did not require a wide time band. In the case of the waxing square, it unfolded no more than 3 months outside of the central time band. In the case of the waning trine, it required no more than 5 months outside of the central time band. Only one other signature correlated to a specific type of cycle with a value greater than 9.00, and that was the conjunction, which had a greater historical correspondence to troughs (-9.08). In all, there were five signatures with a bias towards crests: waxing square, waning trine, waning semi-square, waning square, and waxing sextile. In this case, the fact that both types of squares had a bias towards crests may be of interest. There were four signatures with a bias towards troughs: conjunction, opposition, waxing semi-square, and waxing trine. The fact that they are all between the waxing stage of the conjunction and opposition may be of interest.

There were 34 of the 57 instances in which the Saturn-Uranus aspects correlated with cycles greater than 4-year types (59.65%). Thus there is a nearly 60% probability that a long-term cycle (greater than 4-year types) will unfold within nine months of an aspect between these two planets. In the case of the conjunction and opposition, the historical correspondence has been 100% (11 of 11 cases). The waxing square has an 80% correlation, while the waning trine has a 75% correlation.

The ranking orders changed somewhat when only the central time band was used, according to the criteria outlined for this study (i.e. an orb of only one month outside of cases involving a series of three or more passes, or within three months in cases involving only a single passage). These C/S results are shown in the table below. Also shown are the number of instances in which greater than four-year cycles unfolded in this definition of a central time band.

Aspect	Central Time Band	Cycles > 4-Years
1. Waxing Square	8.70 (+7.50)	3/5 = 60%
2. Opposition	8.625	4/5 = 80%
3. Waxing Sesquiquadrate	8.50	2/4 = 50%
4. Waxing Trine	8.25 (- 8.00)	1/4 = 25%
5. Waning Square	8.00 (+8.00)	1/5 = 20%
6A. Waning Trine	7.75 (+7.75)	2/4 = 50%
6B. Waxing Sextile	7.75 (+7.00)	2/5 = 40%
8. Waning Semi-Square	7.625	2/5 = 40%
9. Waning Sesquiquadrate	6.75 (- 6.75)	1/4 = 25%
10. Waxing Semi-Square	6.33 (- 6.33)	1/5 = 20%
11. Conjunction	5.33	1/6 = 17%
12. Waning Sextile	4.75	0/5 = 0%

In this view, the status of the conjunction has fallen all the way from the strongest signature (allowing a 10-month orb of time) to the next to weakest signature (when viewed only in the central time band). Obviously the very long-term market cycles associated with the Saturn-Uranus conjunction do not fall right on the time of the aspect. They require some leeway. The opposition, however, repeats its place as number two in the ranking. Thus many of the long-term market cycles associated with Saturn opposed to Uranus actually happen in the central time band. One reason for this difference is due to the fact that the conjunction only occurs in a single passage of the aspect in about half of the cases, whereas during the time of the opposition, the aspect frequently occurs in a series of five (and even seven) passes, which takes up to two and even three years to complete.

Using the central time band for this study, the waxing square becomes the most prominent signature correlating with long-term market cycles within its central time band. Not only that, but only this square and the opposition have a greater than 50% frequency of historical correlation to cycles greater than 4-year types during their central time bands. Both the waxing sesquiquadrate and waning trine had a 50% frequency, but all other aspects were less. In the case of the waning sextile, there were no long-term cycles greater than 4-year types which unfolded in the central time band. In the cases of waxing trines, waning squares, waning sesquiquadrates, waxing semi-squares, and conjunctions, there was one instance each of longer than 4-year cycle types unfolding. In all, there were 20 of 57 instances (35%) in which cycles greater than 4-year types unfolded within the central time band.

As far as C/S values were concerned, five of the signatures had a moderately strong rating of 8.00 or greater (waxing square, opposition, waxing sesquiquadrate, waxing trine, and waning square). The top four were all the aspects between the waxing square and opposition, which may be of interest. This suggests that once these planets enter the 90° relationship from one another, all major aspects through the opposition must be watched carefully during their central time bands for major trend reversals. This covers only 90° of the zodiac, but include four aspects (square, trine, sesquiquadrate, and opposition).

Once again there were some instances of a bias towards crests or troughs. The waning square, for instance, has always corresponded to a crest during its central time band. The waxing square, waning trine, and waxing sextile also exhibited a bias more towards crests during their central time band. On the other hand, the waxing trine, waning sesquiquadrate, and waxing semi-square showed a bias towards troughs.

Saturn-Uranus in Cardinal Signs

In the first section of this book, the observation was made that the great bull markets in U.S. stocks began and ended when Saturn, Uranus and/or Pluto were in cardinal signs. This observation was made from the market history point of view. That is, when a great bull market ended, or began, a combination of these planets seemed always to be in cardinal signs. However, these planets are in cardinal signs more frequently than the 51-72 years that it takes a bull market in U.S. stocks to start or end. So the question arises whether or not other major trends in U.S. stocks begin or end when combinations of these planets are in cardinal signs? To test this theory, let's examine the history of U.S. stock market cycles during those times in which Saturn and Uranus were in cardinal signs together, and compare their C/S scores to the average.

First of all, understand that planets can only be in the same quality (i.e. cardinal signs) when the two planets involved are in a hard aspect to one another (conjunction, square, or opposition). If we simply look to those aspects between Saturn and Uranus, and extract the instances in which they were in cardinal signs, we get the following list:

Conjunctions

	Dates & Position of Saturn		Long-Term Cycles
1.	May 14, 1761	07°♈42'	Absolute low (72-year cycle) preceding great bull market run began in 1762.
	Oct. 28, 1761	06°♈03'	
	Jan. 3, 1762	05°♈23'	
2.	Nov. 1, 1805	21°♎32'	18-year cycle crest unfolded August 1806.

Waxing Square

3.	June 7, 1909	20°♈23'	Double top to 18-year cycle crest in November 1909 (double top to the 18-year cycle crest of 1906).
	Nov. 8, 1909	17°♈51'	
	Apr. 7, 1910	25°♈00'	
4.	Dec. 8, 1951	13°♎02'	18-year cycle crest in January 1953.
	Apr. 18, 1952	10°♎20'	
	Oct. 15, 1952	18°♎30'	

Opposition

	Date	Position	Notes
5.	Feb. 15, 1782	29°♐00'	72-year cycle trough in 1784.
	May 9, 1782	00°♑31'	
	Jan. 5, 1783	04°♑56'	
	July 13, 1783	08°♑24'	
	Dec. 2, 1783	11°♑01'	
6.	Aug. 27, 1828	29°♋04'	18-year cycle trough (maybe 54-year) in January 1829.
	Jan. 10, 1829	01°♌41'	
	July 9, 1829	05°♌08'	

Waxing Square

	Date	Position	Notes
7.	June 28, 1885	29°♊01'	4-year cycle crest in December 1886.
	Nov. 30, 1885	06°♋54'	
	Apr. 29, 1886	04°♋19'	
8.	Feb 22, 1930	09°♑15'	72-year cycle crest in Sept. 1929 ended the second great bull market run, and began decline into 72-year cycle trough in July 1932.
	Apr. 9, 1930	11°♑45'	
	Dec. 12, 1930	11°♑28'	
	July 21, 1931	19°♑22'	
	Oct. 16, 1931	17°♑10'	

As one can readily see, seven of these eight cases of cardinal signs between Saturn and Uranus produced either 18-year or greater cycles, or a double top to an 18-year cycle crest. In only one instance was a long-term cycle of less than the 18-year type present (1885-1886). In that instance, the aspect coincided with a 4-year cycle 8 months later. Except for the 1805 case, this was the only instance in which the dominant longer-term cycle fell more than five months outside of the central time band. Thus in 7 of 9 cases, an 18-year or greater cycle fell either within the central time band, or within five months of it (78%).

In this study, we can see there has been an 87.5% correlation to cycles not only greater than the 4-year type, but as well to an 18-year or greater type. In comparison, the total field of Saturn-Uranus aspects had a 59.65% correlation, but this was to cycles simply greater than 4-year types. If we used only 18-year or greater cycles (and double tops/bottoms) for the calculations, then the total field correlation was 27 out of 57 instances, or 47.4%. *The frequency in which an 18-year or greater cycles (or their double tops or bottoms) occurred was therefore almost twice as great when these two planets formed a hard aspect in cardinal signs.*

As far as Total C/S values were concerned, the score of these eight cases was 9.69* Only the conjunction and opposition had a higher value (9.92 and 9.70 respectively), but then again, they were also part of the cardinal sign group since they are both hard aspects. The average C/S value of the entire field of 12 aspects was 8.885. Thus it can be deduced that indeed when Saturn and Uranus form a hard aspect in cardinal signs, the probabilities are much greater than an 18-year or greater cycle will unfold, and probably within five months of the central time band.

SATURN-NEPTUNE: LONG-TERM CYCLES

Just as Saturn and Uranus are contradictory by nature, so too are the principles of Saturn and Neptune, but in a different way. Whereas Saturn represents structure, Neptune represents the abstract. Whereas Saturn's need deals with form and manifestation and cold hard facts, Neptune's need is to visualize and idealize. Saturn is reality, Neptune is illusion. Saturn requires accountability whereas Neptune requires little more than faith and trust. When the two come together there is either the positive potential to make "dreams come true," to bring into form that which was only conceived as an idea (or ideal), or there is the fear that all that was built will come tumbling down because of ambiguous, nefarious causes, or involvement with deceptive and unscrupulous people. This is an aspect of rumors, accusations, judgments based upon false premises or assumptions. When in hard aspect, it can represent either unfounded euphoria causing prices to rise, or selling pressure due to vague and unfounded fears that things will soon get worse. It is, therefore, something of a paranoid time, and perhaps one in which the character of world leaders comes into question. A loss of confidence in the leadership of the country (or the economy) can also have a chilling effect upon equity prices.

The Saturn-Neptune planetary pair cycle lasts approximately 36 years. Its quarter cycles are about 8-10 years apart. In this section, all major and several minor aspects will be examined for possible correlations to long-term stock market cycles, just as performed in the previous section with Saturn and Uranus.

Conjunction (0°)

	Dates & Position of Saturn		**Long-Term Cycles**
1.	Dec. 1, 1809	06°♐40'	Crest of 3rd phase of 18-year cycle in October 1809.
2.	Apr. 4, 1846 Sep. 5, 1846 Dec. 11, 1846	27°♒18' 26°♒20' 25°♒42'	4-year cycle trough in August 1845, and 4-year cycle crest in August 1847; end of 5-year advance from 18-year cycle trough in 1842 (absolute long-term low in 1842). Prices tripled into this aspect.
3.	May 12, 1882	16°♉29'	Half-cycle crest to 18-year cycle in June 1881; end of 4-year advance from 18-year trough in 1877, during which time prices rallied over 60%. June 1882 was a 22.5-mo cycle trough.
4.	Aug. 1, 1917	04°♌45'	4-year cycle trough in December 1917, following 4-year cycle crest in November 1916. Prices fell over 40%. 22.5-month cycle crest in June 1917.

	Date	Position	Comment
5.	Nov. 21, 1952 May 17, 1953 July 22, 1953	22°♎47' 21°♎38' 21°♎12'	18-year cycle crest in January 1953. End of 3-1/2 year rally in which prices advanced over 80% from June 1949 trough. 18-year cycle trough two months later in September 1953. Market was virtually down during the entire aspect t
6.	Mar. 3, 1989 June 24, 1989 Nov. 13, 1989	11°♑55' 11°♑14' 10°♑22'	Crest of 22.5-month cycle in October 1989; Trough of 22.5-month cycle also in October 1989. The crest was the 2nd phase of the 4-year cycle. The crest of the 4-year cycle was not until a few months later, in July
7.	Feb. 20, 2026	00°♈45'	

	Central	+/- 11 months	Total
Relative Strength			
All	2.80	3.75	3.33
Crest	+3.00	+3.33	+3.33
Trough	- 2.00	- 3.67	- 3.00
Consistency			
All	4.17	3.33	5.00
Crest	+3.33	+2.50	+5.00
Trough	- 1.67	- 2.50	- 4.17
C/S Index			
All	6.97	7.08	8.33
Crest	+6.33	+5.83	+8.33
Trough	- 3.67	- 6.17	- 7.17

The Saturn-Neptune conjunction has a definite correlation to long-term cycle crests. In six cases, a 22.5-month or greater cycle crest was the dominant cycle, and unfolded within 11 months of the aspect (8 or less in all but one case). In four instances (66.7%), it was a 4-year cycle crest, or a phase to the 18-year cycle. One case coincided with an 18-year cycle crest. In many cases, the decline which followed was less than 1 year, and in almost all cases these declines were only corrective in nature and did not lead to 18-year or greater cycle troughs, except the 1953 case which was the mildest 18-year cycle trough in history (it was corrective in nature).

Conclusions: 4-year or greater cycle crests tend to unfold slightly before or after the Saturn-Neptune conjunction aspect, or within the period in which it retrograded. The advances from the previous 4-year cycle troughs were quite impressive (i.e. the advances that started within 3-4 years earlier). In some cases these cycles were 18-year crests, and in others, they were simply phases of the 18-year cycle. Investors may use this signature as an opportunity to take profits on long-term holdings if the market is rallying into it, for the probabilities are great that a 4-year cycle will top out within the central time band, or close by.

Waxing Semi-Square (45°)

	Dates & Position of Saturn		Long-Term Cycles
1.	Feb. 2, 1815	04°♒18'	4-year crest in September 1815.
2.	Apr. 7, 1851	23°♈11'	4-year cycle trough in October 1851. Double top to 22.5-month cycle crest in June 1851.
3.	July 3, 1886	11°♋57'	4-year cycle crest in December 1886. This followed a 22.5-month cycle trough in May 1886.
4.	Oct. 12, 1921	00°♎05'	4-year cycle trough in August 1921.
5.	Dec. 31, 1957	19°♐26'	4-year cycle trough in October 1957.
6.	Apr. 10, 1994 Oct. 29, 1994 Dec. 21, 1994	08°♓17' 05°♓47' 07°♓11'	4-year cycle trough and double bottom in April and November 1994.
7.	May 10, 2030	27°♉15'	

	Central	+/- 7 months	Total
Relative Strength			
All	2.60	3.00	3.00
Crest	+2.00	+3.00	+2.67
Trough	- 2.75	- 3.00	- 2.80
Consistency			
All	4.17	2.50	5.00
Crest	+0.83	+1.67	+2.50
Trough	- 3.33	0.83	- 4.17
C/S Index			
All	6.77	5.50	8.00
Crest	+2.83	+4.67	+5.17
Trough	- 6.08	- 3.83	- 6.97

This aspect does not appear to correlate to very powerful cycles, but it is consistent. In all cases a 4-year cycle unfolded in the central time band, or within 7 months. Four of these (67%) corresponded to 4-year cycle troughs, and of those, three were in the central time band (the last three instances of the aspect, in fact). In five cases (83%) a 22.5-month or 4-year cycle occurred within the central time band.

<u>Conclusions</u>: *The waxing semi-square between Saturn and Neptune appears to coincide within seven months to a 4-year cycle, if one is due. In the vast majority of cases, this has been a trough. Therefore if prices are declining into this time band, and a 4-year cycle trough (or its half cycle) is due, investors may look to purchase stocks for the long-term.*

Waxing Sextile (60°)

	Dates & Position of Saturn		Long-Term Cycles
1.	Apr. 13, 1816	22°♒00'	4-year cycle trough in September 1816.
	Sep. 1, 1816	19°♒20'	
	Jan. 17, 1817	23°♒04'	
2.	May 28, 1852	11°♉25'	18-year cycle crest in October 1852. 4-year cycle trough in October 1851.
3.	Aug. 18, 1887	00°♌01'	4-year cycle crest in December 1886. Prices then fell to 4-year cycle trough in April 1888.
4.	Dec. 11, 1922	18°♎03'	22.5-month cycle crest in March 1923, followed by 22.5-month cycle trough in October 1923.
	Apr. 26, 1923	15°♎22'	
	Sep. 13, 1923	19°♎06'	
5.	Mar. 21, 1959	06°♑30'	22.5-month cycle crest in August 1959, followed by 22.5-month cycle trough in September 1959.
	June 17, 1959	04°♑24'	
	Dec. 23, 1959	06°♑09'	
6.	June 27, 1995	24°♓41'	4-year cycle trough in November 1994. 22.5-month cycle crest in May 1996, followed by 22.5-month cycle trough in July 1996 — after aspect.
	Aug. 17, 1995	23°♓22'	
	Mar. 15, 1996	27°♓13'	
7.	June 27, 2031	15°♊30'	

Relative Strength	**Central**	**+/- 8 months**	**Total**
All	2.33	3.67	3.00
Crest	+2.00	+3.33	+2.70
Trough	- 2.33	- 3.00	- 2.67
Consistency			
All	2.50	2.50	5.00
Crest	+1.67	+2.50	+4.17
Trough	- 2.50	- 2.50	- 5.00
C/S Index			
All	5.83	6.17	8.00
Crest	+3.67	+5.83	+6.87
Trough	- 4.83	- 5.50	- 7.67

The waxing sextile appears to be have a consistent correlation to intermediate-term cycle troughs. In every instance a 22.5-month or 4-year cycle trough unfolded within 8 months of the central time band. There were also five crests within the same time frame. But only three of six (50%) instances found these cycles unfolding in the central time band, and of those, only one was of the 4-year or greater cycle type. What may be significant is that in the last three cases, the aspect coincided with a 22.5-month crest, followed shortly after by a 22.5-month cycle trough.

<u>Conclusions</u>: *The waxing sextile between Saturn and Neptune has a consistent correlation to intermediate-term cycle troughs within a time band of 8 months either side of its central time band. There are also a number of intermediate-term crests in the same time band. therefore investors may use this signature as an opportunity to purchase stocks if a 22.5-month or 4-year cycle trough are unfolding.*

Waxing Square (90°)

	Dates & Position of Saturn		**Long-Term Cycles**
1.	Feb. 20, 1783 July 22, 1783 Dec. 12, 1783	09°♑48' 07°♑46' 12°♑08'	72-year cycle trough in 1784 starts just after last sequence; secondary trough that began great bull market run.
2.	May 16, 1819 Oct. 6, 1819 Feb. 29, 1820	28°♓09' 26°♓08' 00°♈34'	Half-cycle crest of 18-year cycle in May 1819; half-cycle trough to 18-year cycle in January 1820. Prices rallied over 60% in following 4 years.
3.	Aug. 26, 1854 Nov. 25, 1854 May 31, 1855	14°♊53' 13°♊10' 18°♊05'	End of 2nd phase trough to 18-year cycle in December 1854.
4.	Nov. 19 1889 Feb. 3, 1890 Aug. 26, 1890	03°♍20' 01°♍46' 06°♍46'	Crest of 36-year cycle in May 1890. Prices dropped about 25% to 4-year cycle trough by December 1890, and eventually about 50% to low in 1896.
5.	Jan. 16, 1926 May 23, 1926 Nov. 6, 1926	24°♏08' 22°♏06' 26°♏50'	4-year cycle crest in February 1926. End of rally in which prices soared almost 100% since low in May 1924. Also 4-year cycle trough in March 1926. Prices fell more than 15% in that month, then began torrid rally to 72-year crest in 1929.
6.	Feb. 18, 1963	15°♒40'	Half-cycle trough in June 1962 to 18-year cycle. Prices rose nearly 40% to 22.5-month cycle crest in May 1963.
7.	June 25, 1998 Nov. 1, 1998 Apr. 6, 1999	01°♉30' 29°♈30' 04°♉07'	4-year cycle crest unfolded in July 1998. 4-year cycle trough may have unfolded in September-October 1998 as this is being written.
8.	Sep. 16, 2033 Jan. 13, 2034 June 15, 2034	19°♋23' 17°♋23' 22°♋07'	

Relative Strength	Central	+/- 8 months	Total
All	3.40	4.50	4.00
Crest	+3.50	0.00	+3.50
Trough	- 3.33	- 4.00	- 3.67
Consistency			
All	4.17	0.83	5.00
Crest	+3.33	+0.00	+3.33
Trough	- 2.50	- 2.50	- 5.00
C/S Index			
All	7.57	5.33	9.00*
Crest	+6.83	0.00	+6.83
Trough	- 5.83	- 6.50	- 8.67

In every case there was at least a 4-year or greater cycle which unfolded nearby to this signature (within 8 months, although the month of the first instance in 1784 cannot be confirmed). In every case there was also a long-term cycle trough. However, in four of the six cases (67%), there was also a long-term cycle crest, although only three of these were a 4-year or greater cycle type. In most instances, whatever cycle unfolded first, the other followed within 1 year. If a long-term cycle crest was due (4-year or greater), it was followed by the 4-year cycle trough within the next 12 months — or vice-versa. The two instances of cardinal signs (1783, then 1820) correlated with a powerful 72-year cycle trough and 18-year half-cycle trough respectively. The current case is unfolding as this book is being written. A 4-year cycle crest has formed in July 1998, and was followed by a possible 4-year cycle trough just before the second pass in Autumn 1998.

Conclusions: The waxing square between Saturn and Neptune is both a powerful and reliable correlation to 4-year or greater cycles in U.S. stocks. The likelihood is greatest that a long-term trough will unfold during the central time band (or very close to it — within eight months, and usually after the last, or only, contact). However a long-term cycle crest is apt to precede or follow this trough, within 12 months, and usually much less. Therefore investors may use this time band as follows: to look for a 4-year or greater cycle crest to unfold either slightly before or during the central time band as an opportunity to sell stocks, and then look for a 4-year or greater trough to happen during or slightly after the central time band as an opportunity to purchase stocks for the long term. Primarily, though, investors will want to use this aspect to time a 4-year or greater trough, and look to purchase stocks on that trough.

Waxing Trine (120°)

	Dates & Position of Saturn		Long-Term Cycles
1.	May 29, 1822	04°♉05'	4-year cycle trough in September 1822.
	Dec. 5, 1822	04°♉09'	
	Mar. 14, 1823	07°♉16'	

2.	Aug. 12, 1857 Feb. 28, 1858 May 23, 1858	22°♋06' 21°♋53' 29°♋26'	18-year cycle trough — and secondary trough — that preceded the second great bull market run in U.S. stocks, in October 1857. 22.5-month cycle crest in February 1858.
3.	Nov. 25, 1892 Apr. 3, 1893 Sep. 20, 1893	10°♎04' 09°♎05' 13°♎34'	4-year cycle trough in July 1893. Prices rallied over 40% to crest 2 years later.
4.	Mar. 6, 1929 May 29, 1929 Dec. 29, 1929	29°♐35' 28°♐42' 03°♑26'	72-year cycle crest — and end of second great bull run in history of U.S. stocks - ended in September 1929. 4-year cycle trough in November 1929 as prices dropped about 50% in just 3 months.
5.	Mar. 27, 1966	21°♐53'	Double top to 18-year (and maybe greater) cycle crest, and first time DJIA tops 1000 mark, February 1966.
6.	June 25, 2001 Jan. 23, 2002 Apr. 1, 2002	08°♊06' 08°♊16' 10°♊31'	

	Central	+/- 0 months	Total
Relative Strength			
All	4.10	0.00	4.10
Crest	+3.83	+0.00	+3.83
Trough	- 3.50	- 0.00	- 3.50
Consistency			
All	5.00	0.00	5.00
Crest	+3.00	+0.00	+3.00
Trough	- 4.00	0.00	- 4.00
C/S Index			
All	9.10*	0.00	9.10*
Crest	+6.83	+0.00	+6.83
Trough	- 7.50	0.00	- 7.50

In three of the five cases, an 18-year or greater cycle (or double top to it) ended close by. In two of these cases (60%), it was a very long-term cycle crest, such as the one in 1929, and 1966. There was also another in September 1824, which was a year and half after the first series of aspects studied. In these instances, bear markets lasting at least 4-5 years commenced, in which prices lost substantial value. In another case (1857), a 22-year bear market ended, and one of the great bull market runs in U.S. history began. Whatever long-term cycle may be due going into this aspect, investors can anticipate it unfolding and being followed by a significant and long-term reversal. In the two cases of fire signs, both coincided with very important long-term cycle crests (1929 and 1966). What is also interesting is the fact that these cycles all fell within the central time band. They did not need an extended orb of time for the cycle to unfold.

<u>Conclusions</u>: Very long-term cycles (at least a 4-year type, but usually even greater) tend to unfold during the central time band of Saturn in waxing trine to Neptune. These will tend to be 18-year or greater cycles, or double tops (or bottoms) to them. It is most significant if prices are rallying into a long-term crest due at this time, for declines lasting 4-5 years have been noted in 60% of the instances so far. In those cases investors may use this time band as an opportunity to sell stocks (take profits on long-term holdings). However if it is apparent that a 4-year or greater cycle trough is forming, then investors would be advised to make purchases of stocks during this time band.

Waxing Sesquiquadrate (135°)

	Dates and Position of Saturn		Long-Term Cycles
1.	July 7, 1823	22°♉49'	18-year cycle crest in September 1824. End of 4-year rally and start of 5-year bear market.
	Nov. 12, 1823	20°♉30'	
	Apr. 27, 1824	24°♉34'	
2.	Sep. 17, 1858	08°♌29'	Double bottom to 18-year cycle trough in June 1859.
	Feb. 5, 1859	08°♌15'	
	July 10, 1859	12°♌08'	
3.	Nov. 7, 1894	00°♏10'	4-year cycle crest in September 1895. Start of sharp 11-month decline where market lost 57% of its value. 22.5-month cycle trough in March 1895.
	June 15, 1895	00°♏50'	
	Aug. 28, 1895	02°♏54'	
4.	Feb. 21, 1931	19°♑29'	22.5-month cycle trough & crest in October and November, 1931. But greater correlation was breakdown in stocks to 72-year cycle low of July 1932.
	July 23, 1931	19°♑12'	
	Dec. 24, 1931	22°♑56'	
5.	May 10, 1967	08°♈06'	22.5-month cycle crest in September 1967, followed by 22.5-month cycle trough in March 1968. Decline was about 14%. However, the bigger cycles involved the 4-year cycle trough in October 1966, followed by the 4-year cycle crest in December 1968.
	Oct. 16, 1967	07°♈57'	
	Mar. 4, 1968	11°♈31'	
6.	July 29, 2002	24°♊40'	
	Dec. 30, 2002	24°♊32'	
	May 20, 2003	28°♊11'	

Relative Strength	Central	+/- 9 months	Total
All	2.875	4.33	4.10
Crest	+2.33	+4.00	+3.25
Trough	- 2.625	- 4.00	- 3.625

Consistency			
All	4.00	3.00	5.00
Crest	+3.00	+2.00	+4.00
Trough	- 4.00	- 2.00	- 4.00
C/S Index			
All	6.875	7.33	9.10*
Crest	+5.33	+6.00	+7.25
Trough	- 6.625	- 6.00	- 6.625

This too is a consistently powerful signature. However, to be so, it requires a much larger extended time band than the previous waxing trine signature. In three of these five cases, the greater cycle unfolded at least 5-7 months outside of the central time band. In fact, only two cycles of a 4-year type or greater fell within the central time band (40%). But, if a 7 month extended orb was allowed, then 4-year or greater cycles unfolded in every case. In three of these five instances, the cycle was an 18-year or greater type, or a double bottom to it. In the last three instances, its central time band seemed to coincide more often with 22.5-month cycles (half cycles to the 4-year cycle), than very long-term types. There seemed to be no difference in bias towards crests versus troughs.

<u>Conclusions</u>: *The waxing sesquiquadrate of Saturn-Neptune has a fairly strong correlation to long-term cycles in U.S. stocks, given an orb of seven months before or after the central time band. In several cases, this has been an 18-year or greater cycle, although the central time band itself tends to produce more of a 22.5-month type of correction to the longer-term trend. Therefore, investors may look to either buy or sell stocks within that 7-month extended time band, depending upon whether it is a long-term cycle trough or crest that is forming. If the longer-term cycle is still pointed up, then investors may use the central time band as an opportunity to buy a 22.5-month cycle low.*

Opposition (180°)

	Dates & Position of Saturn		**Long-Term Cycles**
1.	May 27, 1792 Oct. 14, 1792 Mar. 24, 1793	27°♈30' 29°♈17' 01°♉21'	4-year cycle trough in September 1792. This followed the 4-year cycle crest of January 1792.
2.	Aug. 5, 1827 Jan. 15, 1828 May 29, 1828	14°♋04' 16°♋12' 17°♋09'	4-year cycle crest in October 1827, followed by 18-year cycle low in January 1829, which may have expanded until Saturn's opposition to Uranus was completed (1 year later, 1829).
3.	Nov. 5, 1862 Mar. 11, 1863 Sep. 4, 1863	01°♎27' 03°♎03' 05°♎19'	4-year cycle crest in March 1864. This is also the middle of the U.S. Civil War (1861-64). Possible 22.5-month cycle trough near December 1862.

	Date	Position	Comment
4.	Feb. 16, 1899	22°♐02'	Half-cycle crest to 18-year cycle in April-September 1899. Prices then dropped to 4-year cycle low in September 1900, as prices lost over 30%.
	May 2, 1899	22°♐57'	
	Dec. 14, 1899	25°♐42'	
	Aug. 16, 1900	28°♐40'	
	Oct. 4, 1900	29°♐16'	
5.	Mar. 21, 1936	14°♓59'	22.5-month cycle crest and trough both unfolded in April 1936. However, the bigger cycle was 4-year crest in March 1937, just 2 months after last aspect.
	Oct. 4, 1936	17°♓26'	
	Jan. 17, 1937	18°♓45'	
6.	June 25, 1971	00°♊52'	22.5-month cycle trough in November 1971. Market began 14-month rally in which prices gained 35% as 18-year cycle crest topped out in January 1973.
	Nov. 27, 1971	02°♊53'	
	Apr. 19, 1972	04°♊46'	
7.	Aug. 31, 2006	17°♌53'	
	Feb. 28, 2007	20°♌15'	
	June 25, 2007	21°♌47'	

Relative Strength	**Central**	**+/- 9 months**	**Total**
All	2.67	3.17	3.83
Crest	+3.00	+3.50	+3.50
Trough	- 2.40	- 5.00	- 2.83
Consistency			
All	5.00	4.17	5.00
Crest	+2.50	+3.33	+5.00
Trough	- 4.17	- 0.83	- 5.00
C/S Index			
All	7.67	7.33	8.83
Crest	+5.50	+6.83	+8.50
Trough	- 6.57	- 5.83	- 7.83

This is a very interesting signature. In most cases (67%), the bigger cycle did not unfold within the central time band. More often than not, the long-term stock market cycle unfolded within 1 year *after* the aspect. And in every case, that cycle was at least a 4-year or greater type. In two cases, the aspect unfolded about 9 months to a year before an 18-year cycle (maybe longer). This tendency to unfold before the cycle is completed may be consistent with Neptune's character of "hiding the negative facts" while it is in effect. Maybe the truth of the difficulties in the economy, government, or market in general are not realized (or believed) until the aspect is completed. While it is in effect, it seems to camouflage those difficulties. It is also interesting to note that given a 9 month orb, cycles of both types (crests and troughs) unfolded, thereby suggesting volatility in prices during this extended time band. Although cycles of both types occurred, the crest cycles were stronger. However, the trough cycles were more likely to unfold during the central time band, albeit rather weak in type compared to the crests which occurred slightly outside of the time band.

<u>Conclusions</u>: *The opposition between Saturn and Neptune has a consistently powerful correlation to long-term cycles in the U.S. stock market, but usually those cycles unfold after the aspect is completed, or towards its last passage. In the central time band itself, it appears to have more reliable correlations to troughs. However, those troughs may not be as strong as longer-term cycle crests which unfold within a year after the aspect. Investors may use this aspect to time long-term cycles that are likely to unfold at the end of a central time band, or after the passage of the last aspect. Depending on whether that cycle is a trough or crest, investors can take appropriate action at that time. If an intermediate-term trough appears to be forming within the central time band, and if the longer-term cycle is still pointed up, investors may purchase stocks on this corrective trough cycle.*

Waning Sesquiquadrate (225°)

	Dates and Position of Saturn		Long-Term Cycles
1.	July 5, 1796 Dec. 11, 1796 Apr. 25, 1797	20°♊49' 24°♊44' 24°♊38'	18-year cycle trough in November 1797.
2.	Sep. 15, 1831 Mar. 5, 1832 July 8, 1832	07°♍31' 11°♍24' 11°♍04'	22.5-month cycle trough in November 1831. This was 2 years after 18-year cycle trough, and 6 months before half-cycle crest to new 18-year cycle.
3.	Nov. 25, 1867 June 1, 1868 Sep. 25, 1868	27°♏29' 01°♐42' 01°♐17'	22-month cycle trough in April 1867, followed by 4-year cycle in July-August 1869. Market was in midst of a move up during this period.
4.	Apr. 1, 1904 June 24, 1904 Jan. 23, 1905	18°♒04' 20°♒33' 21°♒05'	4-year cycle trough in November 1903. Prices were moving up under this aspect. 22.5-month cycle crest and trough in April and May 1905 respectively.
5.	May 21, 1940 Oct. 29, 1940 Mar. 14, 1941	07°♉49' 11°♉42' 11°♉24'	22.5-month cycle trough, June 1940, and 22.5-month crest in November 1940. Market was in decline to 4-year cycle trough in April 1942.
6.	July 28, 1975 Feb. 2, 1976 May 15, 1976	24°♋10' 28°♋28' 28°♋05'	4-year cycle crest in September 1976. In midst of move up from 18-year cycle low in December 1974, to 4-year cycle crest in September 1976. Double top in March 1976.
7.	Oct. 27, 2010 Mar. 24, 2011 Aug. 24, 2011	10°♎57' 14°♎40' 14°♎28'	

Relative Strength	Central	+/- 10 months	Total
All	2.17	4.00	3.67
Crest	+2.25	+3.33	+3.00
Trough	- 2.00	- 4.25	- 3.40
Consistency			
All	2.50	4.17	5.00
Crest	+1.67	+2.50	+3.33
Trough	- 1.67	- 2.50	- 4.17
C/S Index			
All	4.67	8.17	8.67
Crest	+3.89	+5.83	+6.33
Trough	- 3.67	- 6.75	- 7.57

The most outstanding quality of this signature is the absence of any long-term cycles within its central time band. This signature correlated mostly with corrections and sub-cycles to the 4-year cycle, in the middle of moves to greater cycles that unfolded at least 4-10 months before or after these aspects began or ended (up to a year beyond the aspect). In four of the last five instances, the market was in the midst of a rally to a greater cycle that happened after the aspect series ended. This is probably due to the fact that the trine, which follows very shortly after, is a more dominant aspect. The distance of only 15 degrees difference is covered rather quickly between Saturn to Neptune and to Pluto (less than a 1-year difference). Thus oftentimes they overlap the same year.

Conclusions: The waning sesquiquadrate between Saturn and Neptune does not appear to be a prominent correlation to long-term stock market cycles while it is in effect. However, it does seem to correlate to long-term cycles (especially troughs) ending just before this signature begins, and the opposite type (usually crest) culminating within a year after these aspects end. Therefore investors may look to purchase stocks if indeed a long-term cycle trough is happening on the early side of this signature, and look to sell stocks if a long-term cycle crest is occurring on the later end — or within a year after — of this signature (and closer perhaps to the trine). More than likely, no cycle greater than a 22.5-month type will unfold during the central time band. Greater cycles are more likely 4-10 months outside of this central time band.

Waning Trine (240°)

	Dates & Position of Saturn		Long-Term Cycles
1.	June 7, 1762	21°♈44'	72-year cycle trough in 1762.
	Aug. 26, 1762	24°♈16'	
	Mar. 20, 1763	24°♈07'	
2.	Aug. 16, 1797	08°♋09'	18-year cycle trough in November 1797.
	Nov. 23, 1797	11°♋15'	
	May 29, 1798	10°♋48'	

3.	Nov. 4, 1832 Feb. 1, 1833 Aug. 21, 1833	24°♍39' 27°♍29' 27°♍11'	Half-cycle crest to 18-year cycle in April - June 1833. Prices fell 25% to half-cycle trough the next year (February 1834).
4.	Feb. 1, 1869 Apr. 7, 1869 Nov. 20, 1869	14°♐56' 17°♐02' 17°♐09'	4-year cycle crest in July-August 1869. Prices fell nearly 20% to 4-year cycle trough in December 1869.
5.	Mar. 14, 1906 Aug. 30, 1906 Jan. 9, 1907	07°♓37' 12°♓03' 11°♓04'	18-year cycle crest in January 1906. Prices declined nearly 50% over next 22 months to 4-year cycle low in November 1907. 22.5-month cycle trough and crest in July and October 1806 respectively.
6.	July 8, 1941 Oct. 5, 1941 Apr. 20, 1942	25°♉12' 27°♉59' 27°♉42'	Secondary trough preceding great bull market run in April 1942.
7.	Sep. 4, 1976 Jan. 12, 1977 June 23, 1977	11°♌15' 15°♌03' 14°♌18'	Half-cycle crest to 18-year cycle in September 1976. Prices then fell 28% to 4-year cycle low 18 months later. 22.5-month cycle trough in November 1976.
8.	Oct. 10, 2012 June 11, 2013 July 19, 2013	00°♏37' 05°♏22' 04°♏55'	

Relative Strength	**Central**	**+/- 6 months**	**Total**
All	3.93	4.50	4.36
Crest	+3.25	+5.00	+4.00
Trough	- 3.58	- 4.00	- 3.93
Consistency			
All	5.00	1.67	5.00
Crest	+3.33	+0.83	+3.33
Trough	- 4.17	- 0.83	- 5.00
C/S Index			
All	8.93	6.17	9.36*
Crest	+6.58	+5.83	+7.33
Trough	- 7.75	- 4.83	- 8.93

This is a very prominent signature — one of the most impressive of the Saturn-Neptune series. In every case but one, a 4-year or greater cycle unfolded in the central time band. In the one case that missed, 1906, it was less than 2 months before the first aspect, but still within the same year of the aspect. In fact, six of these seven cycles were greater than 4-year types (86%). Thus it is not only a reliable signature, but one that correlates with very long-term cycles (powerful) as well. In all 7 cases there was at least a 22.5-month cycle trough, six of them occurring within the central time band. In 4 of the 7 cases (57%), the aspect coincided with a longer-term cycle crest from which prices would then decline sharply 1-2 years into a long-term cycle trough. In three cases it was the opposite — a long-term cycle trough (18-year and 72-year cycles in first two cases, and a secondary low preceding a great bull market run in the third). Thus whatever long-term cycle seems to be forming going into the aspect will probably reverse. The element of the trine did not seem significant.

Conclusions: The waning trine between Saturn and Neptune is a powerful signature correlating to long-term cycles in U.S. stocks. Usually these cycles are greater than the 4-year type. Investors can therefore look for a long-term cycle to culminate during the time of this aspect and for prices to reverse sharply for at least 1-2 years afterwards.

Waning Square (270°)

	Dates & Position of Saturn		Long-Term Cycles
1.	Aug. 12, 1800 Feb. 24, 1801 May 17, 1801	14°♌32' 19°♌24' 17°♌50'	4-year cycle crest in October 1800.
2.	Dec. 11, 1835 Mar. 4, 1836 Sep. 20, 1836	01°♏37' 04°♏56' 03°♏23'	72-year cycle crest in August 1835. End of great bull market run, and start of 22-year bear market.
3	Jan. 12, 1873 Aug. 2, 1873 Oct. 30, 1873	23°♑33' 28°♑35' 26°♑52'	36-year cycle crest January-May 1873. Start of 4-year bear market in which prices declined over 35%. First 4-year cycle trough in November 1873.
4.	Apr. 14, 1909 Oct. 18, 1909 Jan. 24, 1910	14°♈25' 19°♈20' 17°♈31'	Double top to 18-year cycle crest in September 1909. Start of 5-year bear market in which prices declined almost 50%.
5.	July 2, 1944 Jan. 8, 1945 Apr. 6, 1945	01°♋34' 06°♋26' 04°♋45'	Middle of World War II. No long-term stock market cycles culminated at this time. The market was in midst of a great rise from 1942-1946. There was a 22.5-month cycle crest in June 1945, and a 22.5-month cycle trough in July 1945.
6.	Sep. 14, 1979 Mar. 26, 1980 June 22, 1980	17°♍47' 22°♍41' 21°♍01'	Double bottom to half-cycle trough of 18-year cycle in March 1980. Beginning of a major recession, worst since 1930's. Beginning of 13-month rally as prices gained 40+%. 22.5-month cycle crest in February 1980. Half-cycle rest to 18-year cycle 9 months later in March 1981.
7.	Nov. 26, 2015 June 17, 2016 Sep. 10, 2016	07°♐02' 12°♐02' 10°♐25'	

Relative Strength	Central	+/- 9 months	Total
All	3.60	4.50	3.92
Crest	+3.30	+4.50	+3.92
Trough	- 2.83	- 0.00	- 2.83
Consistency			
All	4.17	0.83	5.00
Crest	+4.17	+0.83	+5.00
Trough	- 2.50	- 0.00	- 2.50
C/S Index			
All	7.77	5.33	8.92
Crest	+7.47	+5.33	+8.92
Trough	- 5.33	- 0.00	- 5.33

If it wasn't for World War II, this would have been another very strong correlation to long-term cycles in stock prices in every instance. As it is, five of six (83%) of these instances correlated to 4-year or greater cycles right within the central time band. Three of those five (60%) were 18-year or greater cycles, or double tops to them. Another was a half-cycle to an 18-year cycle trough. In every case except the World War II instance, there was a long-term cycle crest. In all, this is a very powerful signature, usually signifying the completion of a very long-term cycle in U.S. stocks, and usually a crest.

Conclusions: The waning square between Saturn and Neptune has a very high correlation to very long-term cycles in U.S. stock indexes. Most of the time this will be greater than a 4-year cycle type, most of the time the cycle will culminate in the central time band, and most of the time it will be a crest. Once again, investors may use this signature to time long-term cycles according to the trend going into this signature. But since it usually corresponds with a long-term crest, investors may wish to sell stocks if prices are indeed rising into this time period, or within four months of it.

Waning Sextile (300°)

	Dates & Position of Saturn		Long-Term Cycles
1.	Aug. 25, 1803	21°♍08'	Possible 22.5-month crest and trough in October & November 1803 respectively, but if so, it was very minor.
2.	Nov. 10, 1839	09°♐56'	Probable 22.5-month cycle low in November 1839. In midst of big decline 1835-1842.
3.	Mar. 10, 1876 Aug. 19, 1876 Dec. 14, 1876	01°♓14' 05°♓16' 02°♓44'	36-year cycle trough 6 months later in June 1877. 22.5-month cycle crest in February 1876.

4.	Apr. 26, 1912	21°♉09'	4-year cycle crest in September-October 1912. This was 7 months prior to 4-year trough in September 1911.
5.	July 1, 1947	08°♌03'	22.5-month cycle crest in July 1947. This followed 4-year cycle trough in October 1946 and its double bottom in May 1947.
6.	Oct. 14, 1982 June 7, 1983 June 21, 1983	24°♎41' 28°♎11' 27°♎47'	4-year cycle low in August 1982. This was also the secondary trough preceding a great bull run. Prices were rising sharply during this period.
7.	Jan. 31, 2019 June 18, 2019 Nov. 8, 2019		

Relative Strength	**Central**	**+/- 7 months**	**Total**
All	2.125	3.50	3.00
Crest	+2.00	+3.00	+2.25
Trough	- 2.17	- 3.50	- 3.00
Consistency			
All	3.33	3.33	5.00
Crest	+2.50	+0.83	+3.33
Trough	- 2.50	- 3.33	- 5.00
C/S Index			
All	5.475	6.83	8.00
Crest	+4.50	+3.83	+5.58
Trough	- 4.67	- 6.83	- 8.00

This may be another case where the signature is too close to another aspect to be meaningful. It appears that most of the cycles associated with this sextile actually unfolded outside of the central time band. In fact, only one-third of the dominant cycles occurred within the central time band, and two-thirds were anywhere from 2-7 months earlier or later than the aspect series. What is interesting though is that in the last four cases, the aspect correlated with a long-term cycle trough of the 4-year type or greater. In the prior two cases, 22.5-month cycle troughs were present within the central time band.

Conclusions: The waning sextile between Saturn and Neptune has a somewhat reliable correlation to 4-year or greater cycle troughs, if an orb of nine months either side of the aspect's start and finish is allowed. In most cases this cycle will unfold outside the central time band. In most cases, this will be a 4-year cycle. However, the lack of any consistency of long-term cycles unfolding within the central time band itself makes this an unreliable signature for investors to use in devising long-term strategies. Perhaps if the market is trending down to a 4-year cycle trough within seven months of this aspect, investors might look for an opportunity to make long-term purchases.

Waning Semi-Square (315°)

	Dates & Position of Saturn		Long-Term Cycles
1.	Oct. 25, 1804 Apr. 2, 1805 July 18, 1805	09°♎49' 12°♎50' 10°♎28'	18-year cycle crest 1 year later, in August 1806. 22.5-month cycle crest in June 1805, and trough of same type in September 1805.
2.	Feb. 1, 1841 May 18, 1841 Oct. 30, 1841	29°♐28' 02°♑43' 29°♐17'	72-year cycle trough in February 1842 and start of great bull market run.
3.	Feb. 17, 1878	20°♓05'	36-year cycle trough 8 months earlier, in June 1877. 22.5-month cycle crest 7 months later.
4.	June 13, 1913 Jan. 14, 1914 Feb. 9, 1914	09°♊28' 11°♊55' 11°♊13'	36-year cycle trough 10 months afterwards, in December 1914. 22.5-month cycle trough in June 1913, and its crest in March 1914, with a double top in September 1913. Prices then fell 37% to 36-year. cycle trough.
5.	Aug. 18, 1948	26°♌05'	4-year cycle crest in June 1948. Prices then declined 17.4% to 4-year low one year later in June 1949.
6.	Jan. 10, 1984 Mar. 8, 1984 Sep. 24, 1984	14°♏42' 16°♏15' 13°♏43'	22.5-month cycle trough in July 1984. This was end of 8-month decline in which prices fell close to 17%. Prices then rallied almost 200% over next 3 years.
7.	Jan. 20, 2021	03°♒56'	

Relative Strength	**Central**	**+/- 10 months**	**Total**
All	2.25	5.00	3.67
Crest	+2.33	+0.00	+2.33
Trough	- 2.00	- 5.00	- 4.25
Consistency			
All	3.33	2.50	5.00
Crest	+2.50	+0.00	+2.50
Trough	- 1.67	- 2.50	- 3.33
C/S Index			
All	5.58	7.50	8.67
Crest	+4.83	+0.00	+4.83
Trough	- 3.67	- 7.50	- 7.58

As anticipated, this is a more significant correlation to long-term cycles than the sextile. However, like the waning sextile, this aspect also had several cycles culminating outside the central time band. But in this case, that may have been due to fact that two instances had only one occurrence of the aspect (no retrograde factor resulting in three or five passes). Nevertheless, three of these signatures coincided closely to very long-term cycles in U.S. stocks. 18-year or greater cycles unfolded in three cases (67%), but each was at least 4 months before or after the first or last aspect of the series. In a fourth case (1806), an 18-year cycle crest occurred 13 months after the aspect. Most of these long-term cycles were troughs, but not all. When it was a trough, it was the end of a minimum 17% decline from the prior cycle crest. Only three crests occurred, and two of these were the 22.5-month cycle types. Thus this aspect has a higher correlation to troughs.

Conclusions: Given an orb of up to 1 year, the waning semi-square between Saturn and Neptune has a 66.7% correlation to very long-term cycle culminations in U.S. stocks (18-year or greater). In most cases this will coincide with a trough. Investors may use this signature as a guide to time long-term cycle lows, and then adopt bullish long-term investing strategies when that trough is ended.

Summary of Saturn-Neptune Signatures

The following represents the ranking order of Saturn-Neptune aspects in correlation to long-term stock market cycles. This first ranking order is based upon Total C/S values, which includes a time band of up to 10 months (but usually no more than nine) outside of the aspect. In parentheses are those instances in which that particular signature correlated more times with a crests (+) or trough (-), and the respective values of each. Also included is a column indicating how many instances of cycles greater than four-year types which were associated with each aspect (again, within a 10-month orb of time either side of the aspect), and the percentage of times this represents. In the last column, titled **Orb,** are the number of months used outside of the central time band for the extended time band upon which the Total C/S values were based

Aspect	Total		Cycles > 4-Years		Orb
1. Waning Trine	9.36*	(- 8.93)	6/7 =	86%	6
2 Waxing Trine	9.10*	(- 7.50)	3/5 =	60%	0
2 Waxing Sesquiquadrate	9.10*		3/5 =	60%	9
4. Waxing Square	9.00*	(- 8.67)	4/6 =	67%	8
5. Waning Square	8.92	(+8.92)	4/6 =	67%	9
6. Opposition	8.83	(+8.50)	3/6 =	50%	9
7 Waning Sesquiquadrate	8.67	(- 7.57)	3/6 =	50%	10
7 Waning Semi-Square	8.67	(- 7.58)	3/6 =	50%	10
9. Conjunction	8.33	(+8.33)	2/6 =	33%	9
10. Waxing Semi-Square	8.00	(- 6.97)	0/6 =	0%	7
10 Waxing Sextile	8.00	(- 7.67)	1/6 =	17%	8
10. Waning Sextile	8.00	(- 8.00)	1/6 =	17%	9

The Saturn-Neptune signatures are not as strong nor as reliable in their correlation to long-term cycles as the Saturn-Uranus signatures. Although the table above does not show it, only eight of these signatures corresponded to the 14 cycles that were 18-year or greater troughs (57%), as discussed under the Saturn-Uranus summary. The correlation was a little stronger to the 18-year cycle crests. Here nine of 13 instances found Saturn-Neptune contacts close by (69%).

Surprisingly, the trine aspects between Saturn and Neptune were the most powerful and consistent. Also significant were the waxing sesquiquadrate and waxing square signatures. All four had a C/S total value of 9.00 or greater, with the waning trine the strongest at 9.36. What is also noteworthy was the fact that the waxing trine did not require any extended time band for its corresponding long-term cycle to unfold — all five instances produced a long-term cycle right within its central time band.

Almost as powerful was the waning square, whose Total C/S value was a healthy 8.92. This was followed closely by the opposition with a C/S value of 8.83. Thus five of the six most powerful correlations were with both trines, both squares, and the opposition. In fact, it appeared that the closer the aspects were to the conjunction, the weaker their correspondence to long-term cycles. The five weakest signatures were the conjunction, semi-squares, and the sextiles.

There were 71 instances studied in these 12 different aspects. Of those, 33 found correspondences to cycles greater than the 4-year types, given an extended time band of nine months (46.5%). This is considerably less than the Saturn-Uranus associations. However, eight of these aspects had a correlation of 50% or more to these longer-term cycles. If the five weakest aspects mentioned above were removed from the study (i.e. those that were within 60° of the conjunction, or the semi-squares, sextiles, and conjunction), then the correspondence of the other signatures to long-term cycles greater than the 4-year types shoots up to 63.4% (26 of 41 cases). The most prominent relationship to long-term cycles was seen in the waning trine, where six of seven instances correlated (86%).

Almost all of the signatures had a noticeable bias to either crests or troughs. Crest relationships were most frequent in the following aspects: waning square (+8.92), opposition (+8.50), and the conjunction (+8.33). It is most interesting that these three aspects comprise three-fourths of the possible "hard aspect" formations. The other hard aspect, the waxing square, had a bias towards troughs.

There were more aspects correlating with trough cycles than crests. The following represent the Saturn-Neptune signatures which had a bias towards troughs: waning trine (-8.93), waxing square (-8.67), waning sextile (-8.00), waxing sextile (-7.67), waning semi-square (-7.58), waning sesquiquadrate (-7.57), waxing trine (-7.50), and waxing semi-square (-6.97). Interestingly, all the so-called "harmonious" aspects (or "soft" aspects, like the sextile and trine), had a greater correlation to troughs.

The ranking orders changed somewhat when only the central time band was used, according to the criteria outlined for this study (i.e. an orb of only one month outside of cases involving series of three or more passes, or within three months in cases involving only a single passage). These C/S results are shown in the table below. Also shown are the number of instances in which greater than four-year cycles unfolded in this definition of a central time band.

Aspect	Central Time Band		Cycles > 4-Years
1. Waxing Trine	9.10*	(- 7.50)	3/5 = 60%
2. Waning Trine	8.93	(- 7.75)	5/7 = 71%
3. Waning Square	7.77	(+7.47)	3/6 = 50%
4. Opposition	7.67	(- 6.57)	1/6 = 17%
5. Waxing Square	7.57	(+6.83)	2/6 = 33%
6. Conjunction	6.97	(+6.33)	1/6 = 17%
7. Waxing Sesquiquadrate	6.875	(- 6.625)	1/5 = 20%
8. Waxing Semi-Square	6.77	(- 6.08)	0/6 = 0%
9. Waxing Sextile	5.83		0/6 = 0%
10. Waning Semi-Square	5.58		0/6 = 0%
11. Waning Sextile	5.475		0/6 = 0%
12. Waning Sesquiquadrate	4.67		0/6 = 0%

When the more precise time band is used, only one aspect achieves the level of significance as defined by this study. That is the waxing trine (9.10*). Coming very close to it was the waning trine, which had a C/S value of 8.93. However, no other Saturn-Neptune aspects attained a score of greater than 8.00. Only three other signatures attained a score over 7.00 (waning square, opposition, and waxing square). The seven other signatures all had values between 4.67-6.97, which is considered rather weak and non-reliable as a timing indicator. What is somewhat interesting is that all of the hard aspects and the two trines comprised the top six C/S values for the central time band study. These six are considered the major aspects in astrology. The other six (semi-squares, sextiles, and sesquiquadrates) are considered the minor aspects. This scoring supports classical astrology studies. In *The Gold Book: Geocosmic Correlation to Gold Price Cycles*, only the major aspects were studied, and this section on Saturn-Neptune aspects justifies that approach.

Only three Saturn-Neptune aspects had a 50% or greater correlation to cycles greater than 4-year types unfolding within their central time band. They were: waning trine (71%), waxing trine (60%), and the waning square (50%). The waxing square was next with a 33% frequency. All others had 20% or less reliability to these long term cycles within their central time band. In fact, of the 35 instances of minor aspects, only one correlated with a longer than 4-year cycle within its central time band.

In summary, these studies clearly point out the comparative weakness of Saturn-Neptune aspects to long-term cycles, especially within their central time band. The exceptions seem to be with the trine signatures, for they are quite reliable. The squares are also to be considered, and so too somewhat are the conjunction and opposition. But for all intents and purposes, the central time band of minor aspects between Saturn and Neptune can be eliminated as a market timing tool for long-term cycles in the U.S. stock market, at least those that are greater than 4-year cycle types. In a later chapter, we will review how useful these signatures are for timing four-year cycles.

SATURN-PLUTO: LONG-TERM CYCLES

Unlike Saturn to either Uranus or Neptune, these two planets have much in common. Saturn is the principle of authority and firmness. Pluto's principle is strength and power. Together they are very powerful, even forceful. When expressed in a positive fashion, they represent the ability of the collective to reform obsolete structures, thereby making them useful again. The result is to become more productive. But sometimes it is necessary to tear down the old ways in order to accomplish this. That tearing down process can cause negative reactions as well, and this is where bitter "power plays" come in. When negative, the result can be brutal and almost barbaric. This can represent an urge to destroy, to undermine, and to cause ruin. In hard aspect, this combination can coincide with a time when necessary reforms in the banking system, economy, or even government are called for. If done willingly, there is no loss of value to stock indexes. But when resisted, then it becomes a bitter battle between two very stubborn forces, and the result can be a severe decline in equity prices, as the entire economic structure is forced into an overhaul — and oftentimes an overhaul that is not very well planned.

The Saturn-Pluto planetary cycle is erratic, due to Pluto's extremely elliptical orbit. Their cycle ranges from 31-37 years. This is shorter than the previous two planetary pair cycles, so there will be more cases where some of the consecutive aspects may overlap with the same stock market cycle.

Conjunction (0°)

	Dates & Position of Saturn		Long-Term Cycles
1.	May 5, 1819	27°♓04'	Half-cycle crest to 18-year cycle in May 1819.
	Oct. 5, 1819	26°♓15'	Half-cycle trough to 18-year cycle in January 1820.
	Jan. 11, 1820	25°♓42'	Prices dropped 25% from crest to trough.
2.	June 6, 1851	00°♉20'	4-year cycle trough in October 1851. Rally to 18-year crest into January, 1853.
	Nov. 11, 1851	29°♈29'	
	Feb. 10, 1852	28°♈59'	

3.	May 22, 1883	29°♉46'	Half cycle trough to 18-year cycle in June 1884. 22.5-month cycle crest in September 1882. Possible 22.5-month cycle trough in March 1883.
4.	Oct. 4, 1914 Nov. 1, 1914 May 19, 1915	02°♋13' 02°♋04' 00°♋54'	36-year trough in December 1914. End of 5-year bear market in which stocks lost nearly 50%. Start of 5-year bull market in which stocks gained 150%.
5.	Aug. 11, 1947	13°♌07'	22.5-month cycle crest in July 1947. 4-year cycle crest was 10 months later, in June 1948.
6.	Nov. 8, 1982	27°♎35'	4-year cycle trough, and secondary low that preceded great bull market, unfolded 3 months earlier, in August 1982. Prices gained over 250% by 1987.
7.	Jan. 12, 2020	22°♑46'	

Relative Strength	**Central**	**+/- 11 months**	**Total**
All	3.42	4.00	3.92
Crest	+3.00	+5.00	+3.67
Trough	- 3.70	- 3.00	- 3.58
Consistency			
All	5.00	1.67	5.00
Crest	+1.67	+0.83	+2.50
Trough	- 4.17	- 0.83	- 5.00
C/S Index			
All	8.42	5.67	8.92
Crest	+4.67	+5.83	+6.17
Trough	- 7.87	- 3.83	- 8.58

This conjunction correlated with some very important periods in economic and world history. The 1914-15 instance presaged the first World War. The 1947 instance followed the second World War and coincided with the Marshall Plan, an economic package that enabled much of the world's war-torn countries to rebuild and thus begin the long period of prosperity that dominated the last half of the 20th century. The 1982 instance was just 3 months after the start of the greatest bull market in stocks in the history of many countries in the world.

Not surprisingly, this aspect also correlated with the end of long-term cycles in U.S. equities. Most of these cycles culminated within the central time band (83%), and two-thirds of them were greater than 4-year cycle types. There was a trough in every instance, and in five of six of these cases, it was at least a 4-year cycle trough. Also significant is the fact that in each of the instances in which the conjunction took place in cardinal signs, the stock market put in an 18-year or greater cycle, or a secondary low that preceded a great bull market run.

<u>Conclusions</u>: *The Saturn-Pluto conjunction is a powerful economic cycle, and one that has a strong correlation to the end and beginning of long-term cycles in U.S. equities, particularly if it occurs in a cardinal sign. This is most definitely the case when it correlates to a long-term cycle trough, for afterwards the U.S. market embarks upon a very long bull market trend. Investors may use this signature to initiate bullish strategies if long-term cycle troughs appear to be forming during (or close by to) the central time band. It seems more powerful when there are three passages due to a retrograde factor. Perhaps it allows more time for the "big" cycle to culminate.*

Waxing Semi-Square (45°)

	Dates & Position of Saturn		Long-Term Cycles
1.	June 1, 1823	16°♉54'	4-year cycle trough in September 1822, and 18-year cycle crest in September 1824.
2.	June 8, 1855	19°♊10'	4-year cycle trough in December 1854.
3.	Aug. 31, 1886 Feb. 3, 1887 May 12, 1887	19°♋04' 17°♋07' 18°♋15'	4-year cycle crest December 1886.
4.	Sep. 7, 1918	21°♌29'	22.5-month cycle crest in October 1918. This followed 4-year cycle trough of December 1917.
5.	Oct. 2, 1951	05°♎56'	22.5-month cycle crest in September 1951. Prices declined 8 months to 22.5-month cycle trough in May 1952.
6.	Jan. 17, 1988	27°♐21'	54-year cycle trough in October 1987, just three months earlier. 54-year cycle crest was in August 1987.
7.	May 6, 2024 Sep. 25, 2024 Jan. 26, 2025	17°♓06' 14°♓42' 16°♓53'	

Relative Strength	Central	+/- 9 months	Total
All	3.00	3.50	3.17
Crest	+2.33	+5.00	+3.00
Trough	- 5.00	- 3.00	- 3.50

Consistency	Central	+/- 9 months	Total
All	3.33	3.33	5.00
Crest	+2.50	+0.83	+3.33
Trough	- 0.83	- 2.50	- 3.33

C/S Index			
All	6.33	6.83	8.17
Crest	+4.83	+5.83	+6.33
Trough	- 5.83	- 5.50	- 6.83

Only once did a powerful cycle unfold within the central time band. There were two other occasions in which a 22.5-month cycle crest culminated. In three other instances, a 4-year and an 18-year cycle occurred outside the central time band of the aspect. Therefore, this signature does not appear to be a reliable indicator of the end and beginning of very long-term cycles. At best, it seems to coincide with 22.5-month cycle types within its central time band, and 4-year types 3-9 months outside. Even the long-term cycle coinciding with the semi-square of January 17, 1988 appears to have more association with other aspects nearby. What is interesting is that in the four cases of troughs, all occurred 3-9 months *before* the aspect, and in each case, it was a single passage of the aspect (no multiple passes due to the retrograde factor).

Conclusions: The waxing semi-square of Saturn to Pluto does not appear to exhibit a reliable historical correspondence to long-term cycles in U.S. equities. If a 22.5-month cycle crest is due around this period, investors may use the following decline into its trough as a buying opportunity, or vice-versa. Or, if a four-year or greater cycle trough appears to be forming 3-9 months before this aspect, investors may look to buy stocks on that low.

Waxing Sextile (60°)

	Dates & Position of Saturn		Long-Term Cycles
1.	Apr. 22, 1792	23°♈19'	4-year cycle crest in January 1792, followed by 4-year cycle trough in September 1792.
2.	July 5, 1824 Jan. 12, 1825 Mar. 13, 1825	03°♊11' 01°♊15' 02°♊25'	18-year cycle crest in September 1824. Start of 5-year decline.
3.	July 9, 1856	05°♋32'	4-year cycle crest in December 1856. Prices lost about 50% value in next year as 18-year cycle trough unfolded in October 1857.
4.	Oct. 5, 1887 Jan. 22, 1888 June 22, 1888	04°♌51' 03°♌08' 05°♌07'	4-year cycle trough in March-April 1888. Double top to 18-year cycle crest 1 year later in September 1889.
5.	Oct. 15, 1919 Apr. 4, 1920 July 1, 1920	07°♍46' 05°♍42' 07°♍20'	Half-cycle crest to 18-year cycle in October 1919. Prices dropped over 45% in next 14 months.

6.	Nov. 26, 1952	23°♎16'	18-year cycle crest in January 1953. Prices dropped 13.8% to 18-year cycle trough in September 1953.
	May 31, 1953	20°♎59'	
	Aug. 18, 1953	23°♎00'	
7.	May 1, 1989	13°♑51'	22.5-month cycle crest, then trough, in October 1989. Prices fell 11% in that month, then started rally to 4-year cycle crest in July 1990.
	May 18, 1989	13°♑23'	
	Jan. 16, 1990	17°♑26'	
8.	Mar. 28, 2026	05°♈09'	

Relative Strength	**Central**	**+/- 5 months**	**Total**
All	3.67	3.50	3.79
Crest	+3.80	+3.75	+3.79
Trough	- 3.33	- 3.00	- 3.25
Consistency			
All	4.29	2.14	5.00
Crest	+3.57	+1.43	+5.00
Trough	- 2.14	- 0.71	- 2.86
C/S Index			
All	7.96	5.64	8.79
Crest	+7.37	+5.18	+8.79
Trough	- 5.47	- 3.71	- 6.11

This appears to be a significant signature. In all but one instance, there was an observable cycle within the central time band. Also in all seven instances (100%), there was a cycle crest of importance that culminated, usually within the central time band, or within just five months of it. In six cases, this was at least a 4-year cycle crest. And in four instances, it was greater than a 4-year cycle. Thus it seems that this aspect's greatest value might be in timing 4-year or greater cycle crests, if they are forming either within the central time band, or within five months, of this signature.

<u>Conclusions</u>: The waxing sextile of Saturn and Pluto has a fairly reliable correlation to long-term cycle crests within the central time band. In most cases these will be at least a 4-year cycle crest. Investors may thus use this time band as an opportunity to take profits from the long side, should prices be rising into this aspect's time band.

Waxing Square (90°)

	Dates & Position of Saturn		**Long-Term Cycles**
1.	July 6, 1794	26°♉02'	18-year cycle crest in April 1795. Market began 3-year decline in 18-year low in 1797.
	Dec. 11, 1794	24°♉21'	
	Apr. 6, 1795	27°♉12'	
2.	Sep. 8, 1826	04°♋41'	4-year cycle trough in February 1827. Market was in

	Dec. 16, 1826 June 5, 1827	03°♋17' 06°♋15'	midst of decline from 1824-29, although there was a corrective rally to a 4-year cycle crest in October 1827.
3.	Sep. 7, 1858 Mar. 10, 1859 May 29, 1859	07°♌25' 06°♌03' 07°♌44'	Double bottom to 18-year cycle trough (and start of big bull run) in June 1859.
4.	Sep. 4, 1890	07°♍53'	18-year cycle crest in May 1890. This was followed by decline to 4-year cycle trough in December 1890.
5.	Oct. 8, 1922	11°♎13'	50-week cycle crest in October 1922. End of first leg up in 4-year cycle from trough of August 1921 in which prices gained approximately 60%. 22.5-month cycle crest in March 1923.
6.	Dec. 27, 1955 July 2, 1956 Oct. 7, 1956	28°♏26' 26°♏48' 29°♏42'	4-year cycle crest in April 1956. Prices dropped over 20% to 4-year cycle trough 18 months later.
7.	Mar. 19, 1993 Oct. 9, 1993 Jan. 1, 1994	25°♒23' 23°♒56' 27°♒06'	4-year cycle crest in November 1993. Prices dropped 12% to 4-year cycle trough 5 months later, in April 1994.
8.	June 23, 2028 Nov. 15, 2028 Mar. 29, 2029	08°♉22' 06°♉34' 10°♉02'	

Relative Strength	**Central**	**+/- 4 months**	**Total**
All	3.21	3.67	3.50
Crest	+3.00	+4.00	+3.33
Trough	- 3.50	- 3.00	- 3.375
Consistency			
All	5.00	2.14	5.00
Crest	+2.86	+1.42	+4.29
Trough	- 2.14	- 0.71	- 2.86
C/S Index			
All	8.21	5.81	8.50
Crest	+5.86	+5.42	+7.62
Trough	- 5.64	- 3.71	- 6.235

This is a very consistent signature as far as producing a cycle culmination within the central time band (100%). Most of the time (85.7%) this will be a 4-year or greater cycle, and most of the time (85.7%) it will be a crest. There was one instance (1922), however, where the only noticeable cycle produced was a 50-week crest. It was counted in these calculations, as no other cycle was present nearby. This is one case, though, where the cardinal signs of the square were not the most prominent. There were two instances, and one was the 1922 case which produced only the 50-week cycle. The other (1826-27) coincided with a four-year cycle.

<u>Conclusions</u>: *The Saturn-Pluto waxing square is a fairly reliable signature, coinciding with moderately long-term cycle crests within the central time band. Therefore, investors can usually look for a 4-year type of cycle culmination within this time band (usually a crest) and plan their strategy accordingly. If a crest is forming, investors can look to take profits. If prices appear to be declining into a 4-year or greater cycle trough, investors may instead look for opportunities to purchase stocks for the long-term. Historically, though, this aspect has coincided more with crests from which substantial declines have followed.*

Waxing Trine (120°)

	Dates & Position of Saturn		**Long-Term Cycles**
1.	Sep. 16, 1796 Nov. 12, 1796 June 14, 1797	27°♊26' 26°♊52' 00°♋27'	18-year cycle trough in November 1797.
2.	Aug. 4, 1829	08°♌27'	18-year cycle trough in January 1829.
3.	Nov. 12, 1860 Feb. 6, 1861 Aug. 16, 1861	08°♍16' 07°♍34' 10°♍26'	4-year cycle crest in September 1860. 4-year cycle trough in May 1861. Start of U.S. Civil War.
4.	Nov. 15, 1892 Apr. 13, 1893 Aug. 26, 1893	09°♎06' 08°♎19' 10°♎45'	4-year cycle trough in July 1893. Prices rallied for next 2 years to 4-year cycle crest, gaining over 40%
5.	Jan. 5, 1925 Apr. 24, 1925 Oct. 21, 1925	12°♏25' 11°♏34' 14°♏44'	4-year cycle crest 4 months later in February 1926. End of 100% increase in prices that started in May 1924, and lasted 21 months.
6.	Feb. 5, 1959 July 13, 1959 Dec. 3, 1959	03°♑22' 02°♑31' 06°♑09'	22.5-month cycle crest in August 1959, then 10% decline to 22.5-month cycle trough in September 1959. Crest was end of 64% gain over 22 months.
7.	Apr. 27, 1996 Oct. 25, 1996 Feb 19, 1997	02°♈23' 01°♈50' 05°♈31'	22.5-month cycle crest in May 1996, followed by 11% decline to 22.5-month cycle trough in July 1996. Crest was end of 46% advance over prior 20 months.
8.	June 11, 2031	13°♊29'	

Relative Strength	Central	+/-7months	Total
All	2.50	4.00	3.29
Crest	+2.00	+3.00	+2.50
Trough	- 2.50	- 4.33	- 3.29
Consistency			
All	2.85	2.85	5.00
Crest	+1.42	+1.42	+2.85
Trough	- 2.85	2.14	- 5.00
C/S Index			
All	5.35	6.85	8.29
Crest	+3.42	+4.42	+5.35
Trough	- 5.35	- 6.47	- 8.29

This started out being a very significant correlation to 18-year cycle troughs in its first two instances (1797 and 1829). But then it became progressively weaker over the next five occurrences, three of which were 4-year cycles and two which were 22.5-month cycles. In all cases, there was a cycle trough within seven months of this aspect. Thus it had a greater correlation to cycle troughs than crests.

Conclusions: The waxing Saturn-Pluto trine does not have a reliable history of timing long-term cycles in the U.S. stock market. At best, investors may anticipate a 22.5-month cycle within seven months of its central time band, and perhaps a 4-year cycle if one is due. In most cases, this will be a cycle trough. Therefore if a 22.5-month or greater cycle trough is unfolding nearby to this aspect (usually within five months), then investors may plan to purchase stocks.

Waxing Sesquiquadrate (135°)

	Dates & Position of Saturn		Long-Term Cycles
1.	July 13, 1798	16°♋30'	18-year cycle trough 8 months earlier in November 1797.
2.	Sep. 3, 1830 May 5, 1831 May 12, 1831	24°♌08' 24°♌55' 25°♌04'	22.5-month cycle crest in November 1830. Market was in process of huge rally from low in January 1829 through high in August 1835.
3.	Sep. 20, 1862	26°♍07'	Possible 22.5-month cycle crest in October 1862.
4.	Jan. 1, 1894 Mar. 13, 1894 Oct. 9, 1894	24°♎15' 23°♎53' 26°♎38'	22.5-month cycle crest in August 1894. This followed 18-year cycle trough of July 1893.
5.	Dec. 6, 1926 July 31, 1927	00°♐28' 01°♐03'	22.5-month cycle crest in September 1927. End of 18-month rally in which prices climbed 38%. Market

	Date	Position	Notes
	Sep. 5, 1927	01°♐48'	rallied during this whole aspect, then declined modestly only one month afterwards for 22.5-month trough.
6.	Jan. 26, 1961	22°♑35'	Half-cycle crest to 18-year cycle in November 1961. End of 14-month rally, and start of 7-month decline prices lost nearly 30% in this decline.
	Sep. 15, 1961	23°♑22'	
-	Nov. 11, 1961	24°♑53'	
7.	June 16, 1997	18°♈38'	22.5-month cycle crest August 1997, then strong 2-month decline of 16% to 22.5-month trough in October 1997.
	Sep. 22, 1997	18°♈16'	
	Apr. 9, 1998	22°♈50'	
8.	July 10, 2032	29°♊36'	
	Feb. 20, 2033	00°♋18'	
	Apr. 6, 2033	01°♋25'	

Relative Strength	**Central**	**+/- 6 months**	**Total**
All	2.33	5.00	3.14
Crest	+2.40	0.00	+2.40
Trough	- 2.00	- 5.00	- 3.20
Consistency			
All	4.29	1.42	5.00
Crest	+3.57	0.00	+3.57
Trough	- 2.14	- 1.42	- 3.57
C/S Index			
All	6.62	6.42	8.14
Crest	+5.97	0.00	+5.97
Trough	- 4.14	- 6.42	- 6.77

This is a strange signature. There were no discernible long-term cycles during the central time band in the first five instances of this aspect. There were two 18-year cycle troughs the year before, but each of these pertained more to the waxing trine, which was in effect in each case. In five of these seven cases, only a 22.5-month intermediate-term cycle formed within the central time band. This aspect is therefore not a very reliable correlate to long-term cycles in U.S. stock prices. Furthermore there was no bias towards crests or troughs.

<u>Conclusions:</u> *The waxing sesquiquadrate of Saturn and Pluto tends to correspond to 22.5-month cycles, especially toward the end of the series of aspects (if three hits occur). Investors may use this central time band, then, as an opportunity to take profits from some long positions, if prices rally into it, and then wait for a 1-7 month decline into at least a 22.5-month cycle trough in which to re-enter.*

Opposition (180°)

	Dates and Position of Saturn		Long-Term Cycles
1.	Aug. 1, 1768 Jan. 14, 1769 May 22, 1769	11°♋53' 13°♋53' 15°♋26'	18-year cycle crest formed around 1770.
2.	Oct. 13, 1801 Feb. 12, 1802 July 30, 1802	03°♍50' 04°♍59' 06°♍35'	Double bottom to 18-year cycle trough in February 1802. Price more than doubled in next 4 years.
3.	Sep. 30, 1834	12°♎54'	72-year cycle crest in May 1835. This followed 4-year cycle trough in February 1834 and ended first great bull market run in U.S. history. 22-year bear market then began.
4.	Nov. 1, 1866	14°♏16'	22.5-month cycle crest in October 1866.
5.	Dec. 6, 1898	14°♐42'	Double top to half-cycle crest of 18-year cycle in April 1899. Prices declined 45% over next 4 years.
6.	Feb. 17, 1931 July 8, 1931 Dec. 13, 1931	19°♑03' 20°♑17' 21°♑40'	72-year cycle trough 7 months later in July, 1932. "Great Depression" was underway. New structure had to be built as world economy collapsed. 22.5-month cycle trough and crest in October and November 1931 respectively. But trend was down.
7.	Apr. 23, 1965 Aug. 17, 1965 Feb. 19, 1966	13°♓55' 15°♓18' 17°♓34'	Double top to 18-year and perhaps longer-term cycle crest in January 1966. First time DJIA crossed 1000. 4-year bear market began. 22.5-month cycle trough in June 1965.
8.	Aug. 5, 2001 Nov. 2, 2001 May 25, 2002	12°♊37' 13°♊49' 16°♊35'	

Relative Strength	**Central**	**+/- 8 months**	**Total**
All	3.25	4.625	4.21
Crest	+2.83	+4.50	+3.67
Trough	- 2.83	- 4.00	- 3.625
Consistency			
All	2.86	2.86	5.00
Crest	+2.14	+2.14	+4.29
Trough	- 2.14	- 1.43	- 2.86

C/S Index

All	6.11	7.485	9.21*
Crest	+4.97	+6.64	+7.96
Trough	- 4.97	- 5.43	- 6.485

So far, this is by far the strongest correlation to long-term market cycles of the Saturn-Pluto signatures. In every case a very long-term cycle unfolded within 1 year (and probably within 8 months) of Saturn opposite Pluto. In two cases it coincided with either the beginning or end to one of the three great bull market runs in U.S. history. In another case it was a double top to a long-term (over 18-year) stock market cycle. In yet another case it coincided with an 18-year cycle, and yet another, a double bottom to an 18-year cycle trough. When it correlated with a crest, a multi-year bear market followed, lasting at least 4 years. The long-term cycle didn't always unfold in the central time band (only 57%). It was more apt to fall a few months outside of the central time band (57%). Nevertheless, this is a very important signature, and one that oftentimes correlates to major overhauls in the financial structure of the United States, if not the world. Another interesting feature of this aspect was that when it occurred in cardinal signs (3 times), it coincided with 18-year or greater cycles (twice it coincided with 72-year cycles).

<u>Conclusions</u>: *The opposition between Saturn and Pluto is one of the most powerful correlates known to timing very long-term cycles in U.S. stocks. This is especially true if taking place in cardinal signs. Investors may use this aspect as a reliable market-timing indication of the end — or beginning — of very long-term cycles (i.e. 18-year or greater types), given an orb of one year. If the market has been rising for several years going into this signature, then investors should look to exit all holdings. If the market has been declining for several years going into this time band, then investors should prepare to start purchasing stocks aggressively, for a multi-year bull market (perhaps lasting decades) may be about to commence.*

Waning Sesquiquadrate (225°)

	Dates and Position of Saturn		Long-Term Cycles
1.	Nov. 21, 1805	23°♎44'	18-year cycle crest in September 1806. 7-year bear market began and prices dropped 50%, most of it in 1 year.
	Apr. 1, 1806	26°♎13'	
	Sep. 9, 1806	25°♎59'	
2.	Nov. 22, 1838	01°♐10'	4-year cycle crest in September 1838. Market was in midst of severe decline from 1835-1842 when it lost 80% value.
	July 21, 1839	03°♐57'	
	Aug. 18, 1839	03°♐48'	
3.	Jan. 1, 1871	02°♑07'	Possible 22.5-month cycle trough in January 1871. Market rose during this period to crest in 1873
	July 24, 1871	04°♑46'	
	Oct. 13, 1871	04°♑23'	

4.	Feb. 12, 1903 Aug. 7, 1903 Nov. 30, 1903	02°♒45' 05°♒21' 04°♒56'	Half-cycle trough to 18-year cycle in November 1903. End of 2-year bear market and start of 2-year bull market. Prices rose 140%. 22.5-month cycle crest in February 1903 on first contact of aspect. Price went straight down from start to end of aspect.
5.	May 15, 1935 July 1, 1935 Feb. 14, 1936	09°♓08' 10°♓09' 10°♓42'	22.5-month cycle crest and trough 2 months later, in April 1936. Market was up all during this time, and didn't end until 2 months afterwards.
6.	July 17, 1969 Aug. 21, 1969 Apr. 18, 1970	07°♉56' 08°♉57' 10°♉15'	4-year cycle trough in May 1970. End of 4-year bear market in which prices fell 37%.
7.	Sep. 9, 2005 Jan. 1, 2006 June 29, 2006	06°♌50' 09°♌54' 10°♌05'	

Relative Strength	**Central**	**+/- 2 months**	**Total**
All	3.40	2.00	3.17
Crest	+3.33	+2.00	+3.00
Trough	- 3.00	- 2.00	- 2.75
Consistency			
All	4.17	0.83	5.00
Crest	+2.50	0.83	+3.33
Trough	- 2.50	- 0.83	- 3.33
C/S Index			
All	7.57	2.83	8.17
Crest	+5.83	+2.83	+6.33
Trough	- 5.50	- 2.83	- 6.08

The U.S. stock market is usually in decline going into, or during, this aspect series (about 80% of time). In all but two cases (67%), a 4-year or greater cycle unfolded during the central time band. There is no bias towards troughs or crests, although troughs have unfolded in the last four cases.

<u>Conclusion</u>: *The waning sesquiquadrate between Saturn and Pluto has a modest correlation to long-term cycles, given an orb of two months outside of its central time band. Investors may look to purchase stocks if the market is declining into this signature, especially if it looks like a 4-year or greater trough is unfolding. Be especially attentive to a low forming near the end, or slightly after, the last aspect of a series.*

Waning Trine (240°)

	Dates and Position of Saturn		Long-Term Cycles
1.	Oct. 23, 1807	11°♏29'	Triple bottom to 18-year cycle trough in October 1807.
2.	Jan. 10, 1840 May 26, 1840 Oct. 26, 1840	16°♐57' 19°♐27' 18°♐39'	22.5-month cycle crest in October 1840. But market was primarily in huge decline into 1842 trough. There was a 22.5-month cycle trough in November 1839.
3.	Feb. 24, 1872 June 9, 1872 Dec. 7, 1872	18°♑01' 20°♑01' 19°♑22'	36-year cycle crest in January-May, 1873. Possible 22.5-month cycle trough in September 1872. End of 16-year bull market, and start of 4-year bear market.
4.	Apr. 10, 1904 June 25, 1904 Jan. 15, 1905	18°♒56' 20°♒30' 20°♒06'	Half-cycle trough to 18-year cycle in November 1903 (5 months before aspect). Market then rallied 140% to 18-year crest in January 1906, 1 year later.
5.	Mar. 26, 1937 Oct. 16, 1937 Jan. 4, 1938	26°♓32' 00°♈04' 29°♓20'	4-year cycle crest in March 1937. End of 5-year rally after which prices dropped 50% in next 12 months to 4-year trough in March 1938, 2 months after aspect.
6.	May 25, 1971 Dec. 10, 1971 Mar. 10, 1972	27°♉01' 01°♊52' 00°♊59'	22.5-month cycle trough in November 1971. End of 7-month decline from 22.5-month cycle crest in April 1971, 1 month before aspect series began.
7.	Aug. 6, 2007	26°♌33'	

	Central	+/- 5 months	Total
Relative Strength			
All	3.50	3.50	3.42
Crest	+3.00	+0.00	+3.00
Trough	- 2.83	- 3.50	- 3.10
Consistency			
All	4.17	1.67	5.00
Crest	+3.33	+0.00	+3.33
Trough	- 2.50	- 1.67	- 4.17
C/S Index			
All	7.67	5.17	8.42
Crest	+6.33	+0.00	+6.33
Trough	- 5.33	- 5.17	- 7.27

Given an orb of 5 months outside the aspect series, this is a fairly reliable indicator for long-term cycle reversals in U.S. stocks (100%). In most cases this will correlate with a long-term cycle trough (83.3%), but that is not always the only dominant cycle forming.

Twice there were powerful crests which culminated either at the beginning or end of the signature. In fact, the dominant cycle unfolded either right at the beginning or end (within an orb of 0-5 months) in 5 of 6 instances. In 1872, the market kept right on going higher until 2 months after last aspect. Then a 36-year cycle crested and 4-year bear market commenced. In 1904, the half-cycle to the 18-year cycle trough bottomed just 5 months before the aspect began. Then a powerful 2-year bull market commenced. In 1937, a four-year cycle topped out with the first aspect. Then the market declined sharply to the 4-year cycle trough that ended two months after the last "hit" of this aspect. And in the last case, a 22.5-month cycle crest unfolded 1 month before the first aspect. That same cycle bottomed right in the middle of the series, in November 1971. Therefore, it seems that an investor must be very alert to a powerful cycle culminating either right near the beginning or the end of this aspect, and in some cases, both (opposite types).

Conclusions: The waning trine of Saturn and Pluto coincides with the culmination of long-term cycles in U.S. stocks, given an orb of 5 months before and after the first and last aspect of a series. Within this wide time band, investors can gauge whether a 4-year or greater cycle is due, and if so, look for that trend to end, and then take appropriate action. If the trend has been declining throughout the central time band of the aspect, look for it to bottom near the end, probably within 2 months of the last aspect "passage" between the two planets. In this event, investors may look to purchase stocks on that low.

Waning Square (270°)

	Dates and Position of Saturn		Long-Term Cycles
1.	Nov. 16, 1810	14°♐59'	Possible 22.5-month cycle trough in December 1810. 2nd half cycle crest to 18-year cycle in October 1809.
2.	Feb. 5, 1843 July 9, 1843 Nov. 15, 1843	20°♑09' 22°♑55' 21°♑23'	Double bottom to 72-year cycle trough in January-March 1843, from whence second great bull market run in U.S. stocks began.
3.	Mar. 14, 1875 Aug. 4, 1875 Dec. 20, 1875	21°♒00' 23°♒45' 22°♒02'	22.5-month cycle trough in October 1875. Market and economy were in midst of financial panic at this time from 36-year crest in 1873 to trough in 1877.
4.	Apr. 14, 1907 Sep. 8, 1907 Jan. 18, 1908	22°♓00' 24°♓45' 23°♓11'	4-year cycle trough in November 1907. End of 22-month decline as prices lost nearly 50%. Start of 3-year bull market as prices gained over 90%.
5.	Mar. 25, 1940	00°♉40'	Double top to 4-year crest in September 1939, then market dropped 30% in next 9 months to 22.5-month cycle trough in June 1940.
6.	Sep. 14, 1973	03°♋47'	36-year cycle crest in January 1973 (8 months prior

	Oct. 7, 1973	04°♋39'	to aspect), then 46% decline to 36-year cycle trough in December 1974 (7 months after aspect). In between was a 22.5-month trough in August 1973, followed by 22.5-month cycle crest in October 1973.
	May 28, 1974	04°♋08'	
7.	Nov. 15, 2009	01°♎42'	
	Jan. 31, 2010	04°♎21'	
	Aug. 21, 2010	02°♎55'	

Relative Strength	**Central**	**+/- 8 months**	**Total**
All	2.67	3.75	3.25
Crest	+2.00	+3.75	+3.75
Trough	- 2.67	- 5.00	- 3.25
Consistency			
All	5.00	1.67	5.00
Crest	+0.83	+1.67	+1.67
Trough	- 5.00	- 0.83	- 5.00
C/S Index			
All	7.67	5.42	8.25
Crest	+2.83	+5.42	+5.42
Trough	- 7.67	- 5.83	- 8.25

-

If a 15 or even 22-month orb would have been allowed, then in every case (100%), the dominant long-term cycle would have culminated *before* the Saturn-Pluto waning square. In four of the six instances (67%), these would have been very long-term cycles: an 18-year cycle crest, two 36-year cycle crests, and a 72-year cycle trough. In addition, there was also the second half-cycle crest to an 18-year cycle, and a double top to a 4-year cycle. As one can see, in five of six cases (83%), a long-term cycle crest unfolded 6-15 months before the first series of this square aspect occurred. In the other instance, a 72-year cycle trough happened just a few months before this aspect unfolded (1842). This is, therefore, one of the most potent signatures determined so far. But the most dominant cycle (the trend) ends before the aspect gets underway. It is also interesting to note that the square, which occurred prior to the history of the U.S. stock market, was in 1776-1777—the time of the American Revolution. Using a much more reasonable time band, however, this signature has had a 100% correlation to smaller trough cycles. In four cases, a 22.5-month cycle trough has unfolded within the central time band. In the other two cases, it coincided with a 4-year and 72-year cycle trough. What is most interesting is the fact that in the two cases of cardinal signs, a 36 and 72-year cycle trough unfolded nearby.

<u>Conclusions</u>: *The waning square of Saturn to Pluto is powerful, if given a very generous extended time band. Otherwise, using the normal time bands in this study, it is only powerful when the square takes place in cardinal signs. Almost all other cases correlate to just 22.5-month cycle troughs. Given the very wide time band, though, this signature has a reliable history of ending long-term cycles in U.S. stocks about 6-15 months before the onset of the first aspect of the series. In many cases, this will correlate with a very long-term cycle crest, such as the 18-year or longer types. After this, the market declines*

quite severely. The longest-term cycle culminations are especially the case when the aspect takes place in cardinal signs. Investors may use the 6-15 month time band prior to the first "hit" as a high probability zone for a long-term cycle completion. If a long-term bull market has been in effect, then investors may look for that bull market to end, and therefore look to take profits on current holdings. If the underlying longer-term cycle trend is pointed up, then investors can look to purchase stocks on a 22.5-month cycle trough that tends to unfold within the central time band.

Waning Sextile (300°)

	Dates and Position of Saturn		**Long-Term Cycles**
1.	Dec. 16, 1813	18°♑34'	18-year cycle trough in March 1813.
2.	Feb. 27, 1846 Sep. 17, 1846 Nov. 16, 1846	23°♒25' 25°♒29' 24°♒25'	4-year cycle trough in August 1845. 4-year cycle crest in August 1847.
3.	Mar. 20, 1878	23°♓52'	22.5-month cycle crest in September 1878. 36-year cycle trough 9 months earlier, in June 1877.
4.	Apr. 7, 1910	24°♈59'	4-year cycle crest in November 1909, followed by 10-month decline to 22.5-month cycle trough in July 1910. Market lost 27% in that decline.
5.	June 9, 1942 Jan. 3, 1943 Feb. 15, 1943	04°♊04' 06°♊37' 05°♊39'	Secondary low preceding great bull market happened 2 months earlier in April 1942. That ended 3-1/2 year bear market and began very long bull market.
6.	Aug. 26, 1976 Jan. 24, 1977 May 24, 1977	10°♌10' 14°♌10' 11°♌36'	4-year cycle crest in September 1976. Prices then declined 28% over next 18 months. 22.5-month low in November 1976.
7.	Dec. 26, 2012 Mar. 8, 2013 Sep. 21, 2013	09°♏08' 11°♏15' 08°♏59'	

Relative Strength	**Central**	**+/- 9 months**	**Total**
All	3.00	4.10	3.92
Crest	+3.00	+3.00	+3.00
Trough	- 2.00	- 4.375	- 3.90

Consistency			
All	0.83	4.17	5.00
Crest	+0.83	+1.67	+2.50
Trough	- 0.83	- 3.33	- 4.17

C/S Index

All	3.83	8.27	8.92
Crest	+3.83	+4.67	+5.50
Trough	- 2.83	- 7.71	- 8.07

This is a prominent correlate to long-term cycles in U.S. stocks. However, once again, the Saturn-Pluto signature requires an orb outside the central time band for all but one of these cycles to culminate. In five of six instances, the dominant cycle unfolded 2-9 months *before* the aspect. Another interesting feature is that the signature would switch between trough, then crest, on each successive occurrence. In all cases the cycle was at least a 4-year type. In three of the cases (50%), it was a cycle much longer than the 4-year periodicity.

Conclusion: The waning sextile between Saturn and Pluto is important, as 4-year or greater cycles tend to happen within 9 months of this aspect series. When not within the central time band, it tends to unfold 2-9 months prior to the cycle. Therefore investors may use this signature to time either a 4-year cycle or a phase to an 18-year cycle in U.S. stocks, but use a time band extending as much as 9 months prior to the aspect.

Waning Semi-Square (315°)

	Dates and Position of Saturn		**Long-Term Cycles**
1.	Feb. 14, 1815 Aug. 24, 1815 Nov. 2, 1815	05°♒40' 22°♒22' 06°♒05'	4-year cycle crest in September 1815.
2.	May 3, 1847 July 29, 1847 Jan. 17, 1848	10°♓49' 11°♓56' 09°♓57'	4-year cycle crest in August 1847. Then 1 year decline of about 30% to 1st phase trough of 18-year cycle in October 1848.
3.	May 7, 1879 Oct. 8, 1879 Jan. 22, 1880	10°♈43' 12°♈08' 10°♈30'	4-year cycle crest in January 1880.
4.	May 15, 1911	11°♉39'	4-year cycle trough in September 1911. This follows 22.5-month cycle crest of June 1911, and ends 2-year bear market. Starts 1-year bull market.
5.	July 22, 1943 Dec. 10, 1943 Apr. 4, 1944	21°♊37' 23°♊33' 21°♊27'	22.5-month cycle crest in July 1943. followed by 4-month drop to 22.5-month cycle trough in November. Drop was about 12%.
6.	July 18, 1978	29°♌04'	4-year cycle trough in March 1978, and triple bottom to the secondary trough in 1982 which began one of the great bull runs in U.S. stock history. Also end of 18-month bear market in which prices dropped 28%.

7. Nov. 27, 2014 27°♏02'
June 20, 2015 29°♏39'
Aug. 13, 2015 28°♏24'

Relative Strength	**Central**	**+/- 4 months**	**Total**
All	2.60	3.00	2.83
Crest	+2.60	+0.00	+2.60
Trough	- 2.00	- 3.00	- 2.67
Consistency			
All	4.17	1.67	5.00
Crest	+4.17	+0.00	+4.17
Trough	- 0.83	- 1.67	- 2.50
C/S Index			
All	6.77	4.67	7.83
Crest	+6.77	+0.00	+6.77
Trough	- 2.83	- 4.67	- 5.17

This is a fairly consistent signature for timing 4-year cycles within 4 months of its central time band (83%). In the other case it was only a 22.5-month cycle. In all but the last case, this signature correlated with a crest within the central time band. Overall it is weaker than most Saturn-Pluto signatures in terms of the cycle type produced. But, it is consistent.

<u>Conclusions</u>: *The waning semi-square between Saturn and Pluto is a reliable indicator for timing 4-year cycles. It has a greater historical correlation to crests, especially within the central time band, although in some cases both types unfolded, given a 4-month orb. Therefore, investors can look for the trend to a 4-year cycle to end within four months of this aspect. If the market has been rising into it, then look for a 22.5-month or 4-year cycle crest. If declining into this time band, then look for a 22.5-month or 4-year cycle trough to be completed. In that later case, investors might want to use this as a timing tool for purchasing stocks.*

Summary of Saturn-Pluto Signatures:

The following represents the ranking order of Saturn-Pluto aspects in correlation to long-term stock market cycles. This first ranking order is based upon Total C/S values, which includes a time band of up to 11 months (but usually no more than nine) outside of the aspect. In parentheses are those instances in which that particular signature correlated more times with a crests (+) or trough (-), and the respective values of each. Also included is a column indicating how many instances of cycles greater than four-year types which were associated with each aspect (again, within an eleven-month orb of time either side of the aspect), and the percentage of times this represents. In the last column, titled **Orb,** are the number of months used outside of the central time band for the extended time band upon which the Total C/S values were based

	Aspect	Total C/S		Cycles > 4-Years		Orb
1.	Opposition	9.21*	(+7.96)	5/7 =	71%	8
2.	Conjunction	8.92	(- 8.58)	4/6 =	67%	11
2.	Waning Sextile	8.92	(- 8.07)	3/6 =	50%	9
4.	Waxing Sextile	8.79	(+8.79)	4/7 =	57%	5
5.	Waxing Square	8.50	(+7.62)	3/7 =	42%	4
6.	Waning Trine	8.42	(- 7.27)	3/6 =	50%	5
7.	Waxing Trine	8.29	(- 8.29)	2/7 =	28.5%	7
8.	Waning Square	8.25	(- 8.25)	2/6 =	33%	8
9.	Waxing Semi-Square	8.17		1/6 =	17%	9
9.	Waning Sesquiquadrate	8.17		2/6 =	33%	2
11.	Waxing Sesquiquadrate	8.14		3/7 =	42%	6
12.	Waning Semi-Square	7.83		0/6 =	0%	4

One can immediately observe the lack of Saturn-Pluto signatures with a Total C/S value of 9.00 or greater. Only the opposition aspect achieved this level of significance. However, 10 of the remaining 11 signatures recorded a C/S value of at least 8.00. Only the waning semi-square failed to meet this level.

The opposition and conjunction were the two strongest correlations to long-term cycles in U.S. stocks, according to the criteria used in this study. Surprisingly, both the sextiles were next followed by the two squares and two trines. The semi-squares and the sesquiquadrates were the four weakest.

In all, there were 32 instances of Saturn-Pluto aspects to stock market cycles greater than 4-year types, corresponding to the extended time bands used in this study. This represents a frequency of only 41.5% (out of 77 cases to date). That is a much lower correlation than to long-term stock market cycles than witnessed in the Saturn-Uranus and Saturn-Neptune cases. However, if the instances of semi-squares and sesquiquadrates are eliminated from the calculations, the frequency increases to 50%, which is still not high, compared to the Uranus and Neptune contacts with Saturn. Only the opposition and conjunction had a correlation of over 60% to long-term stock market cycles, with the opposition frequency being 71% and the conjunction 67%. Perhaps only in those two instances can investors expect a possible longer-term cycle than the 4-year type to unfold in the stock market.

There were some definite correlations to either crests or troughs. The waxing sextile especially had a strong bias towards crests (+8.79), and within an orb extending only five months outside of the central time band. the opposition (+7.96) and waxing square (+7.62) also had a bias towards crests. Five other signatures were associated more with troughs. In this group were the conjunction (-8.58), waxing trine (-8.29), waning square (-8.25), waning sextile (-.8.07), and waning trine (-7.27).

The ranking orders changed somewhat when only the central time band was used, according to the criteria outlined for this study (i.e. an orb of only one month outside of cases involving series of three or more passes, or within three months in cases involving only a single passage). These C/S results are shown in the table below. Also shown are the number of instances in which greater than four-year cycles unfolded in this definition of a central time band.

	Aspect	Central Time Band		Cycles > 4-Years
1.	Conjunction	8.42	(- 7.87)	3/6 = 50%
2.	Waxing Square	8.21		2/7 = 28.5%
3.	Waxing Sextile	7.96	(+7.37)	3/7 = 42%
4.	Waning Trine	7.67		2/6 = 33%
4.	Waning Square	7.67	(- 7.67)	1/6 = 17%
6.	Waning Sesquiquadrate	7.57		2/6 = 33%
7.	Waning Semi-Square	6.77	(+6.77)	0/6 = 0%
8.	Waxing Sesquiquadrate	6.62		1/7 = 14%
9.	Waxing Semi-Square	6.33		1/6 = 17%
10.	Opposition	6.11		2/7 = 28.5%
11.	Waxing Trine	5.35		0/7 = 0%
12.	Waning Sextile	3.83		0/6 = 0%

In this more defined time band, no Saturn-Pluto signatures attained a C/S value of 9.00 or greater. Only two reached the level of 8.00 or greater. These were the conjunction (8.42) and waxing square (8.21). Close behind was the waxing sextile (7.96). Furthermore, only 17 cases witnessed a cycle greater than a 4-year type unfolding with a Saturn-Pluto central time band (22%). It appears the Saturn-Pluto aspects are not a reliable correlation to cycles greater than the 4-year types in U.S. stocks, especially during their central time band. Unless we consider those instances of hard aspects in cardinal signs.

Saturn-Pluto in Cardinal Signs

Once again we draw your attention to the first section of this book, when the observation was made that the great bull markets in U.S. stocks began and ended when Saturn, Uranus and/or Pluto were in cardinal signs. We already demonstrated how this combination worked extremely well in the case of Saturn to Uranus "hard aspects" in cardinal signs. Their correlation was much greater than the average. To test this theory again, let's examine the history of U.S. stock market cycles during those times in which Saturn and Pluto were in cardinal signs together, making a hard aspect, and compare their C/S scores to the average.

Conjunction (0°)

	Dates & Position of Saturn		Long-Term Cycles
1.	June 6, 1851 Nov. 11, 1851 Feb. 10, 1852	00°♉20' 29°♈29' 28°♈59'	18-year cycle crest in January 1853.
2.	Oct. 4, 1914 Nov. 1, 1914 May 19, 1915	02°♋13' 02°♋04' 00°♋54'	36-year trough in December 1914.
3.	Nov. 8, 1982	27°♎35'	Secondary low that preceded great bull market unfolded 3 months earlier, in August 1982.

Waxing Square (90°)

4.	Sep. 8, 1826 Dec. 16, 1826 June 5, 1827	04°♋41' 03°♋17' 06°♋15'	4-year cycle trough in February 1827. Market was in midst of decline from 1824-29
5.	Oct. 8, 1922	11°♎13'	This is the only case that failed totally.

Opposition (180°)

6.	Aug. 1, 1768 Jan. 14, 1769 May 22, 1769	11°♋53' 13°♋53' 15°♋26'	18-year cycle crest formed around 1770.
7.	Sep. 30, 1834	12°♎ 54'	72-year cycle crest in May 1835.
8.	Feb. 17, 1931 July 8, 1931 Dec. 13, 1931	19°♑03' 20°♑17' 21°♑40'	72-year cycle trough 7 months later in July 1932. "Great Depression" was underway.

Waning Square (270°)

9.	Feb. 5, 1843 July 9, 1843 Nov. 15, 1843	20°♑09' 22°♑55' 21°♑23'	Double bottom to 72-year cycle trough in January-March 1843, from whence second great bull market run in U.S. stocks began.
10.	Sep. 14, 1973 Oct. 7, 1973 May 28, 1974	03°♋47' 04°♋39' 04°♋08'	36-year cycle crest in January 1973 (8 months prior to aspect), then 46% decline to 36-year cycle trough in December 1974 (7 months after aspect).

11.. Nov. 15, 2009   01°♎42'
Jan. 31, 2010   04°♎21'
Aug. 21, 2010   02°♎55'

In all cases except the waxing square, the hard aspects of Saturn to Pluto in cardinal signs produced either a very long-term cycle crest or trough, or double bottom, or secondary low preceding one of the great bull markets in the U.S. stock market history. This is quite remarkable, and supports the findings in the earlier chapters, which was: **long-term bull and bear markets have a much higher probability of ending and beginning when and combination Saturn, Uranus, or Pluto are in cardinal signs together.**

Comparison Summary of Saturn Aspects To Uranus and Beyond

Note how these "scores" compared to the previous Saturn transits. In the table below, remember there were 12 different aspects used for each study, so the sum of each column will be the 12 aspect possibilities under each signature.

Total C/S Score	Sat-Uran	Sat-Nept	Sat-Pluto
> 9.00	5	4	1
8.00 - 8.99	6	8	10
< 8.00	1	0	1

Within a time band extending up 11 months (and usually 9 or less) either side of the central time band of these aspects, one can see that there was a progressive lessening of the number of aspects achieving the 9.00 or greater level of significance as the planetary cycle length lessened. That is, the greatest number of correlations were with the Saturn-Uranus signatures, and the least number of correlations were with the Saturn-Pluto aspects. Saturn-Uranus has the longest planetary cycle of these three groups, while Saturn-Pluto has the shortest. Although the instances between Saturn-Neptune seem close to that shown in the Saturn-Uranus group, the fact is that Saturn-Uranus signatures not only slightly more aspects with a value of 9.00 or greater, but the actual values of four of those aspects were 9.25 or greater. In the four instances of Saturn-Neptune shown here, only one had a value greater than 9.25.

If we looked at the frequency of each planetary pair cycle to market cycles that were greater than 4-year types, we see this same ranking verified. There were 34 of 57 cases (59.6%) in which this occurred under a Saturn-Uranus aspect, 33 of 71 cases (46.5%) under Saturn-Neptune contacts, and 32 of 77 cases (41.5%) under Saturn-Pluto contacts. Thus the Saturn aspects to Uranus are by far the most powerful of these combinations. Yet the Saturn to Neptune and Pluto combinations are frequent enough to bear close observance, and even the formulation of investment strategies, particularly when Saturn is in a hard aspect to Pluto from cardinal signs.

The same ranking results are noted when only the central time band is used — a time band that is about half the average length of the criteria used for the total. In this case, a score of 8.00 would be considered strong, because that means within the central time band, there is a very high probability that a cycle at least as strong as a 4-year cycle periodicity will unfold.

Total Score	Sat-Uran	Sat-Nept	Sat-Pluto
> 9.00	0	1	0
8.00 - 8.99	5	1	2
7.00 - 7.99	3	3	4
< 7.00	4	7	6

Again, one can see more values to Saturn-Uranus of greater than 8.00. Both Saturn-Neptune and Saturn-Pluto have over 80% of their central time band instances with values under 8.00. Saturn-Uranus, on the other hand, finds five out of 12 possible signatures with values of 8.00 or greater in the central time band (42%). It is interesting to note that of the five Saturn-Uranus, and two each of Saturn-Neptune and Saturn-Pluto signatures with values of 8.00 or greater, all were major aspects. There were no instances of minor aspects in either of these three groups that had a C/S value of 8.00 or greater within its central time band.

The frequency of cycles greater than the 4-year type also stood up in this study of central time bands. Saturn-Uranus witnessed 20 of 57 cases of a cycle greater than 4-years in its central time band (35%), while Saturn-Neptune contained 16 of 71 (22.5% frequency), and Saturn-Pluto 17 of 77 (22%).

JUPITER-SATURN SIGNATURES

Like Saturn and Neptune, as well as Saturn and Uranus, the principles of Jupiter and Saturn are diametrically opposite one another. The nature of Saturn is to constrict, reduce, define, and analyze. The nature of Jupiter is to expand, enlarge, and understand the "big picture" but not the details. Jupiter represents growth and exaggeration, increase and hope. Saturn represents under-estimation and reality, is patient and hard-working. In terms of financial markets, the presence of these two planets in aspect to one another may negate one another. Or, in hard aspect, it may suggest a period of increased worry and doubt about the future (falling prices). In a soft aspect, it may represent gradual growth, growth that is well-planned and under control. It is success through agreements of a long-term nature, and moderation and successful blending of different approaches or styles. In the later case, prices might peak out, after which they begin to separate, as the "glue" that held the deal together starts to unravel.

The time between aspects of these two planets will be considerably shorter than anything examined so far (the entire cycle is about 20 years in length). Thus this section will only analyze the conjunction, squares, trines, and opposition (harmonics of one through four). The smaller aspects, such as the sextile, semi-square, and sesquiquadrate, will mostly happen in the same years as one another, or one of the major aspects. Nevertheless, it is important to analyze this planetary pair from a long-term cycles perspective because in the study of mundane astrology, Jupiter and Saturn have been considered the most important for centuries. When their conjunction occurred in earth signs (every even numbered decade from 1840-1960), every U.S.A. president who was either elected or in office at the time of this conjunction died in office before his term ended. That combination returns again in 2000. If Jupiter and Saturn are so important as significators for predicting the time of such major world events, then it seems they should also be important in timing the culmination and beginning of long-term cycles in U.S. stock indexes.

Conjunction (0°)

	Dates and Position of Jupiter		Long-Term Cycles
1.	July 17, 1802	05°♍07'	Double bottom to 18-year cycle in February 1802. Prices gained about 150% in next 4 years.
2.	June 19, 1821	24°♈38'	4-year cycle crest in November 1821.
3.	Jan. 26, 1842	08°♑54'	72-year cycle trough in February 1842. Second great bull market run in U.S. history began from this low. Prices more than quadrupled in next 10 years.
4.	Oct. 21, 1861	18°♍22'	4-year cycle trough in May 1861. U.S. Civil War began.
5.	Apr. 18, 1881	01°♉35'	Half-cycle crest to 18-year cycle in June 1881. 3-year bear market started; market lost about 25%.
6.	Nov. 28, 1901	13°♑59'	Half-cycle crest of 18-year cycle in June 1901. 27-month bear market started then, and prices fell 46%.
7.	Sep. 9, 1921	26°♍35'	Half-cycle trough to 18-year cycle in August 1921. 8-year bull market to end of second great bull market started then.
8.	Aug. 7, 1940 Oct. 19, 1940 Feb. 15, 1941	14°♉27' 12°♉27' 09°♉07'	22.5-month cycle trough in June 1940, followed by 5-month corrective rally to 22.5-month cycle crest in November 1940.
9.	Feb. 18, 1961	25°♑12'	Half-cycle crest to 18-year cycle in November 1961. Prices declined for 7 months and lost about 30%.

10. Dec. 31, 1980 Mar. 4, 1981 July 23, 1981	09°♎29; 08°♎06' 04°♎56	4-year cycle crest (and half-cycle crest to 18-year cycle) in April 1981. 16-month bear market then commenced, as prices dropped 25%.
11. May 28, 2000	22°♉43'	
12. Dec. 21, 2020	00°♒29'	

Relative Strength	**Central**	**+/- 9 months**	**Total**
All	3.80	3.70	3.75
Crest	+3.33	3.67	+3.50
Trough	- 4.50	- 3.75	- 4.13
Consistency			
All	2.50	2.50	5.00
Crest	+1.50	+1.50	+3.00
Trough	- 1.00	- 1.00	- 2.00
C/S Index			
All	6.30	6.20	8.75
Crest	+4.83	+5.17	+6.50
Trough	- 5.50	- 4.75	- 6.13

In nine of ten cases (90%), a 22.5-month cycle culminated within 5 months of this aspect. In eight of those cases, the cycle was a 4-year or greater type. The other instance was a half-cycle crest to the 18-year cycle which unfolded 9 months following the aspect (1961). In 70% of the cases, the nearby cycle was even greater than the 4-year. In fact, most of time this signature corresponded to a half-cycle trough or crest to the 18-year cycle (six instances). If it was a crest (six times), then the market would commence a 7-month to 3-year bear market, and prices would lose about 25%-50%. In cases where a long-term cycle bottomed with this signature, a 4-10 year bull market would commence. In five of these cases, the conjunction occurred in the all-important cardinal signs. In four of these cases (80%), at least a half-cycle to the 18-year cycle would bottom or top out with this aspect. Four of these cycles in cardinal signs (80%) corresponded with crests.

<u>Conclusions</u>: *The Jupiter-Saturn conjunction is a reliable indicator for timing bull and bear market reversals in U.S. stocks (90% frequency), usually of a half-cycle type to the 18-year cycle. Reversals of 16 months to 4 years are common. Reversals are more likely when this conjunction occurs in cardinal signs (100%). When the aspect forms only once, the cycle culmination will tend to be 1-9 months away from the exact date, and usually five months or less. When it occurs three times due to a retrograde factor, then the cycle tends to culminate in the central time band. Thus investors may use this aspect to time a 4-year or greater cycle in U.S. stocks, using an orb of 5 months either side of the contact — or within the central time band if they retrograde back and forth in aspect three times. Whatever 4-year cycle trend is in effect going into this time band, investors may look to take contrary action (plan to purchase if going down, or plan to sell if trend is going up into this time band). This is most true if the conjunction is to take place in cardinal signs.*

Waxing Square (90°)

	Dates and Position of Jupiter		Long-Term Cycles
1.	Apr. 11, 1807 Aug. 17, 1807 Feb. 1, 1808	08°♒24' 05°♒04' 21°♒31'	Triple bottom to 18-year cycle in October 1807. Two-year bull market began.
2.	Nov. 9, 1826 May 22, 1827 Sep. 19, 1827	05°♎41' 04°♎38' 18°♎36'	4-year cycle trough in February 1827, followed by 4-year cycle crest in October 1827.
3.	June 14, 1846	00°♊48'	Closest cycle is 4-year trough in August 1845, a full ten months earlier. But this trough was almost negligible, as market was mostly up.
4.	Mar. 16, 1867	23°♒58'	22.5-month cycle trough in April 1867.
5.	Dec. 25, 1885 Mar. 17, 1886 Nov. 7, 1886	04°♎58' 01°♎37' 22°♎30'	22.5-month cycle trough, May 1886, which followed 22.5-month cycle crest of February 1886. Prices then rallied to 4-year cycle crest in December 1886.
6.	July 28, 1905 Dec. 19, 1905 May 20, 1906	01°♊20' 28°♉14' 13°♊54'	18-year cycle crest in January 1906. Start of 8-year bear market as prices lost almost 50%, with most of it in following 22 months.
7.	Apr. 29, 1926 Aug. 29, 1926 Feb. 17, 1927	23°♒49 20°♒27' 06°♓59'	4-year cycle crest in February 1926, followed by 1-month decline to 4-year cycle trough in March. Loss of 17% in that one month as aspect applied.
8.	Dec. 19, 1945 May 4, 1946 Nov. 4, 1946	23°♎14' 19°♎47' 08°♏39'	4-year cycle crest in May 1946, followed by 5-month decline to 4-year cycle trough in October 1946. Market lost about 25% in that 5-month drop.
9.	July 6, 1965	17°♊09'	Double top to 18-year cycle in February 1966. First time DJIA crossed 1000 mark. There was a 22.5-mo. cycle trough in June 1965. Prices rose 20% to February 1966.
10.	Apr. 2, 1986	09°♓32'	22.5-month cycle crest in July 1986. Prices then fell 10% to 22.5-month cycle low 1 month later.
11.	Dec. 17, 2005 June 22, 2006 Oct. 25, 2006	10°♏44' 09°♏15' 23°♏31'	
12.	Aug. 19, 2024 Dec. 24, 2024 June 15, 2025	17°♊27' 14°♊01' 01°♋18'	

Relative Strength	Central	+/- 10 months	Total
All	3.06	2.88	3.20
Crest	+3.50	+2.83	+3.21
Trough	- 2.64	- 3.00	- 2.69
Consistency			
All	4.00	2.50	5.00
Crest	+2.00	+1.50	+3.50
Trough	- 3.50	- 0.50	- 4.00
C/S Index			
All	7.06	5.38	8.20
Crest	+5.50	+4.33	+6.71
Trough	- 6.14	- 3.50	- 6.69

Given an orb of 10 months, this aspect has a 70% correlation to the culmination of 4-year or greater cycles. In only three cases (30%) were these greater than 4-year cycles. In 70% of the cases, there was a significant crest after which prices dropped sharply, but sometimes only for a short amount of time — usually 1 to 22 months. There were also eight important cycle troughs, but half of them were only the 22.5-month type. When it was a 4-year or greater trough, bull markets tended to unfold, which lasted 2-4 years. In each of the three instances of cardinal signs, a four-year cycle crest occurred within the central time band.

<u>Conclusions</u>: *The waxing square between Jupiter and Saturn has an 70% correlation to 4-year or greater cycles within an orb of 10 months before through 7 months after the aspect (or series). Six of seven times it unfolded within the central time band when there were three contacts due to retrograde. If the aspect unfolds in cardinal signs, it has a greater probability of coinciding with a 4-year cycle crest (100% so far). The cycle is not as powerful as the conjunction, but useful nonetheless. If the 4-year cycle is moving down and due with this aspect, investors are encouraged to look for opportunities to start purchasing on weakness. If the 4-year cycle is moving up and due in this time band, investors would be encouraged to sell, or take profits on long positions in anticipation of 1-22 month decline into the next 4-year cycle trough. This is especially true if the aspect is unfolding in a series of three passages in cardinal signs.*

Waxing Trine (120°)

	Dates and Position of Jupiter		Long-Term Cycles
1.	June 9, 1808 Aug. 12, 1808 Apr. 1, 1809	16°♓48' 16°♓01' 03°♈33'	4-year cycle crest in October 1809. Market then commenced a 4-year bear market. Prices lost over 40% in value. Half-cycle trough to 18-year cycle ended in October 1807, just 8 months before.

2.	Feb. 14, 1828	14°♏05'	18-year cycle trough in January 1829. End of 5-year bear market, and start of 6-year bull market.
	Mar. 25, 1828	13°♏25'	
	Dec. 23, 1828	03°♐00'	
3.	Aug. 15, 1847	19°♋52'	4-year cycle crest in August 1847. 22.5-month cycle trough in December 1847. 4-year bull market began with low in October 1848, as prices gained over 80%.
	Feb. 4, 1848	11°♋57'	
	June 24, 1848	25°♋10'	
4.	May 6, 1868	03°♈36'	2nd phase crest to 18-year cycle in July 1869. End of 4-year bull market, and then 1-year decline.
	Nov. 4, 1868	05°♈17'	
	Mar. 3, 1869	16°♈42'	
5.	Jan. 30, 1888	02°♐29'	4-year cycle trough in March-April 1888.
	May 20, 1888	01°♐45'	
	Dec. 20, 1888	19°♐59'	
6.	Oct. 1, 1906	09°♋45'	18-year cycle crest in January 1906. Possible 22.5-month cycle crest in October 1906 (test of 18-year high), then 13-month decline to 4-year low in November 1907. Prices declined about 45% in that decline.
	Dec. 6, 1906	08°♋48'	
	Aug. 4, 1907	26°♋54'	
7.	June 26, 1927	02°♈15'	22.5-month cycle crest in September 1927, then 1-month decline to 22.5-month cycle trough in October 1927 (loss of only 8%).
	Aug. 29, 1927	01°♈28'	
	Apr. 15, 1928	18°♈51'	
8.	Jan. 26, 1948	20°♐19'	4-year cycle crest in June 1948. Prices declined 17% to 4-year cycle trough 12 months later. It was end to 20-month bull market.
	July 9, 1948	21°♐09'	
	Dec. 13, 1948	06°♑11'	
9.	Sep. 9, 1966	27°♋01'	4-year cycle trough in October 1966. 2-year bull run then began in which prices gained over 35%.
	Feb. 6, 1967	27°♋09'	
	July 25, 1967	12°♌27'	
10.	May 23, 1987	19°♈04'	54-year cycle crest in August 1987, followed by 40% decline to 54-year cycle trough in October 1987. 2-year bull market then started.
	Nov. 21, 1987	20°♈44'	
	Mar. 18, 1988	02°♉05'	
11.	Mar. 16, 2007	19°♐09'	
	May 6, 2007	18°♐23'	
	Jan. 21, 2008	07°♑36'	
12.	Aug. 31, 2026		
	Apr. 3, 2027		
	July 11, 2027		

Relative Strength	Central	+/- 9 months	Total
All	3.25	4.00	3.60
Crest	+3.00	+3.67	+3.43
Trough	- 3.33	- 4.00	- 3.50
Consistency			
All	4.00	1.50	5.00
Crest	+2.50	+1.50	+3.50
Trough	- 3.00	- 1.00	- 4.00
C/S Index			
All	7.25	5.50	8.60
Crest	+5.50	+5.17	+6.93
Trough	- 6.33	- 5.00	- 7.50

This is a very consistent and powerful signature for a Jupiter-Saturn series. Given an orb of 9 months, 90% of the cases yielded a 4-year or greater cycle. In 80% of these cases, a significant long-term cycle unfolded within the central time band, which is quite noteworthy. Three of these cases (30%) coincided with 18-year or greater cycles (given an orb of 9 months again), and two were within the central time band of a three-passage series. If it was a crest, then in most cases a 1-7 year bear market would commence.

<u>Conclusions</u>: *The waxing trine of Jupiter and Saturn has a very reliable correspondence to 4-year or greater cycles (90%). The cycle is just as likely to be a crest as a trough, and in some cases (40% probability), both types will occur within a 9-month extended time band from the central time band. Therefore if the long-term trend is rising into this time band, investors may use it as a market timing indicator to exit long positions (sell), and stand aside until a 1-7 year bear market ends, in which prices decline at least 25%. In some cases (like 1987), the decline may be shorter, but still at least 25% from the crest which forms with this signature. If the market is declining, however, into a potential 4-year or greater cycle trough, investors may use this time band as an opportunity to purchase stocks for the next bull market.*

Opposition (180°)

	Dates and Position of Jupiter		Long-Term Cycles
1.	July 9, 1811 Dec. 31, 1811 May 21, 1812	21°♊39' 00°♋11' 07°♋04'	18-year cycle trough ends in March 1813. End of 7-year bear market, and start of 11-year bull market. 22.5-month cycle crest in June 1811.
2.	Mar 17, 1832 Oct. 4, 1832 Jan. 29, 1833	10°♓26' 21°♓17' 27°♓36'	Half-cycle crest to 18-year cycle in May 1833. Market declined about 25% to half-cycle trough next year in 1834.
3.	Nov. 20, 1850	14°♎46'	4-year cycle trough in October 1851. There was a

	Date	Position	Comment
	Mar. 18, 1851	20°♎39'	22.5-month cycle crest in December 1850, with a double top in June 1851.
	Oct. 17, 1851	01°♏23'	
4.	Aug. 21, 1870	21°♊56'	36-year cycle crest in January-May 1873, 9 months after last contact. Possible 22.5-month cycle trough in January 1871.
	Nov. 5, 1870	15°♊41'	
	June 24, 1871	06°♋55'	
	Mar. 19, 1872	19°♋52'	
	Apr. 11, 1872	20°♋59'	
5.	Apr. 26, 1891	10°♓33'	4-year cycle crest in March 1892. Prices then started 5-year bear market as they fell about 45%.
	Aug. 10, 1891	16°♓16'	
	Mar. 6, 1892	27°♓33'	
6.	Nov. 18, 1910	01°♏24'	4-year cycle trough in September 1911. End of 2-year bear market and start of 1-year bull market in which prices gained about 30%.
	Apr. 30, 1911	09°♏42'	
	Oct. 18, 1911	18°♏28'	
7.	July 26, 1930	06°♋45'	Right in the middle of the "Great Depression" bear market. 72-year cycle crest was in September 1929, and 72-year cycle trough was July 1932. 4-year cycle crest unfolded in April 1930, then prices plunged.
	Jan. 10, 1931	14°♋53'	
	June 10, 1931	22°♋09'	
8.	Apr. 10, 1951	27°♓24'	22.5-month cycle crest in September 1951. Market began modest 8-month decline. Prices fell about 8%.
	Oct. 15, 1951	07°♈28'	
	Feb. 21, 1952	14°♈18'	
9.	Dec. 29, 1969	02°♏04'	4-year cycle trough in May 1970. 32-month bull market begins in which prices gain 70%. 22.5-month cycle crest in April 1971, followed by 22.5-month cycle trough in November 1971. Biggest part of rally was the 14 months after last aspect in which prices gained 35%.
	Mar. 8, 1970	05°♏32'	
	Nov. 18, 1970	18°♏34'	
	June 11, 1971	29°♏11'	
	Oct. 16, 1971	05°♐49'	
10.	Sep. 10, 1989	07°♋18'	4-year cycle crest in July 1990. Market then dropped 22.4% to 4-year cycle trough 3 months later in October 1990. Big bull market then started. This was time of the Persian Gulf conflict.
	Nov. 14, 1989	10°♋26'	
	July 13, 1990	22°♋06'	
	Mar. 15, 1991	03°♌53'	
	May 16, 1991	06°♌50'	
11.	May 23, 2010	27°♓52'	
	Aug. 16, 2010	02°♈26'	
	Mar. 28, 2011	14°♈21'	

Relative Strength	**Central**	**+/- 10 months**	**Total**
All	2.63	4.75	3.60
Crest	+2.33	+4.67	+3.11
Trough	- 2.80	- 5.00	- 3.17

Consistency			
All	4.00	2.00	5.00
Crest	+3.00	+1.50	+4.50
Trough	- 2.50	- 0.50	- 3.00
C/S Index			
All	6.63	6.75	8.60
Crest	+5.33	+6.17	+7.61
Trough	- 5.30	- 5.50	- 6.17

This is yet another consistent and powerful signature between Jupiter and Saturn. If a 10-month orb is used before first aspect or after last aspect, then 4-year or greater cycles unfolded in nine of ten instances (90%). Furthermore 30% of these signature correlated with at least 18-year cycle types. Once again this signature has a greater correlation to long-term cycle crests, as nine of ten unfolded (90%) with this opposition. If the greater cycle did not unfold within the central time band, then it tended to unfold up to ten months *after* the aspect (all but one case). When the correlation was to a long-term crest cycle, the following bear market usually lasted 1-5 years. Five of the last six instances (83%) have witnessed the greater stock market cycle unfolding within the central time band. The strongest cycles occurred when the aspect took place in cardinal or mutable signs.

Conclusions: The Jupiter-Saturn opposition has an 90% correlation to 4-year or greater cycles within a time band that might extend out to 10 months after the aspect. In most cases (90%) there will be a long-term cycle crest associated with this opposition, from which prices commence a 1-5 year bear market. Sometimes it is less. But even so, the decline is usually at least 20% from the preceding long-term cycle crest. However, this crest is not always the strongest cycle, for 40% of the time there was a trough cycle that was stronger. As such, investors may use this signature to time the end of a 4-year or greater cycle trend, depending on the direction of that trend going into the first aspect (or within a few months of it). If the 4-year trend is up going into this time band (usually the case), then investors may wish to sell holdings and wait for a 1-5 year bear market to unfold, in which prices decline at least 20%. If the 4-year cycle trend is declining into this time band, then investors will want to use it as an opportunity to purchase new holdings.

Waning Trine (240°)

	Dates and Position of Jupiter		Long-Term Cycles
1.	Feb. 7, 1795	22°♑56'	18-year cycle crest in April 1795. Two-year bear market then started.
	June 19, 1795	06°♒25'	
	Dec. 22, 1795	08°♒38'	
2.	Sep. 30, 1814	24°♍08'	4-year cycle crest in September 1815. Market then declined 1 year.
	Mar. 6, 1815	07°♎50'	
	Aug. 14, 1815	08°♎04'	

No.	Date	Position	Comment
3.	Aug. 3, 1834	06°♊35'	72-year crest in May 1835. Start of 22-year bear in which most all of it was lost in next 7 years as prices fell 80%. Double top in August 1835.
	Sep. 18, 1834	11°♊27'	
	May 17, 1835	17°♊17'	
4.	Jan. 27, 1855	09°♒04'	4-year cycle trough in December 1854. 4-year cycle crest in December 1856.
	Aug. 21, 1855	27°♒38'	
	Dec. 11, 1855	27°♒09'	
5.	Sep. 16, 1874	08°♎10'	Double top to 36-year cycle crest in February 1874. Prices then declined 37.5% into 36-year low three years later.
	Apr. 30, 1875	25°♎02'	
	July 28, 1875	24°♎02'	
6.	June 24, 1894	18°♊25'	4-year cycle crest in September 1895. 22.5-month cycle trough in March 1895 and 22.5-month cycle crest in August 1894.
	Dec. 6, 1894	03°♋22'	
	May 1, 1895	03°♋22'	
7.	Mar. 16, 1914	12°♒13'	18-year cycle trough in December 1914. Prices up strongly next 2 years (+120+%). 22.5-month cycle crest in March 1914.
	June 17, 1914	22°♒13'	
	Jan. 20, 1915	26°♒35'	
8.	Oct. 25, 1933	09°♎49'	22.5-month cycle crest in February 1934. Prices then fell close to 25% to 22.5-month trough 5 months later in July 1934. Then 32-month bull market started.
	Mar. 6, 1934	21°♎59'	
	Sep. 8, 1934	23°♎17'	
9.	June 7, 1954	03°♋17'	18-year cycle trough ended September 1953. It was the weakest of all 18-year cycle declines. The market rallied strongly during this aspect and afterwards.
	Feb. 17, 1955	21°♋03'	
	Apr. 2, 1955	20°♋19'	
10.	Feb. 26, 1974	27°♒47'	36-year cycle trough in December 1974. 21-month rally gained 80%. Big bull market started here, and lasts several years.
	Aug. 22, 1974	14°♓45'	
	Jan. 10, 1975	15°♒03'	
11.	Oct. 12, 1993	23°♎49'	4-year cycle crest in January 1994, followed by 4-year cycle trough in April, 1994. Prices fell 12% in that 5-month period, then began huge bull market.
	Apr. 28, 1994	09°♏59'	
	Aug. 28, 1994	09°♏18'	
12.	July 17, 2013	04°♋53'	
	Dec. 12, 2013	18°♋27'	
	May 24, 2014	18°♋59'	

Relative Strength	**Central**	**+/- 9 months**	**Total**
All	3.67	4.17	3.95
Crest	+3.14	+3.75	+3.38
Trough	- 3.33	- 5.00	- 3.57

Consistency			
All	4.09	1.37	5.00
Crest	+3.18	+0.91	+3.64
Trough	- 2.72	- 0.45	- 3.18
C/S Index			
All	7.76	5.51	8.95
Crest	+6.32	+4.66	+7.02
Trough	- 6.05	- 5.45	- 6.75

This is another Jupiter-Saturn signature that reaches close to the C/S value of 9.00 (8.95). It is therefore reliable and strong, given a 9-month orb. In the 11 instances to date, six coincided with 18-year or greater cycles, or double tops to them (55%). Four of these unfolded within the central time band. The other two were 7 and 9 months before the aspect. Four of the other five correlations were to 4-year cycles, and only one (1933-34) correlated to a cycle of less than 4-years (9%). That means that given an orb of nine months, 91% of the cases to date coincided with a 4-year or greater cycle (and 55% correlated to 18-year or greater cycles). Both crests and troughs were present.

Conclusions: The waning trine between Jupiter and Saturn is both consistent and powerful as a timer of long-term cycles in the U.S. stock market, given an orb of 8-9 months either side of the first or last aspect in a series. In slightly more than half of the cases that long-term cycle has been an 18-year type or greater. In almost all cases (91%), a 4-year or greater cycle will unfold within this time band. Therefore, investors may use this as a reliable market-timing signature for long-term cycle troughs or crests, depending on the trend going into an orb of 8-9 months before the first of the aspect series, until 4 months after the last. If the 4-year or greater cycle is trending up into this time band, investors may look for a point to sell holdings. If a 4-year or greater cycle trough is forming in this time band, then investors may look to purchase new holdings in anticipation of a new long-term bull market trend.

Waning Square (270°)

	Dates and Position of Jupiter		**Long-Term Cycles**
1.	Feb. 23, 1797	20°♓56'	18-year cycle trough in November 1797. This started 9-year bull market.
	Oct. 28, 1797	12°♈05'	
	Dec. 12, 1797	10°♈00'	
2.	Oct. 29, 1816	17°♏25'	4-year cycle trough in September 1816.
	May 28, 1817	05°♐43'	
	Aug. 29, 1817	02°♐24'	
3.	July 28, 1836	29°♋07'	72-year cycle crest 1 year earlier, August 1835. 7-year bear market began in which prices dropped
	Jan. 13, 1837	15°♌38'	

	Date	Position	Comments
	May 27, 1837	12°♌10'	80%. The top, however, coincided more with the waning trine. There may have been a 22.5-month cycle trough and crest in December 1936 and January 1837.
4.	Apr. 18, 1856 Aug. 7, 1856 Feb. 8, 1857	25°♓44' 09°♈02' 07°♈59'	18-year and secondary low preceding 2nd great bull market run in U.S. history in October 1857. Prices appreciated 350% over next 16-years of bull market. There was a 4-year cycle crest in December 1856.
5.	Dec. 22, 1875 Mar. 17, 1876 Oct. 13, 1876	22°♏16' 01°♐59' 01°♐46'	36-year cycle trough in June 1877. End of 4-year bear market in which prices dropped 37.5%. There was a 22.5-month cycle crest in February 1876.
6.	July 7, 1896	12°♌28'	36-year cycle trough in August 1896. 10-year bull market run started as prices soared over 270%. Prices gained over 180% in next 32 months.
7.	Mar. 24, 1916 Oct. 24, 1916 Jan. 19, 1917	09°♈42' 00°♉16' 26°♈57'	4-year cycle crest in November 1916. Prices dropped over 40% in next 13 months to 4-year trough. There was a 22.5-month cycle trough in February 1917.
8.	Nov. 26, 1935 May 26, 1936 Sep. 28, 1936	03°♐48' 21°♐22' 17°♐54	22.5-month cycle crest and trough in April 1936. Decline was 13% in that month. 4-year cycle crest was 6 months after last aspect in March 1937.
9.	Aug. 24, 1955 Jan. 15, 1956 June 21, 1956	15°♌33' 00°♍14' 27°♌18'	4-year cycle crest in April 1956. Prices then declined next 18 months, losing about 20%. 22.5-month cycle trough in October 1955.
10.	June 3, 1975 July 28, 1975 Mar. 9, 1976	17°♈19' 24°♈14' 26°♈19'	In between 36-year cycle low in December 1974, and 4-year cycle crest in September 1976. Each of these cycles were 6 months outside of the aspect series. Up most of time.
11.	Nov. 10, 1995	18°♐05'	22.5-month cycle crest in May 1996, six months after the single passage of the aspect.
12.	Aug. 3, 2015 Mar. 23, 2016 May 26, 2016	28°♌16' 16°♍24' 13°♍41	

Relative Strength	**Central**	**+/- 11 months**	**Total**
All	3.11	4.17	4.00
Crest	+2.50	+3.25	+3.00
Trough	- 3.00	- 5.00	- 3.60

Consistency			
All	4.09	2.72	5.00
Crest	+2.72	+1.82	+3.64
Trough	- 3.18	- 1.37	- 4.55
C/S Index			
All	7.20	6.89	9.00*
Crest	+5.22	+5.07	+6.64
Trough	- 6.18	- 6.37	- 8.15

This Jupiter-Saturn signature did in fact reach the 9.00 C/S value level, if an orb of 11 months before through 8 months after the aspect (or series) is allowed. It is a bit questionable in cases where the cycle occurred earlier, because in most of those instances, the waning trine was in effect, and during its central time band (i.e. 1835 crest and 1974 low). Nevertheless, if the 11-month allowable orb is used, then there were six instances out of 11 possibilities (55%) in which an 18-year or greater cycle culminated. However this has happened only once in the last five possibilities. In the very last instance (November 1995), only a 22.5-month cycle topped out, and that was 6 months *after* the aspect. In due respect, though, that was only a single passage, whereas nine of the other ten instances involved three passages due to the retrograde factor. In five of the six cases of a long-term cycle culminating (over 18-year types), they were troughs. If it wasn't an 18-year or greater cycle trough, then it was likely to coincide with a 4-year cycle crest (and maybe even 22.5-month crest). In other words, when a trough, it was powerful. But when a crest, it was more on the line of a 4-year type, or even weaker. There were four instances of cardinal signs. In three of them (75%), an 18-year or greater cycle trough unfolded within 8 months. In two of these instances, it was 6-8 months outside of the central time band.

<u>Conclusions</u>: Given an orb of 11 months, the waning square between Jupiter and Saturn is a reliable and powerful market timing indicator. It seems particularly relevant to 18-year or greater cycle troughs that might form in this time band. If so, then investors may use this signature to define a time band for long-term purchases of stocks. However, if the four-year cycle trend is up going into this time band, then investors may wish to take profits on holdings and stand aside for next 1-2 years until the following long-term cycle trough is completed. If it is a crest, it tends to be of the 4-year cycle type.

Summary of Jupiter-Saturn Signatures

The following represents the ranking order of Jupiter-Saturn aspects in correlation to long-term stock market cycles. This first ranking order is based upon Total C/S values, which includes a time band of up to 11 months (but usually no more than nine) outside of the aspect. In parentheses are those instances in which that particular signature correlated more times with a crests (+) or trough (-), and the respective values of each. Also included is a column indicating how many instances of cycles greater than 4-year types which were associated with each aspect (again, within an 11-month orb of time either side of the aspect), and the percentage of times this represents. In the last column, titled **Orb,** are the number of months used outside of the central time band for the extended time band upon which the Total C/S values were based

	Aspect	Total C/S	Cycles > 4-Years		Orb
1.	Waning Square	9.00* (-8.15)	6/11 =	55%	11
2.	Waning Trine	8.95	6/11 =	55%	9
3.	Conjunction	8.75	7/10 =	70%	9
4.	Opposition	8.60 (+7.61)	4/10 =	40%	10
4.	Waxing Trine	8.60 (-7.50)	4/10 =	40%	9
6.	Waxing Square	8.20	3/10 =	30%	10

All signatures examined had a C/S value of greater than 8.00. One (waning square) had a value of 9.00. Thus all Jupiter-Saturn signatures were close to equal in strength and consistency. In fact, five of the six signatures had a C/S value ranging from 8.60-9.00. What may be interesting is the fact that the strongest correlations were those aspects from the waning trine through the conjunction (240° through 360°). This observation might change after more instances unfold in the future. But so far, it indicates that stock market cycles of a longer duration may be more evident with aspects between Jupiter and Saturn which take place *after* the opposition, or during the waning phase of these two planets.

This Total ranking is not quite born out in the number of cycles greater than 4-year types that unfolded with each aspect. The aspect with the greatest frequency to the strongest cycles was the conjunction, in which 7 of 10 cases found these stronger cycles present (70%). The orb for these cycles was only up to nine months (not 11) outside of the aspect. In fact, in six of those cases, it was five months or less. Also in six of those cases, it was either a half-cycle to the 18-year cycle, or a double bottom to it, and not the 18-year or greater cycle itself. This may be an interesting observation to keep in mind as the next conjunction unfolds in May 2000. Aside from the conjunction, only the waning square and waning trine had a correlation of over 50% to greater than 4-year cycle types. The waxing square was by far the weakest correlation to long-term cycles, both in strength and in frequency.

In all, there were 62 cases of aspects studied, of which 30 (48.4%) correlated with cycles greater than 4-years during the extended time band. That means there is almost a 50-50 probability that when Jupiter and Saturn enter into a major aspect, a cycle greater than the 4-year type is likely to unfold within 11 months, and usually nine months or less.

The ranking order changed considerably when only the central time band was used. These C/S results are shown in the table below, which accounts only for cycles that unfolded within the time frame of a three-passage instance, or within three months of single passage instance. Also shown are the number of instances in which greater than four-year cycles unfolded in this definition of a central time band.

Aspect	Central Time Band	Cycles > 4-Years	
1. Waning Trine	7.76	2/11 =	18%
2. Waxing Trine	7.25 (- 6.33)	2/10 =	20%
3. Waning Square	7.20 (- 6.18)	2/11 =	18%
4. Waxing Square	7.06 (- 6.14)	2/10 =	20%
5. Opposition	6.63	0/10 =	0%
6. Conjunction	6.30	4/10 =	40%

These are rather unusual findings. Within the central time band, there are no Jupiter-Saturn aspects with a C/S value greater than 8.00. Interestingly enough, the most consistent and powerful signatures were the trines (first the waning, then waxing), followed by the both squares (first the waning, then the waxing). All four signatures had values greater than 7.00. However the conjunction and opposition were both below 7.00.

But what may be most startling is the fact that the conjunction, which had the lowest C/S score for the central time band as defined in this study, also had the most instances of greater than 4-year cycle types unfolding in that time band. Here, 40% of the time, a cycle greater than a 4-year type occurred within its central time band. No other aspect had more than two such occurrences. Why? Perhaps the answer lies in our criteria. Since we allowed only a three-month orb based on a single passage, and since the conjunction — more than any other aspect — had predominately only single passage cases (whereas the others had more instances of three, and even five passages due to the retrograde factor), the conjunction found a majority of market cycles unfolding outside of its central time band. In fact, if we had allowed a five month orb for single passage instances to be included in the central time band, the conjunction would have been by far the most powerful of all these signatures. Allowing a five month orb, its C/S score within this 5-month time band would have been a whopping 8.22, which is far above the 7.76 value of the waning trine.

Another interesting finding of this part of the study is that there were absolutely *no* cycles greater than the 4-year types that unfolded within the central time band of the opposition.

In all, only 12 of 62 cases of central time bands correlated with a cycle greater than a 4-year type (19.35%).

<u>Conclusions of Jupiter-Saturn Signatures</u>: *There is nearly a 50% probability that a greater than 4-year cycle will culminate within 11 months of Jupiter and Saturn in major aspect to one another. The probability is highest when the aspect is a conjunction. However, given this orb of up to 11 months, the strongest cycles in the U.S. stock market tend to happen with aspects following the opposition (i.e. waning trine, waning square, and conjunction).*

When examined only within the central band, the probability of a cycle greater than a 4-year type shrinks to less than 20%. In fact, only the conjunction has a frequency of over 20%. Its frequency in fact has been 40%, and even 60% if a five-month orb is allowed in single passage instances. The opposition, on the other hand, has a 0% frequency of correlation to such cycles within its central time band.

Therefore investors need to use the time band extending nine months either side of the Jupiter-Saturn aspect series, as a window in which to time the very long-term cycle troughs and crests of the U.S. stock market.

References:

1. Raymond A. Merriman, *The Gold Book: Geocosmic Correlations to Gold Price Cycles,* Seek-It Publications, W. Bloomfield, MI, 1982.

CHAPTER SEVEN

THE "TEENY BOPPERS": CORRELATIONS TO PLANETARY CYCLES OF JUPITER AND BEYOND

The movement of Jupiter through the heavens is quite rapid compared to the planets of Saturn and beyond. Whereas Saturn, Uranus, Neptune, and Pluto take 29, 84, 168, and 248 years respectively to orbit the Sun, Jupiter takes slightly less than 12 years. Whereas Saturn, Uranus, Neptune, and Pluto take between 31–492 years to complete their planetary pair cycles to one another, Jupiter would take between 13–20 years to do the same (hence the term "teeny boppers"). Therefore, major (and minor) aspects between Jupiter to planets beyond its orbit will happen much more frequently than any of the other aspects reported in this study thus far.

Due to the increased frequency of aspects in the Jupiter series, it makes sense to apply two modifications. First, we will primarily only use data after 1873 — data wherein we have reliable monthly figures on the New York Stock Exchange stocks. Prior to that time, our figures and graphs are limited, and may not be reliable for gauging cycles with lengths less than 4-year types. Using the earlier data was fine in our effort to determine very long-term cycles, like the 18-year variety or their half cycles, and in most (if not all) cases even the 4-year cycle. However, the earlier data is not as reliable in determining the presence of 22.5-month or 50-week cycles, which we will now be referred to as *intermediate-term* cycles. By using monthly figures as of 1873, we can identify most — if not all — of the intermediate-term cycles that followed. And, because the aspects between Jupiter and beyond happen more frequently than those studied thus far, we will be able to analyze enough cases to get a sense of potential significance. Conversely, if we had used 1873 as the beginning date to analyze the prior signatures involving Saturn to Uranus, Neptune, and Pluto only after 1873, there would have been too few cases to study — only two or three cases would have been available because they occurred so infrequently. We will use instances prior to 1873, however, if there was a consistent correlation to 4-year or greater cycles with a particular signature.

The second modification to be applied to this section is in terms of the criteria used in our C/S values — at least in terms of the Strength values. Jupiter moves much faster through the heavens than Saturn and beyond, so it is likely that such signatures will not correspond to cycles that are as long-term as the ones studied thus far. In other words, it is very unlikely to find a Jupiter signature that will consistently correspond to 18-year or greater cycles, or even their half cycles (except, perhaps, the Jupiter-Saturn aspects, as already demonstrated). Since these planetary pair cycles will range from 13–20 years in length, each quarter cycle will then average 3–5 years apart. Therefore, it would be more valid to see if any of these signatures would have a high correlation to cycles closer to that average length — which would be the 4-year cycle type.

With this in mind, the "Strength" values of the following studies will be changed to reflect the following scores:

Cycles greater than 4-years	**5.00**
4-year cycles	**4.00**
Double bottom or top to 4-year cycles	**3.50**
22.5-month cycles	**3.00**
Double bottom or top to 22.5-month cycle	**2.50**
50-week cycles	**2.00**
Shorter cycles that involved a 10% or greater move	**1.50**

The allowable orb outside of the central time band will also have to be adjusted, and so will the allowable orb of a central time band in those cases where there is only one instance of the Jupiter signature. In the previous Saturn signatures, an orb of up to 9 months was used in almost all instances, because during that period, Saturn remained in a relatively close orb of aspect to Uranus, Neptune, or Pluto. However, it would not be wise to use the same formula for Jupiter, which moves about 2-1/2 times as fast as Saturn in its orbit around the Sun. Jupiter will therefore stay within a rather close orb of aspect to other planets outside of its orbit for a much shorter length of time than Saturn.

To simplify matters, an orb of 6 weeks will be used when creating a *central time band* in which there is only one passage of a Jupiter aspect to Uranus, Neptune, or Pluto. However, an orb of 2 months will be used in the case of Jupiter in aspect to Saturn, since it is the longest of the cycles being examined in this chapter (the Jupiter-Saturn cycle is about 20 years, whereas the Jupiter to Uranus, Neptune, or Pluto cycles are 13-14 years each). When the exact date of a cycle is unknown (as in cases prior to 1928), and it is uncertain whether it was 6 or more weeks between the aspect and the cycle culmination, the author will use his "best judgment" as to whether it belongs in the central time band or extended time band. When there are three-passage instances due to retrogradation, then an orb of only two weeks prior to the first aspect, and two weeks following the last passage of the aspect, will be used in the calculation for a central time band, plus all the time in between these two dates. Again, in cases prior to 1928 when it is unclear whether it was two weeks or more between an aspect date and a cycle unfoldment, the author will use his "best judgment." An incorrect "best judgment" will not effect the Total values, but may possibly effect some cases of central time band values. As one will see, though, as this book progresses, it is the Total values that will be given greater importance in the final recommended uses from this study.

An orb of up to 6 months from the time of a single or three-passage aspect will be used as the *extended time band* in the "Total" category for counting cases of 4-year or greater cycles. In the case of 22.5-month cycles, orbs of only 4 months will be used in the extended time band. And in cases of 50-week cycles, orbs of only 3 months maximum will be used.

One other point needs to be addressed, and this could again slightly alter the results of these studies. Daily and weekly charts are not available prior to 1928. Thus 50-week cycles may not be evident — or our report of them may be subject to questioning — prior to 1928. When looking only at monthly graphs, the smaller 50-week cycles may not be apparent. An effort was made to consider the "phases" of the 4-year cycle as if they were 50-week or 22.5-month cycles. This is a logical assumption, because usually there are three, four, or five 50-week cycle "phases" to the 4-year cycle, as reported in Volume 1. The emphasis, though, in this chapter, is to attempt to find those Jupiter planetary pair signatures that correlate to 50-week or greater cycles. Given the limitations just discussed, it is believed that this procedure of analysis will represent the "best effort" toward that goal.

Two final points distinguish this chapter's studies from the previous ones. These Jupiter studies will focus only upon the major aspects of the 3rd, 4th, and 6th (sextile) harmonics. This is due to the fact that, when using a 3-month orb, the 8th harmonic frequently overlaps with the 3rd and 6th. For this reason the semi-squares and sesquiquadrates are not included here. Additionally, these studies will not be concerned with sign positions of Jupiter— just the fact that these planets are in aspect to one another.

JUPITER-SATURN SIGNATURES

Although this signature was studied in the last chapter for its correlation to even longer-term stock market cycles — and found to be reliable — it will be studied again using the new criteria for rankings and analysis.

A couple of points need to be discussed here. In order to have enough cases for a study, all instances of the Jupiter-Saturn aspects were used since 1789. However, as mentioned previously, it is difficult to determine the intermediate-term cycles (50-week especially, and to some extent the 22.5-month cycles as well) that may have been present before 1873. Therefore, the Consistency and Relative Strength values for the central time band will be inclusive only of those instances after 1873. Likewise, the Consistency values for the extended time band will also only include instances after 1873. This is because they will include cases of 50-week cycles, whereas cases before 1873 may not. It is the purpose of this book to provide as accurate and as relevant of data and statistics as possible, hence the difference (regarding Jupiter-Saturn signatures only).

However the Total values, and the Strength values in the extended time band, will include *all cases studied* — from the first occurrence of the aspect in this study. This is because the 4-year or greater cycles can be identified prior to 1873, and they oftentimes occurred within an extended time band of 7 months either side of this aspect, and therefore their inclusion makes this part of the study more valuable (and hence useful to investors). In the other Jupiter signatures (to Uranus, Neptune, and Pluto), the studies will not include instances prior to 1873, unless specified. That is because there are enough incidents since that time to produce a meaningful study, since those aspects happen more frequently than Jupiter-Saturn aspects. The result is that some of the crests and trough values in the Total categories for these Jupiter-Saturn signatures may appear distorted. As mentioned, it is the author's opinion that this method will still yield the most accurate results possible, given the fact that 1) an ample number of cases are needed to do the study, and 2) figures prior to 1873 are not sufficient to include accurate identification of possible 50-week cycles.

Conjunction (0°)

	Dates	**Long-Term Cycles**
1.	July 17, 1802	Double bottom to 18-year cycle in February 1802. Prices gained about 150% in next 4 years.
2.	June 19, 1821	4-year cycle crest in November 1821. This followed 18-year cycle trough in January 1820.
3.	Jan. 26, 1842	72-year cycle trough in February 1842. Second great bull market run in U.S. history began from this low. Prices more than quadrupled in next 10 years.
4.	Oct. 21, 1861	4-year cycle trough in May 1861. Prices rallied for next 34 months.
5.	Apr. 18, 1881	Half-cycle crest to 18-year cycle in June 1881. 3-year bear market started; market lost about 25%.
6.	Nov. 28, 1901	50-week cycle trough in December 1901. Half-cycle crest of 18-year cycle in June 1901.
7.	Sep. 9, 1921	Half-cycle trough to 18-year cycle in August 1921.
8.	Aug. 7, 1940 Oct. 19, 1940 Feb. 15, 1941	5-month corrective rally to 22.5-month cycle crest on November 8, 1940. 22.5-month cycle trough in June 1940.
9.	Feb. 18, 1961	22.5-month cycle trough October 25, 1960. Half-cycle to 18-year crest 9 months later in November 1961.
10.	Dec. 31, 1980 Mar. 4, 1981 July 23, 1981	4-year cycle crest (and half-cycle crest to 18-year cycle) in April 1981. 16-month bear market then commenced, as prices dropped 25%.

11. May 28, 2000

12. Dec. 21, 2020

	Central	+/- 5 months	Total
Relative Strength			
All	4.00	4.00	4.40
Crest	+4.33	+4.50	+4.40
Trough	- 3.50	- 3.75	- 3.86
Consistency			
All	4.17	1.67	5.00
Crest	+2.50	+0.83	+3.33
Trough	- 1.67	- 1.67	- 3.33
C/S Index			
All	8.17	5.67	9.40*
Crest	+6.83	+5.33	+7.73
Trough	- 5.17	- 5.33	- 7.19

Using the modified criteria for measurement — in which a 4-year cycle or greater is considered to have a Strength value of 4.00 and anything greater is considered 5.00, and whereas a 50-week cycle is considered to have a Strength value of 2.00 — this signature becomes very significant. A 22.5-month or greater cycle unfolded within 5 months in every instance (100%). In fact, given a 5-month orb, a 4-year or greater cycle unfolded in eight of the ten instances (80%). Within the central time band (2-month orb in cases of single passage, and within two weeks of first and last aspect of a three-passage instance) there were four occurrences of cycles greater than 4-year types (40% — that's high!). In the two cases where there were three passes due to the retrograde factor, a crest of at least the 22.5-month type unfolded within 1 month of the second (retrograde Jupiter) pass (100%). This signature was just as likely to coincide with a long-term cycle crest, as well as a trough, given a 5 month orb. However, since 1881, the bias has been more toward crests. When it is a trough, it is likely to occur *before* the aspect (five of six cases saw this happening).

<u>Conclusions</u>: *Powerful long-term cycles tend to unfold within 5 months of Jupiter conjunct Saturn, or within the central time band of a three-passage series. In most cases, this cycle will be a 4-year or greater cycle (80%), and in all cases it will be at least a 22.5-month cycle. When there are three passes of the aspect, a long-term crest tends to unfold close to the second passage. Long-term investors may thus anticipate a 4-year or greater cycle to unfold very close to the time of the conjunction of Jupiter and Saturn. If a longer-term cycle has trended upward into this time band, then investors may look for a longer-term cycle crest to form and may wish to sell stocks during this period. If per chance a 4-year or greater cycle trough is unfolding (usually <u>before</u> the aspect), then investors may look to purchase stocks.*

Waxing Sextile (60°)

	Dates	Long-Term Cycles
1.	Jan. 29, 1806	18-year cycle crest in August 1806.
2.	Sep. 27, 1824 Mar. 27, 1825 July 8, 1825	18-year cycle crest in September 1824.
3.	July 27, 1844 Aug. 31, 1844 Apr. 5, 1845	4-year cycle crest in May 1844, followed by 4-year cycle trough in June 1845.
4.	Mar. 27, 1865 June 18, 1865 Dec. 30, 1865	Half-cycle trough to 18-year cycle in March 1865. 50-week cycle crest in November 1865.
5.	Sep. 15, 1884	Half-cycle trough to 18-year cycle in June 1884
6.	May 30, 1904	Half-cycle trough to 18-year cycle in November 1903.
7.	Feb. 21, 1925	Primary cycle trough, March 1925. Part of a 10+% reversal. Nothing else noteworthy.
8.	Nov. 12, 1943 Feb. 29, 1944 Sep. 4, 1944	22.5-month cycle trough in November 1943. 50-week cycle crest July 10-14, 1944.
9.	Aug. 18, 1963 Sep. 12, 1963 Apr. 24, 1964	22.5-month cycle trough July 23-26, 1963. 50-week cycle crest on May 7, 1964.
10.	May 5, 1984 June 8, 1984 Jan. 22, 1985	22.5-month cycle trough in July 1984.
11.	Nov. 1, 2003 May 1, 2004 Aug. 17, 2004	

Relative Strength	**Central**	**+/- 7 months**	**Total**
All	2.625	4.50	3.85
Crest	+2.00	+4.00	+3.40
Trough	- 2.625	- 4.33	- 3.57
Consistency			
All	3.33	1.67	5.00
Crest	+1.67	0.00	+1.67
Trough	- 3.33	- 1.67	- 5.00

C/S Index			
All	5.96	6.17	8.85
Crest	+3.67	+4.00	+5.07
Trough	- 5.96	- 6.00	- 8.57

In nine of ten cases (90%), a 22.5-month or greater cycle trough unfolded within 7 months of this aspect. In the tenth case, there was a primary cycle trough within 1 month, which was a point defining a 10+% reversal. In six cases (60%), the cycle was a 4-year or greater type. In the last eight instances, the sextile correlated with a significant trough (compared to only four significant crests nearby). The troughs were also much stronger than the crests. Six of the ten instances were of the three-passage types. Both cycle types were in evidence within 2 months of the first or last aspect in five of these cases.

Conclusions: The waxing sextile between Jupiter and Saturn has a very reliable correlation to 22.5-month cycle troughs, given an orb of 6 months, and usually 3 months or less (if not in central time band of a three-passage type). Investors may use this time band — within 6 months of a single passage or in the central time band of a three-passage sequence — as an opportunity to buy a 22.5-month or greater cycle trough that would appear to be forming.

Waxing Square (90°)

	Dates	**Long-Term Cycles**
1.	Apr. 11, 1807 Aug. 17, 1807 Feb. 1, 1808	Triple bottom to 18-year cycle in October 1807. 2-year bull market began.
2.	Nov. 9, 1826 May 22, 1827 Sep. 19, 1827	4-year cycle trough in February 1827, followed by 4-year crest in October 1827.
3.	June 14, 1846	4-year cycle crest unfolded August 1847. End of 5-year bull run, then 1-year decline. Closer by, a probable 50-week cycle crest occurred in March 1846, and 50-week trough in April.
4.	Mar. 16, 1867	22.5-month cycle trough in April 1867.
5.	Dec. 25, 1885 Mar. 17, 1886 Nov. 7, 1886	4-year cycle crest in December 1886.
6.	July 28, 1905 Dec. 19, 1905 May 20, 1906	18-year cycle crest in January 1906. Start of 8-year bear market as prices lost almost 50%, with most of it in following 22 months.

7.	Apr. 29, 1926 Aug. 29, 1926 Feb. 17, 1927	4-year cycle crest in February 1926, followed by 2-month decline to 4-year cycle trough in March-April. Loss of 17% in that one month as aspect applied. Double top to crest occurred in August-September 1926.
8.	Dec. 19, 1945 May 4, 1946 Nov. 4, 1946	4-year cycle crest in May 1946, followed by 5-month decline to 4-year cycle trough in October 1946. Market lost about 25% in that 5-month drop.
9.	July 6, 1965	Double top to 18-year cycle in February 1966. First time DJIA crossed 1000 mark. There was a 22.5-month cycle trough June 29, 1965, 1 week prior to aspect.
10.	Apr. 2, 1986	22.5-month cycle crest July 2, 1986. Prices then fell 10% to 22.5-month cycle low 1 month later.
11.	Dec. 17, 2005 June 22, 2006 Oct. 25, 2006	

Relative Strength	**Central**	**+/- 7 months**	**Total**
All	3.83	4.00	3.90
Crest	+3.90	+4.50	+4.17
Trough	- 3.67	- 3.00	- 3.50
Consistency			
All	5.00	2,50	5.00
Crest	+4.17	+1.67	+5.00
Trough	- 2.50	- 0.83	- 3.33
C/S Index			
All	8.83	6.50	8.90
Crest	+8.07	+6.17	+9.17*
Trough	- 6.17	- 3.83	- 6.83

This is yet another powerful signature correlating to a long-term cycle in U.S. stocks within an orb of 7 months. In every case but one there was at least a 22.5-month cycle close by, and in several cases (70%) a 4-year or greater cycle. In every case since 1867 (100%), a powerful crest unfolded within 7 months, and in five of those instances it occurred within the central time band. There were six instances in which the aspect occurred in a series of three contacts. In each of those cases (100%), a 4-year or greater cycle unfolded either during that time band, or within 1 month afterwards. In the last five cases, there has always been a crest of at least a 4-year periodicity in the three-passage series.

<u>Conclusions</u>: The waxing square between Jupiter and Saturn has very high correlation to a 4-year or greater cycle within the central time band of three-passage cases, or within 7 months of a single aspect incident (70%). In the last eight cases a powerful cycle crest unfolded. Investors may use this time band as a reliable period for selling holdings if a

22.5-month cycle crest is forming nearby; or if prices are declining, then for making purchases if a 22.5-month cycle trough or greater is forming. Oftentimes both types of cycles form within 3 months. So be alert to a severe but short correction to the cycle of the opposite type that may be forming.

Waxing Trine (120°)

Dates	Long-Term Cycles
1. June 9, 1808 Aug. 12, 1808 Apr. 1, 1809	4-year cycle crest in October 1809. Market then commenced a 4-year bear market. Prices lost over 40% in value.
2. Feb. 14, 1828 Mar. 25, 1828 Dec. 23, 1828	18-year cycle trough in January 1829. End of 5-year bear market, and start of 6-year bull market.
3. Aug. 15, 1847 Feb. 4, 1848 June 24, 1848	4-year cycle crest in August 1847. 1st phase (4-year cycle) trough to 18-year cycle in October 1848. 4-year bull market then began as prices gained over 80%.
4. May 6, 1868 Nov. 4, 1868 Mar. 3, 1869	4-year cycle crest in July-August 1869. End of 4-year bull market, and then 1-year decline.
5. Jan. 30, 1888 May 20, 1888 Dec. 20, 1888	4-year cycle trough in March-April 1888.
6. Oct. 1, 1906 Dec. 6, 1906 Aug. 4, 1907	22.5-month cycle crest in October 1906 (re-test of 18-year high). Half-cycle trough to 18-year cycle unfolded in November 1907.
7. June 26, 1927 Aug. 29, 1927 Apr. 15, 1928	22.5-month cycle crest in September 1927, then 1-month decline to 22.5-month cycle trough in October 1927 (loss of only 8%).
8. Jan. 26, 1948 July 9, 1948 Dec. 13, 1948	4-year cycle crest in June 1948. Prices declined 17% to 4-year cycle trough 12 months later. It was end to 20-month bull market. There was a double bottom in February 1948.
9. Sep. 9, 1966 Feb. 6, 1967 July 25, 1967	4-year cycle trough in October 1966. 2-year bull run then began in which prices gained over 35%.
10. May 23, 1987 Nov. 21, 1987 Mar. 18, 1988	54-year cycle crest in August 1987, followed by 40% decline to 54-year cycle trough in October 1987. 2-year bull market then started.

11. Mar. 16, 2007
May 6, 2007
Jan. 21, 2008

Relative Strength	**Central**	**+/- 6 months**	**Total**
All	3.83	4.20	4.20
Crest	+3.75	+4.00	+4.00
Trough	- 4.00	- 4.33	- 4.14
Consistency			
All	5.00	1.67	5.00
Crest	+3.33	+0.00	+3.33
Trough	- 3.33	- 1.67	- 5.00
C/S Index			
All	8.83	5.97	9.20*
Crest	+7.08	+4.00	+7.33
Trough	- 7.33	- 6.00	- 9.14*

Since 1877 (actually since 1888), a 22.5-month or greater cycle unfolded right within the central time band in every case. In all instances, there were three passages of the waxing trine aspect, and in every case since 1888, the cycle fell within the first and last passage, and usually between the first and within 1 month of the second passage. In four of six of these instances (67%), there was a 22.5-month or greater cycle crest, and in four cases there was also a 22.5-month or greater cycle trough (67%). In two cases (33%) both types of cycles unfolded within the central time band. In four of the cases (67%), the dominant cycle unfolded within 1 month of the middle passage. In the other two cases, it unfolded within a month after the first aspect hit. Utilizing the entire historical data base going back to 1808, there are nine (of ten) instances of a 4-year or greater cycle unfolding within 6 months of a Jupiter waxing trine to Saturn (90%). There were five cases each of crests and troughs (in 1987, both occurred in the central time band). This is undoubtedly a powerful and consistent signature for timing long-term cycles in the U.S. stock market, given a 6-month time band outside the three-passage series.

<u>Conclusions</u>: Powerful 22.5-month or greater cycles unfold within the central time band of Jupiter in a waxing trine to Saturn. This aspect occurs in a series of three passes, and usually the dominant stock market cycle will unfold within 1 month of the second aspect (67%), or within 1 month after the first (33%). Also, given a 6-month time band, there has been a 90% frequency of occurrence with 4-year or greater cycles — both crests and troughs are about evenly divided, though in the past 100 years, there is a slight bias towards troughs. Investors may look to see what type of cycle is unfolding as the aspect series begins, then look to take action within 1 month of the first or second aspect of the series. If the market is trending up, investors may look for a chance to exit holdings, and plan to re-buy on the trough that follows. If prices are headed down into the aspect, investors may use this time band as an opportunity to purchase stocks on a developing cycle trough.

Opposition (180°)

	Dates	Long-Term Cycles
1.	Dec. 6, 1790 Jan. 22, 1791 Oct. 17, 1791 May 2, 1792 Sep. 14, 1792	4-year cycle crest in January 1792, followed by 4-year cycle trough in September 1792.
2.	July 9, 1811 Dec. 31, 1811 May 21, 1812	18-year cycle trough ends in March 1813. End of 7-year bear market, and start of 11-year bull market. 22.5-month cycle crest in June 1811.
3.	Mar. 17, 1832 Oct. 4, 1832 Jan. 29, 1833	1st half-cycle crest to 18-year cycle in April-June 1833. Market declined about 25% to half-cycle trough next year in 1834.
4.	Nov. 20, 1850 Mar. 18, 1851 Oct. 17, 1851	4-year cycle trough in October 1851. End of 2-year bear market and start of 2-year bull market.
5.	Aug. 21, 1870 Nov. 5, 1870 June 24, 1871 Mar. 19, 1872 Apr. 11, 1872	36-year cycle crest ends in February 1873 (10 months after last contact). 2nd phase trough of 18-year cycle in December 1869. Prices rose over 40% to crest 3 years later. 22.5-month cycle trough in January 1871.
6.	Apr. 26, 1891 Aug. 10, 1891 Mar. 6, 1892	Double top to 18-year cycle in March 1892. Prices then started 5-year bear market as they fell about 45%.
7.	Nov. 18, 1910 Apr. 30, 1911 Oct. 18, 1911	4-year cycle trough in September 1911. End of 2-year bear market and start of 1-year bull market in which prices gained about 30%.
8.	July 26, 1930 Jan. 10, 1931 June 10, 1931	72-year cycle crest was September 1929, and 72-year cycle trough was July 1932. However, 50-week cycle trough unfolded December 1930, and followed 4-year cycle crest in April 1930.
9.	Apr. 10, 1951 Oct. 15, 1951 Feb. 21, 1952	22.5-month cycle crest in September 1951. Market began modest 8-month decline. Prices fell about 8%.
10.	Dec. 29, 1969 Mar. 8, 1970 Nov. 18, 1970 June 11, 1971 Oct. 16, 1971	4-year cycle trough in May 1970. 32-month bull market begins in which prices gain 70%. 22.5-month cycle crest in April 1971, followed by 22.5-month cycle trough in November 1971. May 1970 can be considered double bottom to 18-year cycle in 1974.

11.	Sep. 10, 1989 Nov. 14, 1989 July 13, 1990 Mar. 15, 1991 May 16, 1991	4-year cycle crest in July 1990. Market then dropped 22.4% to 4-year cycle trough 3 months later in October 1990. Big bull market then started. This was time of Persian Gulf conflict.
12.	May 23, 2010 Aug. 16, 2010 Mar. 28, 2011	

Relative Strength	**Central**	**+/- 3 months**	**Total**
All	3.67	4.50	3.91
Crest	+3.75	+4.00	+3.88
Trough	- 3.50	- 0.00	- 3.57
Consistency			
All	5.00	0.83	5.00
Crest	+3.33	+0.83	+4.17
Trough	- 3.33	- 0.00	- 3.33
C/S Index			
All	8.67	5.33	8.91
Crest	+7.08	+4.83	+8.05
Trough	- 6.88	- 0.00	- 6.90

Once again this signature unfolded in a series of three passes (and sometimes even five), and in every case since 1892, a 50-week or greater cycle unfolded in the central time band (100%). In 4 of the 6 cases (67%) it was a 4-year or greater cycle. If an orb of 3 months is allowed outside of the central time band, then a 4-year or greater cycle unfolded five times (83%). The last two instances contained five passes, and both 22.5-month and/or 4-year cycle crests and troughs unfolded within the central time band. Unlike the waxing trine where the cycle unfolded within 1 month of the first or second aspect in the series, the opposition found the cycle unfolding within 1 month of the middle or last passages (in the case of three passes). In the last two five-passage instances, both types of cycles — crests and troughs — occurred between the second and fourth passes. If the entire historical data base is studied (since 1790), one will see 11 occurrences of this signature, of which nine contained 4-year or greater cycles within an orb of 8 months (82%), and six within the central time band.

<u>Conclusions</u>: *The opposition between Jupiter and Saturn occurs in a series of either three or five contacts. In all cases, a 50-week or greater cycle has unfolded within that central time band since 1892. In the case of five contacts, both crests and troughs unfold between the second and fourth instance. Otherwise, the cycle unfolds within 1 month of the second or last passage. Usually these cycles are the 22.5-month or 4-year types. Investors may use this time band in anticipation of a 22.5-month or greater cycle culminating, and usually not before the second contact (within 1 month). If a 4-year cycle trough is forming, investors may use this period as an opportunity to buy stocks. If a 4-year cycle crest is forming, investors may wish to look for a spot to sell holdings.*

Waning Trine (240°)

	Dates	Long-Term Cycles
1.	Feb. 17, 1795 June 19, 1795 Dec. 22, 1795	18-year cycle crest in April 1795. Two-year bear market then started.
2.	Sep. 30, 1814 Mar. 6, 1815 Aug. 14, 1815	4-year cycle crest in September 1815. Market then declined 1 year.
3.	Aug. 3, 1834 Sep. 18, 1834 May 17, 1835	72-year crest in May 1835. Start of 22-year bear market, but all of it was lost in next 7 years as prices fell 80%.
4.	Jan. 27, 1855 Aug. 21, 1855 Dec. 11, 1855	4-year cycle trough in December 1854.
5.	Sep. 16, 1874 Apr. 30, 1875 July 28, 1875	Double top to 36-year cycle crest in February 1874. Prices then declined 37.5% into 36-year low 3 years later.
6.	June 24, 1894 Dec.. 6, 1894 May 1, 1895	4-year cycle crest in September 1895. 22.5-month cycle trough in March 1895. Prices gained 28% in those 5 months, but then declined for 1 year.
7.	Mar. 16, 1914 June 17, 1914 Jan. 20, 1915	18-year cycle trough in December 1914. Prices up strongly next 2 years (120+%). 22.5-month cycle crest in March 1914, so market was down mostly.
8.	Oct. 25, 1933 Mar. 6, 1934 Sep. 8, 1934	22.5-month cycle crest in February 1934. Prices then fell close to 25% to 22.5-month trough 5 months later in July 1934. Then 32-month bull market starts.
9.	June 7, 1954 Feb. 17, 1955 Apr. 2, 1955	50-week cycle crest in October 1954, and 50-week cycle trough in November 1954. 18-year cycle trough ended in September 1953.
10.	Feb. 26, 1974 Aug. 22, 1974 Jan. 10, 1975	36-year cycle trough in December 1974. 21-month rally gained 80%. Big bull market started here, and lasted several years.
11.	Oct. 12, 1993 Apr. 28, 1994 Aug. 28, 1994	4-year cycle crest in January 1994, followed by 4-year cycle trough in April 1994. Prices fell 12% in that 5-month period, then began huge bull market.

12. July 17, 2013
Dec. 12, 2013
May 24, 2014

Relative Strength	**Central**	**+/- 7 months**	**Total**
All	3.67	4.50	4.18
Crest	+3.00	+4.00	+3.89
Trough	- 3.67	- 0.00	- 3.71
Consistency			
All	5.00	1.67	5.00
Crest	+3.33	+0.83	+4.17
Trough	- 5.00	0.00	- 5.00
C/S Index			
All	8.67	6.17	9.18*
Crest	+6.33	+4.83	+8.06
Trough	- 8.67	0.00	- 8.71

Once again a 50-week or greater cycle unfolded within the central time band in every case since 1894. In five of the six cases since 1894 (83%), it was a 22.5-month or greater cycle. But the most significant aspect of this signature was the fact that in every case since then, a cycle trough unfolded in the central time band (this cannot be verified for cases prior to 1894). Three of these times (50%) it was a 4-year or greater trough (once it was an 18-year trough, and once a 36-year trough). There was a fourth time in which a 4-year cycle crest unfolded 4 months after the last aspect of a series of three passes, and another case where an 18-year cycle trough ended 9 months before the series began. The actual cycle could occur anywhere in the central time band — sometimes it was 1 month after the first aspect (once), twice it was within 1-2 months of the second contact, and four times (67%) it was within 2 months prior to the last contact when in a series of three passes (which it was every time). Utilizing the entire history of this aspect going back to 1795, one can see that there were ten (out of 11) instances in which a 4-year or greater cycle unfolded, given the 9-month orb (91%). Seven of these occurred within the central time band (64%).

<u>Conclusions</u>: *The waning trine between Jupiter and Saturn has a remarkable correlation to long-term cycle troughs in the last six instances (since 1894). In 83% of the instances, that trough was a 22.5-month type or longer. In 50% of cases, it was at least a 4-year cycle, and in 33% of the cases it was an 18-year cycle trough or greater. Using the longer historical data base, there was an 83% frequency of 4-year or greater cycles unfolding within 9 months, and most of these within only 4 months. Investors are therefore advised to use this time band as an opportunity to buy a 22.5-month or greater cycle trough that will usually unfold within the central time band.*

Waning Square (270°)

	Dates	Long-Term Cycles
1.	Feb. 23, 1797 Oct. 28, 1797 Dec. 12, 1797	18-year cycle trough in November 1797. This starts 9-year bull market.
2.	Oct. 29, 1816 May 28, 1817 Aug. 29, 1817	4-year cycle trough in September 1816.
3.	July 28, 1836 Jan. 13, 1837 May 27, 1837	72-year cycle crest 1 year earlier in August 1835. This began 7-year bear market in which prices dropped 80%. The top, however, coincided more with the waning trine. Probable 22.5-month cycle trough and crest in December 1836 and January 1837 respectively.
4.	Apr. 18, 1856 Aug. 7, 1856 Feb. 8, 1857	18-year and secondary low preceding 2nd great bull market run in U.S. history in October 1857. Prices gained 350% over next 16 years of bull market. 4-year cycle crest in December 1856.
5.	Dec. 22, 1875 Mar. 17, 1876 Oct. 13, 1876	36-year cycle trough in June 1877. End of 4-year bear market in which prices dropped 37.5%. 22.5-month cycle crest in February 1876
6.	July 7, 1896	36-year cycle trough 1 month later, August 1896. 10-year bull market started as prices soared over 270%. Prices gained over 180% in next 32 months.
7.	Mar. 24, 1916 Oct. 24, 1916 Jan. 19, 1917	4-year cycle crest in November 1916. Prices dropped over 40% in next 13 months to 4-year trough.
8.	Nov. 26, 1935 May 26, 1936 Sep. 28, 1936	22.5-month cycle crest and trough in April 1936. Decline was 13% in that month. 4-year cycle crest was 6 months after last aspect in March 1937.
9.	Aug. 24, 1955 Jan. 15, 1956 June 21, 1956	4-year cycle crest in April 1956. Prices then declined next 18 months, losing about 20%. 22.5-month cycle trough in October 1955.
10.	June 3, 1975 July 28, 1975 Mar. 9, 1976	In between 36-year cycle low in December 1974 (6 months earlier than first aspect), and 4-year crest in September 1976 (6 months after last aspect). Up most of time. 50-week cycle crest in July 1975, and 50-week cycle low in October 1975.

11. Nov. 10, 1995	22.5-month cycle crest in May 1996, 6 months afterwards. 50-week cycle low in August, 1995, 3 months before aspect.
12. Aug. 3, 2015 Mar. 23, 2016 May 26, 2016	

	Central	+/- 6 months	Total
Relative Strength			
All	3.50	4.00	4.00
Crest	+3.20	+3.33	+3.57
Trough	- 3.25	- 4.00	- 3.88
Consistency			
All	4.29	2.14	5.00
Crest	+3.57	+2.14	+4.29
Trough	- 2.86	- 1.43	- 3.57
C/S Index			
All	7.79	6.14	9.00*
Crest	+6.77	+5.47	+7.86
Trough	- 6.11	- 5.43	- 7.45

Jupiter in waning square to Saturn is yet another powerful signature. In every case since the beginning of the market, at least a 22.5-month cycle unfolded within 6 months of the aspect. If an 8-month orb was allowed prior to or before the first and last passage, then nine of 11 instances (82%) correlated to a 4-year or greater cycle. In all but one of the last eight cases (87.5%), this signature correlated with a crest within the central time band of a three-passage instance, or within 3 months of a single passage.

<u>Conclusions</u>: *The waning square of Jupiter to Saturn has a high probability of timing a 4-year or greater cycle within an orb of 8 months (usually six months or less), and a very high probability of correlating with a 22.5-month or greater cycle within the central time band (or within 3–6 months if only single passage instance). This cycle will usually correlate with a crest in the central time band. However, given an orb of 8 months before the first or after the last passage, a powerful trough may also occur. Therefore if a 22.5-month or greater cycle crest is unfolding in the central time band, investors may wish to use this signature as a guide to sell stocks (take profits). However, if investors find the market declining into a 22.5-month or greater cycle trough during this central time band, they may prepare to purchase stocks.*

Waning Sextile (300°)

Dates	Long-Term Cycles
1. May 23, 1798 Oct. 8, 1798 Feb. 25, 1799	18-year cycle trough in November 1797

2.	Nov. 16, 1818	4-year cycle crest in May 1819
3.	Aug. 23, 1838	4-year cycle crest in September 1838, followed by 4-year cycle trough in March-April 1838
4.	Apr. 22, 1858	18-year cycle trough in October 1857, and double bottom in June 1859.
5.	Jan. 8, 1878 July 20, 1878 Oct. 12, 1878	36-year cycle trough was 7 months earlier, in June 1877. Market was rising during this period.
6.	Oct. 27, 1897 Jan. 30, 1898 July 29, 1898	22.5-month cycle trough in March 1898.
7.	July 7, 1917 Sep. 27, 1917 Mar. 31, 1918	4-year cycle trough, December 1917.
8.	Dec. 12, 1937	4-year cycle trough 3 months later, in March 1938.
9.	Sep. 20, 1957 Apr. 29, 1958 June 22, 1958	4-year cycle trough, October 1957.
10.	May 27, 1977 Dec. 28, 1977 Feb. 27, 1978	4-year cycle trough 2 days after last aspect on March 1, 1977.
11.	Feb. 9, 1997 July 14, 1997 Nov. 14, 1997	4-year cycle crest in August 1997, followed by 16% decline into 4-year cycle trough in October 1997.
12.	Aug. 27, 2017	

Relative Strength	**Central**	**+/- 7 months**	**Total**
All	3.50	4.50	4.09
Crest	+3.00	+4.00	+3.40
Trough	- 3.80	- 4.60	- 4.10
Consistency			
All	4.29	1.43	5.00
Crest	+1.43	0.00	+1.43
Trough	- 3.57	- 1.43	- 5.00

C/S Index

All	7.79	5.93	9.09*
Crest	+4.43	+4.00	+4.83
Trough	- 7.37	- 6.03	- 9.10*

This is a very interesting signature due to its reliable correlation to 22.5-month or greater cycle troughs in each of the last 9 instances, and 4-year or greater troughs in 7 of those (78%), using a 7-month orb. In the only case of a single passage, the 4-year cycle trough unfolded just 3 months after the aspect (March, 1938).

Conclusions: The waning sextile between Jupiter and Saturn has a strong correlation to 4-year cycle troughs within an orb of 7 months, and usually much less. Investors may therefore use this signature to time purchases of stocks, particularly if a 4-year cycle trough is due and appears to be forming at this time, or within 7 months.

Summary of Jupiter/Saturn Signatures

The following represents the ranking order of the Jupiter-Saturn signatures in terms of their correlation to long-term cycles, via this chapter's new criteria used for the Strength value. This first ranking order is based upon Total C/S values, which includes a time band of up to 7 months (usually 6 or less) outside of the aspect. In parentheses are those instances in which that particular signature correlated more times with a crests (+) or trough (-), and the respective values of each. Also included is a column indicating how many instances of 4-year or greater cycles were associated with each aspect (again, within a 7-month orb of time either side of the aspect), and the percentage of times this represents.

	Aspect	Total		4-Yr or > Cycles		
1.	Conjunction	9.40*		8/10	=	80%
2.	Waxing Trine	9.20*	(- 9.14*)	9/10	=	90%
3.	Waning Trine	9.18*	(- 8.71)	9/11	=	82%
4.	Waning Sextile	9.09*	(- 9.10*)	9/11	=	82%
5.	Waning Square	9.00*		8/11	=	73%
6.	Opposition	8.91*	(+8.05)	8/11	=	82%
7.	Waxing Square	8.90	(+9.17*)	7/10	=	70%
8.	Waxing Sextile	8.85	(- 8.57)	5/10	=	50%

This is a very significant group of geocosmic signatures. In 5 cases the Total C/S value was at (or over) the critical 9.00 mark, and in the other 3 cases, it was very close (8.85 to 8.91). This means that within a 7-month time band of this aspect (and usually much less), there is likely to be a 4-year or greater long-term cycle culmination. In fact, looking at the incidents of 4-year or greater cycles (column to the right), one can see that there were 63 such cases out of 84 incidents studied (or 75% frequency). In every single aspect type there was a 50% or greater correlation to a 4-year cycle. In all but the waxing sextile, the correlation was at least 70%.

It is also interesting to note the correspondence of each aspect with a cycle trend type. Half of the aspects had a higher correlation to troughs than crests. But when examined more closely, it will be seen that each of these aspects correlating primarily with long-term cycle troughs were all the soft aspects (sextiles and trines). This is significant. Two others had a strong bias towards crests (opposition and waxing square), while the remaining two had no observable bias. The waxing square is interesting because it had a +9.17* correlation to crests, and yet its Total C/S value was the second lowest at 8.90. This is due to the manner in which these scores were calculated, whereby Consistency was only measured within the periods after 1877, but Strength was used for all instances since the beginning (1790's). Also reaching the level of significance (by the criteria defined for this study) were the waxing trine (-9.14*) and waning sextile (-9.10*).

When the study was limited to the central time band only, the ranking order was slightly different, as shown by the following table.

	Aspect	Central Time Band		4-Yr or > Cycles		
1.	Waxing Trine	8.83		6/10	=	60%
1.	Waxing Square	8.83	(+8.07)	6/10	=	60%
3.	Waning Trine	8.67	(- 8.67)	7/11	=	64%
3.	Opposition	8.67		6/11	=	55%
5.	Conjunction	8.17	(+6.83)	4/10	=	40%
6.	Waning Square	7.79		6/11	=	55%
6.	Waning Sextile	7.79	(- 7.37)	4/11	=	37%
8.	Waxing Sextile	5.96	(- 5.96)	2/10	=	20%

None of these signatures achieved the very significant 9.00 level, but four attained a C/S value of 8.67 or greater, which is still very high for a central time band. Two aspects actually tied for the highest score at 8.83: the waxing trine, and waxing square. The other two high scores were registered by the waning trine and opposition (8.67 each). The only other signature to register a value greater than 8.00 was the conjunction. What may be noteworthy here is that aspects further away from the conjunction seem more "exact" in coinciding with significant market cycles. Three of the four strongest scores were the opposition and the two trines that surround it.

The weakest correspondence to central time band cycles occurred with the waxing sextile. Yet this aspect had a very high correspondence to trough cycles in every case. So too did the waning sextile — and with much higher scores. The highest correspondence with a trough cycle in the central time band, though, was the waning trine (-8.67). Thus three of the four soft aspects (trines and sextiles) coincided with trough cycles. This was similar to the findings in the extended time band too. In regards to crest cycles within the central time band, the waxing square (+8.07) and conjunction (+6.83) were the only two signatures with a bias in this direction.

The percentage of 4-year or greater cycles during the central time band was, of course, less than that of the extended time band. Still, 5 of these aspects had better than 50% correspondence to 4-year or greater cycles (both trines, both squares, and the opposition). All others had a 20-40% correspondence. Still, this is highly significant. It shows that there is close to a 50% probability (41 of 84 cases) that a 4-year or greater cycle will occur within the central time band of a Jupiter-Saturn aspect. If the two sextiles were omitted, the frequency would have been 55.5% (35 of 63).

Conclusions: Jupiter-Saturn signatures are most noteworthy given a 6-month orb in their correlation to long-term cycles in the U.S. stock market. The most significant correlations may be during the soft aspect time bands, which have a higher probability of coinciding with long-term crest trough cycles. All signatures are reliable in timing long-term cycles within a 7-month extended time band. Within the central time band, the two trines, and the waxing square and opposition are quite reliable. Thus investors may find many advantages to be aware of these signature. If a soft aspect is forming, investors may watch closely for a long-term cycle trough to form, and prepare to buy stocks for the long term (especially if forming within the central time band).

JUPITER-URANUS SIGNATURES

This 13–14 year cycle should be a most interesting signature, because of the explosive nature of both planets. Jupiter's dynamic is expansive and outgoing. Its theme is one of over-reaching, increasing, and making larger or great. It exaggerates, and therefore tends to coincide with periods of hope and confidence (even over-confidence) on the part of the investment community. Stocks may become overvalued if rising, or if falling, the investment community may be given towards hysteria. Uranus' principle is one of suddenness. It tends to break from tradition, which means if there is well-defined support or resistance to the market, it is liable to "break out" of that congestion. When the two planets come together, it is very combustible, but one would think more so from a bullish point of view. Uranus excites and stimulates, Jupiter exaggerates. From a purely astrological point of view, investors may wish to be long a rising market well before an aspect between these two planets culminates. The best of all possible worlds might be to find the market declining into a hard long-term Saturn aspect, that is followed shortly after by a Jupiter-Uranus aspect.

Conjunction (0°)

	Dates	Long-Term Cycles
1.	June 5, 1872	36-year cycle crest 7 months later in January 1873.
2.	Aug. 18, 1886	4-year cycle crest 4 months later in December 1886. End of 30-month rally in which prices gained 65+%. 22.5-month cycle trough in May 1886.

3.	Oct. 20, 1900	4-year cycle trough 1 month earlier, September 1900. Market gained 50% during next 9 months.
4.	Mar. 3, 1914	22.5-month cycle crest in March 1914. Market then closed down last 5 months of this year.
5.	July 15, 1927	22.5-month cycle crest in September 1927, and then market dropped 8% to 22.5-month cycle low in October 1927
6.	May 7, 1941	50-week cycle trough on May 1 1941. Prices rose 14% to 50-week cycle crest 2 months later, July 22, 1941.
7.	Oct. 7, 1954 Jan. 6, 1955 May 10, 1955	Prices finally broke to a new all-time high during this period, breaking above the previous all-time of September 1929 (25 years earlier). 50-week trough on November 1, 1954. Prices soared almost 40% to 22.5-month crest in September 1955.
8.	Dec. 11, 1968 Mar. 11, 1969 July 20, 1969	4-year cycle crest unfolded on December 13, 1968. Prices then dropped sharply, 20.5%, into primary cycle low July 30, 1969. Continued dropping to 4-year low in May 1970.
9.	Feb. 18, 1983 May 14, 1983 Sep. 25, 1983	This was after secondary low of August 1982, which launched a great bull market to new all-time record highs. 50-week cycle crest on June 17, 1983 and 50-week trough August 9, 1983. 22.5-month cycle crest in S&P October 10, 1983. This was another "breakout" period, upwards.
10.	Feb. 15, 1997	50-week cycle crest on March 11, 1997. Prices then fell 842 points in the DJIA (11.8%) to 50-week low April 14, 1997. Prices then rose 31% during the following four months.
11.	June 8, 2010 Sep. 18, 2010 Jan. 4, 2011	

	Central	+/- 7 months	Total
Relative Strength			
All	2.86	3.17	3.30
Crest	+3.00	+3.40	+3.22
Trough	- 2.50	- 2.66	- 2.57
Consistency			
All	3.89	3.00	5.00
Crest	+2.22	+2.50	+4.50
Trough	- 2.22	- 1.50	- 3.50
C/S Index			
All	6.75	6.17	8.30
Crest	+5.22	+5.90	+7.72
Trough	- 4.72	- 4.17	- 6.07

Despite the seemingly low C/S values (compared to Jupiter-Saturn signatures), this was still a very significant aspect. In six cases (60%), the DJIA soared to new all-time highs close to the time this conjunction was unfolding. In nine cases (90%), the market made a significant crest — always in the same month or within 7 months *after* the aspect (and usually 4 months or less). This implies that if the market is rising into the conjunction of Jupiter and Uranus, *it will not top out before the aspect unfolds* — and usually a little afterwards. On the other hand, if the market was declining into this aspect, it would complete its bottom within 1 month and then make a very powerful reversal back upwards.

Conclusions: *The conjunction of Jupiter and Uranus tends to have a very bullish correspondence to U.S. stock prices. If the market is rising into this aspect, it will not top out before the aspect unfolds, and oftentimes in the process it will soar to new record highs. It will tend to end that powerful rally within 7 (and usually 4) months after the aspect is completed — oftentimes only 1. If the market is declining into this aspect, it will tend to bottom within 1 month (usually before or in the month of the aspect), and then commence a powerful reversal back upwards. Thus investors can use this aspect as a guide to buying stocks. If a long-term cycle has bottomed within a year before, be long going into (and maybe slightly beyond), especially if the market is breaking to new record highs. If the market appears to be declining into a 50-week or greater trough within 1 month of the first passage of this aspect (or single pass), then look to purchase stocks in anticipation of very powerful rally about to commence.*

Waxing Sextile (60°)

	Dates	Long-Term Cycles
1.	Oct. 17, 1874	50-week cycle low in September 1874. End of 7-month decline from 36-year cycle crest in February 1874. Rally lasted 7 months.
2.	Dec. 27, 1888	50-week cycle trough in December 1888. End of 2-month decline from 50-week cycle crest, and 1st phase of 4-year cycle which began March-April 1888. Rally lasted 17 months.
3.	Jan. 25, 1903	22.5-month cycle trough in December 1902, and 22.5-month cycle crest 2 months later in February 1903. Decline lasted 9 months.
4.	May 5, 1916	Double bottom to 22.5-month cycle trough in April 1916. End of 4-month decline, start of 7-month rally. 4-year cycle crest unfolded in November 1910, 6 months after aspect.
5.	Aug. 7, 1929 Jan. 3, 1930 Mar. 27, 1930	72-year cycle crest on September 3, 1929; then 49.3% decline to 4-year cycle trough on November 13, 1929. Then 5-month rally to 50-week cycle crest April 16, 1930 (gain was 52%).

6. Aug. 7, 1943 — 22.5-month cycle crest on July 15, 1943. Start of 4-month decline to 22.5-month cycle trough on November 30, 1943. Market dropped 12% — and most of into August 2 primary cycle trough.

7. Sep. 28, 1957 — 22.5-month cycle trough on October 22, 1957. End of 3-month decline for double top to 4-year cycle crest on July 16, 1957. Loss of 20+%. Then started big 10-month rally.

8. Dec. 9, 1971 — 22.5-month cycle trough on November 23, 1971. End of 7-month decline (loss 17.5%), and start of 14-month rally to new all-time highs (gain 35%).

9. May 21, 1985
July 14, 1985
Jan. 8, 1986 — 50-week cycle crest on July 23, 1985, followed by 2-month decline to 50-week cycle trough on September 18, 1985. Loss only 6.4%, then breakout to new all-time high over 1400 in November. Primary top in early January 1986.

10. Apr. 23, 1999

11. July 21, 2012

12. July 21, 2026

	Central	+/- 6 months	Total
Relative Strength			
All	2.83	3.125	3.06
Crest	+3.25	+3.17	+3.21
Trough	- 2.69	- 3.00	- 2.72
Consistency			
All	5.00	2.22	5.00
Crest	+2.22	+1.67	+3.89
Trough	- 4.44	- 0.56	- 5.00
C/S Index			
All	7.83	5.35	8.06
Crest	+5.47	+4.86	+7.10
Trough	- 7.13	- 3.56	- 7.72

This is also a comparatively weak signature, compared to Jupiter-Saturn ones, but it is reliable nonetheless. In every instance a 50-week or greater cycle trough unfolded either in the central time band or within 3 months of the exact aspect. In fact, in eight of nine cases (89%), the trough unfolded within one month of the aspect — and only one of those eight times did it unfold in the month *afterward*. It was usually within 1 month *before* the sextile that the low occurred. However, these troughs were not powerful. Three were only 50-week cycle troughs, and five were 22.5-month cycle troughs. Only one was a 4-year cycle. What is significant, though, is that these troughs were usually the end of declines that started from cycle crests 2–7 months before the aspect. Furthermore, they began strong rallies that lasted 2–17 months, and usually 4–10 months. The crests were not as frequent, but when they occurred, they were oftentimes stronger in cycle type. In all there were six crests within 3 months (out of nine possibilities). There were only two instances of a retrograde causing three passages. In both instances the market first made an all-time high, followed by a sharp 2-month decline, followed by another rally lasting 4-5 months. In the other four cases of crests, three occurred 1–3 months *before* the aspect. Then prices fell sharply into the aspect.

<u>Conclusions:</u> *This is a reliable signature for timing troughs. In eight of nine cases a 50-week or greater cycle trough occurred within 1 month of the waxing sextile between Jupiter and Uranus. In fact, even if a crest coincided, it was usually 1–3 months before the aspect. Normally, though, a significant crest unfolded 2–7 months prior to this sextile, then dropped to form a 50-week or 22.5-month cycle trough within 1 month of it. Then the market would embark upon a strong 4–14 month rally. In these cases, investors may use this signature to time purchases of stocks — if a 50-week or 22.5-month cycle trough appears to be forming within 1 month of the aspect. That cycle trough may be the result of a very sudden and short-lived decline. If the aspect unfolds in a three passage series, then investors may find a crest forming first (after the first passage), then a very sharp 2-month decline, followed by another strong 4-5 month rally.*

Waxing Square (90°)

	Dates	Long-Term Cycles
1.	Dec. 10, 1875	22.5-month cycle trough in October 1875, followed by 22.5-month cycle crest in February 1876. After crest, prices fell hard for 16 months and lost 35%.
2.	Feb. 7, 1890	50-week cycle trough in February 1890. End of 5-month decline. Prices then rallied to 18-year cycle crest in May 1890. A strong 7-month decline then commenced.
3.	June 30, 1903 Aug. 14, 1903 Feb. 27, 1904	"Rich Man's Panic" occurred in 1903, leading to 4-year cycle trough in November 1903. End of big 9-month decline, and start of big 26-month rally to 18-year crest in January 1906.
4.	June 1, 1917	22.5-month cycle crest in June 1917. End of 4-month rally and start of sharp 6 month decline to 4-year cycle trough.
5.	Sep. 5, 1930 Feb. 1, 1931 May 17, 1931	Great Depression in force. Primary cycle crest on September 10, 1930 was followed by sharp 3-month decline to 50-week cycle trough on December 17, 1930. Then 2-month rally to 50-week cycle crest on February 24, 1931.
6.	Sep. 25, 1944	50-week cycle trough September 7 and 14, 1944. End of 2-month decline, and start of 9-month rally.

7.	Nov. 24, 1958	Very sudden 50-week cycle crest on November 17, 1958, followed by 50-week trough on November 25, 1958. Prices then rallied strongly (new all-time highs) for next 9 months.
8.	Jan. 23, 1973	36-year cycle crest on January 11, 1973. End of 14-month rally, and start of bear market lasting 23 months.
9.	June 4, 1986 Sep. 6, 1986 Feb. 12, 1987	22.5-month cycle crest on July 2, 1986 followed by 22.5-month cycle trough September 12, 1986. There was a double bottom on August 14, and double top on September 5. Market then broke out of congestion to cross 2000 in January 1987.
10.	May 20, 2000	
11.	Aug. 21, 2013 Feb. 26, 2014 Apr. 20, 2014	

Relative Strength	**Central**	**+/- 6 months**	**Total**
All	2.89	4.00	3.33
Crest	+3.00	+4.00	+3.29
Trough	- 2.57	- 4.00	- 2.75
Consistency			
All	5.00	1.67	5.00
Crest	+2.78	+1.11	+3.89
Trough	- 3.89	- 0.56	- 4.44
C/S Index			
All	7.89	5.67	8.33
Crest	+5.78	+5.11	+7.18
Trough	- 6.46	- 4.56	- 7.19

Once again this Jupiter-Uranus signature was consistent in forming a 50-week or greater cycle right near the exact date of its occurrence. There were three cases of retrogrades leading to three passes, and in every case a long-term cycle unfolded within the central time band. In the six other cases of single passes, five coincided with a cycle forming in exactly the same month. In the other case, a 22.5-month cycle crest and trough both formed — the crest occurred 2 months before the aspect, and the trough 2 months afterwards (1875-76, the first case studied). In five of the cases (56%), both troughs and crests formed within 3 months, which points to the expected volatility of this aspect. Furthermore, when this aspect occurred in a series of three passes, major "surprises" stunned the economic and political community (panics, depressions), leading to sharp market sell-offs, or "crashes" within that year. In the last example of this, a stock market crashed occurred 8 months afterwards, but in the first two cases, the "crashes" were already in process when the aspect commenced. In another case of a single passage, a 36-year cycle crest unfolded (January 1973), followed by the "Arab Embargo," which led to a severe recession in 1973-74. It was also the time U.S. President Richard Nixon resigned due to the Watergate scandal. In six of the nine cases (67%), this aspect ended a sharp decline. In four of those cases, the decline had lasted 2–5 months. Powerful rallies of 2–11 months then tended to follow. In three cases (33%), powerful rallies of 4–14 months ended with this aspect. They tended to follow with sharp declines lasting 6–24 months. In most cases, the cycle forming may not be very powerful, especially if a trough. There were four instances of 50-week cycle troughs (out of seven total), and three instances of 50-week cycle crests (out of seven total). However, there were two instances of very long-term cycle crests within 3 months of this aspect.

<u>Conclusions:</u> *The waxing square between Jupiter and Uranus has a powerful correlation to a sudden, sharp reversal in U.S. stock indices. In every case a 50-week or greater cycle culminated within 2 months, and usually within <u>the</u> month of a single passage or within the central time band of three-passage instances. When three passes occurred, it usually coincided within 1 year of an historic stock market crash. In more cases than not, the market declines into this aspect from a crest that may be 2–5 months prior. In these cases, investors can prepare to purchase stocks within the month of a single pass of this aspect, on a 50-week or greater trough. This trough may happen suddenly.*

Waxing Trine (120°)

	Dates	Long-Term Cycles
1.	Jan. 22, 1877 Aug. 3, 1877 Oct. 15, 1877	36-year cycle trough in June 1877. End of 16-month decline, and start of 15-month rally.
2.	Mar. 11, 1891	4-year cycle trough 3 months before. Probable 50-week cycle crest in April 1891. End of 4-month rally, start of 3-month decline.
3.	July 7, 1904 Oct. 9, 1904 Mar. 26, 1905	22.5-month cycle crest in April 1905, followed by 22.5-month cycle trough in May 1905. This was a very bullish period. The market was straight up.
4.	July 1, 1918	22.5-month cycle crest in October 1918, and then modest decline 4 months to 22.5-month cycle trough in February 1919. Market was very bullish.
5.	Oct. 10, 1931 Feb. 15, 1932 July 9, 1932	The end of the Great Depression bottom on July 8, 1932 - one day before last aspect! 50-week cycle low October 5, 1931, and 50-week cycle crest on November 9.
6.	Nov. 11, 1945 June 8, 1946 July 30, 1946	4-year cycle crest on May 29, 1946, followed by big 5-month decline to 4-year trough in October 1946.
7.	Jan. 8, 1960	22.5-month cycle crest on January 4. Start of 9-month decline (and end of 2-year rally).

8. Feb. 25, 1974	50-week cycle crest on March 14, 1974, which followed double bottom to 22.5-month cycle on February 12, 1974.
9. June 21, 1987 Oct. 24, 1987 Mar. 12, 1988	54-year cycle crest on August 25, 1987, followed by stock market "crash" into 54-year cycle trough on October 20, 1987. Market lost 40% in that plunge.
10. June 19, 2001	
11. Sep. 25, 2014 Mar. 3, 2015 June 22, 2015	
12. Oct. 27, 2028	

Relative Strength	**Central**	**+/- 3 months**	**Total**
All	3.69	3.50	3.83
Crest	+3.00	+3.00	+3.00
Trough	- 4.375	- 3.67	- 4.07
Consistency			
All	4.44	2.22	5.00
Crest	+3.89	+0.56	+4.44
Trough	- 2.22	- 1.67	- 3.89
C/S Index			
All	8.13	5.72	8.83
Crest	+6.89	+3.56	+7.44
Trough	- 6.60	- 5.34	- 7.96

This is a powerful signature in most cases. Unlike other Jupiter-Uranus aspects, this one has a much greater correlation to cycles greater than 50-week types. In fact, within a 3-month extended time band, a 22.5-month or greater cycle unfolded in every case. There were five cases (56%) of 4-year or greater cycle, and three cases (33%) of 36-year or greater cycles (troughs in each case, though the 1987 episode also contained a 54-year cycle crest). In the last eight cases, the signature coincided with at least a 50-week cycle crest, and usually within the same month as the aspect in a single passage, or within the central time band of a three-passage type. There were five instances of three-passage types due to retrogrades. In four of these (80%), 4-year or greater cycles unfolded. Three coincided with the end of very long-term 36-year or greater cycles. Thus it appears this aspect will usually find a cycle crest unfolding nearby (or within the central time band). But if a 4-year or greater long-term cycle trough is due, it could unfold during the central time band of a three-pass series.

<u>Conclusions</u>: The waxing trine between Jupiter and Uranus is a powerful correlate to long-term cycles in the U.S. stock market. In most cases, a 50-week or greater cycle crest will unfold within the central time band of a three-passage series, or within the month of

a single passage. However, this aspect also has historical correlations to very long-term cycle troughs that may be due (greater than 4-year types). Thus if the stock market does decline into a three-passage instance of this aspect, perhaps forming a long-term cycle trough, investors could use this time band to purchase stocks for the long-term.

Opposition (180°)

	Dates	Long-Term Cycles
1.	Sep. 22, 1837 Apr. 3, 1838 June 25, 1838	4-year cycle trough in March-April 1838. Then 30% rally to 4-year cycle crest 5 months later in September 1838.
2.	Oct. 23, 1851	4-year cycle trough in October 1851. End of 4-month decline and start of 15-month rally.
3.	Feb. 24, 1865 May 15, 1865 Nov. 28, 1865	Half-cycle trough to 18-year cycle in March 1865. End of 1 year decline and start of 8-month rally to 4-year cycle crest in November 1865. Then 7-month decline.
4.	Mar. 29, 1879 Sep. 15, 1879 Dec. 30, 1879	4-year cycle crest in January 1880. Ended 12-month rally and started 5-month decline.
5.	Apr. 30, 1893	Breakout down at this time in "Panic of 1893," which ended with 4-year cycle trough in July 1893. Decline lasted 17 months, and rally that started lasted 26 months.
6.	Aug. 24, 1906 Dec. 15, 1906 May 28, 1907	22.5-month cycle trough in July 1906. 22.5-month cycle crest in October 1906. Then the market collapsed in the "Panic of 1907" with 4-year cycle trough in November 1907
7.	Sep. 10, 1920 May 3, 1921 May 24, 1921	Double bottom to half-cycle of 18-year trough in December 1920. 50-week cycle crest 5 months later in May 1921. Then start of final 3-month decline to big trough in August 1921.
8.	Oct. 10, 1934	22.5-month cycle trough in July 1934, and double bottom to it September 17, 1934. Start of big 3-year rally.
9.	Feb. 6, 1948 June 3, 1948 Nov. 14, 1948	22.5-month cycle trough on February 11, 1948. 4-year cycle crest June 14, 1946. Double top to this crest on October 26, 1948. Prices then declined next 8 months. February 1948 low was double bottom to 4-year cycle troughs of 1946 and 1949.
10.	Mar. 14, 1962 Oct. 8, 1962 Dec. 7, 1962	Half-cycle trough to 18-year cycle on June 25, 1962. Double bottom to it on October 24, 1962. Then powerful 4-year bull market begins.

11. April 18, 1976	Double top to 4-year cycle crest on April 22, 1976. 4-year crest was on September 22, 1976. End of 6-month rally.
12. Aug. 8, 1989 Dec. 29, 1989 May 13, 1990	4-year cycle crest in July 1990, just 2 months after last pass. 22.5-month cycle crest October 10, 1989, and double top in January 3, 1990, with 22.5-month low October 16, 1989 and double bottom January 30, 1990. Final 6-month rally began.
13. Aug. 29, 2003	
14. Dec. 26, 2016 Mar. 2, 2017 Sep. 27, 2017	

Relative Strength	**Central**	**+/- 6 months**	**Total**
All	4.05	3.83	4.125
Crest	+3.36	+4.00	+3.625
Trough	- 4.06	- 3.67	- 4.05
Consistency			
All	4.16	2.50	5.00
Crest	+2.92	+1.25	+3.33
Trough	- 3.33	- 1.25	- 4.17
C/S Index			
All	8.21	6.33	9.125*
Crest	+6.28	+5.25	+6.955
Trough	- 7.39	- 4.92	- 8.22

This is a very strong signature when a time band within 6 months (even 3 months) of the aspect is allowed. For this study we went back a little further — to 1837 — as it was apparent that this was a significant correlate to long-term cycles in U.S. stock indices. In the 12 cases to date, eleven (91.7%) coincided to a 4-year or greater cycle within 6 months, or usually within the central time band in cases involving three passes, or within 3 months in the case of single passages. There were more instances of troughs than crests. In fact, in two-thirds of the instances (8 of 12), a 22.5-month or greater cycle trough unfolded within the central time band. If a 3-month orb outside the central time band was allowed, then this increased to an 83% correlation. The volatile nature of this signature was very much in evidence as five cases (42%) contained both cycle types within the central time band. These were all involving three passage instances, and since there were eight of those, one could argue that there is a 60+% probability that these cases will have a major reversal within their central time band in which both long-term cycle troughs and crests unfold .

<u>Conclusions</u>: The opposition between Jupiter and Uranus has a very high correlation to the culmination of long-term cycles in the U.S. stock indices. In most cases (83%), this will involve a long-term cycle trough of the 4-year periodicity of greater. Thus if a

22.5-month or greater cycle trough is forming during within 3 months of this aspect, investors could prepare to purchase stocks for the long-term. If instead the market is rising to a 22.5-month or greater cycle crest at this time, investors might want to stand aside and wait for a sharp decline into the following long-term cycle trough.

Waning Trine (240°)

	Dates	Long-Term Cycles
1.	May 22, 1881 Dec. 4, 1881 Feb. 8, 1882	Half-cycle crest to 18-year cycle in June 1881.
2.	July 1, 1895	4-year cycle crest, September 1895. End of 6-month rally, start of 3-month decline.
3.	Aug. 15, 1909	Half-cycle crest to 18-year cycle in November 1909, and double top to it in September 1909. End of 7-month rally and start to 8-month decline.
4.	Dec. 13, 1922 Apr. 19, 1923 Sep. 13, 1923	22.5-month cycle crest in March 1923. 7-month decline to 22.5-month cycle trough in October 1923.
5.	Dec. 27, 1936	Half-cycle crest to 18-year cycle on March 10, 1937.
6.	Apr. 26, 1950 July 20, 1950 Jan. 11, 1951	22.5-month cycle crest on June 12, 1950, then sharp decline to 22.5-month cycle trough on July 13, 1950.
7.	May 6, 1964	50-week cycle crest on May 7, 1964 — just one day after aspect! 50-week decline to 50-week cycle trough on June 9.
8.	June 17, 1978	4-year cycle trough in March 1978. Market soared into 50-week cycle crest in September 1978. There was a half-cycle (primary) crest and trough on June 6 and July 6 respectively.
9.	Nov. 11, 1991 Jan. 12, 1992 July 31, 1992	22.5-month cycle crest on June 2, 1992. This followed 50-week cycle trough on December 11, 1991.
10.	Nov. 27, 2005 May 4, 2006 Aug. 29, 2006	
11.	Dec. 15, 2019	

Relative Strength	**Central**	**+/- 4 months**	**Total**
All	3.50	4.00	3.78
Crest	+3.50	+3.67	+3.56
Trough	- 2.33	- 3.33	- 2.83
Consistency			
All	3.33	2.22	5.00
Crest	+3.33	1.67	+5.00
Trough	- 1.67	- 1.67	- 3.33
C/S Index			
All	6.83	6.22	8.78
Crest	+6.83	+5.33	+8.56
Trough	- 4.00	- 5.00	- 6.16

This signature has a definite association with crest cycles. In every case, a 50-week or greater cycle crest unfolded either during the central time band of a three-passage case, or within 3 months of a single passage. Only two of these were 50-week cycles, while three were 22.5-month crests, one was a 4-year crest, and three were half-cycle crests to the 18-year cycle. There were also six cycle troughs, but only three of which unfolded within the central time band. But in only one case was the trough longer in cycle length than the crests which unfolded (1978). There were four instances of three passages due to the retrograde factor. In the last three instances, both crests and troughs unfolded during this time band. In all cases, the crest unfolded either in the month of the aspect, or within 3 months *after* — but never before the aspect or aspect series began.

Conclusions: *The waning trine between Jupiter and Uranus has a very strong correlation to long-term cycle crests (of at least the 50-week type, but more likely the 22.5-month cycle or greater crests). Given an orb of 3 months in the case of single passes, or within the central time band of a three-passage case, these crests unfolded in every instance (100%). Investors may use this signature as a sign to go long (purchase stocks) several months before the aspect unfolds, as the market tends to time a crest within 3 months after the first contact. If instead the market is falling into this signature, then investors may want to purchase at that time. However, that happened only once involving a single passage (1978), and that trough was 3 months before the aspect. A 6-month rally followed. In three-passage cases, the trough unfolded first in one case also, and was immediately followed by a strong 6-month rally again.*

Waning Square (270°)

	Dates	**Long-Term Cycles**
1.	Nov. 5, 1841	72-year cycle trough in February 1842. Absolute low. Started 2nd great bull market run in history of U.S. stocks.
2.	Feb. 12, 1855	4-year cycle trough in December 1854.

3.	Feb. 17, 1869	4-year cycle crest in July-August 1869.
4.	June 25, 1882 Jan. 11, 1883 Mar. 2, 1883	22.5-month cycle trough in June 1882 and crest in September 1882.
5.	Aug. 14, 1896	36-year cycle trough week of August 7, 1896.
6.	Oct. 2, 1910	22.5-month cycle trough in July 1910. Probable 50-week cycle crest in October 1910.
7.	Feb. 16, 1924 Apr. 17, 1924 Oct. 23, 1924	Double bottom to 22.5-month cycle trough in May 1924. This was end of 3-month decline from primary (or greater) cycle crest in February 1924. 22.5-month trough was in October 1923.
8.	Jan. 31, 1938	4-year cycle trough in March 1938.
9.	May 29, 1951 Aug. 31, 1951 Feb. 2, 1952	22.5-month cycle crest on September 14, 1951. This followed 50-week cycle trough on June 29, and DB on May 24. Prices formed double top to 22.5-month cycle on January 23, 1952.
10.	June 8, 1965	22.5-month cycle crest on May 14, 1965, followed by sharp drop to 22.5-month cycle trough on June 29, 1965.
11.	July 29, 1979	No 50-week or greater cycles nearby. Primary cycle low in June, and primary cycle crest and end of 10+% rally on October 5, 1979 (10+% reversal down then began). Very volatile and unstable, large swings, but no cycle long-term cycle reversals.
12.	Sep. 16, 1993	4-year cycle crest in January 1994. This followed 50-week cycle trough on September 21, 1993.
13.	Jan. 22, 2007 May 10, 2007 Oct. 9, 2007	
14.	Sep. 10, 2027	

Relative Strength	**Central**	**+/- 5 months**	**Total**
All	3.19	3.58	3.54
Crest	+3.00	+3.17	+3.58
Trough	- 3.06	- 4.00	- 3.40
Consistency			
All	4.44	2.50	5.00
Crest	+1.67	+1.25	+2.50
Trough	- 4.44	- 1.25	- 4.17

C/S Index

All	7.63	6.08	8.54
Crest	+4.67	+4.42	+6.08
Trough	- 7.50	- 5.25	- 7.57

This signature has a definite preponderance towards troughs. In ten of the twelve cases studied (83%), a 50-week or greater trough unfolded either in the central time band of the three-passage instances, or within 3 months of a single passage instance. In one of the other two instances (July 29, 1979), there was a primary cycle trough a month earlier, but those are not being counted in this study. In the other instance (1869), not enough data is available to determine whether or not a 50-week cycle trough might have transpired nearby. There was a 4-year cycle crest 5 months after the aspect, so there is a possibility that this crest ended a rally that may have started from a 50-week trough 2–8 months earlier. There were only three cases in which the aspect unfolded in a series of three passes. In the first case, the market trended down into the last passage after making a crest 3 months into the central time band. In the second case, the market made a primary cycle crest on the first pass, then dropped to a 22.5-month cycle double bottom on the second pass. In the third case, the market started the first passage with a 50-week cycle low, then proceeded to rally to a 22.5-month cycle crest on the second contact, with a double top to it on the third passage. It seems, though, that its greatest use is in timing a significant trough cycle. There were two 50-week cycle troughs, four 22.5-month cycle troughs (or double bottoms to it), two 4-year cycle troughs, and two cycle troughs that were 36 years or greater in type. All of these occurred within 3 months of a single passage, or within the central time band of a three-passage square.

<u>Conclusions:</u> *The waning square between Jupiter and Uranus has a high correlation to long-term cycle troughs in the U.S. stock market (83%), within an orb of 3 months. Therefore, investors may use this signature to time the occurrence of a 50-week or greater cycle trough and plan to purchase stocks for a healthy rally that usually follows. That rally may only last 4–5 months, unless it is a 4-year type or greater. However, most of these cycles are less in duration than that.*

Waning Sextile (300°)

	Dates	Long-Term Cycles
1.	Aug. 9, 1869 Sep. 10, 1869 Mar. 14, 1870	4-year cycle crest in August 1869. 4-year cycle trough in December 1869.
2.	Aug. 12, 1883 Feb. 2, 1884 Apr. 9, 1884	22.5-month cycle crest in July 1883, followed by drop to half-cycle trough to 18-year cycle in June 1884.
3.	Oct. 12, 1897 Apr. 14, 1898 June 12, 1898	22.5-month cycle trough in March 1898. This followed 22.5-month cycle crest of September 1897.

4.	Nov. 23, 1911	4-year cycle trough in September 1911.
5.	Nov. 27, 1925	4-year cycle crest 3 months later in February 1926, followed by sharp decline to 4-year cycle trough in March 1926. November 1925 may have been a double top to 4-year crest.
6.	Mar. 4, 1939	50-week cycle trough on April 11, 1939. This ended steep plunge of 21.5% from primary cycle crest of March 10, 1939, which was point of a 10+% reversal.
7.	July 1, 1952 Oct. 19, 1952 Feb. 22, 1953	18-year cycle crest on January 5, 1953. Market began sharp 8-month decline.
8.	July 22, 1966	4-year cycle trough 3 months later in October 1966. This followed the double top to 36-year cycle crest in February 1966. Prices dropped 26.5% in those 8 months.
9.	Sep. 22, 1980	50-week cycle crest on November 19, 1980, followed by sharp decline to 50-week cycle trough on December 11, 1980.
10.	Nov. 7, 1994	4-year cycle trough on November 23, 1994 (or double bottom).
11.	Mar. 28, 2008 May 21, 2008 Nov. 13, 2008	
12.	Feb. 17, 2022	

	Central	+/- 5 months	Total
Relative Strength			
All	3.83	3.60	3.80
Crest	+3.375	+3.50	+3.44
Trough	- 3.60	- 4.255	- 3.75
Consistency			
All	3.00	3.00	5.00
Crest	+2.00	+2.00	+4.00
Trough	- 2.00	- 2.00	- 4.00
C/S Index			
All	6.83	6.60	8.80
Crest	+5.375	+5.50	+7.44
Trough	- 5.60	- 6.255	- 7.75

This signature was much stronger than expected, and certainly stronger than the waxing sextile. Within 3 months of a single passage, and within one month of the start of a three-passage type, a 50-week or greater cycle unfolded (100%) in every case. But what is most remarkable is that in seven of ten instances (70%), a 4-year or greater cycle unfolded within this time band. That makes it quite powerful. However, the cycle might just as likely be a crest as a trough, so one will have to know what type of long-term cycle is forming going into this time band. And, in the tradition of Uranus, over half the cases witnessed both types of cycles unfolding within a 5-month time band either side of the aspect (and usually less than 3 months). Thus it again can coincide with volatility and a very sharp price swing reversal.

Conclusions: Long-term cycles of 4-year or greater types tend to unfold within 3 months of Jupiter in waning sextile to Uranus (70%). These may be either crests or troughs. Investors can use this time band to identify a possible culmination of a 4-year or greater cycle that is due. If the market is rising into a 4-year or greater crest within 5 months of this aspect, then investors may wish to take profits on holdings. If instead the market drops into a 4-year or greater cycle trough in this time band, then investors may look to purchase stocks for the next long-term move. There is a 30% probability that cycles of a lesser periodicity may form close by.

Summary of Jupiter-Uranus Signatures

The following represents the ranking order of the Jupiter-Uranus signatures in terms of their correlation to long-term cycles, via this chapter's new criteria used for the Strength value. This first ranking order is based upon Total C/S values, which includes a time band of up to 7 months (usually 6 or less) outside of the aspect. In parentheses are those instances in which that particular signature correlated more times with a crests (+) or trough (-), and the respective values of each. Also included is a column indicating how many instances of 4-year or greater cycles were associated with each aspect (again, within a 7-month orb of time either side of the aspect), and the percentage of times this represents.

	Aspect	**Total**		**4-Yr or > Cycles**		
1.	Opposition	9.125*	(- 8.22)	11/12	=	91%
2.	Waxing Trine	8.83	(- 7.96)	5/9	=	56%
3.	Waning Sextile	8.80		7/10	=	70%
4.	Waning Trine	8.78	(+8.56)	5/9	=	56%
5.	Waning Square	8.54	(- 7.57)	6/12	=	50%
6.	Waxing Square	8.33		4/9	=	44%
7.	Conjunction	8.30	(+7.72)	4/10	=	40%
8.	Waxing Sextile	8.06	(- 7.71)	2/10	=	40%

In the introduction to this signature, mention was made of the possibility that these aspects could be very volatile, with extreme price swings noticed in a short amount of time. This was certainly true as a number of these signatures coincided with both troughs and crests within close proximity of their occurrence. Not only that, but in the case of the waxing square between Jupiter and Uranus, a declining stock market took on the character of a "panic" or "crash" in three instances. With the opposition, there were two instances of a financial "panic." On three occasions, the waxing trine coincided with the end of stock market crashes or economic depressions (probably because every fourth instance of this signature coincides with the 54–56 year Kondratieff wave bottom), while two other stock market crashes ended with the onset of the waning square In the case of the conjunction, the market "broke out" above resistance to score new all-time highs on six of ten occasions. So sudden reversals of very long-term cycles, or breakouts of resistance to new all-time highs, or periods of extreme price swings between cycles of intermediate-length (50-week and 22.5-month types) were all frequent under Jupiter-Uranus contacts. And most of these phenomena will occur within just 1–3 months of a single passage, or within the central time band of a three-passage case. In fact, the very long-term cycles are much more probable under a three-passage instance than a single passage type, particularly when the aspect is an opposition, waxing trine, or waning sextile.

Only the opposition, however, had a Total C/S value over 9.00, and thus in our ranking of significance, it was consistent and powerful. But not far from this level were the waxing and waning trines, as well as the waning sextile, all with values between 8.78–8.83. This is interesting for several reasons. First, the opposition was much more likely to unfold in a three-passage sequence than any of the other signatures. There were eight cases of three-passage oppositions in our studies, compared to only 2–5 for each of the other signatures. Furthermore, these three-passage incidents of the opposition corresponded to a 4-year or greater cycle in each case. This is very significant! It is also impressive that the opposition had a huge bias toward long-term cycle troughs (as opposed to crests) within a 6-month time band — and usually right within the central time band itself (sometimes the central time band correlated with the middle of a panic, and it took a few months after the time band for the market to finally bottom).

The fact that the two trines and the waning sextile had such a high correlation to long-term cycles in U.S. stock indices is also quite noteworthy. These constitute three of the four possible soft aspects between the dynamic duo of Jupiter and Uranus. One of these — the waning trine — had a very high correlation with long-term cycle crests. The conjunction also had a high correlation to crests (+7.72), while the waxing trine (-7.96), waxing sextile (-7.71), and waning square (-7.57) had a bias toward troughs.

The Jupiter-Uranus signatures also has a better than 50% correlation to 4-year or greater cycles (43 of 81 instances, or 53%). Most notable in this correlation were the opposition (83%) and waning sextile (70%). However both the trines (56% each) and the waning square (50%) also had a 50% correlation or higher. The remaining two aspects — the waxing square and conjunction — has a 44% and 40% correlation to 4-year or greater cycles respectively. Thus we can conclude that this signature has a high probability of coinciding nearby to a long-term cycle in U.S. stocks.

When the study was limited to the central time band only, the ranking order was slightly different, as shown by the following table.

	Aspect	Central Time Band		4-Yr or > Cycles
1.	Opposition	8.21	(- 7.39)	7/12 = 58%
2.	Waxing Trine	8.13		4/9 = 44%
3.	Waxing Square	7.89	(- 6.46)	2/9 = 22%
4.	Waxing Sextile	7.83	(- 7.13)	1/9 = 11%
5.	Waning Square	7.63	(- 7.50)	2/12 = 17%
6.	Waning Sextile	6.83		3/10 = 30%
6.	Waning Trine	6.83	(+6.83)	2/9 = 22%
8.	Conjunction	6.75		2/10 = 20%

The major difference is that the waxing square and waxing sextile become more consistent signatures to intermediate-term cycles within its central time band. Still, the opposition and waxing trine are the two most powerful correlations. They are the only two signatures with C/S values of over 8.00. Furthermore, the opposition was the only aspect that had a correlation of over 50% to 4-year or greater cycles within its central time band. The waxing trine (44%) was the only other aspect with a frequency over 30%. In all, the Jupiter-Uranus signatures had a 28.4% correlation to 4-year or greater cycles within their central time band, which is not very reliable.

Conclusions of Jupiter-Uranus Signatures: *Investors can expect sudden events and market turns to unfold near the time of a Jupiter-Uranus aspect. In many cases, like the waxing square and opposition, the economy may enter a panic, or the stock market may crash. In other instances, like the waning square or waxing trine, a crash or "Panic" may come to an end, and the market commences a new long-term bull market. But in most cases, the U.S. stock market undergoes very wide price swings in the 3-month period surrounding a Jupiter-Uranus aspect — or within its central time band in the case of three-passage instances. These cycles will be at least the 50-week types, and usually even 22.5-month cycle types. However, in the case of oppositions and trines (and even waning sextiles), they are apt to be stronger — the 4-year or greater types. The strongest correlation to long-term cycles is with the opposition, if given a 7-month expanded time band, or even if only the central time band was used. This will usually coincide with a long-term cycle trough, and hence investors may look to purchase stocks for the long haul under this time band. The waning trine has a very reliable correlation to long-term cycle crests, and investors may use this time band as an opportunity to cash in on long-term profits, given an orb of only 3 months. Investors may also use this knowledge to position themselves from the long side on dips that occur well before this 3-month time band of the waning trine.*

JUPITER/NEPTUNE SIGNATURES

This should be another interesting study, as these two planets (13-year cycle) have much in common in terms of the collective psychological dynamics. Both are hopeful by nature, positive and optimistic. One would think that the stock market would rise when these two planets are in aspect. However, the rise may get out of hand, for Neptune's nature is also delusional, or one of a "wishful thinking" type. Combined with Jupiter's quality of exaggeration, Neptune's propensity towards idealism and trust can be rather dangerous. Once the glamour wears off, once reality sinks in, stock markets could take a long ride southwards — especially if a long-term Saturn transit follows. These two planets, by the way, co-rule oil. Hence oil-related stocks may move sharply when Jupiter and Neptune aspect one another.

Conjunction (0°)

	Dates	Long-Term Cycles
1.	Feb. 25, 1869	4-year cycle crest in July-August 1869.
2.	June 18, 1881	18-year cycle crest in June 1881.
3.	June 1, 1894	22.5-month cycle crest in August 1894. prices then dropped to 22.5-month cycle trough in March 1895.
4.	May 22, 1907	This was the month the "Panic of 1907" began. Prices fell hard starting that month, all the way to half-cycle trough of 18-year cycle in November 1907.
5.	Sep. 23, 1919 Mar. 8, 1920 Apr. 24, 1920	Half-cycle crest to 18-year cycle in October 1919. Market began 22-month plunge in which it lost half its value.
6.	Sep. 18, 1932	50-week cycle crest on September 8, 1932. This followed 72-year cycle and Great Depression bottom of July 8, 1932.
7.	Sep. 22, 1945	Double bottom to 4-year cycle on July 27, 1945. Prices started soaring into and beyond this aspect, all the way to May 1946.
8.	Sep. 24, 1958	50-week cycle crest October 14, 1958. 2-week decline was very minimal. This was very bullish time.
9.	Feb. 1, 1971 May 21, 1971 Sep. 16, 1971	22.5-month cycle crest on April 28, 1971. Prices then began 7-month decline into 22.5-month cycle trough on November 23, 1971.
10.	Jan. 19, 1984	Double top to 22.5-month cycle on January 10, 1984. Prices then started a 6-month decline.

11. Jan. 9, 1997 — 50-week cycle crest on March 11, 1997. Prices dropped sharply for 1 month into 50-week trough in April 1997.

12. May 27, 2009
July 10, 2009
Dec. 21, 2009

13. Apr. 12, 2022

	Central	+/- 6 months	Total
Relative Strength			
All	3.75	3.21	3.64
Crest	+3.50	+2.75	+3.17
Trough	- 5.00	- 3.83	- 4.125
Consistency			
All	3.00	3.18	5.00
Crest	+2.50	+1.82	+4.09
Trough	- 0.50	- 1.36	- 1.82
C/S Index			
All	6.75	6.39	8.64
Crest	+6.00	+4.57	+7.26
Trough	- 5.55	- 5.19	- 5.95

Given a 6-month orb, an intermediate or long-term cycle unfolded in every case. In nine of eleven cases (82%), this cycle unfolded within 2 months of the conjunction, or within the central time band in a three-passage case. Also nine of these instances correlated with 50-week or greater cycle crests (82%), compared to less than 50% coinciding with troughs. These crests usually unfold in the same month as — or after — the aspect. If it is a three-passage type, then it unfolds after the first passage. The last four instances of this aspect have correlated with only the intermediate-term type of cycles — 50-week and 22.5-month types. However, they have occurred very close in time to the aspect (within 2 months), and all have been crests. After these crests, prices typically decline 6–7 months to next long-term cycle trough — although in two cases the decline lasted less than 1 month, and in another case it lasted 22 months. In the two instances in which the aspect unfolded in a series of three contacts, a 22.5-month or greater cycle crest occurred 1–2 months after the first passage, then began a 7–22 month decline.

<u>Conclusions</u>: *As expected, the Jupiter conjunct Neptune aspect correlated mostly with bullish periods. 82% of the time a long-term cycle crest unfolded with this conjunction — and usually in the month of the aspect or afterward (not before). There were only two instances of troughs alone, and one instance where the more dominant longer-term cycle nearby was a trough (1932 low — which was 2 months before the transit). Investors may thus use this time band for identifying potential intermediate-term crests in the U.S. stock market. As such, they may wish to buy dips prior to this aspect's time band. That is, look to be long on cycle troughs that precede the conjunction a few months. Perhaps going into the aspect investors may look to cash in on some profitable long positions.*

Waxing Sextile (60°)

	Dates	Long-Term Cycles
1.	Aug. 9, 1883	22.5-month cycle crest in July 1883.
2.	Aug. 10, 1896	36-year cycle trough, in first week of August 1896.
3.	Aug. 17, 1909	Double top to half-cycle of 18-year cycle in September 1909. Prices fell hard into July 1910 (for 8 months).
4.	Dec. 18, 1921 Apr. 10, 1922 Aug. 18, 1922	50-week cycle crest in October 1922. This was end of rally that started from half-cycle trough to 18-year cycle in August 1921.
5.	Dec. 19, 1934	50-week cycle crest on February 19, 1935, and double top to it on January 7, 1935. Decline only last one month. This was very bullish time for the market.
6.	Dec. 21, 1947	22.5-month cycle trough on February 11, 1948. Start of 4-month rally. There was a double top to 22.5-month cycle in October 1947.
7.	Dec. 15, 1960	22.5-month cycle trough October 25, 1960. Market was very bullish, on way up to half-cycle crest of 18-year cycle in November 1961.
8.	Apr. 2, 1973 Aug. 19, 1973 Nov. 22, 1973	36-year cycle crest unfolded January 11, 1973. This was the beginning stages to the great "Arab Oil Embargo" crisis that precipitated a the severe recession of 1973-74. Also coincided with Nixon's Watergate scandal. 22.5-month cycle trough on August 22, 1973, and 22.5-month cycle crest on October 29, 1973.
9.	Mar. 16, 1986	22.5-month cycle crest on July 2, 1986. Market was very bullish during this period.
10.	Feb. 26, 1999	
11.	June 8, 2011	
12.	May 23, 2024	

Relative Strength	Central	+/- 4 months	Total
All	3.80	3.42	3.78
Crest	+3.67	+2.90	+3.21
Trough	- 3.67	- 4.00	- 3.80

Consistency			
All	2.77	3.33	5.00
Crest	+1.67	+2.78	+3.89
Trough	- 1.67	- 1.11	- 2.78
C/S Index			
All	6.57	6.75	8.78
Crest	+5.34	+5.68	+7.10
Trough	- 5.34	- 5.11	- 6.58

Very seldom did cycles unfold right near this aspect. At the exact time of this aspect, stock prices were usually soaring, on their way to some sort of cycle crest. Yet the aspect is fairly strong, because within about 4 months, a longer-term cycle usually did unfold. In fact, in four of these cases (44%), the cycles were greater than 4-year types, and usually 3–4 months before. However even when these signatures correlated with a long-term cycle trough, it sometimes was short-lived. In two-thirds of the cases, the market was in the middle of a strong wave upwards. There were two instances of three-passage sextiles. In both cases the very long-term dominant cycle unfolded 3–4 months *before* the series began. The market trended strongly during the series. It is interesting to note that in the last five instances, the Total C/S value would only be 8.20, which is not too strong.

<u>Conclusions</u>: *Intermediate or long-term cycles in U.S. stocks tend to happen within 4 months of the waxing sextile between Jupiter and Neptune. If the market is bullish, it will usually continue bullish through and beyond this aspect. In those cases, investors might use this as an indicator that a bull market will continue until at least this aspect unfolds — and usually a couple months later. However, it is difficult to tell if this aspect is bullish in all cases, and one might be best advised to take a pulse of the collective mood at the time. If it is positive, then prices will continue soaring. But if it is pessimistic, then uncertainty can bring prices down. Despite this aspect's high C/S value in the extended time band, it doesn't seem to be a reliable indicator in forecasting future prices, due to the fact that so few significant cycles unfolded within the central time band.*

Waxing Square (90°)

	Dates	**Long-Term Cycles**
1.	Sep. 12, 1884	Half-cycle trough to 18-year cycle in June 1884.
2.	Sep. 21, 1897	22.5-month cycle crest in September 1897. Prices then dropped next 6 months to trough.
3.	Oct. 2, 1910	Primary cycle crest in October, but dominant cycle was the 22.5-month cycle trough 3 months earlier in July 1910.
4.	Jan. 29, 1923 Apr. 24, 1923 Oct. 7, 1923	22.5-month cycle crest in March 1923, and then 7-month decline to 22.5-month cycle trough in October 1923.

5.	Jan. 24, 1936 July 26, 1936 Sep. 19, 1936	22.5-month cycle crest on April 6, 1936, and 22.5-month cycle trough on April 30, 1936. Decline was 13%.
6.	Jan. 21, 1949	4-year cycle trough 5 months later, June 1949.
7.	Jan. 12, 1962	4-year cycle crest on November 15, 1961, followed by 7-month decline of nearly 30% to 4-year trough on June 25, 1962.
8.	Apr. 19, 1974 Oct. 27, 1974 Dec. 1, 1974	Right in the midst of the "Arab Oil Embargo" recession. 36-year cycle trough was on December 9, 1974, with a double bottom on October 4, 1974. It ended with this last pass.
9.	Apr. 4, 1987	54-year cycle crest on August 25, 1987, followed by crash into October 1987. In early April there was a primary cycle crest.
10.	July 21, 1999 Oct. 11, 1999 Mar. 16, 2000	
11.	June 25, 2012	
12.	June 18, 2025	

Relative Strength	**Central**	**+/- 6 months**	**Total**
All	3.50	4.20	3.89
Crest	+3.00	+4.50	+3.60
Trough	- 3.67	- 4.20	- 4.00
Consistency			
All	2.22	2.78	5.00
Crest	+1.67	+1.11	+2.78
Trough	- 1.67	- 2.78	- 4.44
C/S Index			
All	5.72	6.98	8.89
Crest	+4.67	+5.61	+6.38
Trough	- 5.34	- 6.98	- 8.44

The waxing square has a definite correlation more to troughs than crests. In eight of these nine cases studied (89%), a 22.5-month or greater cycle trough unfolded within 6 months. Three of these were greater then 4-year cycle types, and two were 4-year cycle troughs, and three more were 22.5-month troughs. When it was bad, it was real bad, and the plunge usually lasted a couple of months beyond the aspect (or last aspect of a series). However, there were a fair number of crests also going into this aspect, and sometimes carrying through until slightly afterwards. There were three instances in which the aspect occurred in a series of three contacts. In each case, the market fell hard into the middle, and towards end, of this series. In two cases there were crests right after the first passage. In the last example, 1974, the Arab Oil Embargo was in full force, plus the nation was reeling from the resignation of President Richard Nixon. There had been a violation of trust, and the investment community was not only confused, but shocked and stunned.

<u>Conclusions</u>: *Jupiter in waxing square to Neptune can correlate to a very uncertain market climate. This can — and has — led to a collective hysteria in which prices have fallen hard in some cases. This aspect has a very high correlation to long-term cycle troughs forming within 6 months, and usually after the aspect has passed. Investors would be well advised to wait for that long-term cycle trough surrounding this aspect, as an opportunity to purchase stocks for the long-term. The cycle should be at least a 22.5-month type.*

Waxing Trine (120°)

	Dates	Long-Term Cycles
1.	Oct. 10, 1872 Mar. 2, 1873 June 27, 1873	Double top to 36-year cycle crest in January, March, and May of 1873. prices then dropped to 4-year cycle trough in November 1873.
2.	Oct. 19, 1885	22.5-month cycle crest in February 1886. Decline lasted 3 months.
3.	Oct. 31, 1898	50-week cycle trough in October 1898. End of 2-month decline and then continuation of rally for 6 months.
4.	Nov. 11, 1911	4-year cycle trough 2 months earlier in September 1911.
5.	Mar. 4, 1924 May 14, 1924 Nov. 14, 1924	Double bottom to 22.5-month cycle trough in May 1924. Market was in process of huge bull market run.
6.	Feb. 21, 1937 Aug. 25, 1937 Oct. 26, 1937	Half-cycle crest of 18-year cycle on March 10, 1937. 50-week cycle trough June 17, 1937. Double top to March crest on August 16, 1937. Then huge decline into April 1938 (loss of 50% from market top in August).
7.	Feb. 15, 1950	22.5-month cycle crest on June 12, 1950. Sharp 1-month decline to 22.5-month cycle trough on July 13, 1950.
8.	June 2, 1962 Aug. 6, 1962 Feb. 2, 1963	Half-cycle trough to 18-year cycle on June 25, 1962. Double bottom to this on October 24, 1962. Then the market sky-rocketed up for 3 years.
9.	May 4, 1975	50-week cycle crest on July 15, 1975. This followed 36-year cycle trough on December 9, 1974.

10. Apr. 22, 1988	50-week cycle crest on June 22, 1988. End of first recovery rally following the October 1987 stock market crash.
11. July 27, 2000 Dec. 9, 2000 Apr. 5, 2001	
12. July 17, 2013	
13. July 20, 2026	

Relative Strength	**Central**	**+/- 6 months**	**Total**
All	3.36	4.00	3.95
Crest	+3.50	+3.00	+3.33
Trough	- 2.875	- 4.50	- 3.69
Consistency			
All	3.50	3.00	5.00
Crest	+2.00	+1.00	+3.00
Trough	- 2.00	- 2.00	- 4.00
C/S Index			
All	6.86	7.00	8.95
Crest	+5.50	+4.00	+6.33
Trough	- 4.875	- 6.50	- 7.69

Given a 6-month orb from the single passage incidents, this is a fairly strong signature correlating with long-term cycles in the U.S. stock market — especially troughs. In five cases (50%), cycles greater than 4-year periodicities were present. Four of these occurred in the last five instances, and in the last three cases, they were troughs. However, in the last two instances, these long-term cycle troughs were not the cycle closest to the aspect — they occurred 5 and 6 months prior to the aspect. A smaller cycle crest (50-week cycle crest in each case) was closer to the aspect. There were four occurrences of three-passage signatures. In each case, the dominant cycle unfolded within the central time band, and usually the strongest type was right around the second pass. However, on two occasions, that was a double bottom or top to the greater cycle which unfolded also close to the first passage. Of these aspects, 90% coincided with a cycle trough within 6 months before through 4 months after the single passage instances (or within the central time band, if a three-passage series).

<u>Conclusions</u>: *The waxing trine between Jupiter and Neptune has an 80% correlation to a cycle trough of at least the 50-week cycle type, given an orb of 6 months. However, within the central time band (usually within 2 months), it is just as likely to be a crest, but of a smaller degree. Therefore investors can use this aspect as an indicator to outline a time band for a significant cycle trough, within 6 months, and therefore prepare to purchase stocks on that trough. If it involves a three-passage series, then investors may look for that trough to form within the central time band.*

Opposition (180°)

	Dates	Long-Term Cycles
1.	Dec. 27, 1874 Mar. 25, 1875 Sep. 20, 1875	50-week cycle crest in April-May 1875, followed by 22.5-month cycle trough in October 1875.
2.	Jan. 1, 1888 June 1, 1888 Sep. 25, 1888	4-year cycle trough in March-April 1888. 50-week cycle crest in October 1888.
3.	Jan. 7, 1901	This was 4 months following 4-year cycle trough in September 1900, and 5 months prior to 4-year cycle crest in June 1901.
4.	Jan. 9, 1914	22.5-month cycle crest in February-March 1914. Market sold off to 18-year cycle trough in December 1914.
5.	Apr. 17, 1926 Aug. 2, 1926 Jan. 2, 1927	22.5-month cycle trough in March-April 1926.
6.	Apr. 2, 1939	50-week cycle trough on April 11, 1939. Double top to 4-year cycle crest in September 1939.
7.	Mar. 21, 1952	22.5-month cycle trough on May 1, 1952.
8.	June 18, 1964 Dec. 3, 1964 Feb. 28, 1965	50-week cycle trough on June 9, 1964. Market soared upwards for next 11 months, to crest in May 1965.
9.	June 8, 1977	In middle of a steep decline between 22.5-month cycle crest in January 1977 and 4-year cycle trough in March 1978.
10.	Oct. 1, 1989 Nov. 14, 1989 June 6, 1990	22.5-month cycle crest and trough in October 1989. 4-year cycle crest culminated 1 month after, in July 1990.
11.	Sep. 11, 2002 Feb. 16, 2003 June 2, 2003	
12.	Sep. 17, 2015	

Relative Strength	Central	+/- 5 months	Total
All	2.77	3.625	3.25
Crest	+2.75	+3.83	+3.25
Trough	- 2.83	- 3.50	- 3.00

Consistency			
All	4.50	2.00	5.00
Crest	+2.00	+1.50	+3.00
Trough	- 3.00	- 1.00	- 4.00
C/S Index			
All	7.27	5.625	8.25
Crest	+4.75	+5.33	+6.25
Trough	- 5.83	- 4.50	- 7.00

This is one of the weaker signatures we have seen thus far. There were no instances of a cycle greater than 4 years, and only one of those in a central time band (and two others, but 4–5 months past the single passage instances or 1 month past a central time band involving a series of three passes). If a 4-month time band is allowed, then this signature had a strong bias towards troughs (80%). But once again, these were not necessarily strong — only two 4-year cycles, four 22.5-month cycles, and two 50-week cycles. There were five instances of a three-passage series. In each case the market formed a trough — usually close to the beginning (although once it was 1 month afterwards), and in all but one case it was followed by very powerful rallies.

Conclusions: *The Jupiter opposite Neptune aspect is a rather weak signature. At best it seems to correlate with cycle troughs (80%). Thus investors may use this to time a 50-week or greater low in the stock market as an opportunity to buy stocks, given an orb up to 4 months involving a single passage. Sometimes this trough is the result of a very sharp but short-lived decline. If the aspect forms in a series of three passes, and prices decline to form a trough close to the first pass (usually in the same month), then investors may look to purchase stocks during that time.*

Waning Trine (240°)

	Dates	Long-Term Cycles
1.	Nov. 23, 1877	36-year cycle trough in June 1877.
2.	Mar. 4, 1890 Aug. 5, 1890 Nov. 14, 1890	36-year cycle crest in May 1890. Very sharp 7-month decline followed to 4-year cycle trough in December 1890.
3.	Feb. 24, 1903	22.5-month cycle crest in February 1903, then severe drop as "Rich Man's Panic" takes hold to 4-year trough in November.
4.	Feb. 15, 1916	22.5-month cycle crest in December 1915, followed by 22.5-month cycle trough in April 1916.
5.	May 18, 1928 Dec. 2, 1928 Jan. 12, 1929	Possible 50-week cycle crest in May 1928, followed by corrective 1-month decline. In middle of huge bull market. It didn't really stop it.

6.	May 5, 1941	50-week cycle trough on May 1, 1941. Market rallied two months to 50-week cycle crest on July 22, 1941.
7.	Aug. 19, 1953 Nov. 16, 1953 Apr. 26, 1954	18-year cycle trough on September 15, 1953. Huge bull market then began, first thrust lasting 3 years.
8.	Aug. 2, 1966	4-year cycle trough on October 10, 1966, and double bottom to it on August 30, 1966. End of huge 8-month decline.
9.	Aug. 3, 1979	Double top to 22.5-month cycle crest on October 5, 1979.
10.	Aug. 9, 1992	22.5-month cycle trough on October 5, 1992. This followed the 22.5-month cycle crest of June 2, 1992.
11.	Nov. 29, 2004	
12.	Dec. 2, 2017	

Relative Strength	**Central**	**+/- 5 months**	**Total**
All	3.36	3.67	3.50
Crest	+3.25	+3.00	+2.83
Trough	- 3.50	- 3.80	- 3.71
Consistency			
All	3.50	3.00	5.00
Crest	+2.00	+1.00	+3.00
Trough	- 1.50	- 2.50	- 3.50
C/S Index			
All	6.86	6.67	8.50
Crest	+5.25	+4.00	+5.83
Trough	- 5.00	- 6.300	- 7.21

This is a fairly reliable signature. In nine of the last ten cases (90%), a long-term cycle unfolded within 2 months of this waning trine aspect between Jupiter and Neptune. The cycles were usually of the 22.5-month type, and almost equally dispersed between troughs and crests. There were only three instances of cycles greater than the 4-year type, and two were very long-term cycle troughs. There was also two instances of a 4-year cycle trough. The rest were 22.5-month and 50-week cycle types. Seven of these ten cases involved only a single passage of the aspect. In six of those cases, the cycle unfolded within 2 months. Five of these involved crests, five involved troughs, and two saw both types unfolding — each type within that two-month span around the aspect.

<u>Conclusions</u>: *The waning trine between Jupiter and Neptune is a rather benign signature. Intermediate-term cycles of both types may unfold within 2 months of a single passage of this aspect, or within the central time band of a three-passage series. If the market declines into this time band, investors may use it as an opportunity to purchase stocks for the longer-term.*

Waning Square (270°)

	Dates	Long-Term Cycles
1.	Dec. 16, 1878	22.5-month cycle trough in January 1879. End of 4-month decline from 22.5-month cycle crest in September 1878.
2.	Mar. 27, 1891 Oct. 14, 1891 Nov. 9, 1891	50-week cycle crest in April 1891, and 50-week cycle trough 3 months later in July 1891.
3.	Mar. 14, 1904	March was secondary low to 4-year cycle trough of November 1903 (end of "Rich Man's Panic").
4.	July 7, 1916 Sep. 20, 1916 Feb. 27, 1917	4-year cycle crest in November 1916, followed by decline to 22.5-month cycle trough in February 1917.
5.	June 7, 1929	72-year cycle crest on September 3, 1929. Start of Great Depression and stock market crash.
6.	May 28, 1942	Secondary low preceding great bull market on April 28–29, 1942.
7.	Sep. 17, 1954 Dec. 23, 1954 May 21, 1955	50-week cycle crest on October 7, 1954, followed by 50-week trough on November 1, 1954. Decline was modest — it was a very bullish market throughout this aspect.
8.	Sep. 6, 1967 Apr. 9, 1968 Apr. 20, 1968	22.5-month cycle crest on September 26, 1967, followed by 14% decline to 22.5-month cycle trough on March 22, 1968.
9.	Sep. 9, 1980	Double bottom to 4-year cycle trough on March 27, 1980, followed by 38% rise to 50-week cycle crest on November 19, 1980. It was a very bullish period around this aspect.
10.	Sep. 17, 1993	50-week cycle trough on September 21, 1993, followed by 4-month rally to 4-year cycle crest on January 31, 1994.
11.	Jan. 27, 2006 Mar. 16, 2006 Sep. 24, 2006	

Relative Strength	Central	+/- 6 months	Total
All	3.25	3.75	3.60
Crest	+3.20	+3.67	+3.375
Trough	- 2.86	- 3.75	- 3.055

Consistency			
All	4.00	2.00	5.00
Crest	+2.50	+1.50	+4.00
Trough	- 3.50	- 1.00	- 4.50
C/S Index			
All	7.25	5.75	8.60
Crest	+5.70	+5.17	+7.375
Trough	- 6.16	- 4.75	- 7.555

The waning square oftentimes produced both types of cycles — crests and troughs — within a 6-month time band of the aspect occurrence. This happened seven times (70%). It happened 40% of the time within the central time band — which was every time the aspect unfolded in a series of three contacts. In each of those four instances of three passes, the first cycle was a crest, the second was a trough. Usually the crest unfolded within 1 month (after) the first pass. There were three (30%) instances of 4-year or greater cycles unfolding within the central time band (or within three months of single passage). When extended out to 6 months, there were six (60%) cases of a 4-year or greater cycle (four crests and two troughs).

Conclusions: *The waning square of Jupiter and Neptune is a rather volatile signature. In 70% of cases, both a cycle crest and trough unfolded within 6 months of a single passage or within the central time band of a three-passage series. In fact, in a three-passage series, every instance so far has coincided with a crest first, followed by a cycle trough 1–6 months afterwards, but still within the central time band. In these cases, investors may plan to purchase stocks a few months before the three-passage series begins, and either sell with the first crest that forms early in the series, or plan to add on 1–6 months after that crest when another trough unfolds before the series ends. Otherwise, long-term investors may simply use the time band of this aspect to purchase stocks should a 50-week or greater trough form within 4 months. Usually it will not be greater than a 4-year cycle trough. Only once was it necessary to completely unload long-term holdings due to a crest greater than the 4-year type— in the 1929 instance.*

Waning Sextile (300°)

	Dates	Long-Term Cycles
1.	May 24, 1879 July 24, 1879 Jan. 2, 1880	4-year cycle crest in January 1880. 5-month decline to 4-year cycle trough followed.
2.	Apr. 15, 1892	4-year cycle crest in March 1892. 16-month decline to 36-year cycle trough followed.
3.	Apr. 1, 1905	22.5-month cycle crest unfolded in April 1905. 22-month cycle trough followed one month later, in May 1905.

4.	July 22, 1917 Nov. 24, 1917 Mar. 11, 1918	22.5-month cycle crest in June 1917, at start of this aspect series, then 34% decline to 4-year cycle trough in December 1917 (WW1).
5.	July 3, 1930	4-year cycle crest on April 16, 1930. This was in midst of Great Depression. Prices continued to fall for 2 years.
6.	June 27, 1943	22.5-month cycle crest on July 15, 1943. Market then fell 4 months.
7.	Nov. 2, 1955 Jan. 14, 1956 June 24, 1956	22.5-month cycle trough on October 11, 1955, followed by 21% rally to 22.5-month cycle crest on April 9, 1956, followed by 2-month decline to 50-week low on June 8, 1956.
8.	Oct. 20, 1968 Apr. 15, 1969 June 12, 1969	4-year cycle crest on December 13, 1968, followed by 3-month decline to 50-week cycle trough on February 25–26, 1969. This was followed by rally to 50-week cycle crest on May 14, 1969.
9.	Oct. 23, 1981	50-week cycle trough on September 28, 1981, followed by 3-month rally to 50-week cycle crest on December 11, 1981. Then 8-month decline to 4-year trough.
10.	Oct. 28, 1994	Market tested 4-year cycle crest in September and October, 1994, then fell hard to 4-year cycle trough on November 23, 1994.
11.	Oct. 29, 2007	
12.	Feb. 20, 2020 July 27, 2020 Oct. 12, 2020	

Relative Strength	**Central**	**+/- 5 months**	**Total**
All	3.44	3.25	3.50
Crest	+3.50	+3.00	+3.35
Trough	- 3.00	- 4.00	- 3.14
Consistency			
All	4.50	2.00	5.00
Crest	+3.50	+1.50	+5.00
Trough	- 3.00	- 0.50	- 3.50
C/S Index			
All	7.94	5.25	8.50
Crest	+7.00	+4.50	+8.35
Trough	- 6.00	- 4.50	- 6.64

This was an unexpectedly very reliable signature. In every case a 50-week or greater cycle crest unfolded, either during the central time band, or 1 month before the three-passage series began, or within 3 months of a single passage of the aspect. Once these crests unfolded, a 2–8 month decline would usually follow, although once it lasted only 1 month, and three times it lasted 16–24 months. In six of the ten cases (60%), the cycle was at least a 4-year type. Four of these (40%) were crests. In fact, only one of the crests was the 50-week type — all were 22.5-month or stronger crests. The troughs, however, were usually 50-week or 22.5-month types, except in two instances where they were 4-year cycles. There were four cases of a three-passage series due to the retrograde of Jupiter. In the last three cases, the market made a crest first, followed by a 2–6 month decline into a trough before the last contact of the series. The market then rallied strongly. In 5 of the 6 cases of single passes, the crest formed 1–3 months *before* the aspect (83%). In the sixth case, it unfolded 6 weeks after the aspect.

Conclusions: *The waning sextile between Jupiter and Neptune has a very high correlation to long-term cycle crests (usually 22.5-month or greater) within the central time band of a three-passage series, or within 3 months (usually before) of a single passage. The declines which follow from this crest are usually mild if within the three-passage types. Therefore, investors may use this signature to time rising markets, and plan to be long going into it (or at least be long in plenty of time going into a period that starts up to 3 months before the aspect commences). If the market makes a cycle trough nearby, plan to purchase stocks for the next bull run up. But that's only if the market has come down to form a cycle trough within 1 month of the aspect, or during a three-passage series. Otherwise, investors may use this time band to exit from some long-term profitable holdings on the crest that is likely to form just prior to (or very slightly after) the aspect.*

Summary of Jupiter-Neptune Signatures

The following represents the ranking order of the Jupiter-Neptune signatures in terms of their correlation to long-term cycles, via this chapter's new criteria used for the Strength value. This first ranking order is based upon Total C/S values, which includes a time band of up to 6 months (usually less) outside of the aspect. In parentheses are those instances in which that particular signature correlated more times with a crests (+) or trough (-), and the respective C/S values of each. Also included is a column indicating how many instances of 4-year or greater cycles were associated with each aspect (again, within a 6-month orb of time either side of the aspect), and the percentage of times this represents. Of greatest interest will be those aspects which have a frequency of 50% or more to these long-term cycles.

	Aspect	Total		4-Yr or > Cycles		
1.	Waxing Trine	8.95	(- 7.89)	6/10	=	60%
2.	Waxing Square	8.89	(- 8.44)	5/9	=	55%
3.	Waxing Sextile	8.78	(+7.10)	4/9	=	44%

4. Conjunction	8.64	(+7.26)	5/11 =	45%
5. Waning Square	8.60		6/10 =	60%
6. Waning Sextile	8.50	(+8.35)	6/10 =	60%
6. Waning Trine	8.50	(- 7.21)	4/10 =	40%
8. Opposition	8.25	(- 7.00)	3/10 =	30%

As one can see, no signature achieved the significant C/S level of 9.00 or greater. However, seven of the eight aspects achieved a respectable level of 8.50-8.95 in their Total C/S value summaries. Interestingly enough, the highest Total C/S values belonged to the conjunction and all the waxing aspects. The four weakest belonged to the opposition and all the waning aspects. However, that ranking symmetry disappeared when only the C/S values of the central time band were used.

Nearly one-half (38) of these 79 instances of Jupiter-Neptune aspects correlated with 4-year or greater cycles within an extended time band of six months (49.4%). The strongest of these correlations were the waxing trine, waning square, and waning sextile, which each had a 60% frequency. Only half as consistent in this correlation was the opposition (30%), which in fact was the weakest correlation of all eight aspects studied.

Also noteworthy in their correlation to cycle troughs and crests were the waxing square, which had a -8.44 Total C/S trough value, and the waning sextile, with a Total C/S crest value of +8.35 respectively. Other signatures showing a bias towards troughs were the waxing trine (-7.89), waning trine (-7.21), and opposition (-7.00). Those with a bias more toward crests included the conjunction (+7.26) and the waxing sextile (+7.10).

When the study was limited to the central time band only, the ranking order was different, as shown by the following table.

Aspect	**Central Time Band**		**4-Yr or > Cycles**	
1. Waning Sextile	7.94	(+7.00)	5/10 =	50%
2. Opposition	7.27		1/10 =	10%
3. Waning Square	7.25	(- 6.16)	3/10 =	30%
4. Waxing Trine	6.86		3/10 =	30%
4. Waning Trine	6.86		2/10 =	20%
6. Conjunction	6.75	(+6.00)	3/11 =	27%
7. Waxing Sextile	6.57		2/9 =	22%
8. Waxing Square	5.72		1/9 =	11%

In this central time band, only three signatures achieved a C/S level of 7.00: the waning sextile (7.94), opposition (7.27) and waning square (7.25). All others were below 7.00, and the waxing square was the lowest at a very weak score of 5.72. The weakness of strong cycles unfolding within the central time band is also apparent in the fact that only

20 of the 78 (25.3%) cases coincided with a 4-year cycle or greater. Only one aspect — the waning sextile — had a central time band correlation of 50% to 4-year or greater cycles. There were no others with a frequency greater than 30%. Thus it seems that the central time band might relate more with intermediate-term cycles, and not with longer-term cycles. The longer-term cycles are more apt to occur when a 6-month orb outside of the central time band is allowed. This lack of strong correlation may be due to the fact that the majority of aspects between Jupiter and Neptune are only single passage types. Slightly less than two-thirds (52 of 79) of these aspects fit this phenomenon. Therefore, unlike a three-passage instance, a single contact case will have a far smaller central time band in which a cycle might unfold. If the study was limited to just the 27 cases of central time bands comprised of three-passage contacts, the correlation to 4-year or greater cycles increases to 44.44% (12 instances coincide with 4-year or greater cycles).

Conclusions: *Unless longer-term planetary cycles are present, or longer-term market cycles are in fact due, investors are best advised to use the Jupiter-Neptune signature as outlining a time band in which a 22.5-month or 50-week cycle is most likely to transpire. If a 6-month orb is allowed, then there is about a 50% probability that a 4-year or greater cycle will unfold. But for long-term investors, this time band may be more useful as an opportunity to add onto — or make new purchases for — one's long-term stock portfolio. Nevertheless, there were a couple of noteworthy aspect findings here. First, significant crests tend to be more likely to unfold with the waning sextile aspect, whereas troughs are more likely with the waxing square aspect. Second, in a single passage of a Jupiter-Neptune aspect, the likelihood of a 4-year or greater cycle unfolding is very small (about 15%). However, in three-passage instances, the probabilities increase to nearly 45%. This supports the astrological tenet that retrograde zones (central time bands of three-passage instances) will represent times in which the dynamics of that signature are more evident in mundane (world) events.*

JUPITER-PLUTO SIGNATURES

Unlike the previous two signatures, Jupiter and Pluto have little in common according to astrological understanding. Pluto corresponds to the dynamic of termination, endings, and transformation — even rebirth. When it is present in most aspects, there is either news — or the threat — of danger and destruction, whether natural or human-induced. Pluto brings about obsolescence and the need to reform, rebuild, repair, or re-do. Jupiter, on the other hand, is concerned with growth and going forward. Pluto has to look back and recognize its mistakes, or correct or heal them. Jupiter's energy would just as soon overlook such trivial matters and press onward and upward.

So what happens when these two dynamics come together in an aspect? It's the tug-of-war between the forces of progress at any cost versus the forces that want the inequities and mistakes removed or corrected first before moving forward. The result can be very threatening rhetoric. In terms of the market, the effect depends upon whether these forces are focused upon economic matters. If the economy needs to be re-vamped, it could be treacherous. If the infrastructure (like roads, bridges, etc.) need to be repaired, it could be a boon to the economy. If mother nature strikes and destroys vital properties and business districts, it could also be devastating; but those cases are usually locally contained.

This planetary pair cycle lasts 12–13 years, which makes it the shortest one so far to be examined. Therefore we would expect more cases of single-passage instances.

Conjunction (0°)

	Dates	Long-Term Cycles
1.	July 26, 1869 Oct. 29, 1869 Mar. 4, 1870	4-year cycle crest in July-August 1869, followed by 5-month, 19% decline into 4-year cycle trough in December 1869.
2.	Apr. 12, 1882	22.5-month cycle trough in June 1882, followed by 3-month rally to 22.5-month cycle crest in September 1882.
3.	May 18, 1894	Double top to 22.5-month cycle crest in April-May 1894. 3–4 month decline followed.
4.	June 26, 1906	22.5-month cycle trough in July 1906. End of 6-month decline. 4-year crest in January 1906.
5.	Aug. 10, 1918	22.5-month cycle crest in October 1918. 4-month decline then started.
6.	May 26, 1931	50-week cycle crest on February 24, 1931. Primary cycle trough on June 2 was part of a 10% filtered wave. 22.5-month cycle trough unfolded in October 1931.
7.	Aug. 1, 1943	22.5-month cycle crest on July 15, 1943. 4-month decline to 22.5-month cycle trough in November 1945 followed.
8.	Nov. 2, 1955 Feb. 7, 1956 June 16, 1956	22.5-month cycle trough on October 11, 1955, followed by 4-year cycle crest on April 9, 1956, followed by 50-week cycle trough on June 8, 1956.
9.	Oct. 13, 1968	4-year cycle crest in December 1968.
10.	Nov. 2, 1981	50-week cycle trough on September 28, 1981, and 50-week cycle crest on December 1, 1981. Assassination of Egyptian President Anwar Sadat.
11.	Dec. 2, 1994	4-year cycle trough on November 23, 1994. Default on Orange County (California) Municipal bonds shook the market's confidence.

12. Dec. 11, 2007

13. Apr. 4, 2020
    June 30, 2020
    Nov. 12, 2020

Relative Strength	**Central**	**+/- 5 months**	**Total**
All	3.06	3.14	3.32
Crest	+3.10	+3.20	+3.15
Trough	- 3.00	- 2.92	- 3.125
Consistency			
All	3.64	3.18	5.00
Crest	+2.27	+2.27	+4.55
Trough	- 2.73	-1.36	- 3.64
C/S Index			
All	6.70	6.32	8.32
Crest	+5.37	+5.47	+7.70
Trough	- 5.73	- 4.28	- 6.76

Given an orb of only 2 months, this is a fairly reliable signature corresponding to intermediate-term cycles in U.S. stocks. In every case, at least a 50-week cycle unfolded within 2 months, and usually less. There were more crests (10) than troughs (8), and the following move tended to last about 3-5 months. Given an extended orb of 5 months, there were 5 of 11 cases which contained a 4-year cycle or greater (45%), and two of those occurred in the only two instances of three-passage aspects that transpired. Four of these five were crests (there were two troughs, as one instance had both types nearby).

<u>Conclusions:</u> *The conjunction of Jupiter and Pluto is a fairly reliable signature for intermediate-term cycles in U.S. stocks. However, if the conjunction unfolds in a series of three passes due to retrogradation, then it tends to correspond with a longer-term cycle — like a 4-year cycle type. In both historical cases, a 4-year cycle crest unfolded within the central time band of a three-passage conjunction. In fact, there were four cases of 4-year or greater cycle crests given an orb of 5 months. Therefore, investors may use the conjunction to time the selling of stocks — if in fact the market appears to be rising to a 4-year or greater cycle crest during this time frame. In all other cases, investors can simply use the 2-month orb surrounding a single passage of this conjunction to buy stocks if a 50-week or 22.5-month cycle trough appears to be forming.*

Waxing Sextile (60°)

Dates & Position	**Long-Term Cycles**
1. Oct. 3, 1883 Jan. 21, 1884 May 26, 1884	Half-cycle trough to 18-year cycle unfolded in June 1884.

2.	July 10, 1896	36-year cycle trough unfolded in first week of August 1896.
3.	Aug. 22, 1908	50-week cycle crest in November 1908. A slight 3-month decline then commenced. Not very impressive.
4.	Oct. 8, 1920	Double bottom to half-cycle trough of 18-year cycle in December 1920.
5.	Dec. 21, 1932 Feb. 7, 1933 Aug. 9, 1933	50-week cycle trough on February 27, 1933, followed by double top to 22.5-month cycle crest on July 18, 1933. Market then dropped next 3 months. 72-year cycle trough unfolded just 5 months before first passage of this aspect.
6.	Oct. 18, 1945	22.5-month cycle trough on July 27, 1945. Market was going vertical (straight up) at time of aspect. Topped out in late May 1946 (7 months later and just outside our extended time band).
7.	Feb. 4, 1958 Mar. 14, 1958 Sep. 22, 1958	No cycles in central time band. Market was basing between December 1957 through April 1958, following 4-year low in October 1957. Then it soared upwards into January 1960.
8.	Jan. 12, 1971 July 4, 1971 Aug. 31, 1971	22.5-month cycle crest on April 28, 1971. Prices then declined next 7 months.
9.	Jan. 29, 1984	Double top to 22.5-month cycle crest on January 10, 1984. Then big decline for next 6 months.
10.	Feb. 13, 1997	50-week cycle crest on March 11, 1997. 11.7% decline to 50-week cycle trough on April 14 followed.
11.	Feb. 6, 2010	
12.	May 3, 2022	

Relative Strength	**Central**	**+/- 5 months**	**Total**
All	3.29	3.50	3.60
Crest	+2.50	+2.00	+2.40
Trough	- 3.75	- 3.875	- 4.07
Consistency			
All	3.50	2.50	5.00
Crest	+2.00	+0.50	+2.50
Trough	- 2.00	- 2.00	- 3.50
C/S Index			
All	6.79	6.00	8.60
Crest	+4.50	+2.50	+4.90
Trough	- 5.75	- 5.875	- 7.57

This signature is surprisingly more powerful than expected. Given a 5-month orb, there were five cases (50%) correlating with long-term cycles in U.S. stocks. However, none of these last eight instances found such a cycle unfolding in the central time band. In the cases of single passages, the corresponding cycle (if it occurred) usually fell 1–3 months *after* the aspect. Neither crests nor troughs occurred with any regularity over the other during the central time band, but the troughs were stronger (longer) in cycle length. Using a 5-month time band, however, the correspondence with long-term cycles increased markedly. The correlation with long-term cycles was 75% in the four cases of three-passage types, given the 5-month extended time band.

<u>Conclusions</u>: *The waxing sextile aspect between Jupiter and Pluto appears to be a more reliable correlation to long-term cycles in U.S. stocks than one would expect. In some cases the market would form a crest just afterwards, followed by a sizable 1–6 month decline. In other cases, it would form a significant long-term cycle trough nearby to the aspect. Given a 5-month extended time band, investors may be alert to a possible 4-year or greater cycle trough forming. If so, they can use that trough as an opportunity to purchase stocks for the long term.*

Waxing Square (90°)

	Dates & Position	Long-Term Cycles
1.	Sep. 17, 1872	Double top to 36-year cycle crest in January 1873.
2.	Oct. 28, 1884 Feb. 24, 1885 July 1, 1885	Double bottom to "Panic of 1884" trough (June 1884) in January 1885 (1/2-cycle trough to 18-year cycle).
3.	Aug. 15, 1897	22.5-month cycle crest in September 1897. Began 6-month decline.
4.	Sep. 27, 1909	Half-cycle crest to 18-year cycle in November 1909. Double top to this crest in September 1909.
5.	Nov. 12, 1921 June 7, 1922 June 20, 1922	Straight up during this time, following half-cycle trough to 18-year cycle in August 1921, 3 months before aspect series.
6.	Feb. 5, 1934 Feb. 20, 1934 Sep. 20, 1934	22.5-month cycle crest on February 5, 1934, followed by sharp drop to 22.5-month cycle trough on July 26, 1934.
7.	Nov. 26, 1946	4-year cycle trough on October 30, 1946.
8.	Nov. 3, 1959	22.5-month cycle trough on September 22, 1959, and 22.5-month cycle crest on January 4, 1960. Market then fell next 9 months.

9.	Feb. 15, 1972 July 25, 1972 Oct. 18, 1972	50-week cycle crest on May 30, 1972, followed by drop to 50-week cycle trough on July 18, 1972. Market then soared to 36-year cycle crest on January 11, 1973, and then recession commenced into late 1974.
10.	Feb. 27, 1985	No longer-term cycles. Primary cycle crest unfolded at this time, but it was in between 22.5-month cycle low of July 1984 and 50-week crest of July 1985.
11.	Mar. 9, 1998	No longer-term cycles in central time band, but 4-year crest unfolded 4 months later, on July 17, 1998.
12.	July 24, 2010 Aug. 3, 2010 Feb. 25, 2011	
13.	May 17, 2023	

Relative Strength	**Central**	**+/- 4 months**	**Total**
All	3.29	4.50	4.20
Crest	+3.25	+4.25	+4.00
Trough	- 3.00	- 5.00	- 3.57
Consistency			
All	3.18	2.73	4.55
Crest	+1.82	+1.82	+3.18
Trough	- 2.27	- 0.91	- 3.18
C/S Index			
All	6.47	7.23	8.75
Crest	+5.07	+6.07	+7.18
Trough	- 5.27	- 5.91	- 6.75

This is a strange aspect. In seven of eleven cases (64%), a long-term cycle (4-year or greater type) unfolded within an extended time band of 4 months outside of the aspect (or aspect series). In fact, five of these (45% of total) were greater than 4-year cycles. This is quite a high frequency for this type of Jupiter transit (compared to Jupiter-Neptune and other Jupiter-Pluto aspects). However, within the central time band itself, only twice did anything greater than a 22.5-month cycle unfold. As might be expected, some of these cycles either started or ended very major financial declines (washouts). Remember: Pluto pertains to destruction and the need to restructure, so in a square aspect one might anticipate a severe threat to the economic or financial community. There were panics and depressions with this aspect — sometimes. Other times, there was nothing noteworthy to the financial community. The stock market trend just continued uninterrupted. Thus this signature is unpredictable: it may coincide with a very severe decline (or end one), or it may be nothing. There were four cases of three-passage instances of this aspect. In three cases, very long-term cycles unfolded within 4 months before or after this series. The fourth case was during the Great Depression, so the cycles were already pretty battered.

When the aspect correlates with a market-sensitive event, it is big. But it isn't always a market or economic-oriented event, in which case, nothing happens.

Conclusions: *The waxing square between Jupiter and Pluto has the potential to end and/or begin long-term cycles in the U.S. stock market. It is especially dangerous if the market is making a long-term cycle crest within 4 months of this aspect, for it could suddenly end and a huge decline commence. But there are also instances of long-term declines ending nearby to this same signature, and just as peculiarly, there are also instances where nothing major happens in terms of the stock market. Nevertheless investors need to be very cautious around the time of the waxing square between Jupiter and Pluto. If the market has been trending up into a possible long-term cycle crest within 4 months, investors may wish to sell stocks and stand aside. If instead the market has been mired in a decline for several months going into this aspect, investors may wish to start purchasing stocks that have promise of a recovery — again within 5 months of this aspect. This is especially the case when the aspect unfolds with three passes.*

Waxing Trine (120°)

	Dates & Position	Long-Term Cycles
1.	Oct. 17, 1873	4-year cycle trough in November 1873, followed by half-cycle crest to 18-year cycle in February 1874.
2.	Nov. 29, 1885 Mar. 19, 1886 Aug. 9, 1886	22.5-month cycle crest in February 1886, followed by 3-month decline to 22.5-month cycle trough in May 1886. This was followed by run to 4-year cycle crest in December 1886.
3.	Sep. 20, 1898	50-week cycle crest in August 1898, followed by 2-month decline to 50-week cycle trough in November 1898. A 4-year cycle crest occurred in April 1899, seven months after the aspect, and thus outside of normal 6-month time band.
4.	Oct. 31, 1910	Double top to 22.5-month cycle crest in October 1910. This followed the 22.5-month cycle trough of July 1910.
5.	Dec. 16, 1922 June 9, 1923 Aug. 20, 1923	22.5-month cycle crest in March 1923. Prices then declined 7 months to 22.5-month cycle trough in October 1923.
6.	Oct. 27, 1935	No major cycle close by. Closest is 22.5-month cycle crest on April 6, 1936, followed by 22.5-month trough on April 30. Market was bullish. There was a primary low in October 1935.
7.	Dec. 29, 1947	22.5-month cycle trough on February 11, 1948. Market then rallied to 4-year crest 4 months later in June 1948.

8. Dec. 5, 1960	22.5-month cycle trough on October 25, 1960. Market then rallied for next 13 months.
9. Mar. 11, 1973 Sep. 2, 1973 Nov. 16, 1973	Series began 2 months after 36-year cycle crest on January 11, 1973. Prices then fell 7 months to 22.5-month cycle trough on August 22, 1973, then rallied to 22.5-month cycle crest on October 29, 1973 before falling hard into December 5, 1973.
10. Mar. 21, 1986	22.5-month cycle crest on July 2, 1986, followed by sharp decline to 22.5-month cycle trough on August 4, 1986. Market was very bullish during aspect.
11. Mar. 29, 1999	
12. July 7, 2011 Oct. 28, 2011 Mar. 12, 2012	
13. June 2, 2024	

Relative Strength	**Central**	**+/- 6 months**	**Total**
All	2.94	3.78	3.70
Crest	+2.70	+4.00	+3.72
Trough	- 3.00	- 3.00	- 3.00
Consistency			
All	4.50	4.50	5.00
Crest	+2.50	+3.50	+4.50
Trough	- 3.00	- 1.50	- 4.50
C/S Index			
All	7.44	8.28	8.70
Crest	+5.20	+7.50	+8.22
Trough	- 6.00	- 4.50	- 7.50

This is yet another interesting Jupiter-Pluto signature. Within 6 months, it coincided with an intermediate-term cycle in all cases. In a couple of cases, though, it unfolded in between long-term cycles that occurred 6–7 months away. Yet in most cases (80%) it coincided with 22.5-month or greater cycles given an extended orb of only 4 months. Given a 7-month orb, there were five cases of a 4-year or greater cycle (50%). But within the central time band itself, there was only one instance of a four-year cycle, and that was in 1873, the first case used in this study. There were five instances of 22.5-month cycles, Thus the central time band seems mostly to coincide with 22.5-month cycles. Given an orb of 6 months, there were eight instances of both troughs and crests (80%). Thus this signature indicates a period of sharp swings in price in a relatively short amount of time. There were three cases of a three-passage series, and each time a 22.5-month or greater cycle crest was followed by 22.5-month or greater cycle trough, given an orb of 2 months before or after the aspects of this series.

<u>Conclusions:</u> The waxing trine between Jupiter and Pluto correlates with a volatile time band. Both cycle troughs and crests are present nearby, and in the case of a three-passage series, both unfold (usually crest first followed by trough). This aspect has a high correspondence to cycles of the 22.5-month periodicity. If the market is declining into what appears to be a 22.5-month cycle trough, it may provide an opportunity to buy stocks on that low for the next leg up.

Opposition (180°)

	Dates & Position	Long-Term Cycles
1.	Oct. 11, 1851	4-year cycle trough in October 1851.
2.	Nov. 15, 1863	4-year cycle crest in March 1864.
3.	Dec. 21, 1875 June 15, 1876 Aug. 29, 1876	22.5-month cycle crest in February 1876.
4.	Feb. 3, 1888 May 1, 1888 Oct. 15, 1888	4-year cycle trough March-April 1888.
5.	Nov. 22, 1900	4-year cycle trough in September 1900,
6.	Dec. 28, 1912	4-year cycle crest in September 1912. Big decline into June 1913 (22.5-month cycle trough).
7.	Feb. 9, 1925 Aug. 11, 1925 Oct. 15, 1925	50-week cycle trough in March 1925, but bigger cycle was the 4-year cycle crest in February 1926, followed by 4-year cycle trough in March 1926. But it was after central time band.
8.	Apr. 22, 1937 May 29, 1937 Dec. 18, 1937	50-week cycle trough on June 17, 1937, followed by double top to 4-year cycle on August 16, 1937, after which prices fell nearly 50% to 4-year trough in March 1938.
9.	Feb. 13, 1950	22.5-month cycle crest on June 12, 1950, followed by 1-month decline to 22.5-month cycle trough on July 20, 1950. Market was rising strongly around time of aspect.
10.	May 4, 1962 Aug. 18, 1962 Jan. 15, 1963	Half-cycle trough to 18-year cycle on June 25, 1962. Double bottom to it on October 24, 1962. Then huge bull market started for next 3 years.
11.	Apr. 18, 1975	36-year cycle trough on December 9, 1974. 50-week cycle crest on July 15, 1975.

12. Apr. 27, 1988	50-week cycle crest on June 22, 1988. But bigger cycle was 54-year cycle trough ("crash") on October 20, 1987.
13. Sep. 4, 2000 Oct. 13, 2000 May 6, 2001	Possible long-term cycle trough within 6 months of the first contact (and usually only 2 months). Crest is also likely within central time band, or up to 4 months after last contact.
14. Aug. 7, 2013 Jan. 31, 2014 Apr. 20, 2014	
15. July 20, 2026	

Relative Strength	**Central**	**+/- 6 months**	**Total**
All	3.50	4.00	4.08
Crest	+3.25	+3.17	+3.19
Trough	- 3.40	- 4.67	- 4.17
Consistency			
All	2.50	4.00	5.00
Crest	+1.00	+2.50	+3.50
Trough	- 2.00	- 3.00	- 4.00
C/S Index			
All	6.00	8.00	9.08*
Crest	+4.25	+5.67	+6.69
Trough	- 5.40	- 7.67	- 8.17

This is another very interesting signature. There was not much consistency within the central time band, but with an extended orb of 6 months (and usually only 4 or less), very significant long-term cycles of at least a 22.5-month periodicity unfolded in every case. Given this orb, there were nine of twelve instances in which a 4-year or greater cycle occurred (75%), and given a 6-month orb, there was yet another (the 54-year cycle trough of October 1987). Within the central time band, though, there were only three such long-term cycles (25%). However there were another four instances (33%) in which no cycles of note unfolded within the central time band. The last two instances (1975 and 1988) saw two very long-term cycle troughs (36-year and 54-year) unfold 4 and 6 months before the aspect respectively. Both of these were devastating lows, the result of powerful sell-offs in the U.S. stock market. The instance before that witnessed a half-cycle trough to the 18-year cycle low. Thus when this aspect occurs, there is the potential for great losses — which also means there is a potential to purchase stocks very cheaply after a tremendous decline culminates. There were five instances of a three-passage series of this aspect. In the last four cases, a significant trough unfolded during this central time band — within 2 months after the first passage.

<u>Conclusions</u>: The Jupiter opposition to Pluto aspect is potentially a very powerful correlate to long-term cycles in the U.S. stock market. In many cases a huge market

decline ends within 6 months. There were also several cases in which a 4-year or greater cycle crest coincided around this aspect (usually within 4 months afterwards). Thus it doesn't have a bias as to crests or troughs, but it does seem to time either the beginning or end of a substantial market decline. Therefore, if the market has been rallying into this time band into what looks like a 4-year or greater cycle crest, investors might want to cash in on profits and stand aside for the decline. On the other hand, if the market has taken a beating and fallen substantially into this time band (into a 4-year or greater cycle trough), then investors might want to begin purchasing stocks at these greatly reduced values for the long term. You will have to let the market tell you which strategy to adopt when it gets to that time band.

Waning Trine (240°)

	Dates & Position	Long-Term Cycles
1.	Feb. 11, 1878	No cycles very nearby. Closest was 36-year cycle trough in June 1877 and 22.5-month crest in September 1878.
2.	Mar. 21, 1890 July 27, 1890 Nov. 22, 1890	18-year cycle crest in May 1890, followed by sharp decline to 4-year cycle trough in December 1890.
3.	Dec. 31, 1902	22.5-month cycle trough in December 1902. Prices rallied only 2 months to 22.5-month cycle crest in February 1903, "Rich Man's Panic" commenced.
4.	Feb. 5, 1915	18-year cycle trough in December 1914.
5.	Mar. 17, 1927	No cycles very close by. Closest was 4-year cycle low 1-year before, and 22.5-month cycle crest in September 1927.
6.	May 8, 1939 Oct. 5, 1939 Jan. 8, 1940	22.5-month cycle crest on September 13, 1939. End of 5-month rally, and start of 9-month decline.
7.	Mar. 15, 1952	Double top to 4-year cycle crest on May 1, 1952. End of 8-month decline, start of 7-month rally.
8.	May 31, 1964 Dec. 30, 1964 Jan. 14, 1965	50-week cycle trough on June 9, 1964, followed by 22.5-month cycle crest on May 14, 1965. This was very bullish.
9.	May 26, 1977	Closest intermediate-term cycle is 22.5-month cycle crest on January 3, 1977. Market was in midst of 26-month decline to 4-year cycle trough in March, 1978.
10.	June 13, 1990	4-year cycle crest on July 17, 1990. Started 3-month decline to 4-year cycle trough in October, 1990.

11. Oct. 27, 2002
    Dec. 18, 2002
    July 1, 2003

12. Oct. 11, 2015
    Mar. 16, 2016
    June 26, 2016

13. Sep. 24, 2028

Relative Strength	Central	+/- 7 months	Total
All	3.64	3.17	3.55
Crest	+3.875	+3.00	+3.39
Trough	- 3.50	- 4.00	- 3.60
Consistency			
All	3.50	3.00	5.00
Crest	+2.00	+2.50	+4.50
Trough	- 2.00	- 0.50	- 2.50
C/S Index			
All	7.14	6.17	8.55
Crest	+5.875	+5.50	+7.89
Trough	- 5.50	- 4.50	- 6.10

The figures above are somewhat unreliable. That is because in two instances (1878 and 1927), we stretched our normal criteria by 1-2 months in order to include a cycle, otherwise there would be none. If we exclude these two cases, then the Total C/S value for "All" drops to only 6.95. Like other Jupiter-Pluto signatures, this one is also somewhat unpredictable. There were two cases of 18-year cycles, and two cases of 4-year cycles, unfolding within the central time band. But there were also two instances in which no long- or intermediate-term cycles unfolded within six months of the aspect. The other cycles were mostly 22.5-month types, except one instance of a 50-week cycle. Thus if a cycle falls nearby to this waning trine, it will tend to be fairly strong — at least a 22.5-month type. But sometimes no cycles unfold that close to the aspect. In both cases of no cycles, the market was extremely bullish, having completed a 4-year or greater trough at least 8 months before. In the eight cases that coincided with an intermediate or longer-term cycle, seven were crests — and all were 22.5-month or greater types. There were three instances of a three-passage series of this aspect. Two contained a dominant long-term crest in the central time band. The other contained a 50-week trough within 1 month of the first passage, then bullish through the remainder of the time band — and beyond.

<u>Conclusions</u>: *The waning trine of Jupiter to Pluto tends to coincide more with crests than troughs, or is very bullish before and after the aspect unfolds (in a single passage). Sometimes no cycles culminate here, but rather the market just rises. If a 22.5-month cycle crest is due, this signature may time it within 4 months. But otherwise it may not be very useful to investors.*

Waning Square (270°)

	Dates & Position	Long-Term Cycles
1.	Mar. 1, 1879	22.5-month cycle trough in January 1879
2.	Apr. 4, 1891 Oct. 17, 1891 Nov. 10, 1891	50-week cycle crest in April 1891 and 50-week trough in July 1891. There was also a 4-year cycle trough 4 months earlier in December 1890, followed by a 4-year cycle crest four months after the series, in March 1892.
3.	May 18, 1903 Aug. 25, 1903 Jan. 9, 1904	4-year cycle trough in November 1903. Part of the "Rich Man's Panic" of 1903. 22.5-month cycle crest three months before first contact, in February 1903.
4.	Feb. 18, 1916	22.5-month cycle crest in December 1915, and 22.5-month cycle trough in April 1916.
5.	Mar. 30, 1928	50-week cycle trough in February 1928 and crest of same one month earlier in January - but the decline was minimal in the face of a great bull market "blow off."
6.	May 20, 1940	22.5-month cycle low on May 21, 28, and June 10, 1940.
7.	Mar. 30, 1953	18-year cycle crest on January 5, 1953. Market then began 7-month decline to 18-year trough in September 1953.
8.	June 21, 1965	22-month cycle trough on June 29, 1965, followed 22.5-month cycle crest on May 14, 1965.
9.	June 22, 1978	4-year cycle trough on March 1, 1978. Market soared next 6 months to 50-week crest on September 11, 1978.
10.	July 16, 1991	Double bottom to 50-week cycle on August 19, 1991 (the "Gorbachev Kidnapping" caper). 50-week cycle crest on October 18, 1991, followed by sharp 2-month decline.
11.	Aug. 6, 2004	
12.	Nov. 24, 2016 Mar. 30, 2017 Aug. 4, 2017	

Relative Strength	Central	+/- 6 months	Total
All	2.69	3.50	3.25
Crest	+2.50	+3.00	+3.67
Trough	- 2.69	- 4.33	- 3.25

Consistency			
All	4.00	3.00	5.00
Crest	+1.00	+2.50	+3.00
Trough	- 4.00	- 1.50	- 5.00
C/S Index			
All	6.69	6.50	8.25
Crest	+3.50	+5.50	+6.67
Trough	- 6.69	- 5.83	- 8.25

Although this aspect did not coincide with as many powerful long-term cycles as previous instances of Jupiter and Pluto signatures, it was more consistent. In every case a 50-week or greater cycle trough unfolded within just 6 months, and usually just 3 months, of the aspect. However, there was only one instance of a cycle greater than a 4-year, and only one 4-year cycle type within the central time band (two other 4-year cycles unfolded within 4 months). Three of the occasions could only produce a 50-week cycle in the central time band and four coincided with a 22.5-month type. So the cycles were generally weaker than usual, but at least they happened. The waning square was not so disastrous as might be expected — at least not as often as the opposition (another hard aspect). In nine of the ten cases studied (90%), a cycle trough occurred within 3 months, and usually 2. There were also instances of crests unfolding — 6, or 60% — but these were usually outside of the central time band and not the dominant cycle. There were only two cases of three-passage series types, and in each instance a trough formed. In one case, it was the bottom ending the Panic of 1903, which was the only instance of great apprehension financially (although the 1991 instance coincided with the bizarre kidnapping of Russian President Mikhail Gorbachev).

<u>Conclusions</u>: *The waning square between Jupiter and Pluto has more of a bias toward intermediate-term troughs (50-week and 22.5-month types) within an orb of 2 months in single passage instances. Therefore investors may use this time band to purchase stocks on that trough if the market is in fact declining into what looks like a 50-week or 22.5-month cycle low.*

Waning Sextile (60°)

	Dates & Position	**Long-Term Cycles**
1.	Mar. 15, 1880	4-year cycle crest in January 1880, followed by sharp 4-month decline to 4-year cycle trough in May 1880.
2.	Apr. 16, 1892	4-year cycle crest in March 1892.
3.	May 24, 1904 Nov. 23, 1904 Dec. 26, 1904	22.5-month cycle crest in April 1905, followed the 4-year cycle low of November 1903. Market was straight up bullish in 1904 after the Panic of 1903.

4.	July 20, 1916 Sep. 19, 1916 Feb. 26, 1917	4-year cycle crest in November 1916, followed by decline to 22-month cycle trough in February 1917.
5.	Apr. 14, 1929	Possible 50-week cycle trough in March 1929, but bigger cycle of course was 72-year cycle crest on September 3, 1929.
6.	June 6, 1941	50-week cycle trough on May 1, 1941, and 50-week cycle crest on July 22, 1941.
7.	Aug. 31, 1953 Nov. 14, 1953 Apr. 16, 1954	18-year cycle trough on September 15, 1953. Market just exploded into a new bull market after this — record highs.
8.	July 20, 1966	4-year cycle trough on October 10, 1966. Double bottom was on August 30, 1966. Market then exploded upwards.
9.	July 28, 1979	Closest cycle is a primary cycle crest on October 5, 1979. This ended and began a 10+% reversal
10.	Aug. 26, 1992	22.5-month cycle trough on October 5, 1992. Market then exploded upwards.
11.	Sep. 17, 2005	
12.	Jan. 15, 2018 Apr. 14, 2018 Sep. 12, 2018	

Relative Strength	**Central**	**+/- 6 months**	**Total**
All	4.00	3.67	3.65
Crest	+3.30	+3.50	+3.36
Trough	- 3.08	- 4.00	- 3.375
Consistency			
All	4.00	1.50	5.00
Crest	+2.50	+1.00	+3.50
Trough	- 3.00	- 1.50	- 4.00
C/S Index			
All	8.00	5.17	8.65
Crest	+5.80	+4.50	+6.86
Trough	- 6.08	- 5.50	- 7.375

This was an unexpectedly consistent and rather powerful correlate to long-term cycles in U.S. stock indices. It did require an extension of 6 months on a three-passage series, though, to get these values. If that instance in 1903-04 was removed (since no intermediate or longer-term cycles unfolded within the central time band), the Total C/S value would have dropped to 8.33. But that is still fairly high compared to what one would expect for a waning sextile. Both the extended time band and the central time band had a slightly higher correlation with trough cycles than crests. In fact, there was an 80% probability that an intermediate or longer-term cycle trough would unfold within 6 months of this sextile. There was a 70% probability it would unfold within 2 months of a single passage or within the central time band of a three-passage series. But what is most interesting is that in seven cases (70%), a four-year or greater cycle unfolded within this 6-month time band. The three-passage series were more significant than single passage instances, only in the fact that they correlated with 4-year or greater cycles within 6 months in all three instances.

Conclusions: The waning sextile between Jupiter and Pluto tends to correlate with an intermediate or longer-term cycle trough (80%). However, there is also a 70% correlation to 4-year or greater cycles of both types within a 6-month orb of this aspect. Therefore, investors can use this signature to identify possible long-term cycles (4-year or greater) that may be due within a 6-month period surrounding it. If it is a 4-year or greater trough, then of course, investors should prepare to purchase stocks in that event. Usually this trough will be at least a 22.5-month type, and usually it will unfold within only 2 months of the aspect, which usually is a single passage type.

Summary of Jupiter-Pluto Signatures

The following represents the ranking order of the Jupiter-Pluto signatures in terms of their correlation to long-term cycles, via this chapter's new criteria used for the Strength value. This first ranking order is based upon Total C/S values, which includes a time band of up to 7 months (usually less) outside of the aspect. In parentheses are those instances in which that particular signature correlated more times with a crests (+) or trough (-), and the respective C/S values of each. Also included is a column indicating how many instances of 4-year or greater cycles were associated with each aspect (again, within a 7-month orb of time either side of the aspect), and the percentage of times this represents. Of greatest interest will be those aspects which have a frequency of 50% or more to these long-term cycles.

	Aspect	Total		4-Yr or > Cycles		
1.	Opposition	9.08*	(- 8.17)	10/12	=	83%
2.	Waxing Square	8.75		7/11	=	64%
3.	Waxing Trine	8.70	(+8.22)	5/10	=	50%
4.	Waning Sextile	8.65		7/10	=	70%
5.	Waxing Sextile	8.60	(- 7.57)	5/10	=	50%
6.	Waning Trine	8.55	(+7.89)	3/10	=	30%
7.	Conjunction	8.32	(+7.70)	5/11	=	45%
8.	Waning Square	8.25	(- 8.25)	4/10	=	40%

As one can see, only one signature achieved the significant C/S level of 9.00 or greater: the opposition aspect. All the others were between 8.25-8.75, which is fairly strong. In fact, the waxing square, waxing trine, and waning sextile all achieved a respectable level of 8.60-8.75 in their Total C/S value summaries. It is interesting to note that two of the hard aspects (the opposition and waxing square) were the two most significant in value, as well as most frequent in their association with 4-year or greater cycles, along with the waning sextile.

The opposition had by far the strongest correlation to longer-term cycles. In 10 of 12 cases (83%), a four-year or greater cycle unfolded within six months of a contact. The waning sextile (70%), waxing square (64%), waxing trine (50%), and waxing sextile (50%) also coincided with 4-year or greater cycles in at least half of their occurrences, which supports their importance in this study. In fact, 46 of the total field of 84 instances (55%) coincided with 4-year or greater cycles, which is more than observed in the Jupiter-Neptune signatures. However if only the hard aspects were used, then the frequency increased to 59.1% (26 of 44 cases).

As to the correlation of cycle types, the waning square (-8.25), opposition (-8.17), and waning sextile (-7.57) had a greater bias to cycle troughs than crests. The waxing (+8.22) and waning trine (+7.89), plus the conjunction (+7.70) coincided with crests more than troughs.

When the study was limited to the central time band only, the ranking order was different, as shown by the following table.

	Aspect	**Central Time Band**		**4-Yr or > Cycles**		
1.	Waning Sextile	8.00		4/10	=	40%
2.	Waxing Trine	7.44		1/10	=	10%
3.	Waning Trine	7.14		3/10	=	30%
4.	Waxing Sextile	6.79	(-5.75)	2/10	=	20%
5.	Conjunction	6.70		3/11	=	27%
6.	Waning Square	6.69	(- 6.69)	1/10	=	10%
7.	Waxing Square	6.47		1/11	=	09%
8.	Opposition	6.00		3/12	=	25%

The opposition — which was so strong using an extended six-month time band — now drops from first to last place, from a Total C/S value of 9.08 to a central time band C/S Value of only 6.00. This means that very large, long-term cycles are more likely to unfold *outside* of the central time band of the opposition (more than 6 weeks away). However, within the central time band itself, the waning is the most prominent aspect — the only one with a C/S value of at least 8.00. Two others had values exceeding 7.00, while all the others fell lower.

There were no aspects that had a 50% or greater correlation to 4-year or greater cycles within their central time band. The most consistent correlation to cycles of this strength was the waning sextile, which had a 40% frequency rate. The only other aspects which coincided at least three times with 4-year or greater cycles within their central time band were the conjunction, opposition, and waning trine. The waxing square, waxing trine, and waning square recorded only one instance each of a 4-year or greater cycle in this central time band. One other point of interest in regards to the central time band studies: the waning square and waxing sextile were the only aspects with a bias toward a cycle type. Both correlated more frequently to troughs than crests.

<u>Conclusions</u>: *Jupiter-Pluto aspects have a strong correlation to long-term or intermediate-term cycles in U.S. stock indices. The most noteworthy aspect is the opposition, if using a 6-month orb. All in all, these signatures have a greater correlation to 4-year or greater cycles than either the Jupiter-Uranus or Jupiter-Neptune signatures, given an extended orb of 7 months, although much less in most cases.*

CHAPTER EIGHT

THE "THIRTY-SOMETHING" PLANETARY PAIR CYCLES RE-VISITED

In the last chapter on the intermediate-term planetary cycles, a different weighting criteria was applied than that used for the longer-term planetary pair cycles of Chapters Five and Six. The reason for this was obvious, as verified by the actual result of these studies: the aspects of Jupiter to Uranus, Neptune, and Pluto correlated more with intermediate-term stock market cycles, while those of Saturn, Uranus, Neptune, and Pluto to one another (as well as Jupiter to Saturn) correlated more with long-term market cycles. To have applied the longer-term planetary pair cycles criteria of Chapters Five and Six, to the Jupiter aspects examined in Chapter Seven, would have resulted in very low C/S values, for there were many cases in which no cycles of at least a 22.5-month periodicity were present.

However, it is possible to apply the weighting criteria of the previous chapter to the longer-term planetary pair cycles of Saturn and beyond. Of course, the results will yield even higher C/S values than those reported in Chapters Five and Six, which were already quite significant. Nevertheless, in an effort to present a standard weighting guide that would be consistent with all geocosmic signatures studied in this volume, this chapter will examine the Strength and Consistency Values to the longer-term planetary cycles using the same criteria applied to the intermediate-term planetary pair cycles of Chapter Seven.

The results on the following pages will not repeat the listing of dates of aspects between Saturn, Uranus, Neptune, and Pluto. Nor will these results review the behavior of the market that unfolded during each aspect, or the conclusions that were summarized at the end of each signature. Those factors will not change, and for a review, the reader may simply turn back the pages to each signature. This section will simply re-calculate the Strength, Consistency, and C/S values for each signature based upon the modified weighting criteria set forth in Chapter Seven. The aspects of Uranus, Neptune, and Pluto will not be examined further in this chapter. It will be assumed that they are the most powerful correlates to long-term cycles in the U.S. stock market on the basis of results reported in Chapter 5. We already know that these planetary pair cycles occur infrequently. We already know that many of these aspects — like those between Neptune and Pluto and even Uranus to Neptune — have only unfolded once in the 200+ year history of the U.S. stock market. Most of the others have only unfolded twice. Yet when they do unfold, long-term stock market cycles also unfold nearby with a very high degree of consistency.

SATURN-URANUS

For a description of which cycles were present during each period in which these Saturn-Uranus aspects unfolded, please refer to Chapter Six, beginning on page 59.

Conjunction (0°)

Relative Strength	**Central**	**+/- 10 months**	**Total**
All	3.67	5.00	5.00
Crest	+3.00	+5.00	+4.33
Trough	- 3.75	-5.00	- 4.75
Consistency			
All	2.50	4.17	5.00
Crest	0.83	+1.67	+2.50
Trough	- 1.67	- 3.33	- 5.00
C/S Index			
All	6.17	9.17	10.00*
Crest	+3.83	+6.67	+6.83
Trough	- 5.42	- 8.33	- 9.75*

Waxing Semi-Square (45°)

Relative Strength	**Central**	**+/- 4 months**	**Total**
All	4.33	4.50	4.40
Crest	+0.00	+4.00	+4.00
Trough	- 4.33	- 5.00	- 4.50
Consistency			
All	3.00	3.00	5.00
Crest	+0.00	+1.00	+1.00
Trough	- 3.00	- 1.00	- 4.00
C/S Index			
All	7.33	7.50	9.40*
Crest	+0.00	+5.00	+5.00
Trough	- 7.33	- 6.00	- 8.50

Waxing Sextile (60°)

Relative Strength	**Central**	**+/- 7 months**	**Total**
All	4.25	4.00	4.20
Crest	+3.75	+4.00	+3.80
Trough	- 4.00	0.00	- 4.00

Consistency			
All	4.00	1.00	5.00
Crest	+4.00	+1.00	+5.00
Trough	- 2.00	0.00	- 2.00
C/S Index			
All	8.25	5.00	9.20*
Crest	+7.75	+5.00	+8.80
Trough	- 6.00	0.00	- 6.00

Waxing Square (90°)

Relative Strength	**Central**	**+/- 8 months**	**Total**
All	4.40	4.33	4.80
Crest	+5.00	+4.50	+4.80
Trough	- 4.00	- 4.00	- 4.00
Consistency			
All	5.00	3.00	5.00
Crest	+3.00	+2.00	+5.00
Trough	- 3.00	- 1.00	- 4.00
C/S Index			
All	9.40*	7.33	9.80*
Crest	+8.00	+6.50	+9.80*
Trough	- 7.00	- 5.00	- 8.00

Waxing Trine (120°)

Relative Strength	**Central**	**+/- 9 months**	**Total**
All	4.25	5.00	4.25
Crest	+4.00	5.00	+4.33
Trough	- 4.00	0.00	- 4.00
Consistency			
All	5.00	1.25	5.00
Crest	+2.50	+1.25	+3.75
Trough	- 5.00	0.00	- 5.00
C/S Index			
All	9.25*	6.25	9.25*
Crest	+6.50	+6.25	+8.08
Trough	- 9.00	0.00	- 9.00*

Waxing Sesquiquadrate (135°)

Relative Strength	Central	+/- 9 months	Total
All	4.00	4.00	4.50
Crest	+4.00	+4.00	+4.00
Trough	- 3.67	- 4.00	- 4.00
Consistency			
All	5.00	2.50	5.00
Crest	+2.50	+1.25	+3.75
Trough	- 3.75	- 1.25	- 3.75
C/S Index			
All	9.00*	6.50	9.50*
Crest	+6.50	+5.25	+7.75
Trough	- 7.42	- 5.25	- 7.75

Opposition (180°)

Relative Strength	Central	+/- 9 months	Total
All	5.00	5.00	5.00
Crest	+5.00	0.00	+5.00
Trough	- 4.00	- 5.00	- 4.20
Consistency			
All	4.00	1.00	5.00
Crest	+3.00	0.00	+3.00
Trough	- 4.00	- 1.00	- 5.00
C/S Index			
All	9.00*	6.00	10.00*
Crest	+8.00	0.00	+8.00
Trough	- 8.33	- 6.00	- 9.20*

Waning Sesquiquadrate (225°)

Relative Strength	Central	+/- 9 months	Total
All	4.00	4.50	4.50
Crest	+3.00	+4.67	+4.25
Trough	- 4.00	- 3.50	- 4.00
Consistency			
All	3.75	5.00	5.00
Crest	+1.25	+3.75	+5.00
Trough	- 3.75	- 2.50	- 5.00

C/S Index			
All	7.75	8.50	9.50*
Crest	+4.25	+8.42	+9.25*
Trough	- 7.75	- 6.00	- 9.00*

Waning Trine (240°)

Relative Strength	Central	+/- 5 months	Total
All	4.67	5.00	4.75
Crest	+4.67	+5.00	+4.75
Trough	- 3.50	0.00	- 3.50
Consistency			
All	3.75	1.25	5.00
Crest	+3.75	+1.25	+5.00
Trough	- 2.50	0.00	- 2.50
C/S Index			
All	8.42	6.25	9.75*
Crest	+8.42	+6.25	+9.75*
Trough	- 6.00	0.00	- 6.00

Waning Square (270°)

Relative Strength	Central	+/- 9 months	Total
All	3.80	4.50	4.20
Crest	+3.80	+4.50	+4.20
Trough	- 3.00	- 5.00	- 3.50
Consistency			
All	5.00	2.00	5.00
Crest	+5.00	+2.00	+5.00
Trough	- 3.00	- 1.00	- 4.00
C/S Index			
All	8.80	6.50	9.20*
Crest	+8.80	+6.50	+9.20*
Trough	- 6.00	- 6.00	- 7.50

Waning Sextile (300°)

Relative Strength	Central	+/- 7 months	Total
All	3.17	5.00	3.90
Crest	+3.00	+5.00	+3.50
Trough	- 2.75	- 4.50	- 3.625

Consistency			
All	3.00	2.00	5.00
Crest	+3.00	+1.00	+4.00
Trough	- 2.00	- 2.00	- 4.00
C/S Index			
All	6.17	7.00	8.90
Crest	+6.00	+6.00	+7.50
Trough	- 4.75	- 6.50	- 7.625

Waning Semi-Square (315°)

Relative Strength	**Central**	**+/- 8 months**	**Total**
All	4.50	4.50	4.60
Crest	+4.50	+4.50	+4.50
Trough	- 4.50	- 4.00	- 4.33
Consistency			
All	4.00	2.00	5.00
Crest	+2.00	+2.00	+4.00
Trough	- 2.00	- 1.00	- 3.00
C/S Index			
All	8.50	6.50	9.60*
Crest	+6.50	+6.50	+8.50
Trough	- 6.50	- 5.00	- 7.33

Summary of Saturn-Uranus Signatures

The following represents the ranking order of Saturn-Uranus aspects in correlation to long-term stock market cycles. This first ranking order is based upon Total C/S values, which includes a time band of up to 10 months (but usually no more than nine) outside of the aspect. In parentheses are those instances in which that particular signature correlated more times with a crest (+) or trough (-), and the respective values of each. Also included is a column indicating how many instances of cycles of at least a four-year type were associated with each aspect (again, within a 10 month orb of time either side of the aspect), and the percentage of times this represents. In the last column, titled **Orb,** are the number of months used outside of the central time band for the extended time band upon which the Total C/S values were based

Aspect	**Total**	**4-Year or > Cycles**		**Orb**
1. Conjunction	10.00* (- 9.75*)	6/6 =	100%	10 mo
1. Opposition	10.00* (- 9.20*)	5/5 =	100%	9
3. Waxing Square	9.80* (+9.80*)	5/5 =	100%	3

4. Waning Trine	9.75* (+9.75*)	4/4 =	100%	5
5. Waning Semi-Square	9.60* (+8.50)	5/5 =	100%	8
6. Waning Sesquiquadrate	9.50* (+9.25*)	4/4 =	100%	9
6. Waxing Sesquiquadrate	9.50*	4/4 =	100%	9
8. Waxing Semi-Square	9.40* (-8.50)	5/5 =	100%	4
9. Waning Square	9.20* (+9.20*)	4/5 =	80%	8
9. Waxing Sextile	9.20* (+8.80)	4/5 =	80%	7
11. Waxing Trine	9.25 (- 9.00*)	4/4 =	100%	9
12. Waning Sextile	8.90	3/5 =	60%	7

As one can see, all but one signature achieved the significant C/S level of 9.00 or greater. In fact, seven aspects (50%) made the very significant level of 9.50 or greater. Two of these aspects (the conjunction and opposition) achieved the highest values possible, 10.00, which means long-term cycles greater than the 4-year types unfolded in every instance. Only the waning sextile failed to meet the 9.00 level, but its score was quite close: 8.90.

The Saturn-Uranus signatures were extremely consistent in their correlations to 4-year or greater cycles. In the 57 instances of aspects studied, only three failed to produce a 4-year or greater cycle within an orb of 10 months from the central time band. Most, of course, produced such a cycle in an orb requiring far fewer months. That means there is a 95% frequency of correlation to 4-year or greater cycles when using the extended time band of Saturn-Uranus aspects.

Several of these signatures had definite and significant correlation with crests or troughs. In order of their C/S values, *the following signatures had a definite bias towards crests*: **waxing square (+9.80*), waning trine (+9.75*), waning sesquiquadrate (+9.25*), waning square (+9.20*), waxing sextile (+8.80), and waning semi-square (+8.50)**. *These signatures, in order of their C/S values, had a definite bias towards troughs:* **conjunction (-9.75*), opposition (-9.20*), waxing trine (-9.00*), and the waxing semi-square (-8.50).** The waning sesquiquadrate was perhaps the most volatile signature of all, for it had a high correlation to both crests (+9.25*) and troughs (-9.00*) within 9 months of its central time band.

When only the central time band was used, further interesting results emerge, which can be of use for investors when calculating a more precise time band for potential cycle crest or trough of importance. These C/S results are shown in the table below. Also shown are the number of instances in which four-year or greater cycles unfolded within the definition of a central time band used for this study.

Aspect	Central Time Band	4-Year or > Cycles
1. Waxing Square	9.40* (+8.00)	4/5 = 80%

2.	Waxing Trine	9.25*	(- 9.00*)	4/4 = 100%
3.	Opposition	9.00*		4/5 = 80%
3.	Waxing Sesquiquadrate	9.00*	(- 7.42)	2/4 = 50%
5.	Waning Square	8.80	(+8.80)	3/5 = 60%
6.	Waning Semi Square	8.50		4/5 = 80%
7.	Waning Trine	8.42	(+8.42)	3/4 = 75%
8.	Waxing Sextile	8.25	(+7.75)	3/5 = 60%
9.	Waning Sesquiquadrate	7.75	(- 7.75)	2/4 = 50%
10.	Waxing Semi-Square	7.33	(- 7.33)	3/5 = 60%
11	Conjunction	6.17		1/6 = 17%
11	Waning Sextile	6.17		1/5 = 20%

Even within the central time band, there are four aspects which achieved the level of significance for this study, which was a Total C/S value of 9.00 or greater. These were the waxing square (9.40*), waxing trine (9.25*), opposition and waxing sesquiquadrate (9.00* for each). Note that these are all the major aspects within a tight 90° segment of the zodiac, from the waxing square to the opposition. It appears that when Saturn and Uranus are in this segment of their cycle, the correlation to long-term stock market cycle is much more precise. They do not require the normal extended time band (usually up to nine months from the central time band) to reflect their influence (correspondence) upon the collective market psychology. As these aspects come into exactness, there is a great tendency for a 4-year or greater cycle to culminate. In fact, in the case of the waxing trine, a four-year or greater cycle unfolded in every instance within the central time band, and usually it was a trough.

Both the conjunction and waning sextile had a very weak correlation to long-term cycles unfolding within their central time bands. Investors therefore need to allow more time for long-term cycles to unfold when these two come into effect, especially in the case of the conjunction, which had the greatest C/S values when an extended time band was allowed.

In all, there was a nearly 60% frequency of a 4-year or greater cycle unfolding within the central time band of a Saturn-Uranus signature, as used in this study. **However, if the conjunction and waning sextile are removed from this study, that frequency leaped to about a 70% correlation (32 of 46 instances).** Every signature except those two had a 50% or greater correlation to such a cycle occurring within its central time band.

In conclusion, the Saturn-Uranus aspects have historically had an extremely high correlation to 4-year or greater cycles unfolding nearby (95%). Even within the central time band, the correlation is nearly 60%, and if the conjunction and waning sextile are removed, the correlation increases to about 70%. *This, then, is one of the most powerful and consistent of the geocosmic correlations to long-term cycles in the U.S. stock market.*

SATURN-NEPTUNE

For a description of which cycles were present during each period in which these Saturn-Neptune aspects unfolded, please refer to Chapter Six, beginning on page 82.

Conjunction (0°)

	Central	+/- 9 months	Total
Relative Strength			
All	3.60	4.25	4.17
Crest	+3.75	+4.33	+3.83
Trough	- 3.00	-4.33	- 3.80
Consistency			
All	4.17	3.33	5.00
Crest	2.50	+2.50	+5.00
Trough	- 1.67	- 2.50	- 4.17
C/S Index			
All	7.77	7.58	9.17*
Crest	+6.25	+6.83	+8.83
Trough	- 4.67	- 6.83	- 7.97

Waxing Semi-Square (45°)

	Central	+/- 7 months	Total
Relative Strength			
All	3.60	4.00	4.00
Crest	+3.00	+3.00	+3.00
Trough	- 3.75	- 4.00	- 3.80
Consistency			
All	4.17	2.50	5.00
Crest	+0.83	+1.67	+2.50
Trough	- 3.33	- 0.83	- 4.17
C/S Index			
All	7.77	6.50	9.00*
Crest	+3.83	+4.67	+5.50
Trough	- 7.08	- 4.83	- 7.97

Waxing Sextile (60°)

	Central	+/- 8 months	Total
Relative Strength			
All	3.33	4.33	3.83
Crest	+3.00	+4.00	+3.60
Trough	- 3.33	-4.00	- 3.67

Consistency			
All	2.50	2.50	5.00
Crest	+1.67	+2.50	+4.17
Trough	- 2.50	-2.50	- 5.00
C/S Index			
All	5.83	6.83	8.83
Crest	+4.67	+6.50	+7.77
Trough	- 5.83	- 6.50	- 8.67

Waxing Square (90°)

Relative Strength	**Central**	**+/- 8 months**	**Total**
All	4.20	4.67	4.67
Crest	+4.25	+0.00	+4.25
Trough	- 4.33	- 4.67	- 4.50
Consistency			
All	4.17	2.50	5.00
Crest	+3.33	+0.00	+3.33
Trough	- 2.50	- 2.50	- 5.00
C/S Index			
All	8.37	7.17	9.67*
Crest	+7.58	+0.00	+7.58
Trough	- 6.83	- 7.17	- 9.50*

Waxing Trine (120°)

Relative Strength	**Central**	**+/- 0 months**	**Total**
All	4.60	0.00	4.60
Crest	+4.33	0.00	+4.33
Trough	- 4.25	0.00	- 4.25
Consistency			
All	5.00	0.00	5.00
Crest	+3.00	+0.00	+3.00
Trough	- 4.00	0.00	- 4.00
C/S Index			
All	9.60*	0.00	9.60*
Crest	+7.33	+0.00	+7.33
Trough	- 8.25	0.00	- 8.25

Waxing Sesquiquadrate (135°)

Relative Strength	Central	+/- 9 months	Total
All	3.75	4.67	4.60
Crest	+3.33	+4.50	+4.00
Trough	- 3.50	- 4.50	- 4.25
Consistency			
All	4.00	3.00	5.00
Crest	+3.00	+2.00	+4.00
Trough	- 4.00	- 2.00	- 4.00
C/S Index			
All	7.75	7.67	9.60*
Crest	+6.33	+6.50	+8.00
Trough	- 7.50	- 6.50	- 8.25

Opposition (180°)

Relative Strength	Central	+/- 9 months	Total
All	3.67	4.40	4.50
Crest	+4.00	+4.25	+4.33
Trough	- 3.40	- 5.00	- 3.67
Consistency			
All	5.00	4.17	5.00
Crest	+2.50	+3.33	+5.00
Trough	- 4.17	- 0.83	- 5.00
C/S Index			
All	8.67	8.17	9.50*
Crest	+6.50	+7.58	+9.33*
Trough	- 7.57	- 5.83	- 8.67

Waning Sesquiquadrate (225°)

Relative Strength	Central	+/- 10 months	Total
All	3.17	4.60	4.33
Crest	+3.25	+4.33	+4.00
Trough	- 3.00	- 4.67	- 4.00
Consistency			
All	2.50	4.17	5.00
Crest	+1.67	+2.50	+3.33
Trough	- 1.67	- 2.50	- 4.17

C/S Index			
All	5.67	8.77	9.33*
Crest	+4.89	+6.83	+7.33
Trough	- 4.67	- 7.17	- 8.17

Waning Trine (240°)

Relative Strength	**Central**	**+/- 6 months**	**Total**
All	4.57	5.00	4.86
Crest	+4.25	+5.00	+4.75
Trough	- 4.17	- 5.00	- 4.29
Consistency			
All	5.00	1.43	5.00
Crest	+2.86	+1.25	+2.86
Trough	- 4.29	- 0.71	- 5.00
C/S Index			
All	9.57*	6.43	9.86*
Crest	+7.11	+6.25	+7.61
Trough	- 8.46	- 5.71	- 9.29*

Waning Square (270°)

Relative Strength	**Central**	**+/- 9 months**	**Total**
All	4.30	5.00	4.50
Crest	+4.00	+5.00	+4.50
Trough	- 3.83	- 0.00	- 3.83
Consistency			
All	4.17	1.67	5.00
Crest	+4.17	+1.67	+5.00
Trough	- 2.50	- 0.00	- 2.50
C/S Index			
All	8.47	6.67	9.50*
Crest	+8.17	+6.67	+9.50*
Trough	- 6.33	- 0.00	- 6.33

Waning Sextile (300°)

Relative Strength	**Central**	**+/- 9 months**	**Total**
All	3.125	4.25	3.83
Crest	+3.00	+4.00	+3.25
Trough	- 3.17	- 4.25	- 3.83

Consistency			
All	3.33	3.33	5.00
Crest	+2.50	+0.83	+3.33
Trough	- 2.50	- 3.33	- 5.00
C/S Index			
All	6.455	7.58	8.83
Crest	+5.50	+4.83	+6.58
Trough	- 5.67	- 7.58	- 8.83

Waning Semi-Square (315°)

Relative Strength	**Central**	**+/- 10 months**	**Total**
All	3.25	5.00	4.17
Crest	+3.33	+0.00	+3.33
Trough	- 3.00	- 5.00	- 4.50
Consistency			
All	3.33	2.50	5.00
Crest	+2.50	+0.00	+2.50
Trough	- 1.67	- 2.50	- 3.33
C/S Index			
All	6.58	7.50	9.17*
Crest	+5.83	+0.00	+5.83
Trough	- 4.67	- 7.50	- 7.83

Summary of Saturn-Neptune Signatures

The following represents the ranking order of Saturn-Neptune aspects in correlation to long-term stock market cycles. This first ranking order is based upon Total C/S values, which includes a time band of up to 10 months (but usually no more than nine) outside of the aspect. In parentheses are those instances in which that particular signature correlated more times with a crest (+) or trough (-), and the respective values of each. Also included is a column indicating how many instances of cycles of at least a four-year type were associated with each aspect (again, within an ten-month orb of time either side of the aspect), and the percentage of times this represents. In the last column, titled **Orb,** are the number of months used outside of the central time band for the extended time band upon which the Total C/S values were based

Aspect	**Total**		**4-Year or > Cycles**		**Orb**
1. Waning Trine	9.86*	(- 9.29*)	7/7 =	100%	6
2 Waxing Square	9.67*	(- 9.50*)	7/7 =	100%	8
3. Waxing Trine	9.60*	(- 8.25)	5/5 =	100%	0
3. Waxing Sesquiquadrate	9.60*	(- 8.25)	5/5 =	100%	9
5. Waning Square	9.50*	(+9.50*)	5/6 =	83%	9

5. Opposition	9.50*	(+9.33*)	6/6 =	100%	9
7. Waning Sesquiquadrate	9.33*	(- 8.17)	5/6 =	83%	10
8 Waning Semi-Square	9.17*	(- 7.83)	4/6 =	67%	10
8. Conjunction	9.17*	(+8.83)	5/6 =	83%	9
10. Waxing Semi-Square	9.00*	(- 7.97)	6/6 =	100%	7
11. Waxing Sextile	8.83	(- 8.67)	4/6 =	67%	8
11. Waning Sextile	8.83	(- 8.83)	4/6 =	67%	9

Given a 10 month orb outside of the central time band, the Saturn-Neptune signatures have a very reliable correlation to 4-year or greater cycles in the U.S. stock market. Ten of these 12 aspects achieved the level of significance as defined by a C/S value of 9.00 or greater. Only the two sextiles did not achieve this level. However, they were close with a C/S value of 8.83 each. What is perhaps most important here is that both the trines and the squares achieved values of 9.50 or greater, as did the opposition. In fact, these five signatures were amongst the top six in their correlation to long-term stock market cycles. If we include the two instances of the sesquiquadrates, then we will see that these aspects comprised the top seven in the Total C/S rankings.

What does this mean? It suggests that the aspects formed between the two squares of Saturn and Neptune (the sector between 90° - 270° of their planetary cycle arc) coincide more reliably with the longer-term cycles in U.S. stocks than do the aspects in the other half of their planetary cycle. Or, the aspects closest to the opposition are more consistent with long-term stock market cycles than the half closest to the conjunction. Thus the further away Saturn and Neptune are to one another, the more likely their aspects are to coincide with longer-term stock market cycles, given an orb of 10 months from their central time band.

Also significant is the fact that 63 of these 72 cases coincided with a 4-year cycle or greater, given this 10-month orb (87.5%). There were only two instances which required the full ten months, as most of these aspects required nine or less. Half of these signatures, in fact, had a 100% correlation to four-year or greater cycles. These were the two trines, waxing square, waxing sesquiquadrate, opposition, and waxing semi-square.

There were two signatures each which had a very high correlation to crests and troughs. The waxing square (-9.50*) and waning trine (-9.29*) coincided with long-term cycle troughs, while the waning square (+9.50*) and opposition (+9.33) had a definite bias towards crests.

When only the central time band was used, further interesting findings emerge, which can be of use for investors when calculating a more precise time band for a potential cycle crest or trough of importance. These C/S results are shown in the table below. Also shown are the number of instances in which four-year or greater cycles unfolded within the definition of a central time band used for this study.

	Aspect	Central Time Band		4-Year or > Cycles	
1.	Waxing Trine	9.60*	(- 8.25)	5/5 =	100%
2.	Waning Trine	9.57*	(- 8.46)	6/7 =	86%
3.	Opposition	8.67	(- 7.57)	3/6 =	50%
4.	Waning Square	8.47	(+8.17)	4/6 =	67%
5.	Waxing Square	8.37	(+7.58)	5/7 =	71%
6.	Conjunction	7.77		1/6 =	17%
6.	Waxing Semi-Square	7.77	(- 7.08)	3/6 =	50%
8.	Waxing Sesquiquadrate	7.75	(- 7.50)	2/5 =	40%
9.	Waning Semi-Square	6.58		1/6 =	17%
10.	Waxing Sextile	6.455		0/6 =	0%
11.	Waning Sextile	5.83		1/6 =	17%
12.	Waning Sesquiquadrate	5.67		0/6 =	0%

When the more precise time band is used, only two aspects achieve the level of significance as defined by this study. That is the waxing trine (9.60*) and waning trine (9.57*). Falling in the moderately reliable zone were the opposition (8.67), waning square (8.47), and waxing square (8.37). None of the other Saturn-Neptune aspects attained a score of greater than 8.00. In fact, five aspects had C/S values within their central time band of less than 7.00. As in the earlier section in Chapter Six, this study also demonstrates that the correlation of longer-term cycles in the U.S. stock market is highest when to the major aspects of astrology. The conjunction, squares, trines, and opposition were the six most reliable aspects. The minor ones were all in the grouping of the six least reliable aspects.

Within the central time band of Saturn-Neptune, the frequency of cycles of at least a 4-year type dropped considerably compared to that of the extended time band. In 87.5% of the extended time band aspects, a 4-year or greater cycle unfolded. In the central time band, that frequency was only 43%, or about half. *However, if just the major aspects between the waxing and waning square sectors were used (i.e. squares, trines, and the opposition), then the frequency increased markedly. In this division, there were 23 instances of 4-year or greater cycles out of 31 possibilities (74%). Each aspect had a correlation of 50% or more. In the case of the waxing trine, the frequency of four-year or greater cycles unfolding within its central time band, so far, has been 100%.*

In summary, the Saturn-Neptune signatures are reliable indicators of 4-year or greater stock market cycles if given a 10-month extended orb from their central time band. Within the central time band itself, the squares, trines, and opposition are very reliable market timing tools for potentially identifying the same type of long-term stock market cycles.

SATURN-PLUTO

For a description of which cycles were present during each period in which these Saturn-Pluto aspects unfolded, please refer to Chapter Six, beginning on page 102.

Conjunction (0°)

Relative Strength	Central	+/- 11 months	Total
All	4.17	4.50	4.50
Crest	+4.00	+5.00	+4.33
Trough	- 4.40	-4.00	- 4.33
Consistency			
All	5.00	1.67	5.00
Crest	+1.67	+0.83	+2.50
Trough	- 4.17	- 0.83	- 5.00
C/S Index			
All	9.17*	6.17	9.50*
Crest	+5.67	+5.83	+6.83
Trough	- 8.57	- 4.83	- 9.33*

Waxing Semi-Square (45°)

Relative Strength	Central	+/- 9 months	Total
All	3.75	4.25	4.00
Crest	+3.33	+5.00	+3.75
Trough	- 5.00	- 4.00	- 4.25
Consistency			
All	3.33	3.33	5.00
Crest	+2.50	+0.83	+3.33
Trough	- 0.83	- 2.50	- 3.33
C/S Index			
All	7.08	7.58	9.00*
Crest	+5.83	+5.83	+7.08
Trough	- 5.83	- 6.50	- 7.58

Waxing Sextile (60°)

Relative Strength	Central	+/- 5 months	Total
All	4.33	4.33	4.43
Crest	+4.40	+4.50	+4.43
Trough	- 4.00	-4.00	- 4.00

Consistency			
All	4.29	2.14	5.00
Crest	+3.57	+1.42	+5.00
Trough	- 2.14	-0.71	- 2.86
C/S Index			
All	8.62	6.47	9.43*
Crest	+7.97	+5.92	+9.43*
Trough	- 6.14	- 4.71	- 6.86

Waxing Square (90°)

Relative Strength	**Central**	**+/- 4 months**	**Total**
All	4.00	4.33	4.14
Crest	+3.75	+4.50	+4.00
Trough	- 4.33	- 4.00	- 4.25
Consistency			
All	5.00	2.14	5.00
Crest	+2.86	+1.42	+4.17
Trough	- 2.14	- 0.71	- 2.86
C/S Index			
All	9.00*	6.47	9.14*
Crest	+6.61	+5.92	+8.17
Trough	- 6.47	- 4.71	- 7.11

Waxing Trine (120°)

Relative Strength	**Central**	**+/- 7 months**	**Total**
All	3.50	4.50	4.00
Crest	+3.00	+4.00	+3.50
Trough	- 3.50	- 4.67	- 4.00
Consistency			
All	2.86	2.86	5.00
Crest	+1.42	+1.42	+2.86
Trough	- 2.86	- 2.14	- 5.00
C/S Index			
All	6.36	7.36	9.00*
Crest	+4.42	+5.42	+6.36
Trough	- 6.36	- 6.81	- 9.00*

Waxing Sesquiquadrate (135°)

Relative Strength	Central	+/- 8 months	Total
All	3.33	5.00	3.86
Crest	+3.40	+0.00	+3.40
Trough	- 3.00	- 5.00	- 3.80
Consistency			
All	4.29	1.42	5.00
Crest	+3.57	+0.00	+3.57
Trough	- 2.14	- 1.42	- 3.57
C/S Index			
All	7.62	6.42	8.86
Crest	+6.97	+0.00	+6.97
Trough	- 5.14	- 6.42	- 7.37

Opposition (180°)

Relative Strength	Central	+/- 8 months	Total
All	4.00	4.40	4.875
Crest	+3.67	+4.83	+4.25
Trough	- 3.67	- 4.50	- 4.25
Consistency			
All	2.86	2.86	5.00
Crest	+2.14	+2.14	+4.29
Trough	- 2.14	- 1.42	- 2.86
C/S Index			
All	6.86	7.26	9.875*
Crest	+5.81	+6.97	+8.54
Trough	- 5.81	- 5.92	- 7.11

Waning Sesquiquadrate (225°)

Relative Strength	Central	+/- 2 months	Total
All	4.20	3.00	4.00
Crest	+4.00	+3.00	+3.75
Trough	- 4.00	- 3.00	- 3.75
Consistency			
All	4.17	0.83	5.00
Crest	+2.50	+0.83	+3.33
Trough	- 2.50	- 0.83	- 3.33

C/S Index			
All	8.37	3.83	9.00*
Crest	+6.50	+3.83	+7.08
Trough	- 6.59	- 3.83	- 7.08

Waning Trine (240°)

Relative Strength	Central	+/- 5 months	Total
All	4.00	4.50	4.17
Crest	+3.75	+0.00	+3.75
Trough	- 3.67	- 4.50	- 4.00
Consistency			
All	4.17	1.67	5.00
Crest	+3.33	+0.00	+3.33
Trough	- 2.50	- 1.67	- 4.17
C/S Index			
All	8.17	6.17	9.17*
Crest	+7.08	+0.00	+7.08
Trough	- 6.17	- 6.17	- 8.17

Waning Square (270°)

Relative Strength	Central	+/- 8 months	Total
All	3.50	4.25	3.92
Crest	+3.00	+4.25	+4.25
Trough	- 3.50	- 5.00	- 3.92
Consistency			
All	5.00	1.67	5.00
Crest	+0.83	+1.67	+1.67
Trough	- 5.00	- 0.83	- 5.00
C/S Index			
All	8.50	5.92	8.92
Crest	+3.83	+5.92	+5.92
Trough	- 8.50	- 5.83	- 8.92

Waning Sextile (300°)

Relative Strength	Central	+/- 9 months	Total
All	4.00	4.60	4.50
Crest	+4.00	+4.00	+4.00
Trough	- 3.00	- 4.75	- 4.40

Consistency			
All	0.83	4.17	5.00
Crest	+0.83	+1.67	+2.50
Trough	- 0.83	- 3.33	- 4.17
C/S Index			
All	4.83	8.77	9.50*
Crest	+4.83	+5.67	+6.50
Trough	- 3.83	- 8.09	- 8.57

Waning Semi-Square (315°)

Relative Strength	**Central**	**+/- 4 months**	**Total**
All	3.67	4.00	3.83
Crest	+3.60	+0.00	+3.60
Trough	- 3.50	- 4.00	- 3.67
Consistency			
All	5.00	0.83	5.00
Crest	+4.17	+0.00	+4.17
Trough	- 1.67	- 0.83	- 2.50
C/S Index			
All	8.67	4.83	8.83
Crest	+7.77	+0.00	+7.77
Trough	- 5.17	- 4.83	- 6.17

Summary of Saturn-Pluto Signatures

The following represents the ranking order of Saturn-Pluto aspects in correlation to long-term stock market cycles. This first ranking order is based upon Total C/S values, which includes a time band of up to 11 months (but usually no more than nine) outside of the aspect. In parentheses are those instances in which that particular signature correlated more times with a crest (+) or trough (-), and the respective values of each. Also included is a column indicating how many instances of cycles of at least a four-year type were associated with each aspect (again, within an 11 month orb of time either side of the aspect), and the percentage of times this represents. In the last column, titled **Orb,** are the number of months used outside of the central time band for the extended time band upon which the Total C/S values were based

	Aspect	**Total**		**4-Year or > Cycles**			**Orb**
1.	Opposition	9.875*	(+8.54)	6/7	=	86%	8
2.	Conjunction	9.50*	(- 9.33*)	5/6	=	83%	11
2.	Waning Sextile	9.50*	(- 8.57)	6/6	=	100%	9
4.	Waxing Sextile	9.43*	(+9.43*)	6/7	=	86%	5
5.	Waning Trine	9.17*	(- 8.17)	4/6	=	67%	5
6.	Waxing Square	9.14*	(+8.14)	6/7	=	86%	4

7. Waxing Trine	9.00*	(- 9.00*)	5/7 =	71%	7
7. Waxing Semi-Square	9.00*		5/6 =	83%	9
7. Waning Sesquiquadrate	9.00*		4/6 =	67%	2
10. Waning Square	8.92	(- 8.92)	3/6 =	50%	8
11. Waxing Sesquiquadrate	8.86		3/7 =	42%	8
12. Waning Semi-Square	8.83	(+7.77)	5/6 =	83%	4

Given an 11 month extended orb outside of the central time band (and usually nine months or less), there are 9 Saturn-Pluto signatures that achieved a Total C/S value of 9.00 or greater. Even the other three (waning square, waxing sesquiquadrate, and waning semi-square) were very close, with values between 8.83 - 8.92. Thus it appears that the Saturn-Pluto signatures are reliable in identifying time bands for probable four-year or greater cycles in the U.S. stock market.

Most noteworthy were the conjunction, opposition, and "harmonious aspects" of the sextile and trine. All achieved C/S values of 9.00 or greater, and in the case of the sextiles, opposition and conjunction, the values were an extremely high 9.43 - 9.875!

All but one aspect (the waxing sesquiquadrate) actually had a 50% or greater correlation to 4-year or greater cycles in this extended time band. In fact, 58 of the 77 total aspects of Saturn-Pluto studied in the history of the U.S. stock market (75.3%) coincided with a 4-year or greater cycle. This suggests that there is a 75% probability that a 4-year or greater cycle in U.S. stocks will unfold when Saturn and Pluto enter an aspect time band as used in this study. That frequency increases to nearly 80% if the semi-squares and sesquiquadrates are not counted.

There were also levels of significance achieved with certain types of cycles among several of these aspects. For instance, the waxing sextile had a C/S value of +9.43*, implying a very strong bias towards the unfolding of very strong crests during its extended time band. The conjunction (-9.33*) and waxing trine (-9.00*), on the other hand, had a very pronounced bias towards long-term trough cycles. So too did the waning square, whose value was just slightly under -9.00, at -8.92.

When only the central time band was studied, the values changed slightly, yielding further interesting findings which can be of use for investors when calculating a more precise time band for potential cycle crest or trough of importance. These C/S results are shown in the table below. Also shown are the number of instances in which four-year or greater cycles unfolded within the definition of a central time band used for this study.

Aspect	**Central Time Band**		**4-Year or > Cycles**
1. Conjunction	9.17*	(- 8.57)	4/6 = 67%
2. Waxing Square	9.00*		6/7 = 86%
3. Waning Semi-Square	8.67	(+7.77)	4/6 = 67%

4. Waxing Sextile	8.62	(+7.97)	5/7 = 71%
5. Waning Square	8.50	(- 8.50)	2/6 = 33%
6. Waning Sesquiquadrate	8.37		4/6 = 67%
7. Waning Trine	8.17	(+7.08)	2/6 = 33%
8. Waxing Sesquiquadrate	7.62	(+6.97)	1/7 = 14%
9. Waxing Semi-Square	7.08		2/6 = 33%
10. Opposition	6.86		2/7 = 28.5%
11. Waxing Trine	6.36		2/7 = 28.5%
12. Waning Sextile	4.83		1/6 = 17%

The results are still impressive, certainly compared to the cycles of Jupiter and beyond. There were two signatures that reached the critical 9.00 level in the central time band: the conjunction (9.17*) and the waxing square (9.00*). Thus one can anticipate a 4-year or greater cycle type will likely unfold within the central time band of these two aspects. Also rated fairly high in reliability would be the waning semi-square, waxing sextile, and waning square, each with C/S values of 8.50 or higher. However, the opposition (6.86), waxing trine (6.36), and especially the waning sextile (4.83) were not reliable at all as market timing indicators within their central time bands.

In the 77 instances of Saturn-Pluto aspects studied, 35 coincided with 4-year or greater cycles within their central time band (45.5%). However, if one only considered the conjunction, waxing sextile, and waxing trine signatures, the frequency of occurrence increased to 75%. Additionally the waning semi-square and sesquiquadrate also had a high correlation to 4-year or greater cycles unfolding within their central time band. They each had a 66.7% frequency. No other Saturn-Pluto aspects produced a correlation of over 33.3%.

Thus it seems that some, but not all, of the Saturn-Pluto aspects can be used as a reliable market timing indicator. They can reliably identify certain time bands that will have a greater than 50% probability of coinciding with a 4-year or greater cycle within their central time band. These include the conjunction, waxing sextile, waxing square, waning sesquiquadrate, and waning semi-square. When these signatures are due, investors may look to take appropriate action, as a 4-year or greater cycle trough or crest in the U.S. stock market is likely to occur.

CHAPTER NINE

GEOCOSMIC LEVELS 1, 2 AND 3 IN LONG-TERM STOCK MARKET CYCLES

In *The Gold Book: Geocosmic Correlations To Gold Price Cycles*, various geocosmic signatures were categorized into Levels 1, 2, and 3, based upon their frequency of occurrence nearby to primary cycles. Those signatures that had a 50% or greater frequency nearby to primary cycles were categorized as Level 1 types. This meant that 1) when Level 1 signatures unfolded, there was a greater than usually probability that a primary cycle would occur within eight trading days, or 2) if a primary cycle time band was in effect (crest or trough), that time band could be narrowed to a specific date, give or take three trading days, if at least one Level 1 signature was present therein.

Level 2 signatures had a less than 50% frequency of occurrence nearby to primary cycles, but greater than 32%. Level 3 signatures were those that had less than a 32% frequency of correlating to primary cycles.

These various levels were then used to create a market timing strategy for traders, based around the primary cycle of Gold. After years of working with this methodology, it was clearly observed that this strategy for timing — and hence trading — of the Gold market, also worked equally well for other financial and commodity markets.

But that strategy, and that book, was designed for traders, not investors. This book, on the other hand, is being written with the investor in mind. And, as already determined, longer-term planetary pair cycles have a very definite correlation to long-term cycles in the U.S. stock market, given an orb of just a couple of months. However, not all of these signatures are equal. That is, some have a very high correlation to 4-year or greater cycles, and others do not. Those that do not correlate frequently to 4-year or greater cycles, do have a correlation with 22.5-month or 50-week cycles. In essence, then, there seems to be a hierarchy of correlation, and the understanding of this hierarchy can be instrumental in timing the unfolding of various types of long-term and intermediate-term cycles in the U.S. stock market.

This chapter, then, will attempt to delineate that hierarchy. This will be done by analyzing the frequency of occurrence of planetary pair signatures to 4-year or greater cycles in the U.S. stock market that occurred nearby. A list will be generated in the order of those frequencies, and categories of Levels 1, 2 and 3 signatures will be created, according to their correlation to the long-term geocosmic signatures studied in this book.

RANKING OF CORRELATIONS TO CYCLES

The following, then, is a listing which ranks all the signatures in terms of their correlation to 4-year or greater cycles in the U.S. stock market. Please note that the orbs of Jupiter-Saturn signatures has been expanded to nine months so that they will be more consistent with the longer-term aspects between Saturn, Uranus, Neptune, and Pluto to one another, per criteria used in Chapter 6.

GROUP 1

	Signature	4-Year or Greater Cycles	Orb of Time
1.	♄△♆ - 240°	7/7 = 100%	6 Months
1.	♄□♆ - 90°	7/7 = 100	8 "
3.	♄☌♅ - 0°	6/6 = 100	10 "
3.	♄☍♆ - 180°	6/6 = 100	9 "
3.	♄∠♆ - 45°	6/6 = 100	7 "
3.	♄⚹♇ - 300°	6/6 = 100	9 "
7.	♄☍♅ - 180°	5/5 = 100	9 "
7.	♄□♅ - 90°	5/5 = 100	3 "
7.	♄∠♅ - 45°	5/5 = 100	4 "
7.	♄∠♅ - 315°	5/5 = 100	8 "
7.	♄△♆ - 120°	5/5 = 100	0 "
7.	♄⚼♆ - 135°	5/5 = 100	9 "
13.	♄△♅ - 120	4/4 = 100	9 "
13.	♄△♅ - 240°	4/4 = 100	5 "
13.	♄⚼♅ - 135°	4/4 = 100	9 "
13.	♄⚼♅ - 225°	4/4 = 100	9 "

GROUP 2

	Signature	4-Year or Greater Cycles	Orb of Time
17.	♃☍♅ - 180°	11/12= 91	6 "
18.	♃△♄ - 120°	9/10 = 90	6 "
19.	♄☍♇ - 180°	6/7 = 86	5 "
19.	♄⚹♇ - 60°	6/7 = 86	5 "
19.	♄□♇ - 90°	6/7 = 86	4 "
22.	♃△♄ - 240°	10/12= 83	9 "
22.	♃☍♇ - 180°	10/12= 83	6 "
24.	♄□♆ - 270°	5/6 = 83	9 "
24.	♄⚼♆ - 225°	5/6 = 83	10 "
24.	♄☌♆ - 0°	5/6 = 83	9 "
24.	♄☌♇ - 0°	5/6 = 83	11 "
24.	♄∠♇ - 45°	5/6 = 83	9 "
24.	♄∠♇ - 315°	5/6 = 83	4 "

30. ♃□♄ - 270° 9/11 = 82 8 "
30. ♃☍♄ - 180° 9/11 = 82 8 "
30. ♃⚹♄ - 300° 9/11 = 82 7 "
33. ♃☌♄ - 0° 8/10 = 80 5 "
34. ♄□♅ - 270° 4/5 = 80 8 "
34. ♄⚹♅ - 60° 4/5 = 80 7 "

GROUP 3

36. ♄△♇ - 120° 5/7 = 71 7 "
37. ♃□♄ - 90° 7/10 = 70 7 "
37. ♃⚹♅ - 300° 7/10 = 70 5 "
37. ♃⚹♇ - 300° 7/10 = 70 6 "

40. ♄∠♆ - 315° 4/6 = 67 10 "
40. ♄⚹♆ - 60° 4/6 = 67 8 "
40. ♄⚹♆ - 300° 4/6 = 67 9 "
40. ♄△♇ - 240° 4/6 = 67 5 "
40. ♄⚼♇ - 225° 4/6 = 67 2 "
45. ♃□♇ - 90° 7/11 = 64 5 "
46. ♃⚹♄ - 60° 6/10 = 60 7 "
46. ♃△♆ - 120° 6/10 = 60 9 "
46. ♃⚹♆ - 300° 6/10 = 60 3 "
46. ♃□♆ - 270° 6/10 = 60 6 "
46. ♄⚹♅ - 300° 3/5 = 60 7 "

GROUP 4

51. ♃△♅ - 120° 5/9 = 56 3 "
51. ♃△♅ - 240° 5/9 = 56 3 "
51. ♃□♆ - 90° 5/9 = 56 6 "
54. ♃☌♆ - 0° 6/11 = 55 6 "
54. ♃☌♇ - 0° 6/11 = 55 6 "
56. ♃□♅ - 270° 6/12 = 50 3 "
57. ♃☌♅ - 0° 5/10 = 50 7 "
57. ♃△♆ - 240° 5/10 = 50 9 "
57. ♄□♇ - 270° 3/6 = 50 8 "

GROUP 5

60. ♃⚹♆ - 60° 4/9 = 44 4 "
61. ♄⚼♇ - 135° 3/7 = 42 8 "
62. ♃□♇ - 270° 4/10 = 40 4 "
63. ♃△♇ - 120° 4/11 = 36 6 "

64.	♃□♅ - 90°	3/9 =	33	3	"
65.	♃☍♆ - 180°	3/10 =	30	9	"
65.	♃△♇ - 240°	3/10 =	30	4	"

GROUP 6

67.	♃⚹♅ - 60°	2/9 =	22	2	"
68.	♃⚹♇ - 60°	2/10 =	20	4	"

There are several ways to group these results for analysis. First, one could consider just those 16 signatures that, so far, have had a 100% correlation to a 4-year or greater cycle in the U.S. stock market (Group 1). As expected, the longest planetary pair cycles again had the greatest correlation. That is, there were 9 instances of Saturn-Uranus signatures with a 100% correlation. There were 6 instances of Saturn-Neptune signatures, one instance of a Saturn-Pluto signature, and none involving the Jupiter signatures to any planet. The orbs for all of these ranged anywhere from zero to ten months. However, the majority of these required an 8-9 month orb.

A second group (Group 2) can be identified as those signatures which had an 80-91% correlation to 4-year or greater cycles. In this group of 18 signatures, one can note the appearance of many Saturn-Neptune (6 cases) and Saturn-Pluto (9 cases) signatures emerging. Additionally, we now also find several Jupiter-Saturn signatures present (7 out of a possible 8). There was also one case of a Jupiter-Uranus signature (opposition), and the final two cases of Saturn-Uranus.

Thus, in all, there are 35 geocosmic signatures that so far, have had an 80% or greater correlation to long-term cycles in the U.S. stock market. These, then, will be considered the **Level 1** signatures correlating with 4-year or greater cycles in U.S. stock indices. *This simply means that when any one of these signatures are present, there is an 80% or greater probability that a 4-year or greater cycle trough or crest in U.S. stock indices is likely to form within 11 months, and more than likely 9 months or less.* If we were to add the Uranus, Neptune, and Pluto combinations to this study, it would of course increase the number of valid signatures within Level 1. Furthermore, their orb of allowance would also have to increase to one year. However, the number of times these signatures unfold is very few in comparison to those used in this study.

A list of these Level 1 signatures can be created as shown below:

LEVEL 1 SIGNATURES

1. **Neptune-Pluto** (all signatures)
2. **Uranus-Neptune** (all signatures)
3. **Uranus-Pluto** (all signatures)
4. **Saturn-Uranus** (all signatures except the waning sextile).

5. **Saturn-Neptune** (conjunction, waxing semi-square, squares, trines, sesquiquadrates, and opposition).
6. **Saturn-Pluto** (conjunction, semi-squares, sextiles, waxing square, and opposition)
7. **Jupiter-Saturn** (conjunction, waning sextile, waning square, trines, and opposition).
8. **Jupiter-Uranus** (opposition only).
9. **Jupiter-Pluto** (opposition only)

There were only four signatures that had a 70 or 71% correlation to 4-year or greater cycles — one each of a Saturn-Pluto, Jupiter-Saturn, Jupiter-Uranus, and Jupiter-Neptune signature. However, there were 11 signatures with a 60-67% correlation, and another nine with a 50-56% correlation. These comprised the categories of Groups 3 and 4. In all, there were 24 signatures with a 50-71% correspondence to long-term cycles in the U.S. stock market. These, then, will be considered **Level 2** geocosmic signatures to long-term stock market cycles. Their correlation is not as consistent as the Level 1 signatures. It is more likely that when they unfold, 22.5-month or 4-year cycles may occur nearby. However when Level 1 signatures unfold, 4-year or greater cycles are more likely to occur nearby. A Level 2 signature can be useful, however, in the timing of a long-term cycle if a Level 1 signature is also present near the same time. In order of their importance, the Level 2 signatures are listed below.

LEVEL 2 SIGNATURES

1. **Saturn-Neptune** (only the sextiles and the waning semi-square).
2. **Saturn-Pluto** (only the waning square, both trines, and the waning sesquiquadrate).
3. **Jupiter-Saturn** (only the waxing sextile and waxing square).
4. **Saturn-Uranus** (only the waning sextile).
5. **Jupiter-Uranus** (conjunction, waning sextile, waning square, and both trines)
6. **Jupiter-Neptune** (conjunction, waning sextile, both squares, and both trines)
7. **Jupiter-Pluto** (only conjunction, waning sextile, and waxing square)

The weakest signatures would be those with less than a 50% correlation to 4-year or greater cycles in the U.S. stock market. There were 9 such signatures, and their correspondences ranged from 20-44% (groups 5 and 6). The weakest two — Jupiter in waxing sextile to both Uranus and Pluto — had only a 22% and 20% correlation respectively (Group 6). Thus they would have to be considered highly unreliable correlates. The other seven had a 30-44% correlation (Group 5), which means they have enough historical correspondences that they warrant consideration when they occur. However, their reliability as an accurate market timing indicator for long-term stock market cycles is less than 50%, so they will be considered as **Level 3** types. They are as follows:

LEVEL 3 SIGNATURES

1. **Saturn-Pluto** (only the waxing sesquiquadrate).
2. **Jupiter-Uranus** (only the waxing square).

3. **Jupiter-Neptune** (only the waxing sextile and opposition).
4. **Jupiter-Pluto** (only the waning square and both trines).

The **waxing sextiles of Jupiter-Uranus and Jupiter-Pluto** are too weak to place in even Level 3.

USING LEVELS 1-3 FOR MARKET TIMING

The methodology for timing a long-term cycle in the U.S. stock market, using these geocosmic signatures, is quite simple. The first step is to simply identify the occurrence of a Level 1 long-term signature. A chronological listing of all Level 1, 2, and 3 long-term signatures from 1998 - 2030 is provided in the appendices at the back of this book. Those that were in effect prior to 1998 can be found simply by looking up that signature's history in the earlier chapters of this book. Once a signature is identified, determine its orb of influence historically (as listed earlier in this chapter), and create a time band around this date. This time band represents a zone that has an 80% or greater probability of coinciding with a 4-year or greater cycle crest or trough in the U.S. stock market. In fact, in the 28 instances of 4-year cycle troughs or crests since 1946 (1946-1998), fully 25 of them (89.3%) found at least one Level 1 long-term geocosmic signature present within 5 months, and usually less than 3 months.

The length of the time band in which a 4-year or greater cycle trough or crest is likely to unfold, can be narrowed considerably if other Level 1 signatures are located nearby. In other words, if two or more Level 1 signatures occur close in time to one another, then their time bands can be overlapped to create a shorter time frame for an expected cycle culmination. In fact, even the presence of Level 2 signatures within a time band of a Level 1 signature, can be used to narrow the expected time frame for a long-term cycle culmination. In short, wherever multiple geocosmic time bands overlap with one another, therein lies the most likely time period for a long-term cycle to unfold in U.S. stocks.

When a geocosmic time band for a cycle culmination overlaps with the stock market's own time band for a cycle trough or crest, the probabilities of a significant reversal increase markedly. In fact, this is the first place to begin outlining a potential time frame for a 4-year cycle trough or crest. As an example, we know that the vast majority of 4-year cycle troughs occur at a 36-56 month interval from one another. If we were to draw a time band 36-56 months following a 4-year cycle trough, we would in essence have the time band in which the next 4-year cycle trough was due. If we then identified Level 1 long-term geocosmic signatures whose time bands (orbs) were in effect during this 36-56 month period, we would likely be able to narrow it down by several months. This is the technique that will be expanded upon in the next chapter.

CHAPTER TEN

THE ART OF INTEGRATION: COMBINING LONG-TERM CYCLES IN STOCKS WITH LONG-TERM GEOCOSMIC CYCLES

Volume 1 of this series identified the long, intermediate, and short-term cycles in the U.S. and Japanese stock markets. It identified the characteristics and time bands of those cycles. It demonstrated specific technical studies and chart formations to watch for, which have a high probability of occurring at the time of long-term stock market reversals. *Volume 2* has shown the correlation of those long and intermediate-term cycles to the long and intermediate-term geocosmic — or planetary — cycles. The task now is determining how to merge these two studies together to produce a successful investment strategy.

A large part of such a strategy requires accurate market timing — which is the subject of this series of books. Although timing is not everything (contrary to popular jargon), it is important, and if understood properly, can indeed enhance one's investment or trading performance. The intent of this chapter, then, is to determine just how the combination of these two studies can create a more accurate time band for identifying long-term cycle troughs and crests.

START WITH THE 18-YEAR CYCLE

The task of outlining the narrowest time band in which the market has the highest probability of changing a long or intermediate-term trend begins with the correct labeling and application of cycles. Cycles are to geocosmics what a forest is to a tree, or what a war is to a battle. It is the bigger picture. It is the map of the whole territory and not just a small microcosm of a single part of it.

Geocosmics identify a specific point in time when the momentum of something is likely to climax. However, in terms of markets, one never knows if that climax is the end of a bout of selling (trough) or buying (crest) until the time arrives. With the study of cycles, one is more able to correctly forecast which it is likely to be — a trough or a crest. With cycles, you have a map and know *where* you are going, what your destination is to be. With geocosmics, you are more able to tell exactly *when* you are arriving at your destination. But without cycles, it is like hitting many cities along the route, and never knowing for sure which city is the "correct one" you have been striving to reach.

Thus the process of determining when a long-term trend is likely to climax involves watching for significant planetary cycles overlapping onto the time band of when a long-term stock market cycle is due. Where the two time bands overlap narrows the zone of greatest probability as to where the market trend will end — and a new one begin.

The first step in this process involves identifying an 18-year cycle as a starting point. From there, count forward 15-21 years, outlining a time band for the next 18-year cycle. One must keep in mind that after two consecutive 18-year cycles unfolding in this "normal" time band, the probabilities increase that the third (and fourth and fifth) such cycle may "distort." That means it could unfold earlier than 15 years ("contraction"), or greater than 21 years ("expansion"). As discussed in *Volume 1*, the probabilities are greater that such a distortion will be of the "contraction" type, and most likely not less than 13 years. However, of the 11 instances of 18-year cycles to date, only one has clearly contracted to 13 years (1842), and possibly a second (1987). However, it is possible that 1990 — 16 years and normal — may have been the correct starting point as well. All other instances were 15-21 years.

THE 4-YEAR CYCLE TIME BAND

The next step — and here is where an investor's strategy really begins — involves identifying the 4-year sub-cycles that are due within this 18-year cycle. Historically, the 18-year cycle usually consists of five 4-year phases, or sub-cycles. Of the 11 cases of 18-year cycles in the history of U.S. stocks as of this writing, eight have contained five phases of 4-year cycles (72.7%). The other three have each contained three phases of the 4-year cycle. Two of those involved the only 13-year (contracted) instances of the 18-year cycle.

The crest of the 18-year cycle is not likely to top out in the first 4-year phase. In fact, in the 11 historical cases, the 18-year cycle topped out only twice in the second 4-year cycle phase. It peaked twice in the third 4-year cycle phase, four times in the fourth phase, and three times in the fifth. Therefore we can conclude that an 18-year cycle has the greatest probability of topping out in the fourth or fifth 4-year cycle phase. The reason this is important is because it gives the investor an edge in knowing when to look for a crest in a 4-year cycle. If it is one of the first three 4-year cycles of an 18-year cycle, then the probability is great that the cycle will not top out until it passes its midway point (*right translation* — see *Volume 1* for description). Therefore, when investing via the 4-year cycle, the investor looks for buying opportunities in at least the first two years — except when it is the fourth or fifth 4-year cycle phase of the longer-term 18-year cycle.

As discussed in great detail in *Volume 1*, all first phases of longer-term cycles will have a predominance of bullish characteristics. Furthermore, they will not tend to distort — although there are occasions when they will distort following even longer-term cycles, like a 36-, 54-, or 72-year cycle. Therefore, the first 4-year cycle phase (in fact, the first three 4-year cycle phases) of the 18-year cycle will tend to 1) exhibit "right translation," which means the crest will occur past the midway point in time between the troughs that define this cycle, and/or 2) not take out the low of the 18-year cycle itself, and 3) will have an 84.6% probability of unfolding between 36-56 months. Therefore, this first step involves identifying a time band that is 36-56 months after the 18-year cycle trough. This can be repeated for the next two 4-year cycles. This, then, is the time band which has the highest probability of coinciding with the next 4-year cycle trough.

GEOCOSMIC TIME BANDS

Now enters geocosmics. Within the 36-56 month period following the 18-year cycle (or, the time band for the next 4-year cycle trough), one needs to now identify the dates in which any Level 1 long-term geocosmic signature time bands will unfold. The list of Level 1 signatures can be found in the previous chapter. That is, are there any dates in this time band in which certain aspects between Jupiter, Saturn, Uranus, Neptune, or Pluto will form to one another? If so, then mark that date on the chart. Then, go into the prior chapters of this book, and see 1) what the allowable extended time band has been historically for this signature to correlate to a long-term stock market cycle, and 2) what type of cycle does it tend to correlate with (trough, crest, 4-year or greater, or shorter than 4-year types).

In most cases, there are more than one of these geocosmic signatures present. This makes the task of narrowing the time band even more possible. For that is the primary purpose of this exercise — to outline the shortest time band possible in which a long-term cycle is most likely to unfold. Therefore at this stage of the process, one outlines time bands in which these geocosmic signatures are in effect. Although the reader is advised to create an outline for both the central time bands and their extended time bands, in reality it may be sufficient to start with just the extended time band.

The next step is then identifying the time frame in which these geocosmic time bands overlap with the cycle time band for the 4-year trough. In some cases it may be advantageous to examine the 6-month time period before the 36 month interval, and/or after the 56-month interval. If there are very large signatures nearby — such as Jupiter to Saturn, or Saturn to any planet beyond — but outside of the 36-56 month interval, it is possible that their unique planetary orb time bands will still intersect the cycle time band, either at the very beginning or very end. This is especially useful in those cases where there is a lack of other long-term planetary pair cycles within the 36-56 month interval itself. Therefore, it is suggested that the reader not only look within the 36-56 month time band interval for long-term geocosmic signatures, but also be aware of such signatures unfolding slightly before or after this time band — especially in the cases of Saturn in aspects to planets beyond, as well as to Jupiter (the other Jupiter transits are not as important as its aspects to Saturn).

When the 4-year cycle being examined represents the fifth phase of the greater 18-year cycle, it is recommended to use the greater 32-72 month interval. The probability of the

4-year cycle distorting increases considerably when the 18-year cycle is due. It may therefore either contract to less than 38 months, or expand to more than 56 months.

Within the 4-year cycle, though, are two very important shorter-term cycles: the 22.5-month, and the 50-week cycle. These too need to be analyzed to optimally time additional periods for potentially profitable entrances into the stock market.

THE 22.5-MONTH CYCLE TIME BAND

The time band for the 4-year cycle trough can be narrowed even further as the market completes it sub-cycles, or phases. Within the 4-year cycle are usually two, but sometimes three, phases known as the 22.5-month cycle (or sub-cycle). After the 4-year cycle starts, there is a very reliable trough that unfolds around the 22.5-month interval (actually it is 18-27 months). One's analysis of this cycle is fine up until here. In fact, one can outline this time band and have a fairly high confidence of a half-cycle trough (to the 4-year cycle) unfolding 18-27 months following a 4-year cycle trough. And, within this time band, one may search for the presence of long and intermediate-term geocosmic signatures (just as performed before), and use these to narrow even further the probable time band for this sub-cycle. However, the second (and third) instance of this sub-cycle is not very reliable. Its orb varies greatly. Occasionally there is even a third such instance of this cycle within the 4-year cycle, and it is *very* prone to great distortion (sometimes as short as 8 months).

So the 22.5-month sub-cycle **will not help** greatly in identifying — or narrowing — the time band for the next 4-year cycle trough. It **will help** in defining an important half-cycle trough to the 4-year cycle, but not the final 4-year cycle itself, for the second half of the 4-year cycle is not comprised of clearly defined and reliable 22.5-month sub-cycle phases.

THE 50-WEEK CYCLE TIME BAND

But there is help, and it is in the form of yet a smaller but very reliable cycle, known as the 50-week cycle. To aid in the task of further narrowing the time band of a probable 4-year cycle, it is necessary to scale down further to the analysis of this 50-week cycle. Within the 22.5-month cycle are usually two 50-week cycles — except in the second half of the 4-year cycle where the 22.5-month cycle can contract greatly, as it sometimes does in its third instance. In these cases there is only one 50-week cycle to the 22.5-month cycle. They are the same.

What is useful, though, is the knowledge that within the 4-year cycle there will usually be four or five of these 50-week cycles. In 15 instances of 4-year cycles since 1938, three have contained only three 50-week cycles, seven have contained four 50-week cycles, and five have contained five 50-week cycles. Thus 12 of 15 instances have contained either four or five phases known as this 50-week cycle. The probabilities thus favor a 4-year cycle comprised of either four or five 50-week sub-cycles, or phases.

THE INVESTOR'S "STRATEGY"

Why is the knowledge of 50-week cycle phases important to our task? Well, the task is to buy stocks at the 4-year cycle troughs, and carry them to the crest of the four-year cycle. As long as it is not the last 4-year cycle to an even greater 18-year cycle, an investor can usually depend upon the trend of the 4-year cycle to be bullish, until at least the third 50-week cycle phase within this 4-year cycle. That means the investor can not only buy stocks as prices drop into a time band for the 4-year cycle trough, but he/she can also buy as prices drop into the first, second, and even third 50-week cycle trough (end of first, second, and third phases) of the 4-year cycle. This will be true for the first three 4-year cycle phases of the even greater 18-year cycle. Once the market starts the fourth 4-year cycle phase of an 18-year cycle, then this strategy needs to be altered whereby the buying stops after the second 50-week cycle phase of the 4-year cycle.

In most cases, the trough of the second 50-week cycle phase will coincide with the 22.5-month cycle — the first of this sub-cycle's two or three phases to the 4-year cycle. Where this 22.5-month cycle and the second 50-week cycle time bands overlap defines a narrower time band for the lows of each, which will provide an outstanding point to either buy — or add onto existing — stock positions, especially if the market is in one of the first three 4-year cycles of the greater 18-year cycle.

There is yet a second importance to knowing about the 50-week cycle. As stated earlier, there is an 80% probability (12 of 15 cases since 1938) that the 4-year cycle trough will coincide with the fourth or fifth instance of this 50-week phase. Thus once the market completes its third or fourth 50-week cycle phase, the projection of its next occurrence (time band) will overlap the time band for the 4-year cycle trough itself. This 4-year cycle trough time band has already been narrowed considerably through the use of geocosmic time bands in effect during that interval. By applying the fourth or fifth 50-week cycle time band on top of that, this 4-year cycle trough time band can be reduced even further.

However, there is the matter of distortion to consider at the end. As with all long-term cycles, the last phase of the 4-year cycle has a higher-than-usual tendency to distort. As explained and demonstrated thoroughly in *Volume 1*, there have been 71 cases of 50-week cycles in the U.S. stock market between November 1929 and October 1997, which have unfolded in the 29-78 week interval. 73.2% of them have unfolded between the 38-62 week interval, which is considered the normal time band. Of the 19 instances that distorted (occurred outside of the normal 38-62 week interval), eight of these coincided with the 4-year cycle. Because there are only 16 cases of 4-year cycles since 1929, that means there is a 50-50 chance that the last 50-week cycle phase of the 4-year cycle will distort. Furthermore, seven of those eight instances were the expansion type of distortion. The length of the expansion varied up to 72 weeks. In fact, nine of these 16 cases unfolded between the 61-72 week interval. The other seven cases ranged from 36-62 weeks (mostly in the normal time band). Thus in the last 50-week phase of a 4-year cycle, we need to outline a projected time band that is 32-72 weeks following the last such instance.

Therefore, once the third or fourth 50-week cycle phases to the 4-year cycle are completed, one should project 32-72 weeks out into the future. This time band represents its next scheduled due period. Even though this 40-week interval may seem like a long time frame to consider, the fact is that it will very likely intersect only partially with the previously defined time band for the 4-year cycle. The overlap of the two cycle time bands will very often be less than the time band of each one individually, and this overlap then becomes the most likely period for the actual cycle to unfold. One's task of identifying the time band for the next 4-year cycle trough has just been defined more narrowly — which is the goal of this methodology.

THE 4-YEAR CYCLE CREST

Identifying the probable time band for the crest of the first four-year cycle phase of the 18-year cycle requires knowledge and application of certain cycle characteristics just discussed. Again this subject was covered at length in *Volume 1*, and the reader is encouraged to review those sections. As the first phase is more apt to be bullish, and as one of the characteristics of a bull market is *right translation*, it can be assumed that the 4-year cycle crest will occur past the halfway point between the start of the 4-year (and 18-year) cycle and the time band determined for the probable "next" 4-year cycle trough.

In the first 4-year cycle of the greater 18-year cycle, the probabilities are greatest that the 4-year cycle crest will occur 1) after the 22.5-month half cycle, and 2) in at least the third 50-week cycle phase (or later — the fourth, or even fifth). *The probability of the first 4-year cycle crest (of a new 18-year cycle) unfolding in the first two 50-week cycle phases is very remote, unless it is also a longer-term cycle, like the 36-, 54-, or 72-year cycle. Therefore, the time to begin searching for the 4-year cycle crest is only after the third 50-week cycle has begun. It is even better to look for this crest in the fourth 50-week phase, for the likelihood of it unfolding here is greatest.* Even if the 4-year cycle tops out in the third 50-week cycle, probabilities are great that the rally in the fourth 50-week cycle will challenge the previous high, perhaps forming a double top. The greatest decline of a 4-year cycle in the early phase of a larger 18-year cycle is not until its last 50-week cycle phase. In the last 50-week cycle phase, the market is apt to exhibit more bearish characteristics than the previous phases, such as lower highs than the previous 50-week cycle, and/or lower lows than the prior 50-week cycle, and/or a *left translation* chart pattern.

There are two things we know from history about the rallies in even the last 50-week cycle phase of the 4-year cycle. First, the rally to the crest of the 50-week cycle will last at least 9 weeks. There have been no instances of 50-week cycles topping out before the ninth week. Secondly, we know the market will top out several weeks before the bottom of the 4-year (and final 50-week phase) is achieved. In fact, the shortest duration of declines from the crest of the last 50-week cycle phase to the trough of the 4-year cycle has been 8 and 9 weeks (1987 and 1994, respectively). The one in 1990 declined 12 weeks. These are the shortest on record since 1929. All other final phases have declined 14-59 weeks.

Thus this methodology of forecasting the 4-year cycle crest requires outlining a time band that starts 9 weeks after the fourth 50-week cycle commences, and lasts until 8 weeks prior to the end of the time band outlined for the 4-year cycle trough. This then becomes an extended time band for a 4-year cycle crest — which we know will precede the trough by at least 8 weeks.

Within this time band, the analyst once again identifies the presence of intermediate and long-term planetary cycles. The history of these cycles is reviewed in the earlier chapters of this book. Time bands are outlined in which these signatures have coincided with the culmination of long-term stock market cycles in the past. Furthermore, each cycle is studied to see if it has a more probable association with long-term cycle crests in U.S. stocks. If so, then that (or those) time band(s) are given greatest priority. The interval of time where these geocosmic time bands overlap with the cycle crest time band previously determined, then, becomes the most probable period in which the 4-year cycle will form its crest — or at least a significant crest in which the investor may exit stock holdings prior to a potentially severe decline to the trough of the 4-year cycle itself. Sometimes this crest time band just outlined will produce a lower high than the crest of the preceding 50-week cycle, but generally it is either 1) the 4-year cycle crest or 2) a test of it.

INVESTMENT STRATEGY SUMMARY

Thus the strategy to be employed by long-term investors for this first 4-year cycle phase of the new 18-year cycle is to buy as prices decline into the time band outlined for this long-term 18-year and 4-year cycle. Positions on the long side can be added on as prices decline into the first two — and probably three — 50-week cycle troughs that follow this 4-year cycle, and especially at the 22.5-month cycle trough, which will probably coincide with the second 50-week cycle phase. Investors can remain long until the time band for the crest of the fourth or fifth 50-week cycle can be outlined, as just described. That will usually be at least 9 weeks after it starts. In none of the cases studied has the crest of the final 50-week cycle in a greater 4-year cycle topped out before the 9th week of the cycle. Furthermore, it will top out at least 8 weeks prior to the end of the time band outlined for the trough of the forthcoming 4-year cycle. This time band can be narrowed considerably using long-term geocosmic signatures. When prices form a crest in this "most probable time band" for a crest, investors can sell stocks and prepare to re-enter when the market declines into the time band outlined for the next 4-year cycle trough.

TECHNICAL INDICATORS AND CHART PATTERNS

In *Volume 1*, six technical indicators were identified that frequently occur at — and can help identify — primary cycle troughs and crests. Although this current book does not discuss the shorter-term primary cycle, the fact is that every 50-week, 22.5-month, and 4-year cycle is also a primary cycle. Therefore these same chart patterns will likely unfold when these longer-term cycles culminate. Most notable of these indicators will be the following five:

1. **Long-term Support and Resistance**
2. **Double Bottoms or Double Tops**
3. **Head and Shoulders Formations**
4. **Intermarket Divergences**
5. **Critical Moving Averages**

This book will not repeat in detail the descriptions given in *Volume 1.* However, suffice it to say that 50-week cycles will generally correct 38-62% of their swing up as they form their troughs — except when they coincide with the 4-year cycle itself. In those cases, the decline will more often be a 38-62% correction of the whole 4-year swing up. Furthermore, the decline to the 4-year cycle trough will 1) usually be represent a loss of at least 20% from the crest of the 4-year cycle, and 2) test or penetrate the low of the prior 50-week cycle. As a 4-year cycle tops out or bottoms, it will very frequently do so with a double top or double bottom formation within 18 months, and usually less than 4 months. If a long-term head and shoulders pattern is forming following a potential 4-year cycle crest or trough, it should be given great importance. When the neckline of that pattern breaks, it is a confirmation signal that the 4-year cycle is over, and the trend reversal is in process. Also, as the Dow Jones Industrial Averages forms its 4-year cycle trough or crest, it will frequently do so on a different date that the S&P futures, or some other prominent and related stock market index. The time difference between the two indices can be as much as several months, or as short as one week. And finally, one can use the 23-month moving average as a confirming indicator. When the stock market has completed its 4-year cycle crest, prices will typically decline to at least test, and usually penetrate below, this moving average. After the 4-year cycle trough is in, the market will then rally back above this average. The 23-month average is the one of choice because it represents half the length of the cycle being confirmed. This is a general rule that can be applied to all markets and all cycles. When it is broken, it generally confirms that cycle has either topped or bottomed, if such a top or bottom occurred in the time band that was projected as its potential due date. Occasionally there are "fake-outs" to these indicators, but they usually occur in time periods that do not coincide with the calculated cycle top or bottom as outlined in the series of this book.

EXAMPLE 1

To demonstrate this methodology, let's examine the first 4-year cycle of an 18-year cycle in U.S. stocks, using examples since 1953. The reader can view the discussion by observing the weekly charts provided on pages 246 and 253.

The 18-year cycle trough of 1953 occurred on September 15. The first step in determining the due date of the next 4-year cycle is to go forward in time 36-56 months. This gives a time band of **September 1956 - May 1958** as the most likely period for the first 4-year cycle trough of this new 18-year cycle.

Now let's look in the ephemeris for that time frame and locate any major transiting aspects between Jupiter, Saturn, Uranus, Neptune, and Pluto that occurred during this

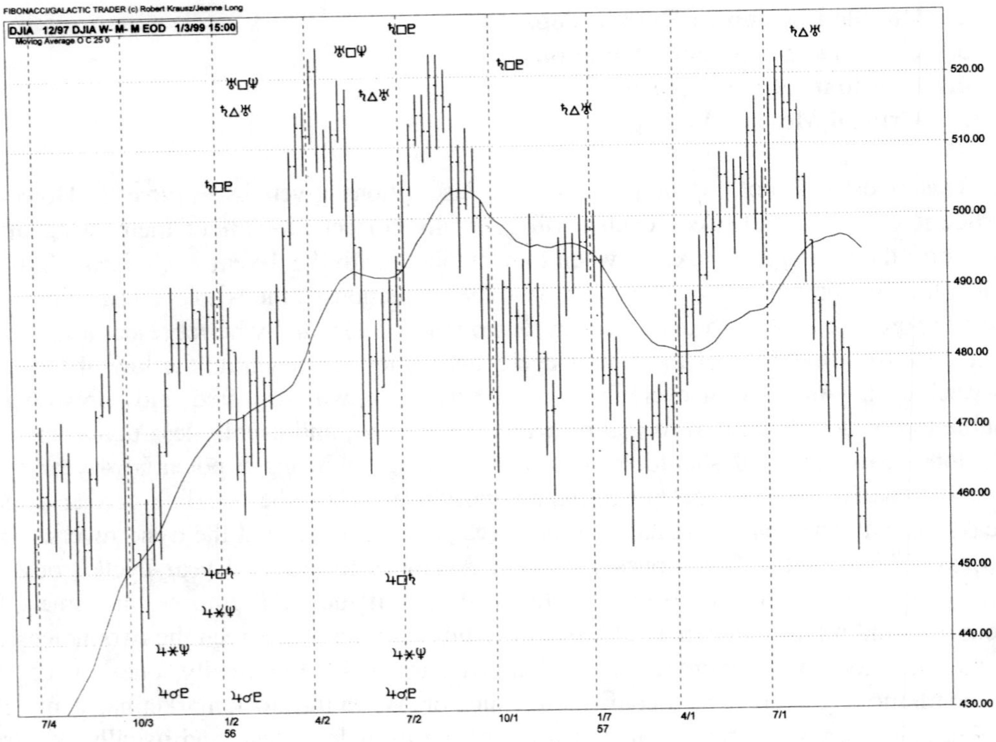
FIBONACCI/GALACTIC TRADER (c) Robert Krausz/Jeanne Long
DJIA 12/97 DJIA W- M- M EOD 1/3/99 15:00
Moving Average O C 25 0
520.00
510.00
500.00
490.00
480.00
470.00
460.00
450.00
440.00
430.00
7/4
10/3
1/2
56
4/2
7/2
10/1
1/7
57
4/1
7/1

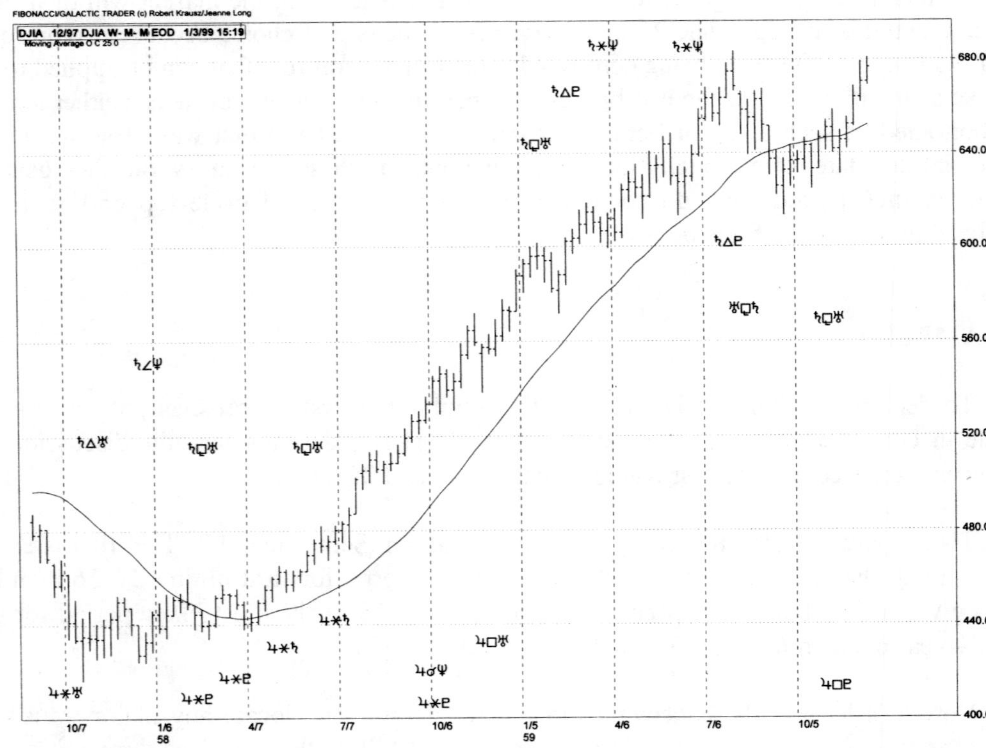
FIBONACCI/GALACTIC TRADER (c) Robert Krausz/Jeanne Long
DJIA 12/97 DJIA W- M- M EOD 1/3/99 15:19
Moving Average O C 25 0
680.00
640.00
600.00
560.00
520.00
480.00
440.00
400.00
10/7
1/6
58
4/7
7/7
10/6
1/5
59
4/6
7/6
10/5

period. Below is a list, outlining the central time bands, and the expanded time bands, as determined by the criteria stated in the earlier chapters of this book. The numbers in parentheses next to signatures represent the Level 1, 2, or 3 types.

Signature & Type	Central Time Band	Expanded Time Band
♅□♆ - 270° (1)	7/15/54 – 5/5/56	July 1953 – May 1957
♃□♄ - 270° (1)	8/24/55 – 6/21/56	December 1954 – February 1957
♃⚹♆ - 300° (2)	11/2/55 – 6/24/56	August 1955 – September 1956
♃☌♇ - 0° (2)	11/2/55 – 6/16/56	May 1955 – December 1956
♄□♇ - 90° (1)	12/27/55 – 10/7/56	August 1955 – February 1957
♄△♅ - 120° (1)	1/17/56 – 10/20/57	March 1956 – July 1958
♃⚹♄ - 300° (1)	9/20/57 – 6/22/58	February 1957 – January 1959
♃⚹♅ - 60°	9/28/57, +/- 2 months	July 1957 – November 1957
♄∠♆ - 45° (1)	12/31/57 +/- 3 months	May 1957 – July 1958
♃⚹♇ - 60°	2/4/58 – 9/22/58	October 1957 – January 1959
♄⚼♅ - 135° (1)	2/16/58 - 12/2/59	May 1957 - September 1960
♃☌♆ - 0° (2)	9/24/58, +/- 2 months	March 1958 – March 1959
♃□♅ - 90° (3)	11/24/58, +/- 2 months	August 1958 – February 1959

One way to go about our task is to determine which parts of these geocosmic signatures overlap with the cycle time band itself for a 4-year stock market trough. Earlier we identified this cycle time band as September 1956 - May 1958. We are only concerned with those parts of geocosmic signatures that overlap during this period. As a point of tact, the reader is advised to first do this exercise using only the central time band. See if that alone produces a couple of smaller time bands within the 4-year cycle time band. If not, then go to the extended time bands and do the same.

In this manner, we can eliminate the first four geocosmic signatures because their central time bands do not overlap the cycle time band for a trough. They all end prior to September 1956, which is when the cycle time band starts. We can also eliminate the last two signatures, for the time bands of the last two — even with a 2-month orb — commence after the cycle time band ends. We would only consider those six signatures if we did not have a sufficient number of geocosmic signatures unfolding within this cycle time band. As it turns out, there are still seven major geocosmic signatures whose central time bands overlap the time band outlined for the 4-year cycle. Let's look at them and where they overlap.

Five of these seven are Level 1 geocosmic signatures. As stated in the previous chapter, there is a nearly 90% probability that a Level 1 signature will occur nearby to a 4-year cycle in U.S. stocks. The Saturn-Pluto waxing square overlaps our cycles time band for a 4-year cycle trough for only 2 months — **September and October 1956**. The Saturn-Uranus waxing trine overlaps between **September 1956 - October 1957**. Next is the Jupiter waning sextile to Saturn, which overlaps the cycle time band between **September 1957 - May 1958.** The fourth signature to consider is the Saturn in waxing semi-square to Neptune. The central time band here is in effect **September 1957 - March 1958.** And finally there is the Saturn in waxing şesquiquadrate to Uranus, which will overlap the cycle time band from **February - May 1958.**

A close analysis of the overlap of these time bands with the 4-year cycle time band will reveal three distinct periods for consideration. The first is the overlap of the Saturn square Pluto and Saturn trine Uranus signatures with the 4-year cycle, which occurs between **September - October 1956**. Therefore, this has to be considered a possible trough (or crest) time band. Next we must consider the fact that Saturn trine Uranus, Jupiter sextile Saturn, and Saturn semi-square to Neptune, all overlap between **September - October 1957,** so this too has to be considered a prime candidate for the 4-year cycle trough. And finally, the last three Level 1 signatures can be seen to overlap between **February - March 1958**, so this too must be considered as a possibility. The other two signatures in this group — Jupiter sextile Uranus and Jupiter sextile Pluto — need not be considered at all since their historical correspondence to long-term stock market cycles was so weak that it did not qualify for any Level designation.

By looking back into the study sections of this book, one can see that these five Level 1 signatures have the greatest probability of coinciding with 4-year cycles. In fact, whenever one does this method of outlining a time band for a 4-year or greater cycle, one must keep in mind that the Saturn and beyond transiting aspects, along with Jupiter-Saturn signatures, will far outweigh the shorter Jupiter transiting aspects under consideration. It is therefore most likely that a 4-year or greater cycle will coincide with these Level 1 signatures and the periods of time in which their "orb of influence" will overlap with the long-term projected cycle time band.

Now, mark down these calculated time bands for a potential 4-year cycle trough— **September - October 1956, September - October 1957, and February–March 1958**. Let's then proceed into the cycle itself, and identify the 50-week sub-cycles, or phases, in an effort to further minimize the time band for this possible 4-year bottom.

The 18-year cycle bottomed on September 15, 1953. It is thus also the starting point of a new 4-year cycle. A probable 50-week cycle trough was thus due 38-62 weeks later. In fact it occurred 59 weeks later on **November 1, 1954**. Although this illustration will not go into detail, there is a great likelihood that one or more of these trans-Jupiter signatures would have been present nearby to this period. In fact, within two months, there were four such signatures: Jupiter waning □ Neptune (September 17, and December 23, 1954), and Jupiter ☌ Uranus (October 7, 1954, and January 6, 1955). The midpoint of this cluster is November 11, 1954. The purpose of this chapter in this book, however, is to locate 4-year cycles crests and troughs for investment purposes. In the next book we will study shorter-term cycles for shorter-term trading purposes. Nevertheless, this low was significant in the respect that it would have allowed investors to make further long-term purchases of stocks.

The next step is to outline the time band for the second 50-week cycle phase, which would probably coincide with the 22.5-month cycle trough. The 22.5-month cycle is due in the 18-27 month interval of the 4-year cycle, or **March - December 1955.** That time band may be narrowed simply by counting forward 38-62 weeks past the November 1, 1954 date. This would provide a time band for the second 50-week cycle trough. This projects out to **July 25, 1955 - January 6, 1956.** By overlapping these two projected time bands, one can narrow the probable time for the 22.5-month and second 50-week cycle trough to **July 25, 1955 - December 31, 1955.** A glance at the weekly charts will confirm that the 22.5-month and 50-week cycles unfolded on **October 11, 1955**. This was the 25th month of the 4-year and 22.5-month cycle, and the 49th week of the 50-week cycle. It was also within two months of three major Jupiter signatures discussed in this book — Jupiter waning □ to Saturn on August 24, 1955; Jupiter waning ⚹ to Neptune on November 2, 1955; and Jupiter ☌ Pluto on November 2, 1955. The midpoint of this cluster was about September 28, 1955. Once again, as this 50-week cycle trough unfolded, investors may look to purchase additional stocks, for the crest of the 4-year cycle is most likely still ahead. Ideally investors will look to take profits in the time band for the crest of the fourth 50-week cycle. However, even at the crest of third 50-week cycle, investors might want to start unloading some stocks.

The third 50-week cycle can thus be projected out 38-62 weeks from the October 11, 1955 date. This comes out to **July 2, 1956 - December 28, 1956.** This one actually came in early, on **May 28, 1956**, the 33rd week. Interestingly enough, there were the same three Jupiter aspects nearby as occurred in the prior 50-week cycle, and no Jupiter aspects further along into the cycle. These were: Jupiter ☌ Pluto June 16, 1956; Jupiter waning □ to Saturn on June 21, 1956; and Jupiter waning ⚹ Neptune on June 24, 1956. The midpoint of this cluster was June 20, about three weeks after the actual cycle unfolded, and only 12 calendar days after June 8, which was a re-test to the May 28 trough (double bottom). The fact that the 50-week cycle contracted here would serve as an alert signal, that perhaps the market was ready to top out — or perhaps did in fact top out, since this was already the third 50-week cycle phase. In hindsight, it did top out in April 1956, with a re-test of that top in August 1956 and again in July 1957. However May 28, 1956 is too early for the 4-year cycle itself, which was not due until September, 1956 or later.

Therefore, investors would now create a time band for a cycle crest in which to exit all (or most) long positions and stand aside until the formation of the forthcoming 4-year cycle crest. May 28, 1956 would thus begin the fourth 50-week cycle phase of the 4-year cycle. We would therefore start looking for major geocosmic signatures that would start unfolding 9 weeks later, through March 1958. Why through March 1958? Because earlier we calculated three time bands for the probable 4-year cycle trough. The last one ended May 1958. And, we know that the crest must unfold at least 8 weeks (2 months) before the completion of the 4-cycle cycle trough.

Therefore our optimal time band for a 4-year cycle crest (or double top fro which the greatest decline would commence) would be **August 1956 (at least 9 weeks after May 28, 1956) through March 1958.** We also realize that since the 50-week cycle contracted, the 4-year cycle crest may have already unfolded at the crest of the third 50-week cycle, which was at 524.40 on April 9, 1956. Even if it was, we still expect a challenge to that high on the crest of the fourth 50-week cycle — unless prices first start falling below the 50-week trough of May 28. If that happens, it may be too late to exit near the top, and investors will simply have to wait for a corrective rally to a smaller cycle yet — the primary cycle — to exit.

This time band can be narrowed down even further by projecting the time band for the next 50-week cycle trough. Since this would be the fourth 50-week cycle phase of the 4-year cycle, it could very well be the last one. Therefore, we must calculate a time band of 32-72 weeks from May 28, 1956. This comes out to **January 7, 1957 - October 18, 1957**. The crest will therefore unfold at least 8 weeks prior to the trough, which means it would likely unfold before August 23, 1957. *Therefore, our ideal time for a 4-year cycle crest (or double top) would be August 1956 - August 1957, and for the trough it would be January 7, 1957 - October 18, 1957.* The most ideal part of that time band for the trough would be the last 10 weeks, for that would mean it was an expansion, which would provide a high confidence factor that there would not be a fifth 50-week cycle phase.

Once again, the market timer searches for geocosmic signatures present between August 1956 - August 1957 (and even a couple months before and after), which is the projected time band for the crest — or test — of the 4-year cycle, based on the assumption that it is most likely to unfold in this, the fourth 50-week cycle phase. Using this time band, the following signatures are present:

♅□♆	7/15/54 - 5/5/56
♃□♄	8/24/55 - 6/21/56
♃⚹♆	11/2/55 - 6/24/56
♃☌♇	11/2/55 - 6/16/56
♄□♇	12/27/55 - 10/7/56
♄△♅	1/17/56 - 10/20/57
♃⚹♄	9/20/57 - 6/22/58
♃⚹♅	9/28/57+/- 2 months

These are the same first eight signatures used in calculating the 4-year cycle trough. The first four signatures can be used here, because they are within three months of the starting point. However, they are not necessary, because there is a sufficient number of the other signatures present, and their central time bands do not overlap with our time bands for this cycle crest. Now we can expand the first group of geocosmic signature from the previous pages to overlap with the cycles time band between **August - October 1956.** We still may use the second and third time bands as found in the projection of the trough: **September - October 1957 and February - March 1958.**

As one knows, the crest will come first. Therefore, if these signatures are to coincide with 4-year cycle crests and troughs and they are all in the time band for each, it is most likely that the first time band will not be the 4-year cycle trough, and it is also likely that the final time band will not be the 4-year cycle crest. Troughs follow crests.

An examination of the weekly charts reveals that the crest we were looking for in this exercise actually unfolded on **August 2 and 9, 1956**, at 523.20. This was within the first time band outlined. It was not a new 4-year cycle high, but a double top to the crest that occurred earlier on April 9 at 524.40. As expected, though, it indeed was a challenge to the prior high and gave investors an opportunity to exit near the then all-time high, the 4-year cycle crest.

The market then declined to the fourth 50-week cycle trough on **February 12, 1957**. This was right at the beginning of our calculated time band for a the 50-week cycle trough (it was the 37th week, and was one week early than a "normal" 50-week time band). It is thus possible that this could be the 4-year cycle trough, as it occurred between the outlined time band for such a cycle: **September 1956 - May 1958**. Furthermore this 50-week cycle distorted, as it unfolded at a contracted 37-week interval (normal would have been 38-62 weeks). However this date did not coincide with our greatest overlap periods from the geocosmic signatures. In fact, there were no geocosmic aspects from Jupiter or beyond within two months. Therefore, it is quite possible that a fifth 50-week cycle might yet unfold. Investors now have to make a choice. They can either start purchasing at this time, as the fourth 50-week cycle unfolds in this fourth 50-week cycle phase time band (which was indeed a distortion), and/or wait until another cycle unfolds — a fifth one — that may take prices even lower, and also coincide with the desired presence of long-term geocosmic signatures. The strategy employed by this book would advise investors to make some purchases now and make further purchases on the next 50-week cycle trough, which may find prices falling even lower since this particular 50-week cycle was not the "highest confidence" date for a 4-year cycle trough, due to the fact that it did not have the most geocosmic signature time bands for a long-term stock market cycle overlapping at this time.

The analyst must now outline yet another time band (actually two). First, once again draw a line 32-72 weeks past February 12, 1957. This becomes the time band for a potential fifth 50-week cycle phase, and thus 4-year cycle trough. This comes out to **September 20, 1957 - July 3, 1958.** We can immediately deduct the last two months from this time band, for we know the cycle itself ends in May 1958. Thus we have to be cognizant of the period between **September 20, 1957 - May 1958** as the probable time band for a 4-year cycle trough.

We can also outline a period for yet another possible 4-year cycle crest (or test of it) nine weeks after February 12, through 2 months prior to May 1958. This would yield a time band of **April 1957 - March 1958.**

Here is what happened. The market declined to the final 4-year cycle trough during the most preferred time band outlined for this important cycle low, September – October 1957. It fell on **October 22, 1957**, at 416.20. It was during the fifth 50-week cycle phase. It was a 36-week interval from the prior 50-week cycle trough, which means it was a contraction (distortion). And it occurred in the geocosmic time band and cycle time band overlap, as calculated above. Prior to that, the market tested the 4-year cycle crest again at the crest of the fifth 50-week cycle, on July 16, 1957 at 523.10. This too was within our time band for a projected 50-week (and possible 4-year) cycle crest, and as expected, it was at least 2 months prior to the 4-year cycle trough. Additionally, on August 6, 1957, Saturn formed a waxing Δ to Uranus, which is the type of major geocosmic signature expected nearby to a 4-year or greater cycle crest or trough. It returned for the fifth and final time on October 20, 1957, just two days prior to the actual 4-year cycle trough. Around that same time, Jupiter formed a sextile to both Saturn and Uranus (September 20, 1957, and September 28, 1957, respectively).

Thus the market timing techniques outlined in this book worked very well for identifying time bands for the major crests and troughs within this 4-year cycle, and certainly the 4-year cycle crest and trough themselves. Let's now proceed to the next example, in which we will use the expanded geocosmic time bands.

EXAMPLE 2

Let's continue with the next 4-year cycle that followed October 22, 1957. You may wish to refer to the charts on pages 246 and 253.

The first step is to identify which phase it will be of the greater 18-year cycle, for this will enable us to anticipate whether this particular 4-year cycle will be a bullish or bearish phase. If bullish, then we can anticipate that 1) the crest of this 4-year cycle will likely be higher in price than the previous 4-year cycle crest, 2) the trough which ends this 4-year cycle will likely be higher in price than the trough which ended the last 4-year cycle (and began this one), and in fact will most likely be a 38-62% correction of the swing up to its crest, and 3) it will likely form its crest after the 22.5-month cycle unfolds, or in other words, it will likely exhibit a right translation pattern wherein its crest occurs in the second half of the cycle. If, on the other hand, this 4-year cycle phase of the 18-year cycle was to be bearish, we would expect several of the aforementioned expectations to be the opposite. That is, 1) the crest might be lower in price than the previous 4-year cycle, 2) the trough which ends the 4-year cycle might also be the 18-year cycle trough, and hence it may fall lower in prices than the trough of the previous 4-year cycle, and 3) it may very well form a left translation pattern, wherein the crest unfolds in the first 22.5-month sub-cycle.

Since the 1953–1957 cycle was the first 4-year cycle phase of a new 18-year cycle, then we know that the end of that cycle (October 22, 1957) will begin the second 4-year cycle phase of this same greater 18-year cycle. We can therefore assume that this 4-year cycle phase will also be bullish, since historically, no 18-year cycles have topped out before their second 4-year cycle phase. In fact, since 1842, no 18-year cycles have topped out before their third 4-year cycle phase. With this knowledge, then, the investor looks for buying opportunities at the beginning of this 4-year cycle, and on the first two (and possibly three) 50-week cycle phases to it. The market is not due to top out *before* the third 50-week cycle phase of a bullish 4-year cycle. Therefore, the strategy is to buy all the sub-cycle troughs into the first 22.5-month cycle, and then look to exit these positions in either the third, fourth, or fifth 50-week cycle phase.

FIBONACCI/GALACTIC TRADER (c) Robert Krausz/Jeanne Long
DJIA 12/97 DJIA W- M- M EOD 1/3/99 15:27
Moving Average O C 25 0
♄✶♆
♄△♇
♄□♅
♃△♅
♄□♇
♃☌♄
♃✶♆
♃△♇
♄□♇
♄□♇
♃□♆
740.00
720.00
700.00
680.00
660.00
640.00
620.00
600.00
580.00
560.00
1/4
60
4/4
7/4
10/3
1/2
61
4/3
7/3
10/2
1/1
62

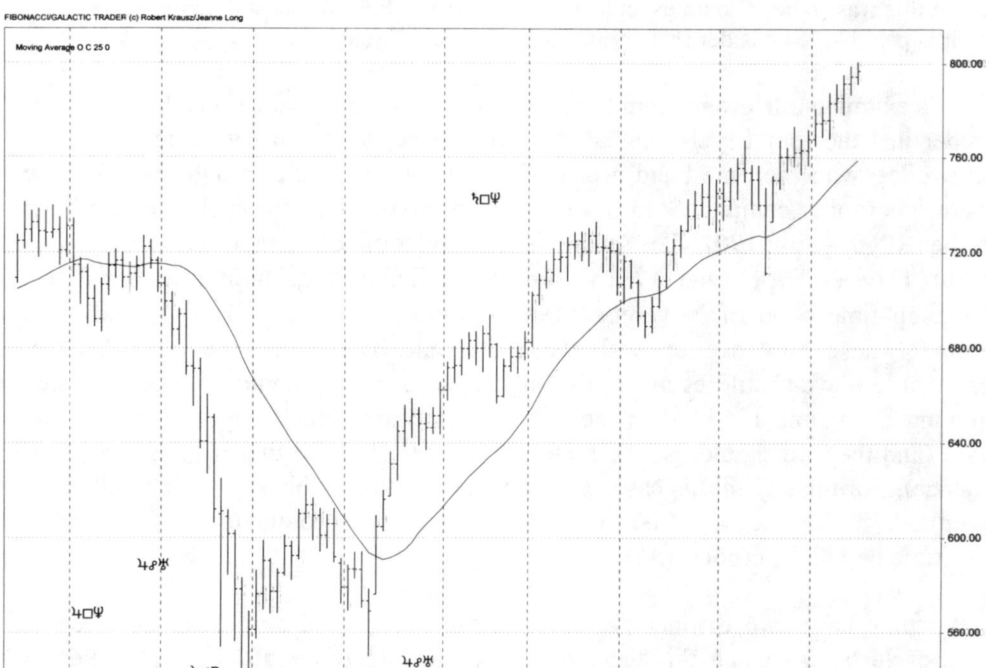
FIBONACCI/GALACTIC TRADER (c) Robert Krausz/Jeanne Long
Moving Average O C 25 0
DJIA 12/97 DJIA W- M- M EOD 1/3/99 15:[illegible]
♄□♆
♃☍♅
♃□♆
♃☍♇
♃☍♇
♃△♆
♃☍♅
♃☍♅
♃△♆
♃☍♇
800.00
760.00
720.00
680.00
640.00
600.00
560.00
520.00
1/1
62
4/2
7/2
10/1
1/7
63
4/1
7/1
10/7
1/6
64

Our initial task is to outline time bands that have the highest potential of coinciding with the forthcoming 4-year cycle trough. We begin by counting forward 36-56 months following the start of the current 4-year cycle. *This provides a time band of October 1960 – June 1962 that has a high probability of containing the next 4-year cycle trough.*

The next step is to create a list of geocosmic signatures whose orbs will unfold during this cyclic time band. In particular, we wish to locate Level 1 signatures within this time band. Below is a list of all the long-term geocosmic signatures that have an orb of influence between **October 1960 - June 1962**:

Signature & Type	**Central Time Band**	**Expanded Time Band**
♃△♇ - 120° (3)	12/5/60 +/- 2 months	June 1960 – June 1961
♃⚹♆ - 60° (3)	12/16/60 +/- 2 months	August 1960 - April 1961
♄⚼♇ - 135° (3)	1/26/61 – 11/11/61	May 1960 – July 1962
♃☌♄ - 0° (1)	2/18/61 +/- 2 months	September 1960 – July 1961
♃□♆ - 90° (2)	1/13/62 +/- 2 months	July 1961 – July 1962
♃☍♅ - 180° (1)	3/14/62 – 12/7/62	September 1961 – June 1963
♃☍♇ - 180° (1)	5/4/62 – 1/15/63	November 1961 – July 1963
♃△♆ - 120° (2)	6/2/62 - 2/2/63	September 1961 – Nov. 1963
♄□♆ - 90° (1)	2/18/63 +/- 3 months	June 1962 – October 1963*

* The Saturn square Neptune came within 4' of a degree of an exact square on June 4, 1962. Because this was so close to an exact aspect, and because Saturn was stationary Retrograde at the time, it is possible to consider this period also as a central time band.

Let's examine this group from the perspective of their extended time bands. First of all consider just the four Level 1 signatures, and the period of time in which their extended orbs overlap with the time band projected for the 4-year cycle trough. The first Level 1 signature is Jupiter conjunct Saturn. Its extended orb overlaps the cycle time band between **October 1960 – July 1961**. The second is the Jupiter oppose Uranus signature, whose orb overlaps between **September 1961 – June 1962.** Third is the Jupiter oppose Pluto, with an overlap time band of **November 1961 – June 1962.** And finally is Saturn square Neptune, whose only overlap with the cycle time band would be **June 1962.** It is questionable if we should even use this signature, or if we should use the period of time beginning from June 1962, when the two planets came within only 4' of arc to an exact square (and then we should use the 8 months prior to that, for that is its acceptable orb of influence). Fortunately in this case, it isn't necessary to use this signature at all. If we did, the author's preference would be to use the 8 months preceding June 1962, which would give a time band of **October 1961 – June 1962.**

We thus have two distinct periods that are highlighted as possible periods for the 4-year cycle trough using this technique. They are: **October 1960 – July 1961** (which involves only one Level 1 signature, but this is OK), and **November 1961 – June 1962** (which involves two, and possibly three, Level 1 signatures in overlap). If we use just the actual extended time band of the only exact Saturn-Neptune square, then the later three signatures only overlap in one month: **June 1962.**

In the first date, there are four supporting signatures (Level 2 and 3 types). These involve Jupiter trine Pluto, Jupiter sextile Neptune, Saturn sesquiquadrate Pluto, and Jupiter square Neptune. The last signature overlaps the greater time period in only the month of **July 1961.** However, the first three of these signature all overlap with the Jupiter conjunct Saturn time band between **October 1960 – April 1961.** This, then, becomes an even more narrow time band of a potential long-term cycle

The second time band — **November 1961 – June 1962** — also has supportive Level 2 and 3 signatures overlapping, and they too can be used to perhaps create an even more narrowly defined time band for this potential 4-year cycle trough. The Saturn sesquiquadrate Pluto, Jupiter square Neptune, and Jupiter trine Neptune all have extended orbs in effect during the same time band as indicated above.

These, then, will be our two most ideal time bands for the next 4-year cycle trough: **October 1960 – April 1961 and November 1961 – June 1962**. To refine this further, we must now let the market unfold, and identify various 22.5-month and 50-week cycles within the 4-year cycle.

The first 50-week cycle phase would most likely unfold 38-62 weeks after October 22, 1957. This projects out to **July 14, 1958 – January 2, 1959.** A look at the weekly charts will reveal that this 50-week cycle trough unfolded in the last week of October 1958, in the 53rd week. The crest unfolded two weeks earlier, so it was a very bullish right translation cycle, which is what one would expect in the first 50-week cycle phase of a new 4-year cycle. At the time of the crest and the trough, there were three signatures nearby: Jupiter conjunct Neptune, sextile Pluto, and square Uranus, all within just a couple of weeks.

The second 50-week cycle, then, would be due 38-62 weeks afterwards. This projects out to **July 20, 1959 – January 8, 1960.** Furthermore, there is a strong likelihood that this 50-week cycle will coincide with the longer 22.5-month cycle. Measured from October 1957, the 22.5-month cycle would be due **April 1959 – January 1960.** As one can see, the 50-week cycle time band narrows this longer cycle time band by three months. A look at the weekly chart of the DJIA will show that this 22.5-month and 50-week cycle unfolded on time, on **September 22, 1959.** The crest to this cycle occurred 7 weeks earlier, on **August 3.** At the time of the crest, there were three powerful signatures nearby: Saturn waxing sextile Neptune, Saturn waxing trine Pluto, and Saturn waxing sesquiquadrate Uranus. The first two are level 2 signatures, while the later is Level 1. These same signatures returned by retrograde nearby to the time of the trough in September.

Now comes the more challenging part of market timing. Our primary task is to identify the 4-year cycle trough, and the crest which will proceed it. We know the 4-year cycle crest could be due in this next 50-week cycle, the third phase of the 4-year cycle. However, it is very unlikely that the 4-year cycle trough would occur in this phase.

Our first task, then, is to outline a period of time when the crest could occur. Since this is the first possible 50-week cycle in which the crest could occur, we must count forward at least 9 weeks from the trough, for all 50-week cycle crests take at least 9 weeks to unfold. Nine weeks from September 22, 1959, comes out to November 23, 1959. This, then is the *earliest* possible date that we might look for a 4-year cycle crest. However, we also know that the 4-year cycle trough is *not likely* in this third 50-week cycle phase, so we might choose to ignore trying to time this crest in this cycle, and instead wait for the next 50-week cycle crest, which has a high probability of at least testing the crest of the third 50-week cycle. At the same time, though, we should also be cognizant of any bearish technical patterns that might form, such as a double top or head and shoulders pattern, for these could be powerful indicators that indeed the cycle may be topping out.

A look at the weekly chart will denote that a double top did indeed form on **January 4, 1960.** The DJIA soared to 688.20, just slightly above the crest of the first 22.5-month cycle back on August 3, 1959, at 683.90. This was very close in time to Saturn waxing sesquiquadrate Uranus (Level 1), Saturn waxing trine to Pluto (Level 2), Saturn waxing sextile to Neptune (Level 2), and Jupiter waxing trine to Uranus (Level 2). This was our first indication that the 4-year cycle might be topping out. We must now consider the possibility that perhaps this will be one of those rare cases of a three-phase 4-year cycle (only three 50-week cycles).

Therefore, the next step is to calculate the third 50-week cycle. Since it might correspond with the 4-year cycle itself, we need to allow it a 32-72 week time band, counted forward from the previous trough of September 22, 1959. This projects a time band of **May 2, 1960 – February 6, 1961.** *Note that this overlaps our first calculated time band for a potential 4-year cycle trough between October 1960 – February 1961!* In other words, this time band is 1) 36-40 months into the 4-year cycle, 2) it contains an important Level 1 geocosmic signature (Jupiter conjunct Saturn), 3) it contains three supporting Level 3 signatures, and 4) it falls within a time band for a 50-week cycle. In fact, the last ten weeks of this time band would constitute an expansion (distortion) to the 50-week cycle, which is something that we like to see as the 4-year cycle bottoms. This means that if the stock market bottoms between **November 28, 1960 – February 6, 1961,** it would fulfill many of our criteria for a 4-year cycle trough.

On **October 25, 1960,** the stock market made a significant trough at 564.20. This was four weeks following a prior low at 565.50 (double bottom). Thus the market made a new 4-year cycle low in a projected time band, and with a chart pattern (double bottom) that is consistent with 4-year cycle troughs. The only things it didn't do, which would make it "perfect," was bottom in the fourth or fifth 50-week cycle phase, and/or distort at the 50-week level. It bottomed in the 57th week, which is "normal."

So was it the 4-year cycle bottom or not? The low occurred in the 36th week, which is acceptable, but just barely. The 50-week cycle was a left translation pattern, which fits. In the final analysis, one would have to assume it was, because both our time and price criteria were met — at least many of these criteria were met. One would then begin to purchase stocks. At the same time, one must keep open to the possibility that there might be another one or two 50-week cycles before this 4-year cycle trough is finally realized. If there were to be lower lows, then investor would simply use them as opportunities to add onto long-term stock positions.

The next step is to outline the time band for the next 50-week cycle. Once again we should count 32-72 weeks forward, since we are not certain that the last trough was indeed the end to the 4-year cycle. Measured from October 25, 1960, this projects out to **June 5, 1961 – March 16, 1962.** A double bottom did in fact occur on June 27 and July 19 at around the 675 mark on the DJIA. Another low occurred on September 25 at 688.90. Either of these could be counted as a 50-week cycle, as both represented substantial declines from the crest which preceded them on May 22 and September 7 at 714.70 and 733.50 respectively. These lows, however, were considerably higher than the previous trough of October 25, 1960. The highs were also higher than the previous 50-week cycle crest. Furthermore, this 50-week cycle exhibited right translation. So either this was the first 50-week cycle of a new 4-year cycle, or it was the fourth 50-week cycle, and there would yet be a fifth 50-week cycle that would contain even more bearish qualities than the third 50-week cycle.

Once again, the market timer must outline a 32-72 week time band measured from the low of either July 19, 1961 or September 25, 1961. Our preference would be to measure from July 19. This projects a time band out to **February 26, 1962 – December 7, 1962.** The first thing we should note is that this time band does indeed overlap with our second (of two) previously defined time bands of potential 4-year cycle troughs as measured from the low of October 1957. In fact, this second time band (November 1961 – June 1962) contained the most Level 1 signatures of the two considered. Therefore, if this 4-year cycle was to be comprised of five 50-week cycle phases, this fifth one would most likely occur when these two time bands overlapped. This would be **February – June 1962.**

Here is what happened. On November 15, 1961, the DJIA topped out at 741.30. This was 17 weeks into the new 50-week cycle. The market then fell back to the 685 area during the last week of January 1962, thus forming a double bottom to the low of September 25, 1961. The market then rallied for six weeks, back up to the 730 area, thus forming a right shoulder to the crest of September 7. That created a head and shoulders pattern, with September 7 as the left shoulder, November 15 as the head, and mid-March as the right shoulder. The neckline (support) was thus the lows around 685-690 in late September and late January. This is a very bearish chart formation, and one that — if it occurs when a long-term cycle crest is due — should be taken seriously when prices start falling below the neckline. This is exactly what happened. The market broke below the neckline by mid-April, and prices collapsed all the way down to 524.60 on June 25, 1962.

In retrospect, one can see that this trough fits better for a 4-year cycle than the one of October 1960. It is still within the 36-56 month interval for a 4-year cycle. It contained three Level 1 signatures nearby, compared to only one in the first projected time frame. It also contained supportive Level 2 signatures. The crest unfolded in a very bearish head and shoulders pattern. And the decline fell to the lowest price of the entire cycle. It turns out that this trough was 20 months following the October 1960 one, which means it also fell in the time band for the 22.5-month cycle. And, as the trough formed, a reverse head and shoulders pattern developed, which pointed to the powerful rally that followed.

Again, in retrospect, one can see that forecasting this 4-year cycle time band was not so difficult. However, determining what to do when these time bands were entered was not so simple. Yet, even if one started to purchase at the first trough (October 1960), it was not too devastating. True, the market went lower 20 months later — but not by much. As a long-term investor looking for ideal times to buy stocks, one would have used both periods to purchase. And if he foresaw the development of the bearish head and shoulders pattern in the fifth 50-week cycle, he could have exited as the neckline was broken (around 680), which is still far ahead of the first trough that was considered in October 1960, when prices were in the 565 area.

This, then, will complete our examples. The process used to outline a time band for a potential 4-year or greater cycle in these examples, is exactly the same process one would use for all examples, and in real life. Of course, using these signatures in past cases for examples, will beg the criticism that, of course, they will work — the studies and results were based upon those very cases that created these values. Well, that is true to some extent. Except, in so many cases, these signatures were present with similar results time and time again. Unless there is some phenomenal coincidence that caused all of these signatures to behave so consistently as they have in the past, there is more than adequate reason to believe that most (if not all) of these signatures will behave in similar fashion in the future. That is, if they have a high correlation to long-term cycles in the past, given a clearly identifiable orb of time, there is every reason to suspect that they will correlate with similar long-term cycles in the future. Unless the universe suddenly becomes detached from its correlation to cycles in human activity, and humankind is no longer directly or indirectly, consciously or unconsciously, connected to that universe. Unless that Divine Intelligence, which created this wonderful orderliness to the solar system, suddenly goes senile!

This book is about timing, and the techniques just illustrated worked beautifully in timing long-term cycles in the stock market. But in the real world of investing, one needs to use all the complimentary tools to market timing. And these involve full understanding of a few important technical studies and chart recognition patterns as described herein, and in *Volume 1*. By integrating these tools with the knowledge of market timing indicators demonstrated in this book, one's probability of success as an investor in the U.S. stock market increases greatly.

No one promised that it would be easy. Making money in the markets never is. But with the use of this book as a reference for many, many years (and even decades), the task has just become easier.

EPILOGUE

This book turned out to be much larger in scope than anticipated. For that I am very grateful, for the process of writing *Volume 2* resulted in a greater revelation than ever expected. I hope I have been able to convey this excitement of "new discovery" to you, the reader. And more importantly, I trust that these findings, conclusions, and illustrations will provide you with additional skills in your quest to be a successful investor.

Because of the vast amount of material uncovered in the undertaking of this effort, it was not possible to include all the studies originally intended. In the beginning, I anticipated *Volume 2* to include an analysis of all the geocosmic cycles, not just the long-term ones. However, that was not to be. The amount of information on just the long-term and intermediate-term planetary cycles was huge, and to do it properly, required a separation from the shorter-term cycles.

Therefore the sequence of this series has to be changed from that originally stated in *Volume 1.* Frankly, I don't think anyone will mind, since the results are so remarkable. Of course, this also means that as I proceed onto *Volume 3*, I might once again discover treasures never imagined, and thus find it necessarily to again change the projected topics for the future volumes.

With that in mind, I can confidently state that the topic for *Volume 3* will be *Geocosmic Correlations for Trading Cycles.* The focus will be on the shorter-term planetary signatures for timing primary, half-primary, major, and trading cycles in the U.S. stock market. The same format used in this book will be used in *Volume 3.* That is, transiting aspects from the Sun, Mercury, Venus, and Mars, to one another and to the farther-out planets, will be analyzed in terms of their correlation to the aforementioned cycles. Additionally, retrograde and direct periods of each planet will be analyzed.

Once that study is completed, we should have a fairly good understanding of cycles in the U.S. stock market, and geocosmic correlations to both the long-term, intermediate-term, and short-term cycles. Used in combination with certain technical tools, that will enable us to differentiate when to invest and when to trade. And even as investors, the material in *Volume 3* will aid us in identifying other periods along the way in which we may add onto our long-term holdings, in the event that 1) we missed getting in (or out) right at the 4-year cycle trough (or crest), or 2) we earn or find additional monies to make purchases after the 4-year cycle trough has already passed. Whatever our circumstances, and whenever our investment monies increase, we should realize that properly calculated timing bands for cyclic troughs and/or crests (although not everything) can play a very important role in enhancing the profitability of our activities in financial markets.

APPENDIX 1

On the next two pages is a Table, showing the ranking order, of all the geocosmic signatures in this book that have a C/S value of over 8.00, according to criteria described in Chapter 7.

On the basis of the studies shown in earlier chapters of this book, we can immediately assume that the aspects between Uranus, Neptune, and Pluto have the most reliable and powerful correlation to very long-term cycles in the U.S. stock market, given an orb of one year from their occurrence. Hence they are not included in this list. The lists that follows then, are the strongest signatures — in order of their consistency and strength combinations — found to correlate with long-term cycles in the U.S. stock market throughout its entire history since 1789.

On the two pages which follow Table 10 is another Table which lists all 4-year and greater cycles, and their double bottoms and tops, that were used in the calculations of the Strength, Consistency, and C/S values for planetary signatures as reported in this book.

TABLE 10

RANKING OF C/S VALUES (9.00 or Greater)

	Signature	C/S Value	Orb of Time
1.	♄☌♅ - 0°	10.00	10 months
1.	♄☍♅ - 180°	10.00	9 "
3.	♄☍♇ - 180°	9.875	8 "
4.	♄△♆ - 240°	9.86	6 "
5.	♄□♅ - 90°	9.80	8 "
6.	♄△♅ - 240°	9.75	5 "
7.	♄□♆ - 90°	9.67	8 "
8.	♄∠♅ - 315°	9.60	8 "
8.	♄⚼♅ - 135°	9.60	9 "
8.	♄△♆ - 120°	9.60	0 "
8.	♄⚼♆ - 135°	9.60	9 "
12.	♄☍♆ - 180°	9.50	9 "
12.	♄□♆ - 270°	9.50	9 "
12.	♄⚼♅ - 225°	9.50	9 "
12.	♄☌♇ - 0°	9.50	11 "
12.	♄✶♇ - 300°	9.50	9 "
17.	♄✶♇ - 60°	9.43	5 "
18.	♃☌♄ - 0°	9.40	5 "
18.	♄∠♅ - 45°	9.40	4 "
20.	♄⚼♆ - 225°	9.33	10 "
21.	♄△♅ - 120°	9.25	9 "
22.	♄✶♅ - 60°	9.20	7 "
22.	♄□♅ - 270°	9.20	7 "
22.	♃△♄ - 120°	9.20	6 "
25.	♃△♄ - 240°	9.18	7 "
26.	♄☌♆ - 0°	9.17	9 "
26.	♄∠♆ - 315°	9.17	10 "
26.	♄△♇ - 240°	9.17	5 "
29..	♄□♇ - 90°	9.14	4 "
30.	♃☍♅ - 180°	9.125	6 "
31.	♃✶♄ - 300°	9.09	7 "
32.	♃☍♇ - 180°	9.08	6 "
33.	♄∠♆ - 45°	9.00	7 "
33.	♄△♇ - 120°	9.00	7 "
33.	♄∠♇ - 45°	9.00	9 "
33.	♄⚼♇ - 225°	9.00	2 "
33.	♃□♄ - 270°	9.00	6 "

RANKING OF C/S VALUES
(8.00 or Greater)

38.	♃△♆ - 120°	8.95	6 "
39.	♄□♇ - 270°	8.92	8 "
40.	♃☍♄ - 180°	8.91	3 "
41.	♄⚹♅ - 300°	8.90	7 "
41.	♃□♄ - 90°	8.90	7 "
43.	♃□♆ - 90°	8.89	6 "
44.	♄⚼♇ - 135°	8.86	6 "
45.	♃⚹♄ - 60°	8.85	7 "
46.	♄∠♇ - 315°	8.83	4 "
46.	♄⚹♆ - 60°	8.83	8 "
46.	♄⚹♆ - 300°	8.83	9 "
46.	♃△♅ - 120°	8.83	3 "
50.	♃⚹♅ - 300°	8.80	5 "
51.	♃△♅ - 240°	8.78	4 "
51.	♃⚹♆ - 60°	8.78	4 "
53.	♃□♇ - 90°	8.75	4 "
54.	♃△♇ - 120°	8.70	6 "
55.	♃⚹♇ - 300°	8.65	6 "
56.	♃☌♆ - 0°	8.64	6 "
57.	♃⚹♇ - 60°	8.60	5 "
57.	♃□♆ - 270°	8.60	6 "
59.	♃△♇ - 240°	8.55	7 "
60.	♃□♅ - 270°	8.54	5 "
61.	♃△♆ - 240°	8.50	5 "
61.	♃⚹♆ - 300°	8.50	5 "
63.	♃□♅ - 90°	8.33	6 "
64.	♃☌♇ - 0°	8.32	5 "
65.	♃☌♅ - 0°	8.30	7 "
66.	♃☍♆ - 180°	8.25	5 "
66.	♃□♇ - 270°	8.25	6 "
68.	♃⚹♅ - 60°	8.06	6 "

TABLE 11

4-YEAR OR GREATER CYCLE TROUGHS AND CRESTS AS USED IN THIS BOOK

Troughs		Crests
December, 1789		January, 1792
September, 1792	(33)	April, 1795*
		DT September, 1794
November, 1797	(62)*	October, 1800
February, 1802	(51)	Aug/Sept, 1806*
October, 1807	(68) - 1/2	October, 1809
		DT February, 1810
March, 1813	(65)*	September, 1815
September, 1816	(42)	May, 1819 - 1/2
		DT December, 1819
January, 1820	(40) - 1/2	November, 1821
September, 1822	(33)	September, 1824*
February, 1827	(53)	October, 1827
January, 1829	(23)*	April, May, June, 1833 - 1/2
February, 1834	(61) - 1/2	May, 1835*
		DT August, 1835
Mar/April, 1838	(50)	September, 1838
February, 1842	(47)*	May, 1844
DB Jan-Mar, 1843		
June-August, 1845	(42)	August, 1847
Oct/November, 1848	(39)	June/July, 1849
October, 1851	(35)	January, 1853*
		DT Oct/Nov, 1852
December, 1854	(38)	December, 1856
October, 1857	(34) *	September, 1860
DB June, 1859		
May, 1861	(43)	March, 1864 - 1/2
March, 1865	(46) - 1/2	July/August, 1869
December, 1869	(57)	January/March/May, 1873*
November, 1873	(47)	February, 1874
June, 1877	(43)*	January, 1880
May/June, 1880	(36)	June, 1881 - 1/2
June, 1884	(48) - 1/2	December, 1886
March/April, 1888	(46)	May, 1890*
		DT September, 1889
December, 1890	(32)	March, 1892
July, 1893	(31)	September, 1895
August, 1896	(37)*	April, 1899 - DT to 1/2 of 1901
		DT September, 1899
September, 1900	(49)	June, 1901 - 1/2
November, 1903	(38) - 1/2	January, 1906*

November, 1907	(48)	November, 1909
		DT September, 1909
September, 1911	(46)	September, 1912
DB July, 1910		
December, 1914	(39)*	November, 1916
December, 1917	(36)	October, 1919 - 1/2
August, 1921 - 1/2	(44)	February, 1926
DB December, 1920		DT Aug/Sept, 1926
March, 1926	(55)	September, 1929*
November, 1929	(44)	April, 1930
July, 1932	(32)*	March, 1937
		DT August, 1937 - 1/2
March, 1938	(68)	November, 1938
		DT September, 1939
April, 1942	(49) - 1/2	May, 1946
October, 1946	(54)	June, 1948
DB July, 1945		
June, 1949	(32)	January, 1953*
DB February, 1948		
September, 1953	(51)*	April, 1956
		DT July, 1957
October, 1957	(49)	November, 1961 - 1/2
June, 1962	(56) - 1/2	February, 1966
October, 1966	(52)	December, 1968
May, 1970	(43)	January, 1973*
December, 1974	(55)*	September, 1976
		DT January, 1977
March, 1978	(39)	April, 1981 - 1/2
DB March, 1980		
August, 1982	(53) - 1/2	August, 1987*
October, 1987	(62)*	July, 1990
October, 1990	(36)	January, 1994
		DT September, 1994
April, 1994	(42) or November, 1994 (49)	July 1998
October, 1998	(54) or (47)	

Asterisks(*) refer to 18-year or greater cycles. DB refers to a double bottom. DT refers to a Double top. 1/2 refers to a half-cycle to the 18-year cycle.

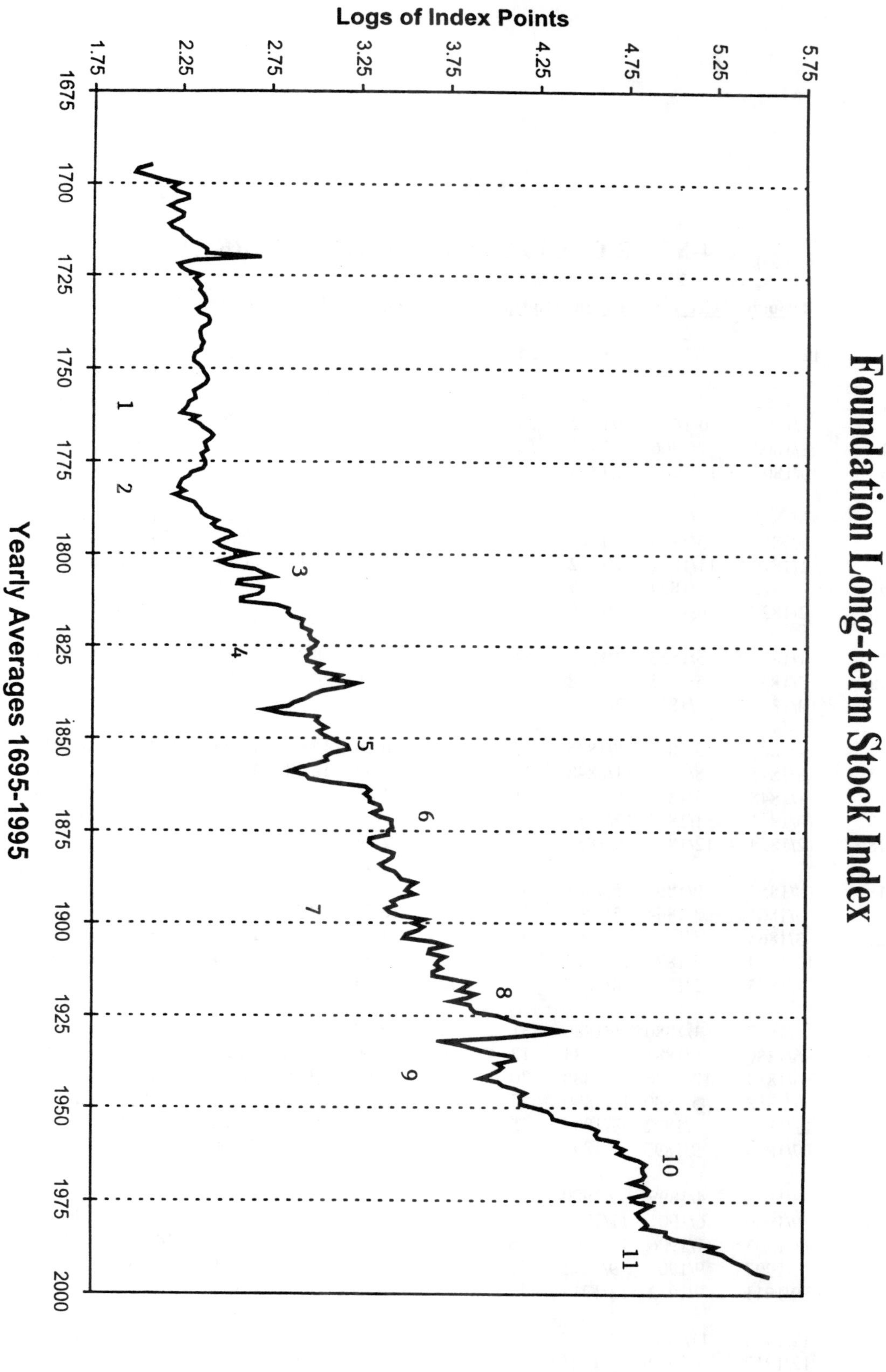

Figure 5: Yearly Averages of the Foundation's Long-Term Stock Index, which includes the British stock prices (from the Course of the Exchange) prior to 1789.

TABLE 12

4-YEAR CYCLES IN U.S. STOCK MARKET

Cycle #	Trough	Crest	Trough	Mo Up	Mo Dn	Low*	High*	Low*	% Up*	%Dn*
1.	12/1789	1/1792	9/1792	25	8	2.76	3.69	2.96	33.7%	19.8%
2.	9/1792	4/1795	11/1797	31	31	2.96	4.52	3.19	52.7%	29.4%
3.	11/1797	10/1800	2/1802	35	16	3.19	5.57	3.36	74.6%	39.7%
4.	2/1802	9/1806	10/1807	55	13	3.36	7.56	3.57	125.0%	52.8%
5.	10/1807	10/1809	3/1813	24	41	3.57	6.91	4.43	93.6%	35.9%
6.	3/1813	9/1815	9/1816	30	12	4.43	9.05	8.29	104.3%	08.4%
7.	9/1816	5/1819	1/1820	32	8	8.29	11.03	9.59	33.1%	13.1%
8.	1/1820	11/1821	9/1822	22	10	9.59	12.15	11.19	26.7%	07.9%
9.	9/1822	9/1824	2/1827	24	29	11.19	14.38	11.11	28.5%	22.7%
10.	2/1827	10/1827	1/1829	8	15	11.11	12.33	10.46	11.0%	15.2%
11.	1/1829	5/1833	2/1834	52	9	10.46	18.33	13.31	75.2%	27.4%
12.	2/1834	5/1835	4/1838	15	35	13.31	23.48	10.70	76.4%	54.4%
13.	4/1838	9/1838	2/1842	5	41	10.70	13.83	6.26	29.3%	54.7%
14.	2/1842	5/1844	8/1845	27	15	6.26	14.61	12.00	133.4%	17.9%
15.	8/1845	8/1847	11/1848	24	15	12.00	16.18	12.26	34.8%	24.2%
16.	11/1848	6/1851	10/1851	31	4	12.26	17.48	15.91	42.6%	9.0%
17.	10/1851	1/1853	12/1854	15	23	15.91	21.13	12.87	32.8%	39.1%
18.	12/1854	12/1856	10/1857	24	10	12.87	15.94	7.99	23.9%	49.9%
19.	10/1857	9/1860	5/1861	35	8	7.99	13.81	10.50	72.8%	24.0%
20.	5/1861	3/1864	3/1865	34	12	10.50	27.23	21.07	159.3%	22.6%
21.	3/1865	8/1869	12/1869	53	4	21.07	31.33	25.35	48.7%	19.1%
22.	12/1869	5/1873	11/1873	41	6	25.35	35.27	28.74	39.1%	18.5%
23.	11/1873	2/1874	6/1877	3	40	28.74	35.68	22.28	24.1%	37.6%
24.	6/1877	1/1880	6/1880	31	5	22.28	31.24	28.60	40.2%	08.5%
25.	6/1880	6/1881	6/1884	12	36	28.60	36.24	27.21	26.7%	24.9%
26.*	6/1884	12/1886	4/1888	30	16	56.00	93.50	76.50	66.7%	18.2%
27.	4/1888	5/1890	12/1890	25	7	76.50	99.50	77.50	30.1%	22.1%
28.	12/1890	3/1892	7/1893	15	16	77.50	94.00	62.00	21.3%	34.0%
29.	7/1893	9/1895	8/1896	26	11	44.00	63.00	27.00	43.2%	57.1%
30.	8/1896	4/1899	9/1900	32	17	27.0	78.0	52.5	188.9%	32.7%
31.	9/1900	6/1901	11/1903	9	29	52.5	79.0	42.5	50.5%	46.2%
32.	11/1903	1/1906	11/1907	26	22	42.5	102.0	53.0	140.0%	48.0%
33.	11/1907	9/1909	9/1911	22	24	53.0	101.5	72.0	91.5%	29.1%
34.	9/1911	9/1912	12/1914	12	27	72.0	93.0	52.0	29.2%	44.1%
35.	12/1914	11/1916	12/1917	23	13	52.0	115.0	66.0	121.2%	42.6%
36.	12/1917	10/1919	8/1921	22	22	66.0	125.0	64.0	89.4%	48.8%
37.	8/1921	2/1926	3/1926	54	1	64.0	175.0	145.0	173.4%	17.1%
38.	3/1926	8/1929	11/1929	41	3	145.0	386.1	195.0	166.3%	49.5%
39.	11/1929	4/1930	7/1932	5	27	195.4	297.3	40.6	52.1%	86.3%

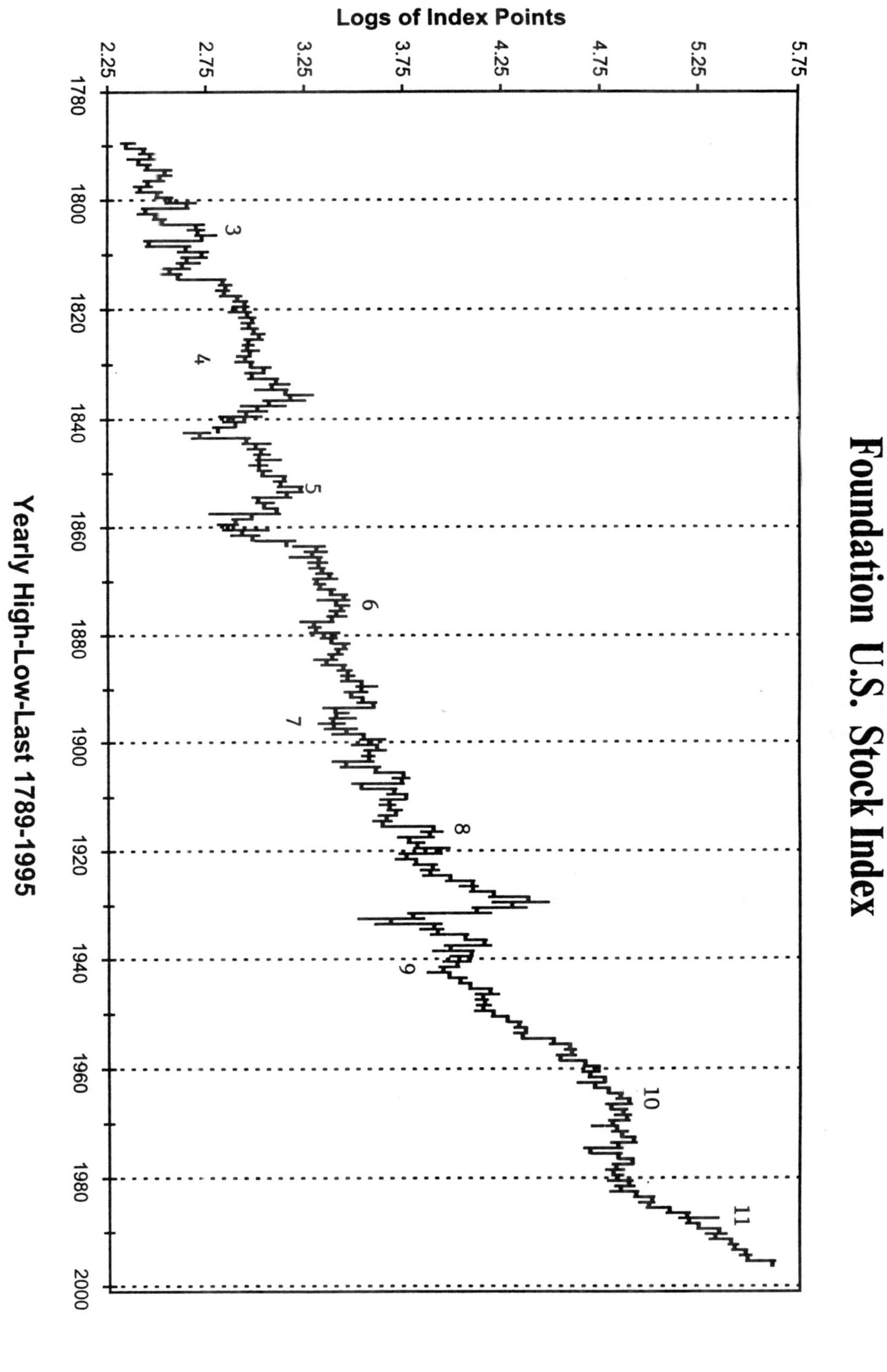

Figure 4: Long-Term Chart of yearly highs and lows (in log form) in U.S. stocks

40.	7/1932	3/1937	3/1938	56	12	40.6	195.6	97.5	381.8%	50.2%
41.	3/1938	11/1938	4/1942	8	41	97.5	158.9	92.7	63.0%	41.7%
42.	4/1942	5/1946	10/1946	49	5	92.7	213.4	160.5	130.2%	24.8%
43.	10/1946	6/1948	6/1949	20	12	160.5	194.5	160.6	21.2%	17.4%
44.	6/1949	1/1953	9/1953	43	8	160.6	295.1	254.4	83.7%	13.8%
45.	9/1953	4/1956	10/1957	31	18	254.4	524.4	416.2	106.1%	20.6%
46.	10/1957	11/1961	6/1962	49	7	416.2	741.3	524.6	78.1%	29.2%
47.	6/1962	2/1966	10/1966	44	8	524.6	1001.1	735.7	90.8%	26.5%
48.	10/1966	12/1968	5/1970	26	17	735.7	994.7	627.5	35.2%	36.9%
49.	5/1970	1/1973	12/1974	32	23	627.5	1067.2	570.0	70.1%	46.6%
59.	12/1974	9/1976	3/1978	21	18	570.0	1026.3	736.8	80.1%	28.2%
51.	3/1978	4/1981	8/1982	37	16	736.8	1031.0	770.0	39.9%	33.9%
52.	8/1982	8/1987	10/1987	60	2	770.0	2746.7	1616.2	256.7%	41.1%
53.	10/1987	7/1990	10/1990	33	3	1616.2	3024.3	2344.3	87.1%	22.5%
54.A.	10/1990	1/1994	4/1994	39	3	2344.3	4002.8	3520.5	70.7%	12.0%
54.B.	10/1990	1/1994	11/1994	39	10	2344.3	4002.8	3612.1	70.7%	9.8%
55.A.	4/1994	7/1998	9/1998	51	2	3520.5	9412.6	7379.7	167.4%	21.6%
55.B.	11/1994	7/1998	9/1998	44	2	3612.1	9412.6	7379.7	160.6%	21.6%
56.	9/1998									

4-year cycles with prices and percent of increase and decline from trough to crest, then down to next trough. *Asterisk represents where different charts were used, and hence values are rounded off to nearest half point.

APPENDIX 2

On the next pages are the long-term yearly charts of the U.S. and World stock prices. These are the same charts from the Study for the Foundation of Cycles as presented in *Volume 1*, pages 4 and 7. The very long-term cycles in the U.S. stock market, referred to throughout this edition of *Volume 2*, can be seen most clearly ion these charts.

The numbers 1-11 refer to the dates of the Saturn-Uranus conjunctions and oppositions in the Foreword of this book.

On the back of these pages (268-269) are the dates and various statistics of the 4-year cycles in the U.S. stock market.

APPENDIX 3

The following 5 pages contains a chronological listing of all the major transits of Jupiter and beyond between 1998-2030. These include only the conjunction, sextile, square, trine, and opposition aspects.

The source of this list comes from the "Hit List" of the Pathfinder Astrology System, created by John Woodsmall of AstroCybernetics in Los Angeles, California.

In the far left column is the date of the aspect.

In the second column is the exact time of the aspect, basis Eastern Standard Time zone (EST).

In the third column is a listing of the two planets in aspect and the aspect which they make to one another. The faster moving planet is given first in the case of direct motion. In the case of retrograde, the slower moving planet is given first. "T" stands for "Transit." These are "Transits to Transits," hence the "T" prior to the first planet, and following the last planet.

The fourth column is the zodiacal position of the first planet listed in the row.

TRANSITS OF JUPITER AND BEYOND
January 3, 1998 at:21:31:15 PM(5) in
From:January 3, 1999 To:January 3, 2000
TRANSITING ACTIVITY (ZONE 5):

Date	Time	Aspect	Position
3/ 9/1998	8:24PM	T ♃ □ ♇ T	8♓03
6/25/1998	6:24PM	T ♄ □ ♆ T	1♉29
10/31/1998	7:29PM	T ♆ □ ♄ T	29♑30
2/26/1999	7:52PM	T ♃ ⚹ ♆ T	3♈08
3/29/1999	8:48AM	T ♃ △ ♇ T	10♈25
4/ 6/1999	11:02AM	T ♄ □ ♆ T	4♉07
4/23/1999	11:47AM	T ♃ ⚹ ♅ T	16♈27
7/17/1999	10:42PM	T ♄ □ ♅ T	15♉36
7/21/1999	11:34AM	T ♃ □ ♆ T	3♉06
10/11/1999	1:03AM	T ♆ □ ♃ T	1♒35
11/14/1999	4:46AM	T ♅ □ ♄ T	13♒04
3/16/2000	12:44PM	T ♃ □ ♆ T	5♉50
5/13/2000	3:23AM	T ♄ □ ♅ T	20♉45
5/20/2000	8:08AM	T ♃ □ ♅ T	20♉48
5/28/2000	10:59AM	T ♃ ☌ ♄ T	22♉43
7/27/2000	6:52AM	T ♃ △ ♆ T	5♊11
9/ 4/2000	5:33AM	T ♃ ☍ ♇ T	10♊12
10/13/2000	3:43AM	T ♇ ☍ ♃ T	10♐54
12/ 9/2000	8:40AM	T ♆ △ ♃ T	4♒36
4/ 5/2001	10:01AM	T ♃ △ ♆ T	8♊26
5/ 6/2001	5:34AM	T ♃ ☍ ♇ T	14♊39
6/19/2001	7:17AM	T ♃ △ ♅ T	24♊39
6/25/2001	3:02AM	T ♄ △ ♆ T	8♊16
8/ 5/2001	11:53AM	T ♄ ☍ ♇ T	12♊37
11/ 2/2001	1:16AM	T ♇ ☍ ♄ T	13♐49
1/23/2002	1:42AM	T ♆ △ ♄ T	8♒15
4/ 1/2002	11:15PM	T ♄ △ ♆ T	10♊31
5/25/2002	9:25PM	T ♄ ☍ ♇ T	16♊35
8/21/2002	2:06AM	T ♄ △ ♅ T	26♊48
9/11/2002	7:35AM	T ♃ ☍ ♆ T	8♌35
10/27/2002	6:24PM	T ♃ △ ♇ T	15♌55
12/16/2002	4:44PM	T ♅ △ ♄ T	25♒39
12/18/2002	8:53AM	T ♇ △ ♃ T	17♐46
2/16/2003	3:31AM	T ♆ ☍ ♃ T	11♒17
6/ 2/2003	10:36PM	T ♃ ☍ ♆ T	13♌06
6/24/2003	6:22PM	T ♄ △ ♅ T	2♋41
7/ 1/2003	7:31AM	T ♃ △ ♇ T	18♌02
8/29/2003	11:29PM	T ♃ ☍ ♅ T	0♍36
11/ 1/2003	12:10PM	T ♃ ⚹ ♄ T	13♍11
5/ 1/2004	3:31PM	T ♄ ⚹ ♃ T	8♋55
8/ 6/2004	4:15PM	T ♃ □ ♇ T	19♍41
8/17/2004	11:30AM	T ♃ ⚹ ♄ T	21♍50
11/29/2004	4:10AM	T ♃ △ ♆ T	12♎58
3/14/2005	1:58AM	T ♆ △ ♃ T	16♒27
8/17/2005	3:11PM	T ♃ △ ♆ T	15♎57
9/17/2005	10:39PM	T ♃ ⚹ ♇ T	21♎53

11/27/2005	6:46AM	T ♃ △ ♅ T	6♏53
12/17/2005	12:14AM	T ♃ □ ♄ T	10♏44
1/27/2006	10:04PM	T ♃ □ ♆ T	16♏56
3/16/2006	12:24AM	T ♆ □ ♃ T	18♒39
5/ 4/2006	10:57PM	T ♅ △ ♃ T	13♓55
6/22/2006	1:43PM	T ♄ □ ♃ T	9♌15
8/29/2006	4:02AM	T ♃ △ ♅ T	13♏01
8/31/2006	5:42AM	T ♄ ☍ ♆ T	17♌53
9/24/2006	4:06PM	T ♃ □ ♆ T	17♏21
10/25/2006	12:23PM	T ♃ □ ♄ T	23♏31
1/22/2007	4:29PM	T ♃ □ ♅ T	12♐25
2/28/2007	5:55AM	T ♆ ☍ ♄ T	20♒14
3/16/2007	5:37PM	T ♃ △ ♄ T	19♐09
5/ 6/2007	2:13AM	T ♄ △ ♃ T	18♌23
5/10/2007	10:44PM	T ♅ □ ♃ T	17♓56
6/25/2007	12:00PM	T ♄ ☍ ♆ T	21♌46
8/ 6/2007	5:11AM	T ♄ △ ♇ T	26♌33
10/ 9/2007	1:13PM	T ♃ □ ♅ T	15♐35
10/29/2007	11:34PM	T ♃ ⚹ ♆ T	19♐15
12/11/2007	2:17PM	T ♃ ☌ ♇ T	28♐23
1/21/2008	4:12AM	T ♃ △ ♄ T	7♑36
3/28/2008	6:49PM	T ♃ ⚹ ♅ T	19♑46
5/21/2008	1:31PM	T ♅ ⚹ ♃ T	22♓07
9/ 8/2008	6:19PM	T ♄ △ ♃ T	12♍32
11/ 4/2008	8:20AM	T ♄ ☍ ♅ T	18♍57
11/13/2008	12:29AM	T ♃ ⚹ ♅ T	18♑49
11/21/2008	7:09AM	T ♃ △ ♄ T	20♑19
2/ 5/2009	6:09AM	T ♅ ☍ ♄ T	20♓39
5/27/2009	5:16PM	T ♃ ☌ ♆ T	26♒28
7/10/2009	1:57AM	T ♆ ☌ ♃ T	26♒02
9/15/2009	7:40AM	T ♄ ☍ ♅ T	24♍42
11/15/2009	9:26AM	T ♄ □ ♇ T	1♎42
12/21/2009	4:35AM	T ♃ ☌ ♆ T	24♒17
1/31/2010	5:20PM	T ♇ □ ♄ T	4♑21
2/ 6/2010	12:32PM	T ♃ ⚹ ♇ T	4♓31
4/26/2010	6:35PM	T ♅ ☍ ♄ T	28♓46
5/23/2010	12:33AM	T ♃ ☍ ♄ T	27♓52
6/ 8/2010	6:09AM	T ♃ ☌ ♅ T	0♈17
7/24/2010	7:13PM	T ♃ □ ♇ T	3♈23
7/26/2010	11:51AM	T ♄ ☍ ♅ T	0♎24
8/ 3/2010	4:35AM	T ♇ □ ♃ T	3♑12
8/16/2010	3:46PM	T ♄ ☍ ♃ T	2♎26
8/21/2010	4:45AM	T ♄ □ ♇ T	2♎55
9/18/2010	8:23PM	T ♅ ☌ ♃ T	28♓42
1/ 4/2011	7:37AM	T ♃ ☌ ♅ T	27♓02
2/25/2011	3:20PM	T ♃ □ ♇ T	7♈02
3/28/2011	4:53PM	T ♃ ☍ ♄ T	14♈21
6/ 8/2011	10:17PM	T ♃ ⚹ ♆ T	0♉55
7/ 7/2011	8:43AM	T ♃ △ ♇ T	5♉57
10/28/2011	11:52AM	T ♇ △ ♃ T	5♑20
3/12/2012	11:21PM	T ♃ △ ♇ T	9♉20
6/24/2012	3:09AM	T ♅ □ ♇ T	8♈23
6/25/2012	3:30AM	T ♃ □ ♆ T	3♊02

7/21/2012	10:54PM	T ♃ ⚹ ♅ T	8♊30
9/19/2012	1:49AM	T ♇ □ ♅ T	6♑57
10/10/2012	10:39PM	T ♄ △ ♆ T	0♏37
12/26/2012	7:25PM	T ♄ ⚹ ♇ T	9♏08
3/ 8/2013	3:21AM	T ♇ ⚹ ♄ T	11♑15
5/20/2013	5:18PM	T ♅ □ ♇ T	11♈14
6/11/2013	2:39PM	T ♆ △ ♄ T	5♓22
7/17/2013	12:29PM	T ♃ △ ♄ T	4♋53
7/17/2013	7:48PM	T ♃ △ ♆ T	4♋57
7/19/2013	12:06PM	T ♄ △ ♆ T	4♏55
8/ 7/2013	6:27PM	T ♃ ☍ ♇ T	9♋26
8/21/2013	2:07AM	T ♃ □ ♅ T	12♋03
9/21/2013	12:07AM	T ♄ ⚹ ♇ T	8♏59
11/ 1/2013	6:10AM	T ♇ □ ♅ T	9♑25
12/12/2013	7:00PM	T ♄ △ ♃ T	18♏27
1/31/2014	4:42AM	T ♇ ☍ ♃ T	12♑17
2/26/2014	2:45AM	T ♅ □ ♃ T	10♈33
4/20/2014	2:09AM	T ♃ □ ♅ T	13♋29
4/20/2014	5:55PM	T ♃ ☍ ♇ T	13♋34
4/21/2014	1:34PM	T ♅ □ ♇ T	13♈33
5/24/2014	12:45PM	T ♃ △ ♄ T	18♋59
9/25/2014	1:11PM	T ♃ △ ♅ T	14♌59
12/15/2014	1:14AM	T ♇ □ ♅ T	12♑35
3/ 3/2015	7:33AM	T ♅ △ ♃ T	14♈34
3/16/2015	8:44PM	T ♅ □ ♇ T	15♈17
6/22/2015	8:36AM	T ♃ △ ♅ T	20♌02
8/ 3/2015	5:34AM	T ♃ □ ♄ T	28♌16
9/17/2015	2:30AM	T ♃ ☍ ♆ T	7♍58
10/11/2015	6:28PM	T ♃ △ ♇ T	13♍02
11/26/2015	8:31AM	T ♄ □ ♆ T	7♐02
3/16/2016	3:33PM	T ♇ △ ♃ T	17♑12
3/23/2016	5:15AM	T ♄ □ ♃ T	16♐24
5/26/2016	7:24AM	T ♃ □ ♄ T	13♍41
6/17/2016	8:11PM	T ♆ □ ♄ T	12♓02
6/26/2016	7:00AM	T ♃ △ ♇ T	16♍29
9/10/2016	10:14AM	T ♄ □ ♆ T	10♐24
11/24/2016	5:32PM	T ♃ □ ♇ T	15♎46
12/24/2016	7:09PM	T ♄ △ ♅ T	20♐33
12/26/2016	1:22PM	T ♃ ☍ ♅ T	20♎33
3/ 2/2017	8:25PM	T ♅ ☍ ♃ T	22♈11
3/30/2017	1:49PM	T ♇ □ ♃ T	19♑17
5/19/2017	1:21AM	T ♅ △ ♄ T	26♈23
8/ 4/2017	1:20PM	T ♃ □ ♇ T	17♎31
8/27/2017	7:12AM	T ♃ ⚹ ♄ T	21♎11
9/27/2017	11:18PM	T ♃ ☍ ♅ T	27♎22
11/11/2017	4:35AM	T ♄ △ ♅ T	25♐37
12/ 2/2017	10:03PM	T ♃ △ ♆ T	11♏30
1/15/2018	10:33PM	T ♃ ⚹ ♇ T	19♏17
4/14/2018	5:39AM	T ♇ ⚹ ♃ T	21♑16
5/25/2018	3:40AM	T ♆ △ ♃ T	16♓20
8/19/2018	3:54AM	T ♃ △ ♆ T	15♏36
9/12/2018	2:28AM	T ♃ ⚹ ♇ T	18♏50
1/13/2019	2:49PM	T ♃ □ ♆ T	14♐23

1/31/2019	11:13AM	T ♄ ⚹ ♆ T	14♑55
6/16/2019	9:07AM	T ♆ □ ♃ T	18♓43
6/18/2019	4:20AM	T ♆ ⚹ ♄ T	18♓43
9/21/2019	12:49PM	T ♃ □ ♆ T	17♐00
11/ 8/2019	11:36PM	T ♄ ⚹ ♆ T	16♑01
12/15/2019	1:55PM	T ♃ △ ♅ T	2♑56
1/12/2020	11:11AM	T ♄ ☌ ♇ T	22♑46
2/20/2020	11:51AM	T ♃ ⚹ ♆ T	17♑46
4/ 4/2020	9:00PM	T ♃ ☌ ♇ T	24♑53
6/30/2020	1:33AM	T ♇ ☌ ♃ T	24♑06
7/27/2020	9:32AM	T ♆ ⚹ ♃ T	20♓39
10/12/2020	3:31AM	T ♃ ⚹ ♆ T	18♑45
11/12/2020	4:07PM	T ♃ ☌ ♇ T	22♑51
12/21/2020	1:16PM	T ♃ ☌ ♄ T	0♒29
1/17/2021	5:43PM	T ♃ □ ♅ T	6♒43
2/17/2021	1:58PM	T ♄ □ ♅ T	7♒13
6/14/2021	5:06PM	T ♅ □ ♄ T	13♉06
12/24/2021	2:10AM	T ♄ □ ♅ T	11♒05
2/17/2022	7:07PM	T ♃ ⚹ ♅ T	11♓12
4/12/2022	10:30AM	T ♃ ☌ ♆ T	23♓59
5/ 3/2022	5:08PM	T ♃ ⚹ ♇ T	28♓35
5/17/2023	7:48PM	T ♃ □ ♇ T	0♉17
6/19/2023	10:49AM	T ♃ ⚹ ♄ T	7♉12
4/20/2024	9:22PM	T ♃ ☌ ♅ T	21♉49
5/23/2024	5:29PM	T ♃ ⚹ ♆ T	29♉31
6/ 2/2024	6:51PM	T ♃ △ ♇ T	1♊52
8/19/2024	4:42PM	T ♃ □ ♄ T	17♊27
12/24/2024	5:00PM	T ♄ □ ♃ T	14♓01
4/ 4/2025	11:17AM	T ♄ ⚹ ♅ T	24♓55
6/15/2025	9:32AM	T ♃ □ ♄ T	1♋18
6/18/2025	11:01PM	T ♃ □ ♆ T	2♋06
8/11/2025	10:30PM	T ♅ ⚹ ♄ T	1♊11
8/29/2025	1:05AM	T ♅ ⚹ ♆ T	1♊26
11/20/2025	3:39AM	T ♆ ⚹ ♅ T	29♓29
1/20/2026	12:17AM	T ♄ ⚹ ♅ T	27♓33
2/20/2026	2:01PM	T ♄ ☌ ♆ T	0♈45
3/28/2026	4:29PM	T ♄ ⚹ ♇ T	5♈09
7/15/2026	7:23PM	T ♅ ⚹ ♆ T	4♊24
7/17/2026	10:29PM	T ♅ △ ♇ T	4♊29
7/20/2026	3:08AM	T ♃ △ ♆ T	4♌22
7/20/2026	9:23AM	T ♃ ☍ ♇ T	4♌26
7/21/2026	6:07AM	T ♃ ⚹ ♅ T	4♌37
7/24/2026	6:12AM	T ♆ ⚹ ♇ T	4♈20
8/31/2026	5:14PM	T ♃ △ ♄ T	13♌41
9/16/2026	3:24PM	T ♇ ⚹ ♆ T	3♒15
11/29/2026	7:32AM	T ♇ △ ♅ T	3♒31
1/14/2027	11:55PM	T ♆ ⚹ ♅ T	1♈56
4/ 3/2027	8:00AM	T ♄ △ ♃ T	17♈08
6/ 6/2027	9:34AM	T ♅ ⚹ ♆ T	6♊21
6/15/2027	2:02AM	T ♅ △ ♇ T	6♊51
6/28/2027	8:45AM	T ♆ ⚹ ♇ T	6♈37
7/11/2027	6:11PM	T ♃ △ ♄ T	27♌10
9/10/2027	11:39AM	T ♃ □ ♅ T	9♍56

10/16/2027	7:58PM	T ♇ ⚹ ♆ T	4♒44
1/13/2028	3:01AM	T ♇ △ ♅ T	6♒19
5/ 9/2028	8:36PM	T ♅ △ ♇ T	8♊49
6/ 8/2028	2:47PM	T ♆ ⚹ ♇ T	8♈37
6/23/2028	9:15PM	T ♄ □ ♇ T	8♉22
9/24/2028	2:22AM	T ♃ △ ♇ T	6♎32
9/28/2028	3:00PM	T ♃ ☍ ♆ T	7♎31
10/27/2028	4:04AM	T ♃ △ ♅ T	13♎38
11/ 8/2028	5:44AM	T ♇ ⚹ ♆ T	6♒30
11/15/2028	8:45AM	T ♇ □ ♄ T	6♒34
3/29/2029	5:21PM	T ♄ □ ♇ T	10♉02
5/22/2029	5:53AM	T ♆ ⚹ ♇ T	10♈25
10/31/2029	7:18PM	T ♃ □ ♇ T	8♏04
12/ 1/2029	1:23AM	T ♇ ⚹ ♆ T	8♒25
12/22/2029	1:59AM	T ♃ ☍ ♄ T	18♏48
4/23/2030	8:56PM	T ♄ ☍ ♃ T	25♉07
5/ 4/2030	1:29AM	T ♆ ⚹ ♇ T	12♈02
11/19/2030	8:03PM	T ♃ ☍ ♄ T	6♐04
12/ 8/2030	1:16AM	T ♃ ⚹ ♇ T	10♐08
12/10/2030	3:48AM	T ♃ △ ♆ T	10♐37
12/26/2030	8:59PM	T ♇ ⚹ ♆ T	10♒35

APPENDIX 4

The following three pages contain a chronological listing of major and minor Saturn and beyond transits that occur between 1998 and 2040. These include the conjunction, semi-square, sextile, square, trine, sesquiquadrate, and opposition aspects. Most of these rated a Level 1 classification in this book.

The source of this list comes from the "Hit List" of the Pathfinder Astrology System, created by John Woodsmall of AstroCybernetics in Los Angeles, California.

TRANSITS OF SATURN AND BEYOND
January 3, 1998 at:21:47:20 PM(5) in
From:January 3, 1999 To:January 3, 2000
TRANSITING ACTIVITY (ZONE 5):

Date	Time	Aspect	Position
4/ 9/1998	4:33AM	T ♄ ⚻ ♇ T	22♈49
6/25/1998	6:24PM	T ♄ □ ♆ T	1♉29
10/31/1998	7:29PM	T ♆ □ ♄ T	29♑30
4/ 6/1999	11:02AM	T ♄ □ ♆ T	4♉07
7/17/1999	10:42PM	T ♄ □ ♅ T	15♉36
11/14/1999	4:46AM	T ♅ □ ♄ T	13♒04
5/13/2000	3:23AM	T ♄ □ ♅ T	20♉45
6/25/2001	3:02AM	T ♄ △ ♆ T	8♊16
8/ 5/2001	11:53AM	T ♄ ☍ ♇ T	12♊37
11/ 2/2001	1:16AM	T ♇ ☍ ♄ T	13♐49
1/23/2002	1:42AM	T ♆ △ ♄ T	8♒15
4/ 1/2002	11:15PM	T ♄ △ ♆ T	10♊31
5/25/2002	9:25PM	T ♄ ☍ ♇ T	16♊35
7/29/2002	10:29PM	T ♄ ⚻ ♆ T	24♊39
8/21/2002	2:06AM	T ♄ △ ♅ T	26♊48
12/16/2002	4:44PM	T ♅ △ ♄ T	25♒39
12/30/2002	4:30PM	T ♆ ⚻ ♄ T	9♒31
5/20/2003	3:02AM	T ♄ ⚻ ♆ T	28♊11
6/24/2003	6:22PM	T ♄ △ ♅ T	2♋41
8/ 7/2004	3:15AM	T ♄ ⚻ ♅ T	20♋36
2/17/2005	3:09PM	T ♅ ⚻ ♄ T	6♓19
6/11/2005	10:09PM	T ♄ ⚻ ♅ T	25♋45
9/ 9/2005	6:23PM	T ♄ ⚻ ♇ T	6♌50
1/ 1/2006	3:21AM	T ♇ ⚻ ♄ T	24♐53
6/29/2006	8:15PM	T ♄ ⚻ ♇ T	10♌04
8/31/2006	5:42AM	T ♄ ☍ ♆ T	17♌53
2/28/2007	5:55AM	T ♆ ☍ ♄ T	20♒14
6/25/2007	12:00PM	T ♄ ☍ ♆ T	21♌46
8/ 6/2007	5:11AM	T ♄ △ ♇ T	26♌33
11/ 4/2008	8:20AM	T ♄ ☍ ♅ T	18♍57
2/ 5/2009	6:09AM	T ♅ ☍ ♄ T	20♓39
9/15/2009	7:40AM	T ♄ ☍ ♅ T	24♍42
11/15/2009	9:26AM	T ♄ □ ♇ T	1♎42
1/31/2010	5:20PM	T ♇ □ ♄ T	4♑21
4/26/2010	6:35PM	T ♅ ☍ ♄ T	28♓46
7/26/2010	11:51AM	T ♄ ☍ ♅ T	0♎24
8/21/2010	4:45AM	T ♄ □ ♇ T	2♎55
10/27/2010	6:33AM	T ♄ ⚻ ♆ T	10♎57
3/24/2011	1:15PM	T ♆ ⚻ ♄ T	29♒40
8/24/2011	8:53PM	T ♄ ⚻ ♆ T	14♎28
6/24/2012	3:09AM	T ♅ □ ♇ T	8♈23
9/19/2012	1:49AM	T ♇ □ ♅ T	6♑57
10/10/2012	10:39PM	T ♄ △ ♆ T	0♏37
12/26/2012	7:25PM	T ♄ ⚹ ♇ T	9♏08
3/ 8/2013	3:21AM	T ♇ ⚹ ♄ T	11♑15
5/20/2013	5:18PM	T ♅ □ ♇ T	11♈14

6/11/2013	2:39PM	T Ψ △ ♄ T	5♓22
7/19/2013	12:06PM	T ♄ △ Ψ T	4♏55
9/21/2013	12:07AM	T ♄ ⚹ ♇ T	8♏59
11/ 1/2013	6:10AM	T ♇ □ ♅ T	9♑25
4/21/2014	1:34PM	T ♅ □ ♇ T	13♈33
11/27/2014	11:04AM	T ♄ ∠ ♇ T	27♏02
12/ 3/2014	5:35AM	T ♄ ⚼ ♅ T	27♏42
12/15/2014	1:14AM	T ♇ □ ♅ T	12♑35
3/16/2015	8:44PM	T ♅ □ ♇ T	15♈17
5/ 4/2015	1:20AM	T ♅ ⚼ ♄ T	17♈59
6/20/2015	8:32AM	T ♇ ∠ ♄ T	14♑39
8/13/2015	3:30PM	T ♄ ∠ ♇ T	28♏23
10/22/2015	10:49AM	T ♄ ⚼ ♅ T	3♐04
11/26/2015	8:31AM	T ♄ □ Ψ T	7♐02
6/17/2016	8:11PM	T Ψ □ ♄ T	12♓02
9/10/2016	10:14AM	T ♄ □ Ψ T	10♐24
12/24/2016	7:09PM	T ♄ △ ♅ T	20♐33
5/19/2017	1:21AM	T ♅ △ ♄ T	26♈23
8/12/2017	3:01AM	T ♅ ∠ Ψ T	28♈29
10/ 6/2017	3:54PM	T Ψ ∠ ♅ T	12♓02
11/11/2017	4:35AM	T ♄ △ ♅ T	25♐37
6/16/2018	9:19AM	T ♅ ∠ Ψ T	1♉29
12/15/2018	12:29AM	T Ψ ∠ ♅ T	13♓49
1/31/2019	11:13AM	T ♄ ⚹ Ψ T	14♑55
5/ 2/2019	3:14AM	T ♅ ∠ Ψ T	3♉03
6/18/2019	4:20AM	T Ψ ⚹ ♄ T	18♓43
11/ 8/2019	11:36PM	T ♄ ⚹ Ψ T	16♑01
1/12/2020	11:11AM	T ♄ ☌ ♇ T	22♑46
1/20/2021	1:43PM	T ♄ ∠ Ψ T	3♒56
2/17/2021	1:58PM	T ♄ □ ♅ T	7♒13
6/14/2021	5:06PM	T ♅ □ ♄ T	13♉06
12/24/2021	2:10AM	T ♄ □ ♅ T	11♒05
5/ 6/2024	5:53AM	T ♄ ∠ ♇ T	17♓05
9/25/2024	7:18PM	T ♇ ∠ ♄ T	29♑41
1/26/2025	6:45PM	T ♄ ∠ ♇ T	16♓53
4/ 4/2025	11:17AM	T ♄ ⚹ ♅ T	24♓55
8/11/2025	10:30PM	T ♅ ⚹ ♄ T	1♊11
8/29/2025	1:05AM	T ♅ ⚹ Ψ T	1♊26
11/20/2025	3:39AM	T Ψ ⚹ ♅ T	29♓29
1/20/2026	12:17AM	T ♄ ⚹ ♅ T	27♓33
2/20/2026	2:01PM	T ♄ ☌ Ψ T	0♈45
3/28/2026	4:29PM	T ♄ ⚹ ♇ T	5♈09
7/15/2026	7:23PM	T ♅ ⚹ Ψ T	4♊24
7/17/2026	10:29PM	T ♅ △ ♇ T	4♊29
7/24/2026	6:12AM	T Ψ ⚹ ♇ T	4♈20
9/16/2026	3:24PM	T ♇ ⚹ Ψ T	3♒15
11/29/2026	7:32AM	T ♇ △ ♅ T	3♒31
1/14/2027	11:55PM	T Ψ ⚹ ♅ T	1♈56
4/12/2027	6:21PM	T ♄ ∠ ♅ T	18♈19
6/ 6/2027	9:34AM	T ♅ ⚹ Ψ T	6♊21
6/15/2027	2:02AM	T ♅ △ ♇ T	6♊51
6/28/2027	8:45AM	T Ψ ⚹ ♇ T	6♈37
10/15/2027	8:58PM	T ♅ ∠ ♄ T	9♊33

10/16/2027	7:58PM	T ♇ ⚹ ♆ T	4♒44
1/12/2028	1:20AM	T ♄ ∠ ♅ T	21♈21
1/13/2028	3:01AM	T ♇ △ ♅ T	6♒19
5/ 9/2028	8:36PM	T ♅ △ ♇ T	8♊49
6/ 8/2028	2:47PM	T ♆ ⚹ ♇ T	8♈37
6/23/2028	9:15PM	T ♄ □ ♇ T	8♉22
11/ 8/2028	5:44AM	T ♇ ⚹ ♆ T	6♒30
11/15/2028	8:45AM	T ♇ □ ♄ T	6♒34
3/29/2029	5:21PM	T ♄ □ ♇ T	10♉02
5/22/2029	5:53AM	T ♆ ⚹ ♇ T	10♈25
12/ 1/2029	1:23AM	T ♇ ⚹ ♆ T	8♒25
5/ 4/2030	1:29AM	T ♆ ⚹ ♇ T	12♈02
5/10/2030	2:40PM	T ♄ ∠ ♆ T	27♉15
12/26/2030	8:59PM	T ♇ ⚹ ♆ T	10♒35
4/12/2031	5:28AM	T ♆ ⚹ ♇ T	13♈24
6/11/2031	8:59AM	T ♄ △ ♇ T	13♊28
6/27/2031	5:51AM	T ♄ ⚹ ♆ T	15♊30
9/ 1/2031	2:07PM	T ♅ ⚼ ♇ T	26♊50
11/18/2031	12:29AM	T ♇ ⚼ ♅ T	11♒23
2/13/2032	7:07AM	T ♇ ⚹ ♆ T	13♒33
2/26/2032	8:58AM	T ♆ ⚹ ♇ T	13♈56
6/28/2032	7:13AM	T ♄ ☌ ♅ T	28♊01
7/10/2032	2:59PM	T ♄ ⚼ ♇ T	29♊35
7/21/2032	8:50PM	T ♅ ⚼ ♇ T	29♊21
1/ 5/2033	8:16PM	T ♇ ⚼ ♅ T	13♒57
2/20/2033	12:08AM	T ♇ ⚼ ♄ T	15♒17
4/ 6/2033	5:32PM	T ♄ ⚼ ♇ T	1♋24
6/18/2033	6:15AM	T ♅ ⚼ ♇ T	1♋33
9/16/2033	7:10AM	T ♄ □ ♆ T	19♋22
1/13/2034	8:55AM	T ♆ □ ♄ T	17♈23
3/ 1/2034	9:30AM	T ♇ ⚼ ♅ T	17♒03
5/ 2/2034	6:27PM	T ♅ ⚼ ♇ T	3♋14
6/25/2034	11:52AM	T ♄ □ ♆ T	22♋07
10/17/2035	6:04AM	T ♄ ☍ ♇ T	17♌30
1/ 1/2036	2:34PM	T ♇ ☍ ♄ T	18♒18
7/27/2036	7:13PM	T ♄ ☍ ♇ T	20♌28
9/12/2036	2:48PM	T ♄ △ ♆ T	26♌22
4/ 8/2037	9:20PM	T ♆ △ ♄ T	26♈16
6/23/2037	2:30PM	T ♄ △ ♆ T	28♌43
9/13/2037	3:35PM	T ♄ ∠ ♅ T	8♍15
10/22/2037	2:14AM	T ♄ ⚼ ♆ T	12♍40
3/ 9/2038	5:05AM	T ♆ ⚼ ♄ T	27♈22
8/16/2038	11:51PM	T ♄ ⚼ ♆ T	16♍20
12/ 6/2038	9:40AM	T ♄ ⚹ ♅ T	28♍19
4/ 1/2039	1:45PM	T ♅ ⚹ ♄ T	24♋40
9/26/2039	2:28PM	T ♄ ⚹ ♅ T	2♎36
10/ 2/2039	11:34PM	T ♅ □ ♆ T	2♌49
11/15/2039	5:33PM	T ♄ ⚼ ♇ T	8♎24
1/31/2040	4:51PM	T ♆ □ ♅ T	0♉56
2/29/2040	10:48PM	T ♇ ⚼ ♄ T	25♒40
8/29/2040	10:54AM	T ♅ □ ♆ T	5♌45
8/31/2040	1:01PM	T ♄ ⚼ ♇ T	10♎40

APPENDIX 5

The following pages contain weekly charts of the DJIA from 1948-1998, with major geocosmic signatures as used in this book. The charts do not reflect presence of semi-squares or sesquiquadrates, which were also used in cases of Saturn and beyond for the studies reported in this book.

Cycle crests and troughs are numbered according to the criteria used in Chapters 7 and 8 as follows:

Cycles greater than 4-years	**5**
4-year cycles	**4**
Double bottom or top to 4-year cycles	**3.5**
22.5-month cycles	**3**
Double bottom or top to 22.5-month cycle	**2.5**
50-week cycles	**2**
Shorter cycles that involved a 10% or greater move	**1.5**

The charts in the pages that follow are printed from the Galactic Trader Program, created by Jeanne Long of P.A.S. in Ft. Lauderdale, Florida.

The data used to compute these charts is provided by Commodities Systems Inc. (CSI) of Boca Raton, Florida.

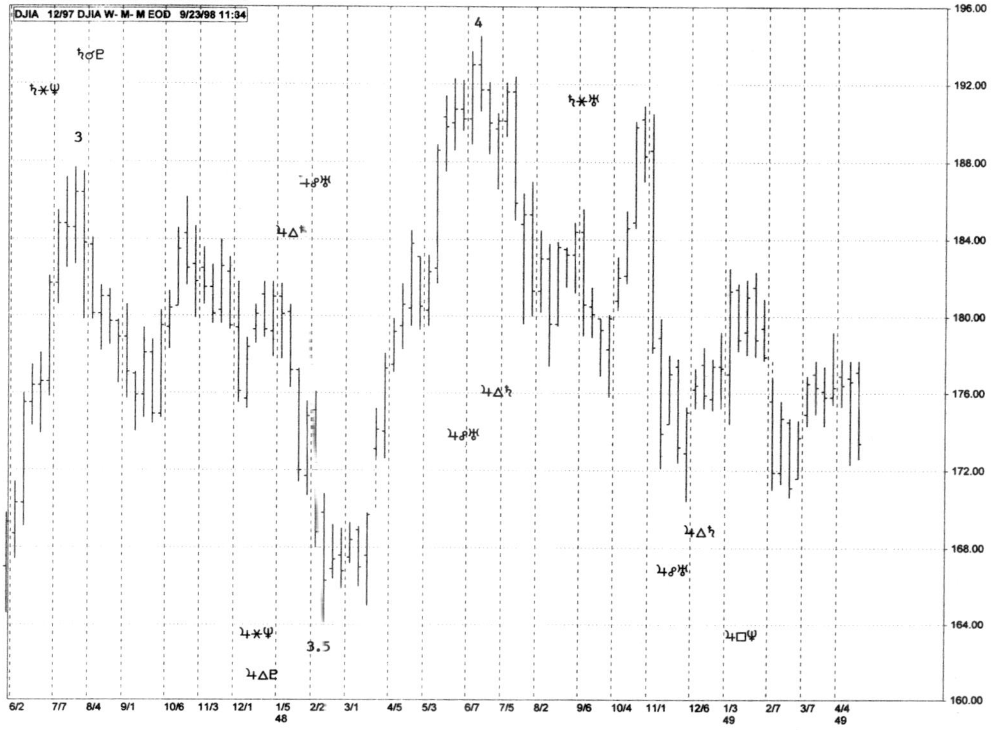
FIBONACCI/GALACTIC TRADER (c) Robert Krausz/Jeanne Long
DJIA 12/97 DJIA W- M- M EOD 9/23/98 11:34
3
3.5
4
196.00
192.00
188.00
184.00
180.00
176.00
172.00
168.00
164.00
160.00
6/2
7/7
8/4
9/1
10/6
11/3
12/1
1/5
48
2/2
3/1
4/5
5/3
6/7
7/5
8/2
9/6
10/4
11/1
12/6
1/3
49
2/7
3/7
4/4
49

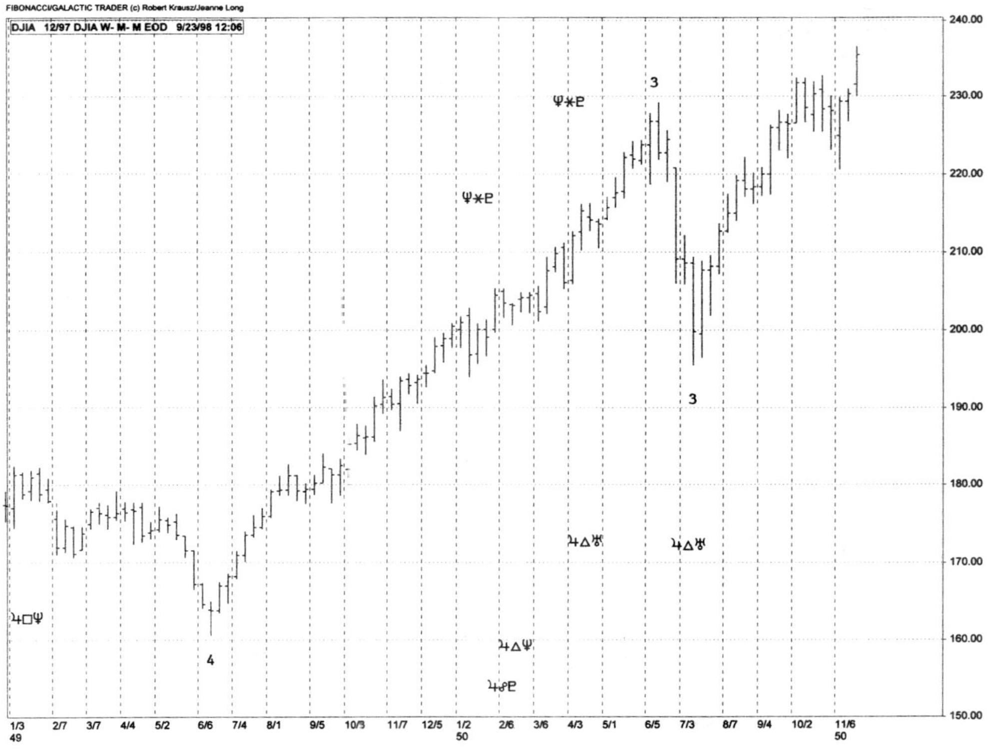
FIBONACCI/GALACTIC TRADER (c) Robert Krausz/Jeanne Long
DJIA 12/97 DJIA W- M- M EOD 9/23/98 12:06
3
3
4
240.00
230.00
220.00
210.00
200.00
190.00
180.00
170.00
160.00
150.00
1/3
49
2/7
3/7
4/4
5/2
6/6
7/4
8/1
9/5
10/3
11/7
12/5
1/2
50
2/6
3/6
4/3
5/1
6/5
7/3
8/7
9/4
10/2
11/6
50

FIBONACCI/GALACTIC TRADER (c) Robert Krausz/Jeanne Long
DJIA 12/97 DJIA W- M- M EOD 9/23/98 13:42

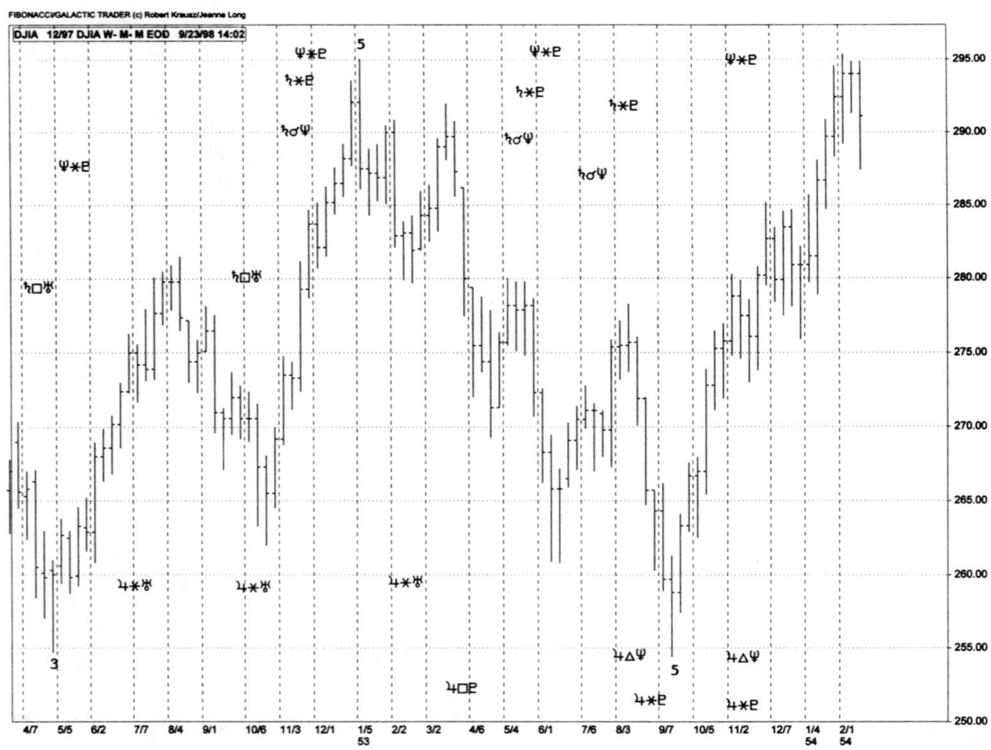
FIBONACCI/GALACTIC TRADER (c) Robert Krausz/Jeanne Long
DJIA 12/97 DJIA W- M- M EOD 9/23/98 14:02

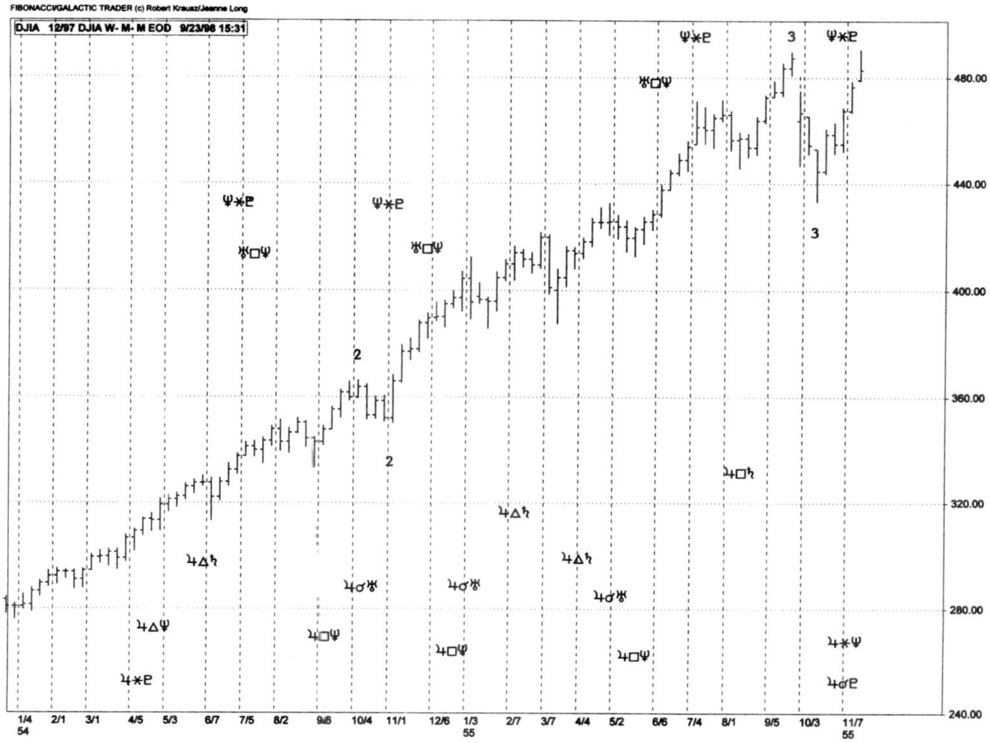
FIBONACCI/GALACTIC TRADER (c) Robert Krausz/Jeanne Long
DJIA 12/97 DJIA W- M- M EOD 9/23/98 15:31
480.00
440.00
400.00
360.00
320.00
280.00
240.00
1/4 54
2/1
3/1
4/5
5/3
6/7
7/5
8/2
9/6
10/4
11/1
12/6
1/3 55
2/7
3/7
4/4
5/2
6/6
7/4
8/1
9/5
10/3
11/7 55

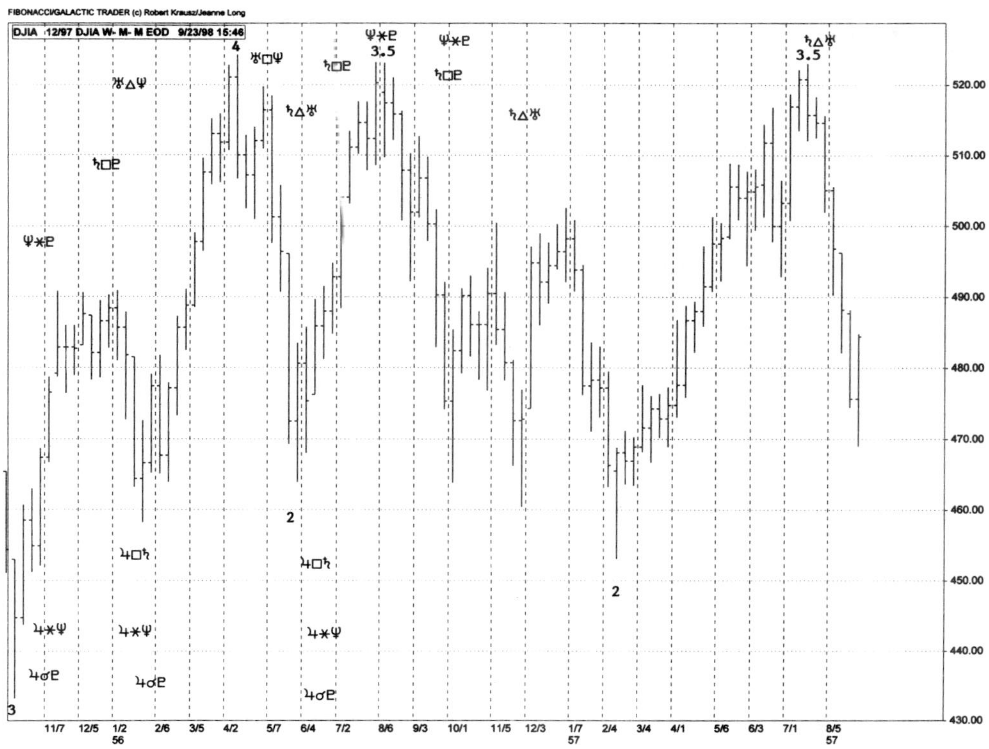
FIBONACCI/GALACTIC TRADER (c) Robert Krausz/Jeanne Long
DJIA 12/97 DJIA W- M- M EOD 9/23/98 15:46
520.00
510.00
500.00
490.00
480.00
470.00
460.00
450.00
440.00
430.00
11/7
12/5
1/2 56
2/6
3/5
4/2
5/7
6/4
7/2
8/6
9/3
10/1
11/5
12/3
1/7 57
2/4
3/4
4/1
5/6
6/3
7/1
8/5 57

FIBONACCI/GALACTIC TRADER (c) Robert Krausz/Jeanne Long
DJIA 12/97 DJIA W- M- M EOD 9/24/98 13:36
♄△♅
♄△♅
3.5
2
2
♄△♇
♄✶♆
♃✶♄
♃✶♅
4
♃✶♇
♃✶♇
♃✶♄
♃✶♄
♃□♅
♃☌♆
♃✶♇
640.00
600.00
560.00
520.00
480.00
440.00
400.00
7/1
8/5
9/2
10/7
11/4
12/2
1/6
58
2/3
3/3
4/7
5/5
6/2
7/7
8/4
9/1
10/6
11/3
12/1
1/5
59
2/2
3/2
4/6
5/4
59

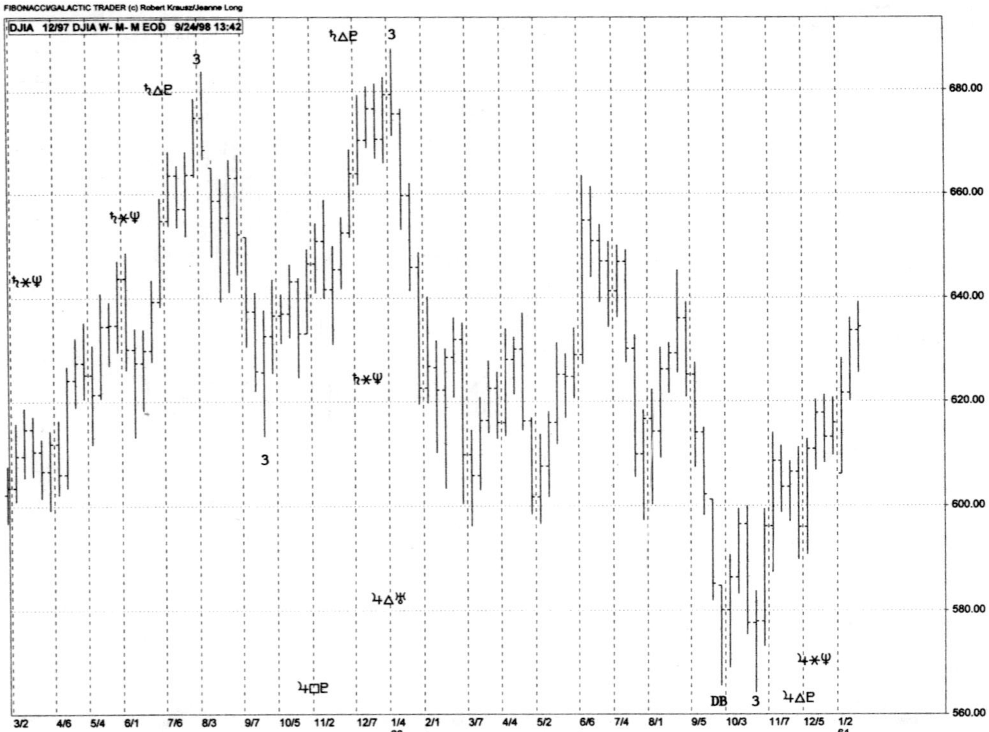
FIBONACCI/GALACTIC TRADER (c) Robert Krausz/Jeanne Long
DJIA 12/97 DJIA W- M- M EOD 9/24/98 13:42
♄△♇
3
3
♄△♇
♄✶♆
♄✶♆
♄✶♆
3
♃△♅
♃□♇
DB
3
♃△♇
♃✶♆
680.00
660.00
640.00
620.00
600.00
580.00
560.00
3/2
4/6
5/4
6/1
7/6
8/3
9/7
10/5
11/2
12/7
1/4
60
2/1
3/7
4/4
5/2
6/6
7/4
8/1
9/5
10/3
11/7
12/5
1/2
61

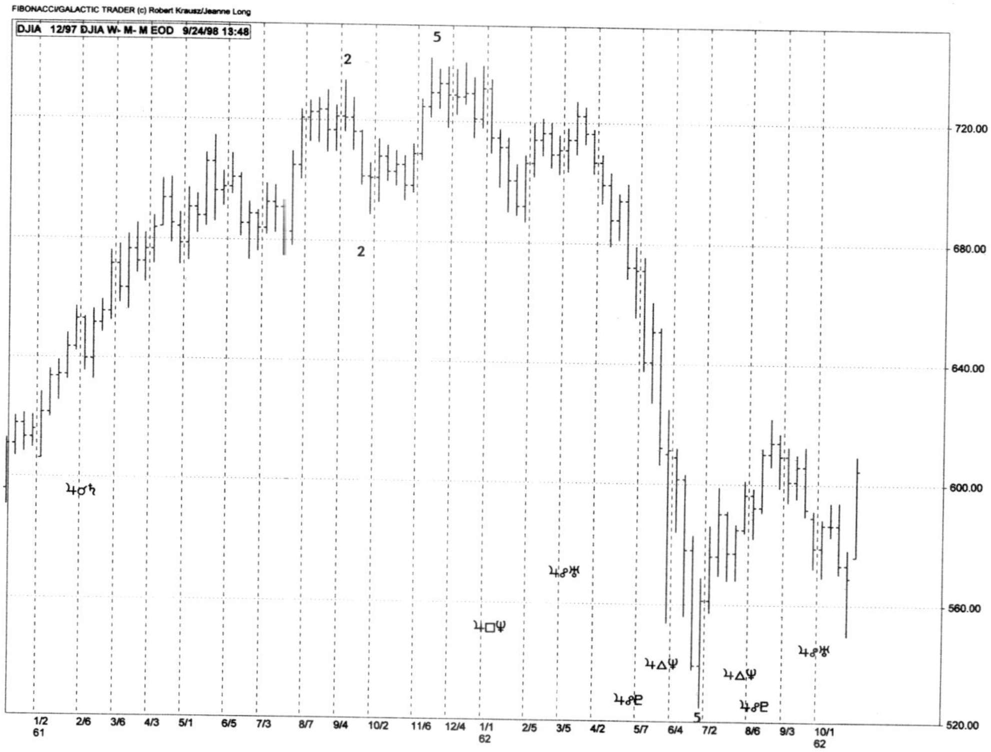
FIBONACCI/GALACTIC TRADER (c) Robert Krausz/Jeanne Long
DJIA 12/97 DJIA W- M- M EOD 9/24/98 13:48

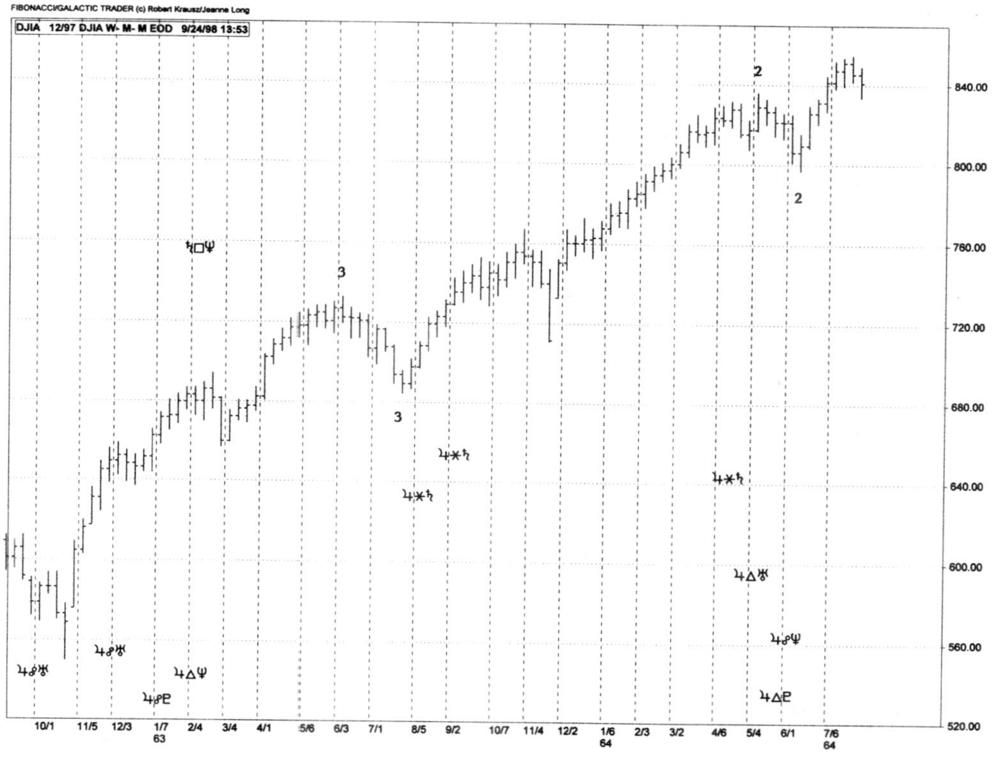
FIBONACCI/GALACTIC TRADER (c) Robert Krausz/Jeanne Long
DJIA 12/97 DJIA W- M- M EOD 9/24/98 13:53

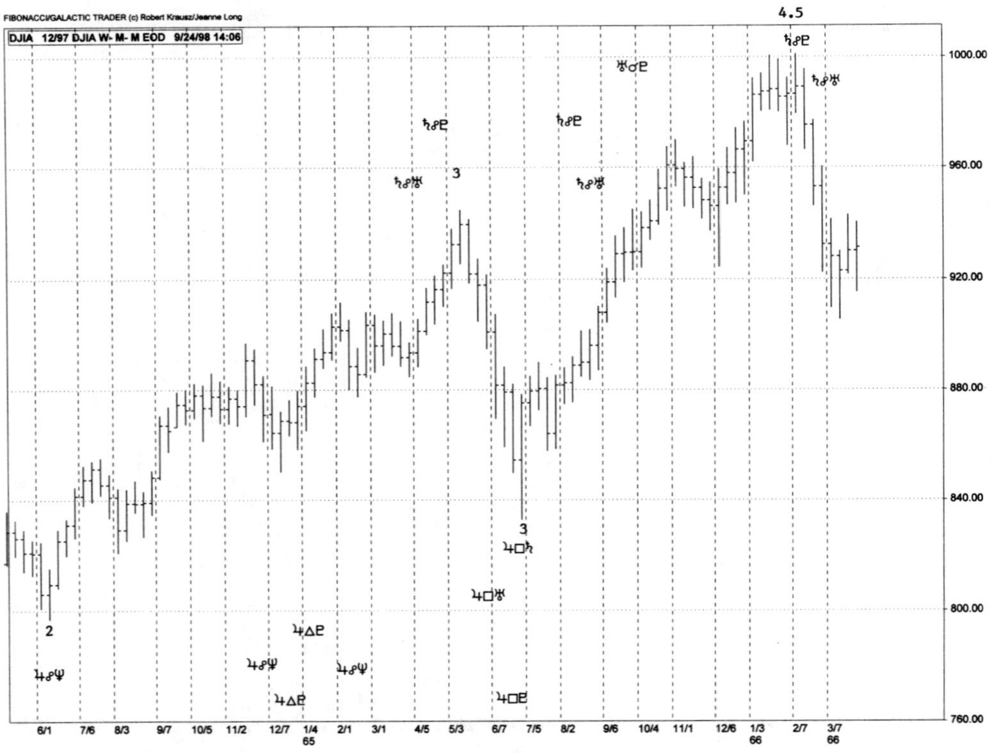
FIBONACCI/GALACTIC TRADER (c) Robert Krausz/Jeanne Long
DJIA 12/97 DJIA W- M- M EOD 9/24/98 14:06

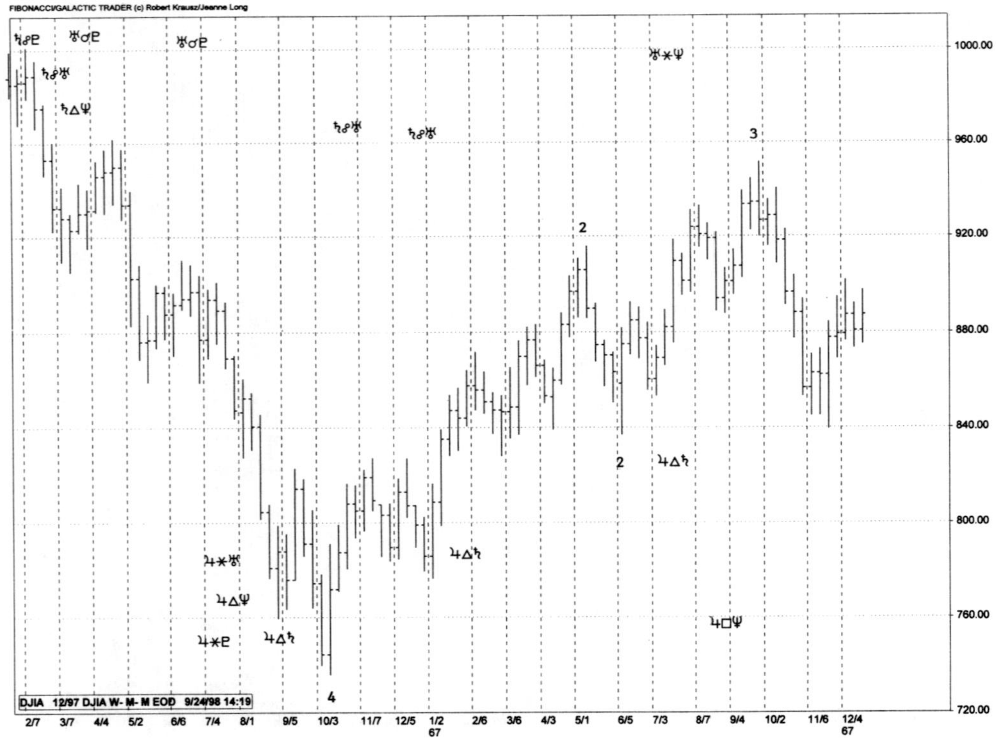
FIBONACCI/GALACTIC TRADER (c) Robert Krausz/Jeanne Long
DJIA 12/97 DJIA W- M- M EOD 9/24/98 14:19

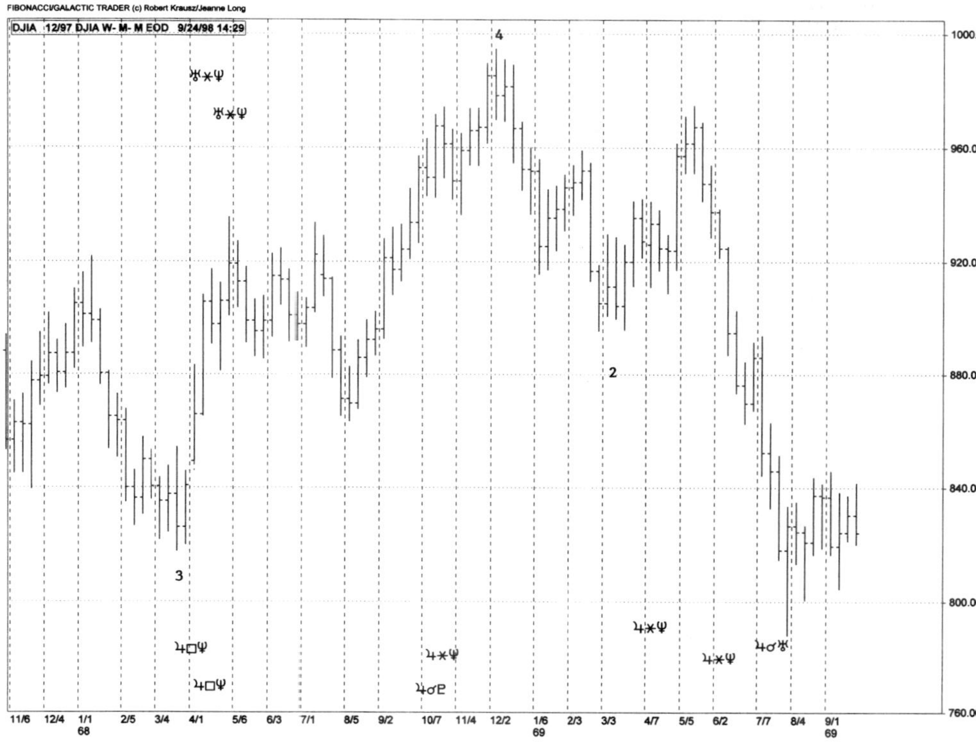
FIBONACCI/GALACTIC TRADER (c) Robert Krausz/Jeanne Long
DJIA 12/97 DJIA W- M- M EOD 9/24/98 14:29
1000.00
960.00
920.00
880.00
840.00
800.00
760.00
11/6 12/4 1/1 68 2/5 3/4 4/1 5/6 6/3 7/1 8/5 9/2 10/7 11/4 12/2 1/6 69 2/3 3/3 4/7 5/5 6/2 7/7 8/4 9/1 69
3
4
2

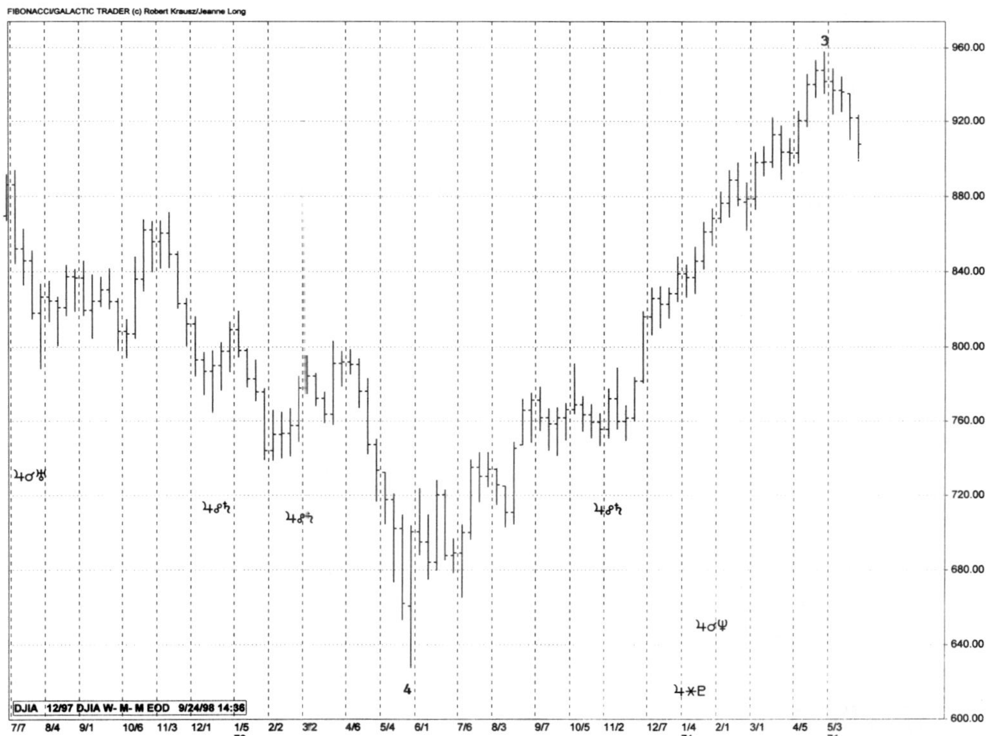
FIBONACCI/GALACTIC TRADER (c) Robert Krausz/Jeanne Long
DJIA 12/97 DJIA W- M- M EOD 9/24/98 14:36
960.00
920.00
880.00
840.00
800.00
760.00
720.00
680.00
640.00
600.00
7/7 8/4 9/1 10/6 11/3 12/1 1/5 70 2/2 3/2 4/6 5/4 6/1 7/6 8/3 9/7 10/5 11/2 12/7 1/4 71 2/1 3/1 4/5 5/3 71
3
4

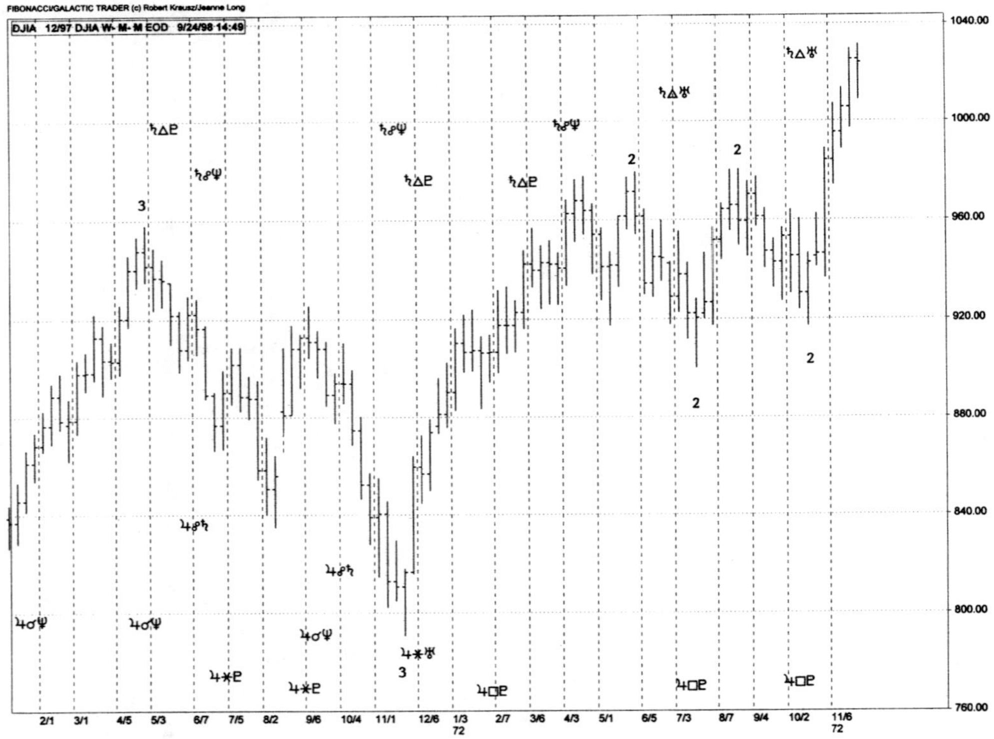
FIBONACCI/GALACTIC TRADER (c) Robert Krausz/Jeanne Long
DJIA 12/97 DJIA W- M- M EOD 9/24/98 14:49

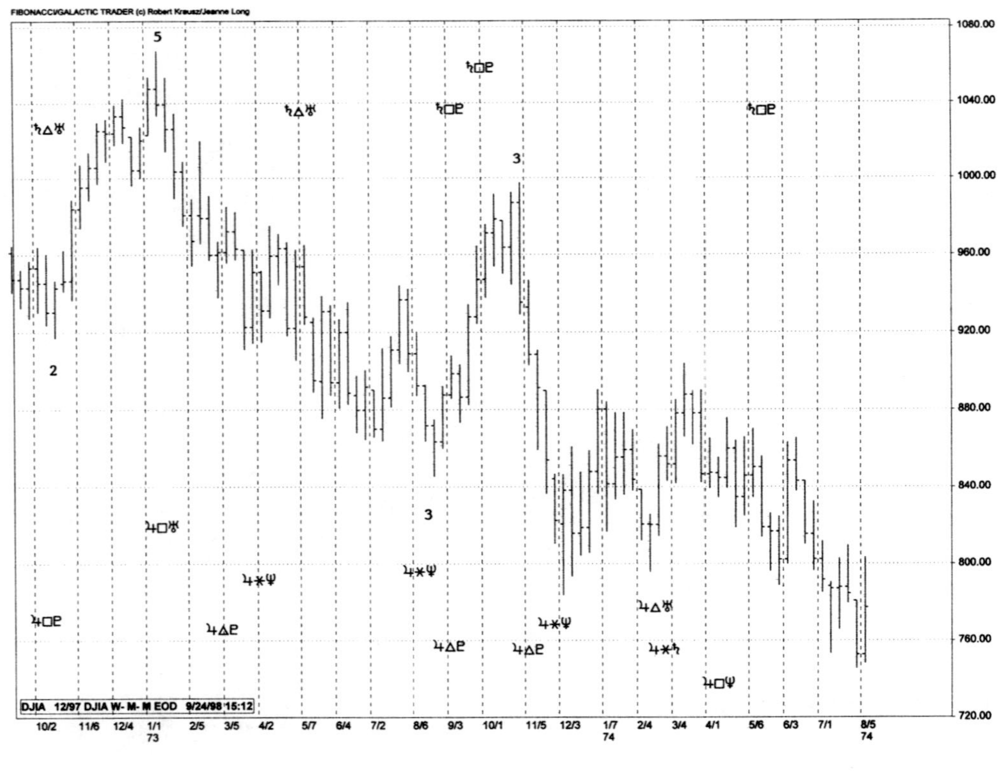
FIBONACCI/GALACTIC TRADER (c) Robert Krausz/Jeanne Long
DJIA 12/97 DJIA W- M- M EOD 9/24/98 15:12

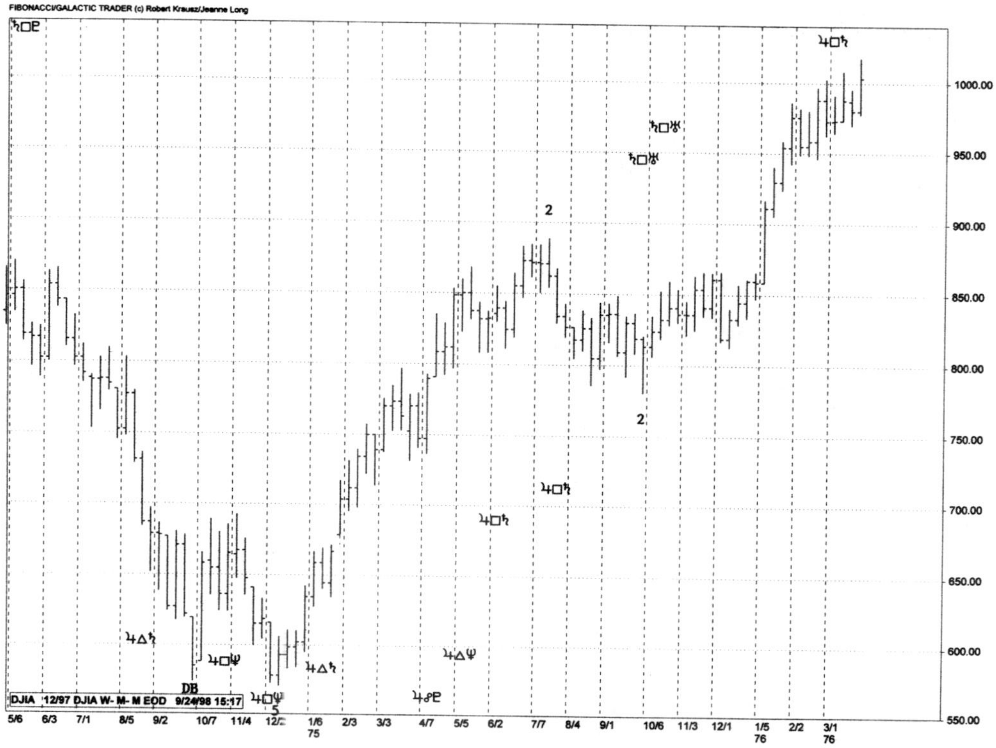

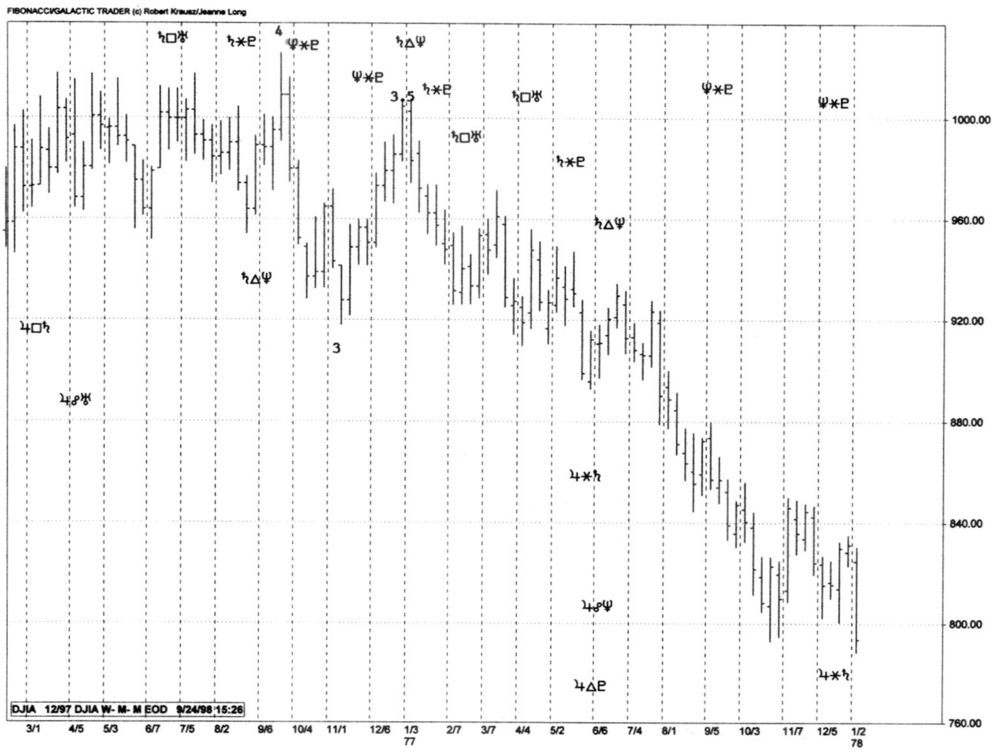

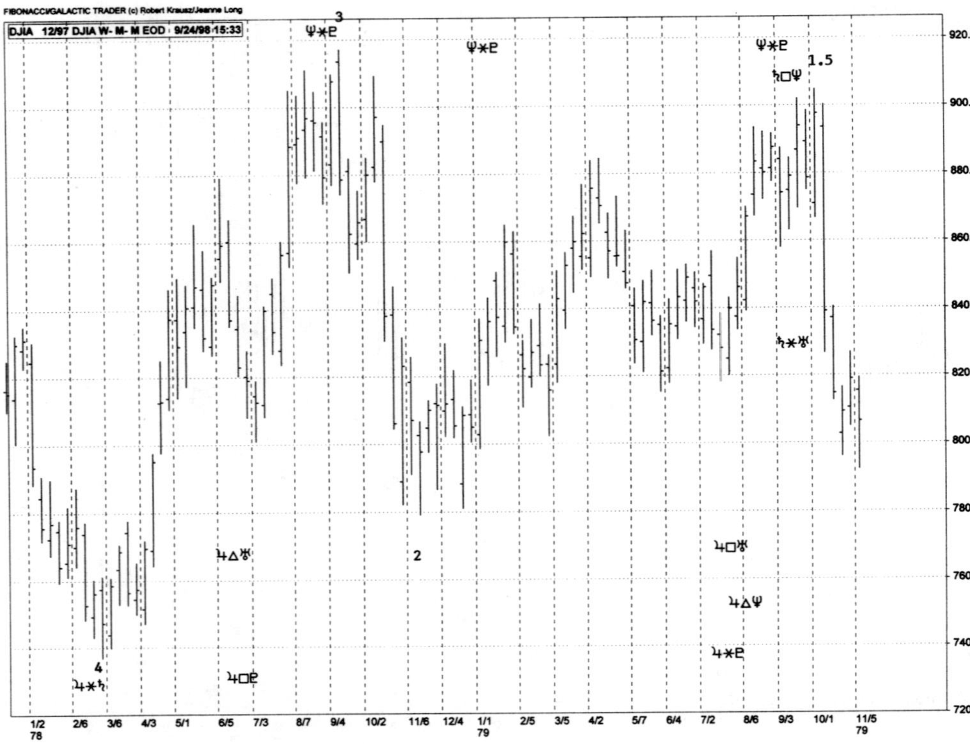
FIBONACCI/GALACTIC TRADER (c) Robert Krausz/Jeanne Long
DJIA 12/97 DJIA W- M- M EOD 9/24/98 15:33

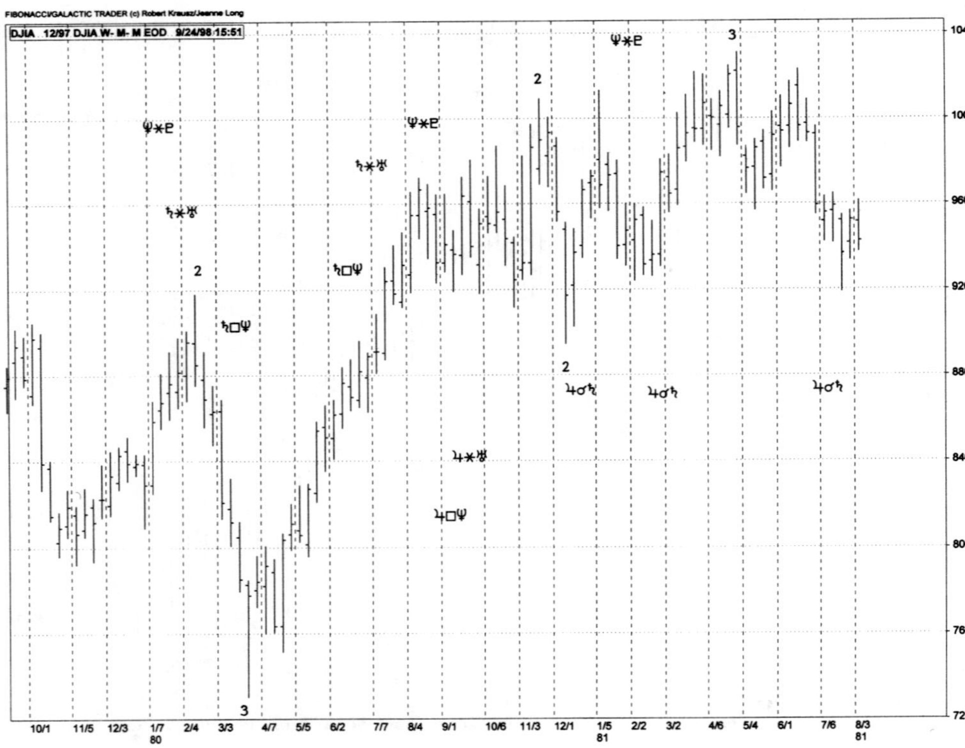
FIBONACCI/GALACTIC TRADER (c) Robert Krausz/Jeanne Long
DJIA 12/97 DJIA W- M- M EOD 9/24/98 15:51

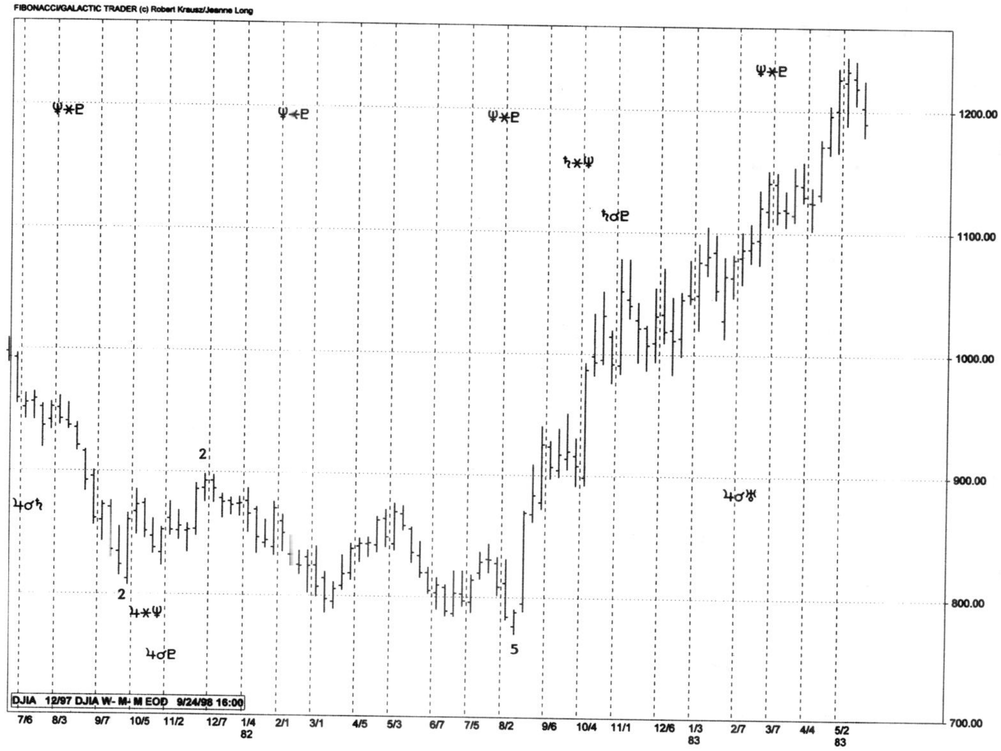
FIBONACCI/GALACTIC TRADER (c) Robert Krausz/Jeanne Long
DJIA 12/97 DJIA W- M- M EOD 9/24/98 16:00

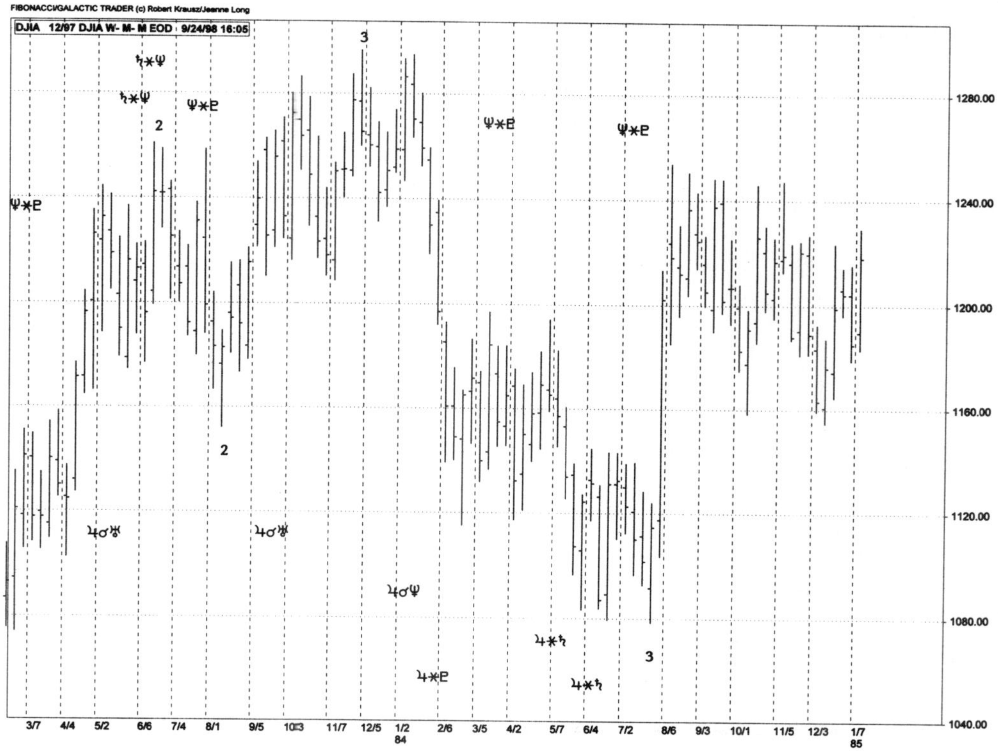
FIBONACCI/GALACTIC TRADER (c) Robert Krausz/Jeanne Long
DJIA 12/97 DJIA W- M- M EOD 9/24/98 16:05

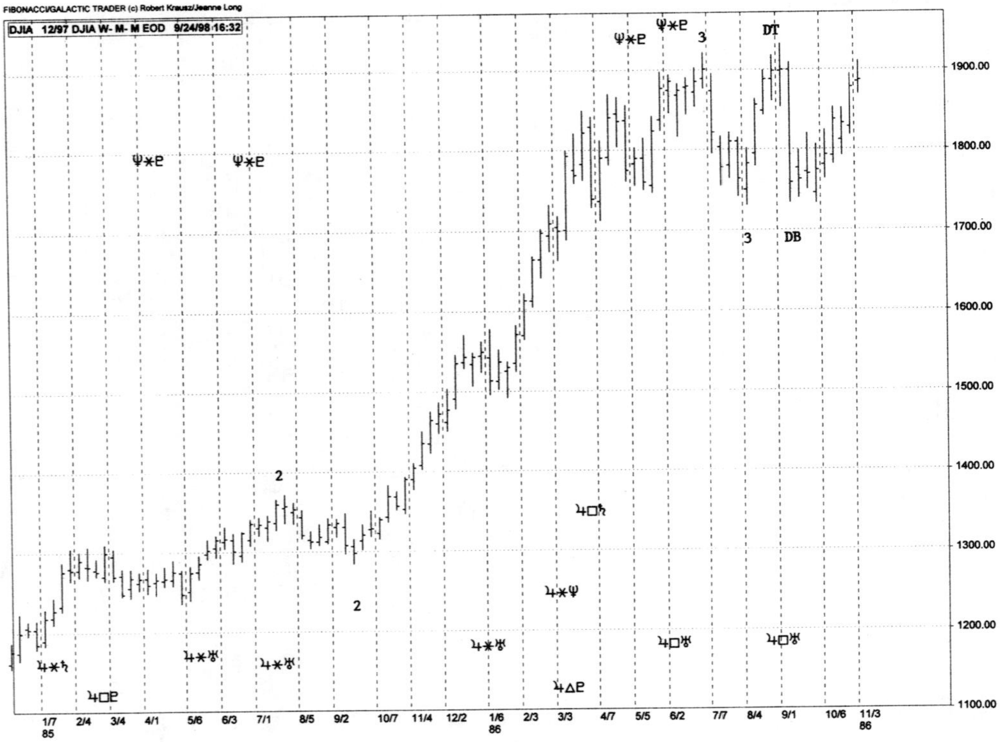
FIBONACCI/GALACTIC TRADER (c) Robert Krausz/Jeanne Long
DJIA 12/97 DJIA W- M- M EOD 9/24/98 16:32
1900.00
1800.00
1700.00
1600.00
1500.00
1400.00
1300.00
1200.00
1100.00
1/7 85
2/4
3/4
4/1
5/6
6/3
7/1
8/5
9/2
10/7
11/4
12/2
1/6 86
2/3
3/3
4/7
5/5
6/2
7/7
8/4
9/1
10/6
11/3 86
2
3
DT
DB

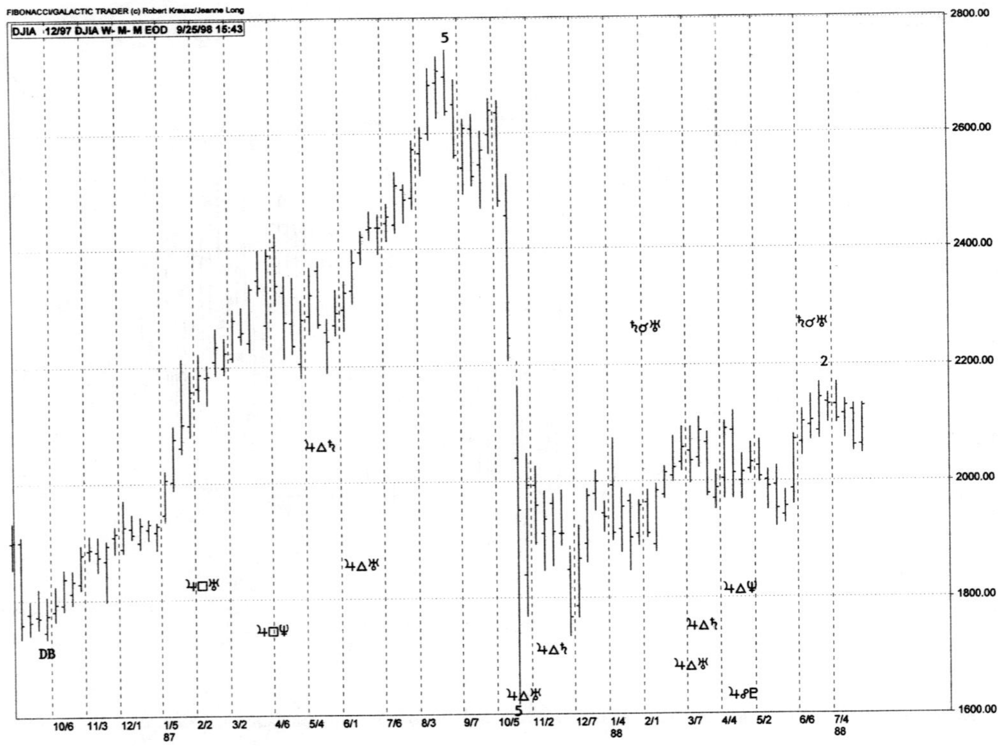
FIBONACCI/GALACTIC TRADER (c) Robert Krausz/Jeanne Long
DJIA 12/97 DJIA W- M- M EOD 9/25/98 15:43
2800.00
2600.00
2400.00
2200.00
2000.00
1800.00
1600.00
10/6
11/3
12/1
1/5 87
2/2
3/2
4/6
5/4
6/1
7/6
8/3
9/7
10/5
11/2
12/7
1/4 88
2/1
3/7
4/4
5/2
6/6
7/4 88
5
2
DB

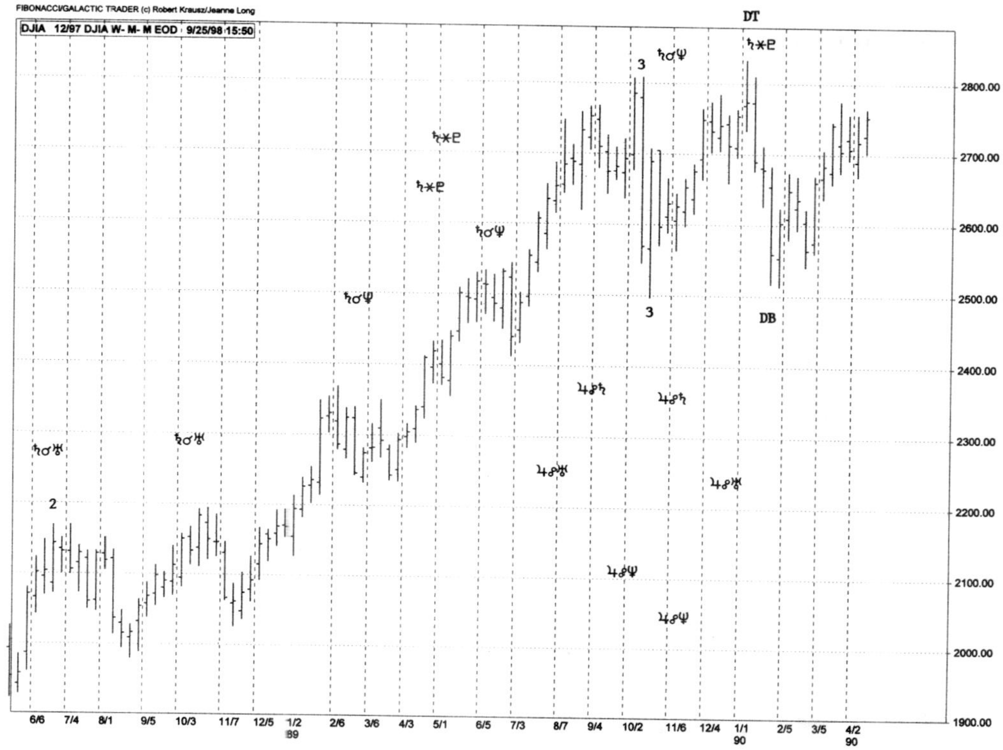
FIBONACCI/GALACTIC TRADER (c) Robert Krausz/Jeanne Long
DJIA 12/97 DJIA W- M- M EOD 9/25/98 15:50
DT
DB

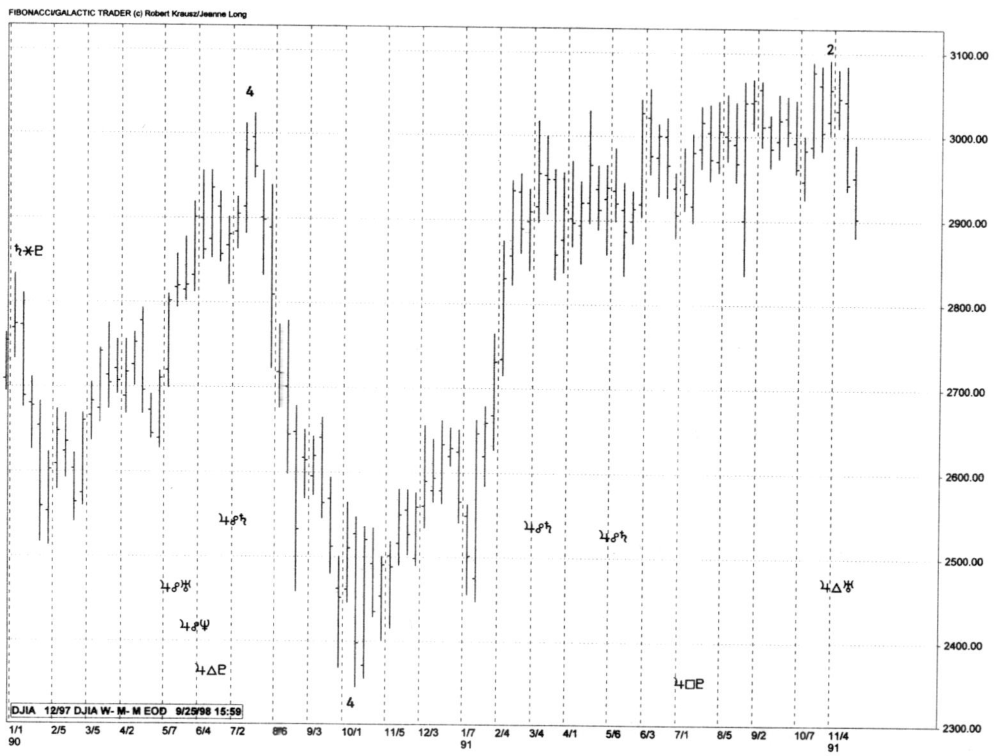
FIBONACCI/GALACTIC TRADER (c) Robert Krausz/Jeanne Long
DJIA 12/97 DJIA W- M- M EOD 9/25/98 15:59

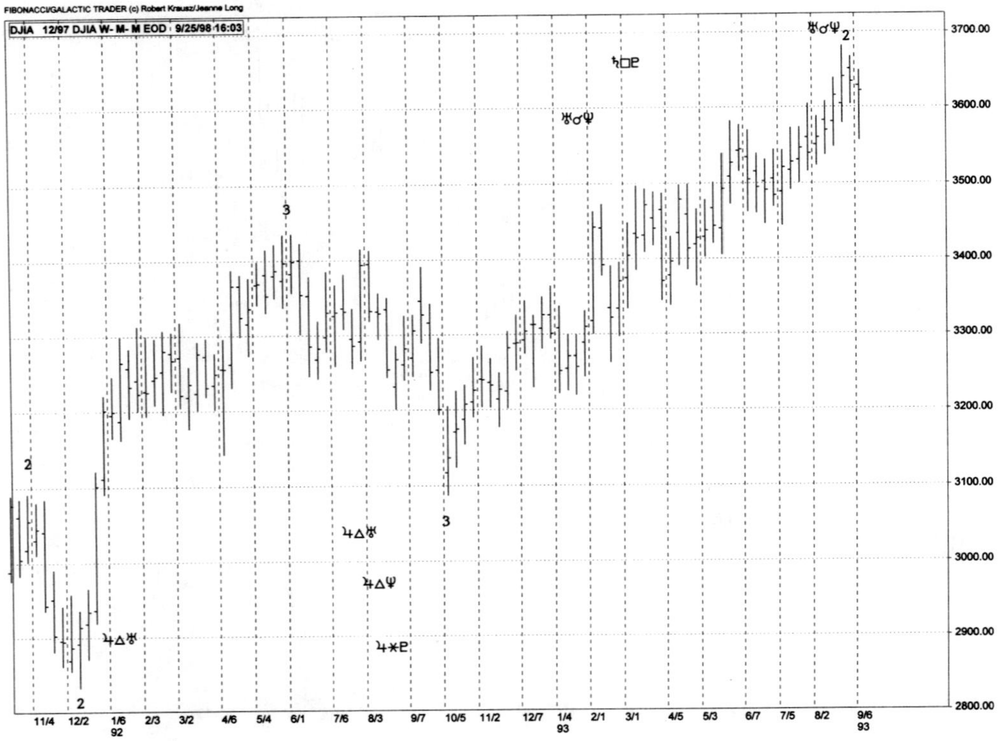
FIBONACCI/GALACTIC TRADER (c) Robert Krausz/Jeanne Long
DJIA 12/97 DJIA W- M- M EOD 9/25/98 16:03

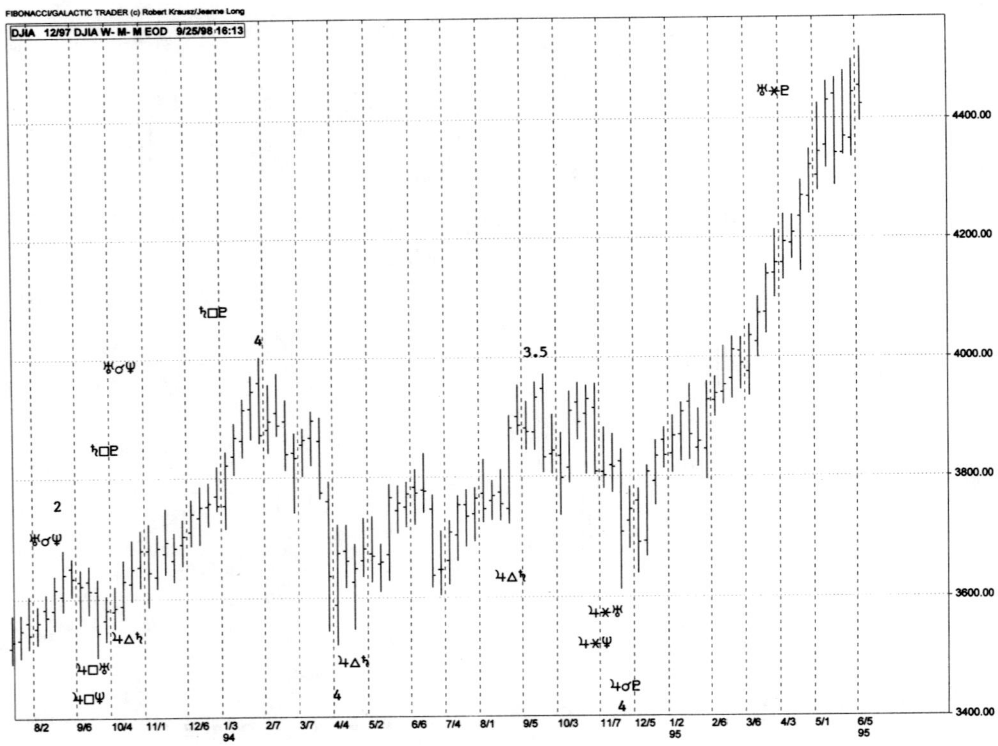
FIBONACCI/GALACTIC TRADER (c) Robert Krausz/Jeanne Long
DJIA 12/97 DJIA W- M- M EOD 9/25/98 16:13

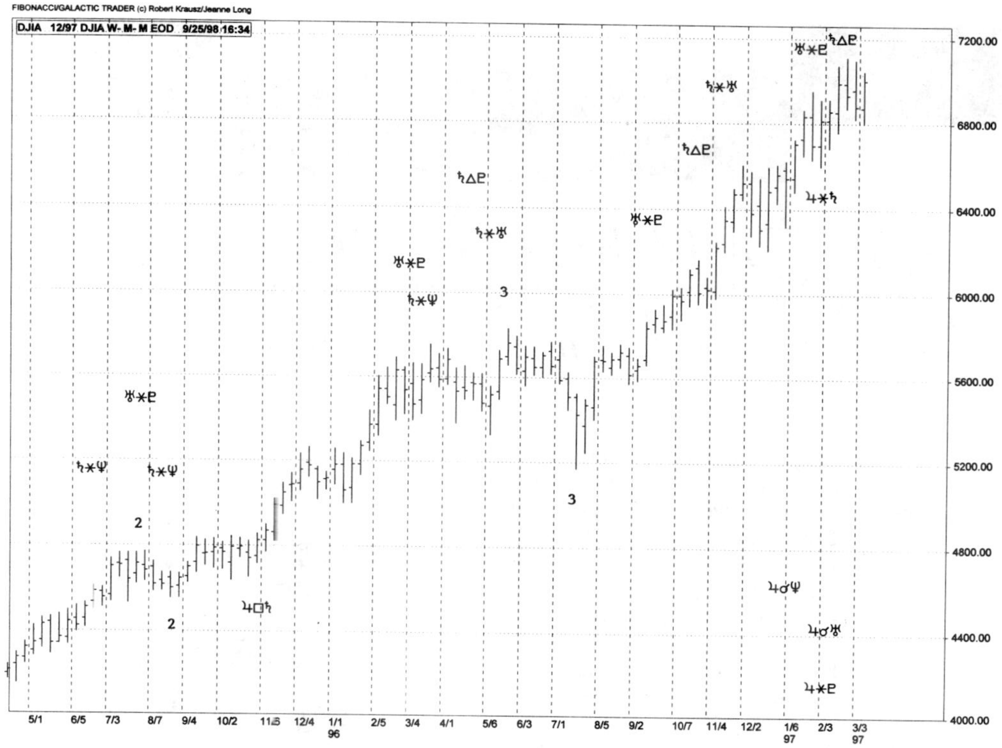
FIBONACCI/GALACTIC TRADER (c) Robert Krausz/Jeanne Long
DJIA 12/97 DJIA W- M- M EOD 9/25/98 16:34

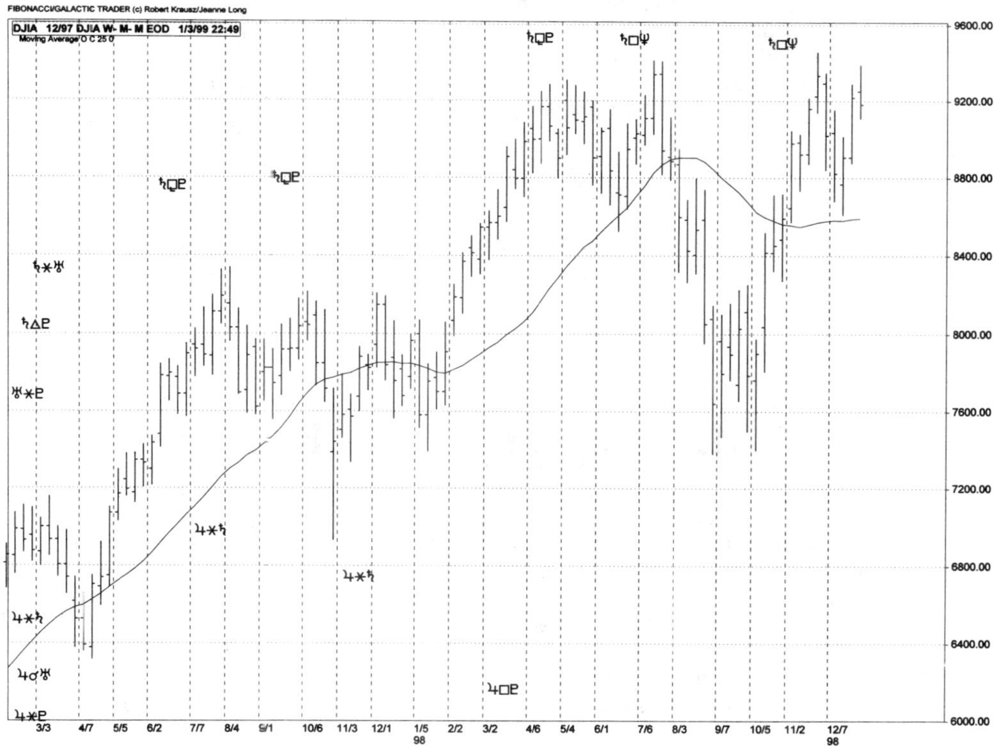
FIBONACCI/GALACTIC TRADER (c) Robert Krausz/Jeanne Long
DJIA 12/97 DJIA W- M- M EOD 1/3/99 22:49
Moving Average O C 25 0

MMA REPORTS

The S.O.S. Special Stock Market Report

By popular demand, MMA now has a new and exclusive stock market "Special Update" report. Issued every six week (8 times per year), this report provides an in-depth update of the phasing of longer-term cycles in the U.S. Stock Market. It also covers specific stocks that are prone to rise or fall in the intermediate-term, based upon an integration of cycles, geocosmics, and technical studies. Although short-term and options traders will find this valuable, SOS is designed with emphasis upon long-term investments in the U.S. Stock Market.

"Ray's work has class, integrity, and outstanding results. His accurate timing and analysis have an excellent cyclic technical foundation. The results of his cyclic analysis put him at the top of the ladder."

–David Marantette
Editor of the *Gold Stock Letter* and *Dear Dow Letter*

Subscription Prices: 1 year/sub: $150.00 •3 issue trial: $60.00 • Fax: add 50% if U.S. or Canada, 75% elsewhere. Postal delivery overseas add 10%. No extra cost for e-mail.

OTHER SERVICES

MMA WEEKLY and Daily Market Comments and Trade Recommendations (by Fax or E-mail only):

2-3 page update on 10 markets: Gold, Silver, U.S.A.. Stock Market, T-Bonds, D-Mark, Swiss Franc, Japanese Yen, Corn, Wheat, and Soybeans. Commentary on what to expect in each market in the forthcoming week or day, with specific buy and sell recommendations, by Raymond A. Merriman

Weekly Updates: $1,000.00/yr - $360.00/3 mo.
Daily Updates: $2,500/yr - $250.00/mo.
Fax: add 50% if U.S. or Canada, 75% elsewhere. No extra cost for e-mail.

Weekly Update of Japanese Nikkei - Fax or E-mail Only

Delivered by fax or e-mail every Friday afternoon (Eastern Time), this update gives in-depth analysis of what to expect in the Japanese Stock Market the following week. Highly accurate.

$1500.00/year - $450.00/3mo.
Fax: add 50% if U.S. or Canada, 75% elsewhere. No extra cost for e-mail.